The Daring Decade

The Exciting, Influential, and Bodaciously Fun American Movies of the 1970s

VOLUME ONE: 1970–1974

Chris Strodder

Pulp Hero Press
The Most Dangerous Books on Earth
www.PulpHeroPress.com

The views expressed in this book are those of the author and do not necessarily reflect the views of Pulp Hero Press.

Pulp Hero Press publishes its books in a variety of print and electronic formats. Some content that appears in one format may not appear in another.

Editor: Bob McLain
Layout: Artisanal Text

ISBN 978-1-68390-214-0
Printed in the United States of America

Pulp Hero Press | **www.PulpHeroPress.com**
Address queries to bob@pulpheropress.com

Contents

FOREWORD

Leigh Taylor-Young's long movie career includes starring roles in a '60s favorite, *I Love You, Alice B. Toklas* (1968) with Peter Sellers; a '70s science-fiction classic, *Soylent Green* (1973) with Charlton Heston; and a thrilling '80s hit, *Jagged Edge* (1985) with Jeff Bridges. On television, she's had important recurring roles on everything from *Peyton Place* and *Beverly Hills 90210* to *Dallas*, supplemented with guest-starring appearances on dozens of other shows. In 1994 *Picket Fences* brought her an Emmy Award as the Outstanding Supporting Actress in a Drama Series. Leigh has also acted on Broadway and off-Broadway, she has modeled for Richard Avedon for *Vogue* magazine, and she has avidly pursued spiritual interests, leading her to India to study and to her current life, often traveling the world with her husband, John Morton, presenting seminars, facilitating workshops on spirituality, and being of service through counseling. She is an ordained minister in the Movement of Spiritual Awareness (read about her remarkable adventures at lty.com). Leigh penned the following observations about '70s movies for us from her Pacific Palisades home.

The 1970s were a time of liberation. Politically, spiritually, socially, and cinematically, we were breaking free from many traditions of the past. After the 1960s, when there were still big studio-driven epics, in the '70s we were moving toward more intimate cutting-edge independent movies that broke through the boundaries of what you could do and what you could reveal. Not just in terms of the new language, sexuality, and violence, but suddenly in the '70s you could have small, off-beat movies like *Harold and Maude*, or movies without traditional happy endings like *The Godfather* and *Chinatown*, or gritty, urban movies like *The French Connection*, or exciting new experiences like *Star Wars* that made everybody cheer with joy for a space fantasy we had not yet seen. We were breaking down barriers for women with movies like *Klute*, and we also had wild, rebellious departures like *Animal House*. It felt like a big shift in our cinematic culture.

I think film illustrates our collective consciousness, and at the time it felt like everything was shaking loose and new forces were being unleashed. After the success of *Easy Rider*, the genie was out of the bottle, and the revolution of change was begun. The '70s were filled with exuberant, youthful, imaginative new directors who were ready to fly. They dared to use the emerging technology, the newest special effects, handheld cameras, and "guerrilla" techniques that gave them a fresh approach to filmmaking. Everything went

Leigh in the 1960s. Photo courtesy LTY.

to extremes, whether the movies were on the dark, realistic side, like Martin Scorsese's *Taxi Driver*, or on the lighter yet provocative side, like Steven Spielberg's *Close Encounters of the Third Kind.*

For me, Steven is a perfect representative of the stunning energy in the '70s. I love the movies he makes and the enthusiasm and passion he brings to his projects. He's always "all in," nothing is halfway. The story of how he innovated his way through *Jaws* to overcome all the problems they had with the mechanical shark is almost mythical. I had a memorable movie experience with Steven. My husband of that time was his agent, and I was sitting next to Steven the first time *E.T.* was premiered. We were in Pacific's Cinerama Theatre, the huge domed showplace in Hollywood, and every seat was filled. At one point toward the end of the film Steven squeezed my hand nervously, waiting to see what the audience thought. I knew right away that it was extraordinary and wonderful, but as the film ended, the audience was completely silent. They stayed that way for a minute. Then from the back of the theater came this growing wave of sound, a roar of cheering that swept over us and engulfed the entire theatre. We both smiled in relief and some amazement with the power of the response.

I can remember some of my '70s movie-going experiences very clearly. *Harold and Maude*, for instance, which most people didn't get at first, though it found its audience. I immediately loved its message, which is simply "to live." Whether you're young or old, no matter your situation, don't limit yourself, the movie is saying, go for the gold in your life. Then there was *The Exorcist*. Normally I prefer non-violent movies, but all my friends had been talking about *The Exorcist*, so I went along with a group to see a midnight show in Westwood Village near UCLA. The show was virtually sold out, so we had to split up, and I ended up in a seat in the middle of a crowded row surrounded by strangers. I watched the movie and felt frozen in horror, with no place to go. The man next to me with this big box of popcorn totally freaked out, flinging his hands up across his eyes and spilling his popcorn everywhere. At the opposite end of the spectrum was my experience seeing *Star Wars* when it opened in Hollywood. Lines formed around the block, and I think they showed it twenty-fours

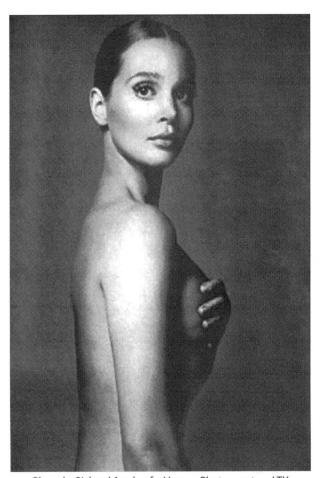

Photo by Richard Avedon for Vogue. *Photo courtesy LTY.*

With Charlton Heston in Soylent Green.

a day for a while. I loved it, and I remember people in the theater expressing their joy as the movie ended.

The most important movie I made in the 1970s was *Soylent Green*. Ironically, I did not believe it would be very successful. It was about a dark time in our future when the environment would be destroyed by human greed, and people would be eating people to survive. I thought it was a stretch and a bit of a folly, but *Soylent Green* today is seen as a highly regarded environmental cult film. Edward G. Robinson's death scene is one of the most poignant on film. My sweetest memory of this movie was working with "Eddie," who died only a few months after we finished filming. He was short, and I was very tall. (Of course my height was aided by my four-inch platforms of that time!) I remember our final photo shoot with Charlton Heston, Chuck Connors, Eddie, and me. Eddie snuggled into my chest, put his arm around my waist, looked up and declared, "I am standing right here!" In the midst of his playful mischief with me there was a precious and sensitive regard. At the cast party, he wanted me to sit next to him. It was the last time I would see him, and I knew it. I cried driving home that night, so touched by his refinement and kindness. He was an oasis.

Soylent Green was actually the end of one aspect of my life. A week after I completed the film, I was on a plane to India and an ashram in the Himalayas where a new chapter of my life would soon open. The '70s was a time when people pursued self-exploration and spiritual adventures, whether that was with Indian gurus, meditation, yoga, or even drugs. Again, there was this sense of liberation, of breaking free of past expectations and norms. There were new health trends to try, like aerobics, supplements, acupuncture, and fasting. I hit the ground running and was probably ahead of the curve, thanks to my '60s experiences.

On the set of Soylent Green. *Photo courtesy LTY.*

As odd as this might sound, the '70s were a remarkably positive and innocent decade, because there was joyful creativity and strong desire for purpose and fulfillment without the materialistic desires that came later in the more glamorous and superficial 1980s. I think of my favorite musicians of the '70s—Cat Stevens, Carole King, early Elton John, James Taylor, and Dave Mason (one of the great unsung guitarists); all of them were sincere artists making beautiful music that I loved. It's like we were all trying to answer what I consider to be the main questions we must all ask, "Who are we? And, who am I?"

I am delighted to participate in Chris' book and I am glad that my friend is celebrating the 1970s. It is my favorite movie decade.

—Leigh Taylor-Young

The Horsemen *(1971)*.

Leigh Taylor Young today.
Photo courtesy LTY.

INTRODUCTION

Don't Start the Revolution Without Me

Writers often get asked how long it takes to write their books. This one took almost fifty years. I began it in January 1970 when I was a newly minted teenager, right after I saw *M*A*S*H* (1970) in a theater. My adventurous parents had already taken me to some excellent "grown-up" movies—*A Hard Day's Night* (1964) at age seven, *Bonnie and Clyde* (1967), age ten—but *M*A*S*H* was the first '70s movie I saw just with my friends. Dazzled and motivated, I immediately wrote up a list of every movie I'd ever seen away from the couch-sized TV console in our living room, starting with *The Great Escape* (1963) at a drive-in and ending with *Butch Cassidy and the Sundance Kid* (1969) on a Boeing 707. Then I ranked them in categories: Best Musical, *A Funny Thing Happened on the Way to the Forum* (1966); Best Sci-Fi Movie, *2001: A Space Odyssey* (1968), etc. I listed *M*A*S*H* as Best Anti-War Movie (which still might be true) and for the next few years steadily added more '70s movies, with each one taking its turn as a new favorite: Best Car Movie, *Vanishing Point* (1971); Best Comedy, *American Graffiti* (1973), and more.

Fortunately, my county, Santa Cruz, was thick with theaters, and just one highway away were San Jose's Century dome theaters for special events like *Jaws* (1975). So, when I wasn't doing homework, or working at the neighborhood market, or playing baseball, I was going to movies. To my astonishment I even made the local newspaper when I was the first patron ever at the brand-new

Aptos Twin Theaters and was awarded a shiny ten-speed Schwinn Varsity, all because I was so eager to see *Sleuth* (1972). Moving on to UCLA, I indulged in Ackerman Union's $1 double-features and the dozen theaters in nearby Westwood Village. And thanks to my internship at *Movieline* magazine, I was visiting the Margaret Herrick Library at the

Academy of Motion Picture Arts and Sciences regularly. My movie list grew rapidly, the award-winners evolved—*Cabaret* (1972) over *Forum*, *Annie Hall* (1977) over *Graffiti*, *Star Wars* (1977) over *2001*—and I added rudimentary notes to the titles: "*Taxi Driver* (1976), not for dates." Over the decades, those notes gradually expanded into this book.

It's important to note that I didn't arrive late to the '70s party. I was right there, watching and studying and reading about these new movies, cringing in my theater seat the first week *The Exorcist* (1973) came out, laughing out loud with everyone else at *Young Frankenstein* (1974), holding my breath like the rest of the audience near the end of *Close Encounters of the Third Kind* (1977), and immediately sneaking back into the theater with my friends to roar once more with *Animal House* (1978). Experience like this is vital for someone writing about a not-so-distant decade—readers should expect first-hand knowledge.

Looking back, I appreciate how fortunate I was to be going to movies in a golden era when a new pantheon of movie gods was starting to walk the earth. These were energetic directors— Scorsese, Spielberg, Woody—and dynamic actors—De Niro, Pacino, Jack—you knew by just one name. Fired up by *The Graduate* (1967), *Easy Rider* (1969), *Midnight Cowboy* (1969), and other provocative catalysts, these insurgents torched the old bloated studio system being run

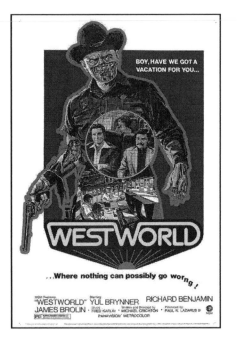

by conservative executives who had wheezed to the end of the 1960s with safe-and-sane products like *Hello, Dolly!* (1969). Instead, the rebels created bold, stylish movies that felt more independent and irreverent, more personal and powerful. Momentous

star-driven entertainments still thrived, obviously (see 1973's Best Picture winner, *The Sting*), but the Little Movies That Could—small, vivid outsiders like *Harold and Maude* (1971)— were flourishing, too. What an exciting time to be a young movie fan. It's no coincidence that many American universities introduced new film-studies programs during the decade.

With the collapse of the regulating Hays Code in 1968, Hollywood could now include sex, violence, and language not previously permissible; furthermore, a surge of technological advancements throughout the '70s, such as the first CGI (computer-generated imagery) in *Westworld* (1973) and the invention of the Steadicam in 1975, enabled special effects not previously possible. The revolution seeded everything from police dramas (*The French Connection*, 1971), to musicals (*The Rocky Horror Picture Show*, 1975), to sports movies (*Slap Shot*, 1978), to horror (*Alien*, 1979), with whole new genres and subgenres—disaster epics like *Airport* (1970), blaxploitation movies like *Shaft* (1971), and superhero extravaganzas like *Superman* (1978), for example—sprouting from the decade's fertile soil.

In the next few years all of these '70s movies will have reached their fiftieth anniversaries, so this seems like an auspicious time to celebrate Hollywood's "daring decade."

With thousands of movies released between January 1, 1970, and December 31, 1974, to choose from, the trick was to pick. I narrowed my volume-one selections like this:

▪ Theatrically released feature-length American movies, so no TV movies, no short films, no Hammer horrors or Monty Pythons from England, and no subtitled foreign films.

▪ Incendiary movies that ignited controversies, like *Straw Dogs* (1971), or sparked new genres, like *The Last House on the Left* (1972).

▪ Movies that advanced cinema's aesthetic, either with their influential style, a la *The Last Picture Show* (1971), or with their new technology, a la *Earthquake* (1974).

▪ Movies that jump-started the careers of important directors, actors, or actresses, like Clint Eastwood's directorial debut, *Play Misty for Me* (1972).

▪ Movies with overwhelming, though sometimes perplexing, popular appeal, like *Love Story* (1970).

▪ Fallible guilty pleasures, like *The Golden Voyage of Sinbad* (1974).

▪ No pornographic movies—sorry, *Deep Throat* (1972).

So, some masterpieces, many popular hits, a few controversial shockers, the occasional quirky oddity, and even some really bad movies that somehow survived ... overall a pretty wide-ranging representation that embraces movies I overly admired back then, like *Start the Revolution Without Me* (1970) and *Silent Running* (1972), and reaches to the more challenging, artful movies I could only appreciate as an adult, like *Five Easy Pieces* (1970) and *The Conversation* (1974). This balance of the nostalgic with the profound means that dopey Disney comedies, which millions of fans and I fondly recall, are alongside intense, indisputable classics like *The Godfather* (1972) and *Chinatown* (1974), which virtually everybody reveres. Right on.

For each year I've selected five movies that I deem FAR-OUT—a decade-spanning superlative used in the documentary *Woodstock* (1970), *Apocalypse Now* (1979), and many others in between—so look for that appellation and be sure to watch these extra-special movies (twenty-five in each volume, so fifty '70s movies in total). Actually, that's good advice for all the movies that follow: watch them. Collectively, they're the greatest ever, according to the American Film Institute, an esteemed body of critics and filmmakers that created a greatest-hits list called "100 Years ... 100 Movies" in 1998 and again in 2007. Both times, there were more movies from the '70s on the list than from any other decade. I hope this book inspires renewed attention to the movies I've loved now for five decades.

My thanks to publisher Bob McLain, who got it, and his Pulp Hero Press team, who crafted it. Endless appreciation goes to Leigh Taylor-Young and Tom Skerritt, who generously took time from their busy lives to write the foreword and afterword of this book (it's sheer coincidence that they're both here and that both of these wonderful actors won Emmy Awards for the same show, *Picket Fences*, in consecutive years, what synchronicity!)

In addition, while researching and writing *The Daring Decade*, my gratitude drifted from the present to the past as I thought about the people I saw these '70s movies with. They don't all know it, but in some ways we did this book together. As the character named G.T.O. says in the last line of *Two-Lane Blacktop* (1971), "Those satisfactions are permanent."

—Chris Strodder

Notes on the Text

In the following text, the movies are presented chronologically with a theater-style format. They open with a listing of main credits and a seventy-character "Preview" (never exceeding *exactly* seventy characters), continue with an opinionated four-hundred-word critical essay, and finish with an "Added Attraction" that further develops something from the movie. For each separate year, I've expanded five noteworthy FAR-OUT movies with a longer format that adds a "Fine Line" (an important quote), a "Close-Up" (a specific scene), and a nine-hundred-word essay. Everything is based on my own original research (not on recycled internet trivia), and I've copied the quotes exactly as they're spoken in the movies (you'd be amazed how often movie quotes are transcribed incorrectly in print and on the internet).

This book makes reference to various copyrighted titles, trademarks, and registered marks (including Academy Award, movies like *The Wizard of Oz*, and publications like *People* magazine) that are the properties of their respective owners and are used here solely for editorial and informational purposes under the Fair Use Doctrine. Neither the author nor the publisher makes any commercial claim to their use. All images were acquired via the Movie Stills Database (moviestillsdb.com).

James Joyce called errors "the portals of discovery." I think of them the same way. Should you doubt a fact or notice a possible "portal of discovery," please do two things: first, forgive my mistake (and it is my mistake, nobody else's); and second, let me know what you found by politely writing to me via www.encycoolpedia.com. I'll reply with interest and gratitude.

—C.S.

1970

In Film

- Oscar for Best Picture: *Patton*.
- Most Oscar wins (seven): *Patton*.
- Most Oscar nominations (ten): *Airport*, *Patton*.
- Top-grossing movie*: *Love Story*.
- Top-grossing comedy: *M*A*S*H*.
- Top-grossing horror or sci-fi: *Beneath the Planet of the Apes*.
- *Airport* launches the decade's disaster genre.

- Average adult movie-ticket price = approximately $1.50
- Five memorable actors: Elliott Gould, Jack Nicholson, Donald Sutherland, Ryan O'Neal, George C. Scott.
- Five memorable actresses: Karen Black, Glenda Jackson, Sally Kellerman, Ali MacGraw, Carrie Snodgress.
- Movie debuts: Diane Keaton, Susan Sarandon, Arnold Schwarzenegger, director Hal Ashby.
- Deaths include composer Alfred Newman.

* Throughout the book, box-office rankings are for domestic releases, shown at Box Office Madness: https://boxofficemadness.wordpress.com.

In America

- National Guardsmen shoot four students at Kent State, intensifying nation-wide protests.
- Voting age lowered to eighteen.
- Environmental Protection Agency formed; first Earth Day.
- *Apollo 13* disaster.
- Average price for a gallon of gasoline: thirty-six cents.
- New transportation: Boeing 747, AMC Gremlin, Ford Pinto, Earth Shoes.
- Over 50,000 women gather in New York, and protests are held around the country, to support the Women's Strike for Equality.
- New York sports: the Knicks beat the Los Angeles Lakers in seven games for the NBA championship, and the first New York City Marathon is held.
- Gary Gabelich sets a new land-speed record of 622 mph in the rocket-powered *Blue Flame*.
- First issue of *National Lampoon* magazine.
- *Doonesbury* debuts as a daily syndicated comic strip.
- Bestselling novel: *Love Story*.

- Music: The Beatles break up; Simon and Garfunkel's last studio album, *Bridge Over Troubled Water*; Casey Kasem's *American Top 40* radio show debuts.
- TV debuts: PBS, *The Mary Tyler Moore Show*, *Monday Night Football*, *The Partridge Family*.
- Deaths include Jimi Hendrix, Janis Joplin, Vince Lombardi.

M*A*S*H

(One of 1970's five **FAR-OUT** movies)

Released: January 1970

Director: Robert Altman

Stars: Donald Sutherland, Elliott Gould, Tom Skerritt

Academy Awards: One win (Best Writing), plus four more nominations (Best Picture; Best Supporting Actress—Sally Kellerman; Best Director; Best Editing)

PREVIEW: Doctors at an army hospital cope with war's horrors by defying military authority.

FINE LINE: "This isn't a hospital! It's an insane asylum!" (Nurse "Hot Lips" O'Houlihan, screaming in frustration at Colonel Henry Blake.)

CLOSE-UP: Watch the first surgical scene closely. Even though his character hasn't arrived at the camp yet, that's Elliott Gould behind the anesthesiologist's mask supplying gas to Hawkeye's patient.

NOW SHOWING: War Movies Meet Their *M*A*S*H*

How interesting that two great but totally different war movies, the irreverent *M*A*S*H* and the more traditional *Patton*, would be duking it out at the Oscars for honors as Best Picture of 1970. *Patton* won, of course, and deservedly so, but it's possible that *M*A*S*H* had the more lasting impact. There had simply been nothing like it, and the unorthodox storytelling techniques it introduced were quickly absorbed into the industry and refreshed in director Robert Altman's later movies, particularly *Nashville* (1975).

Premiering in January 1970, *M*A*S*H* gets the decade off to a radical start. Ostensibly the *M*A*S*H*-maker was screenwriter Ring Lardner, Jr., who won an Oscar for his adaptation of Richard Hooker's 1968 novel about doctors operating and partying near the front lines of the Korean War. Lardner, however, later said he barely recognized any of his dialogue in the finished movie. That's because *M*A*S*H* is the successful result of Altman's aleatoric style of filmmaking in which he sets up situations and then lets seemingly random, spontaneous events and conversations happen in front of his camera. It's the polar opposite of the perfectionistic direction of someone like Stanley Kubrick, who meticulously planned and tightly controlled every aspect of his movies. Altman defiantly jettisons a conventional plot with a traditional leading man and leading lady in favor of wildly careening episodic action, an ensemble cast of mostly fresh faces, improvised over-lapping dialogue, gallows humor amidst realistic operating-room gore, an up-to-the-minute youthful spirit and anti-war attitude, a famous theme song, casual sex, and even a quick glimpse of a doobie being passed around. It all added up to a brash, free-wheeling revolution that attracted blockbuster-size audiences and poster-worthy praise from major critics who recognized that it represented a type of filmmaking for which major American movies had no precedent.

As good as *M*A*S*H* is, however, it could've been better. Once all the doctors have arrived at the camp and the audience has become familiar with how things work in their unusual world, one of the seemingly significant characters is suddenly extracted mid-movie. The young Korean aide, Ho-Jon, seems like he's being groomed for some important role in the story and is friends with the main doctors, but he's dropped off in a Korean hospital and disappears for good. Some viewers guess that it's Ho-Jon's body seen near the end while the boys are playing poker, though this is never clear (the book's Ho-Jon is drafted, wounded, successfully operated on by Hawkeye and Trapper, and sent to Hawkeye's alma mater). It seems odd that he'd be given scenes and dialogue in the first half of the movie but none in the second.

More alarming is the doctors' cruel treatment of Frank Burns. Okay, he's a little older (though the actor, Robert Duvall, is just two years older than Tom Skerritt, playing Duke); true, he prays unabashedly, he doesn't drink, he's not always nice to subordinates, and he may not be the surgeon the others are. But Hawkeye (Donald Sutherland) and Duke, and later Trapper John (Elliott Gould), all instantly hate him on sight. Hawkeye and Duke go to the colonel to have him removed, Trapper physically assaults him with impunity (Burns is a superior officer, remember), and they vulgarly taunt him in public to provoke him into a violent retaliation that puts him in a career-destroying strait-jacket. These mean-spirited scenes are played for laughs with a smug hipper-than-thou attitude, but some viewers remember them as the ugliest of the doctors' arrogant antics (second-ugliest would be the public humiliation of Hot Lips in the shower, but at least they later embrace her into their group, and Duke even falls for her).

Still, the doctors are heroic with their patients and always pull together to overcome difficult conditions and limited resources. They unite to help the suicidal Don Juan dentist, and the entire camp is involved in the entertaining thirteen-minute-long football game that dominates the last act. This rousing contest, which features abundant cheating, taunting, and physical punishment, is true to the book's spirit, though not to its final score (the book has the M*A*S*H men winning 28–24, Lardner's screenplay called for a 14–7 M*A*S*H victory, and Altman settles on an 18–16 game won on the last play when the doctors pull the hidden-ball trick). The movie's last scenes show the gang breaking up when two of the stars are sent home (the book's last thirty pages actually show a month of Hawkeye and Duke's travel adventures after they leave the camp). Sutherland and Gould, both relatively unknown at the time, are appealing in their star-making roles (Gould would go on to four more movies with Robert Altman); Sally Kellerman got an Oscar nomination as Hot Lips; and quiet Gary Burghoff as Radar is the glue that holds everything together (he's the only the cast member who went on to the hit TV show).

And throughout, Altman implements a brilliant device—the camp's P.A. system—to add humorous touches and clever musical flourishes, even letting the tinny speakers deliver the end credits.

Dedicated fans of the later *M*A*S*H*-tastic TV series may be underwhelmed, or they may have forgotten what a groundbreaking, iconoclastic triumph

Donald Sutherland and Elliott Gould.

the movie was. But in 1970 *M*A*S*H* was a monster. It still turns up on various "best" lists, and today it can rightly be regarded as the first movie milestone of the decade.

ADDED ATTRACTION: More War Comedies

The term "war comedies" seems like an oxymoron, but more of these hybrid movies followed *M*A*S*H*'s lead throughout the 1970s. Not all show combat scenes, and not all involve twentieth-century conflicts, but all of the following chronologically listed American movies use military characters and settings to generate comedy. (*M*A*S*H*'s Elliott Gould stars in *Whiffs*.)

- *Kelly's Heroes* (1970)
- *Catch-22* (1970)
- *Which Way to the Front?* (1970)
- *Suppose They Gave a War and Nobody Came* (1970)
- *The Last Detail* (1973)
- *Love and Death* (1975)
- *Whiffs* (1975)
- *Hawmps!* (1976)
- *The Last Remake of Beau Geste* (1977)
- *The Apple Dumpling Gang Rides Again* (1979)
- *1941* (1979)

The Molly Maguires

Released: January 1970
Director: Martin Ritt
Stars: Sean Connery, Richard Harris, Samantha Eggar
Academy Awards: One nomination (Best Art Direction)

PREVIEW: To protest conditions in their 1876 coal mines, a secret group sabotages the mines.

NOW SHOWING: James Bomb

The Molly Maguires (1970) could be nominated for the Most Underrated Movie of 1970 Award. Despite having two stars (Sean Connery and Richard Harris), an Oscar-nominated director (Martin Ritt), powerful action, a well-intentioned social message, effective cinematography by a multiple Oscar winner (James Wong Howe), and an atmospheric score by another multiple Oscar winner (Henry Mancini), somehow this explosive big-budget movie was a dud with audiences. It's their loss.

Based on true events, the movie tells the story of nineteenth-century miners rebelling against the appalling conditions experienced daily by the despairing adults and soot-blackened children working in Pennsylvania's claustrophobic coal mines. A small band of radicals, the Molly Maguires (named after a group of nineteenth-century protestors in Ireland), expresses its outrage by sabotaging the mines with explosives, derailing a train, burning down the company store, assassinating a supervisor, and killing cops. Into their midst comes a stranger (Richard Harris) who's actually an undercover detective. "Don't get confused about which side you're on," he's told, but that's exactly what happens when this infiltrator experiences the miners' difficult, unhealthy life first-hand and falls for a local girl (Samantha Eggar). He joins in on several destructive missions and gets bruised and battered for his troubles, all while informing on the Mollies to the Coal and Iron Police. There's genuine tension as the Mollies start to suspect the traitor among them, and audience sympathies are torn between the tragic miners and the crime-fighters trying to stop the murderous outlaws. Eventually the Mollies are caught, to their horror the detective testifies against them, and the gallows await.

So why was it a flop? Well, there's little levity (though there's a terrific football/rugby game in the middle). Sean Connery, an international superstar from his James Bond movies, is a formidable presence throughout, but he doesn't utter a single word until forty minutes have passed, and the story isn't really about him anyway, it's about the detective (for once Harris isn't his usual over-emoting self, instead playing it low-key and charming so he can win over the Mollies and the girl). Maybe 1970 audiences were uninterested in 1876 social problems, maybe they were confused about whom they should be rooting for (Connery and Harris, both with thick moustaches and accents, are almost like opposing brothers), maybe the ending felt a little drawn-out and deflating. Whatever its flaws, *The Molly Maguires* holds up as a bold accomplishment.

ADDED ATTRACTION: The Great *Great White Hope*

Later in 1970, a second movie by director Martin Ritt was released. *The Great White Hope* fictionalizes the early-twentieth-century story of black boxer Jack Johnson and his fight against racism. After defeating the white heavyweight champ, Jack Jefferson (James Earl Jones) becomes the brash titleholder, but his brazen romance with a dignified white woman, Eleanor (Jane Alexander), brings scandal and arrest. Jefferson jumps bail, and he and Eleanor visit different countries before making a last stand in Mexico, where they both meet defeat. This powerful movie is based on the acclaimed Broadway play that brought Jones and Alexander Tony Awards; their screen performances—Jones is formidable and defiant, Alexander quiet and loyal—earned them both Oscar nominations. For Ritt, *The Great White Hope* is one of his highlights in a decade-long run of noble dramas that include the excellent *Sounder* (1972), *The Front* (1976), and *Norma Rae* (1979).

Patton

(One of 1970's five **FAR-OUT** movies)

Released: February 1970

Director: Franklin J. Schaffner

Stars: George C. Scott, Karl Malden, Paul Stevens

Academy Awards: Seven wins (Best Picture; Best Actor—George C. Scott; Best Director; Best Writing; Best Editing; Best Art Direction; Best Sound), plus three more nominations (Best Cinematography; Best Visual Effects; Best Music)

PREVIEW: General Patton leads daring attacks across Europe while generating controversy.

FINE LINE: "Now, I want you to remember that no bastard ever won a war by dying for his country. He won it by making the other poor dumb bastard die for his country." (Patton, addressing the troops in the first scene.)

CLOSE-UP: The tone-setting six-minute speech that opens the movie is actually a composite of several Patton speeches. As vulgar as Patton's language is in the scene, this version is still somewhat sanitized from what he actually said. As evidenced by the stars on his helmet, Patton is a four-star general at this point, placing this speech in 1944; the speech is followed by the movie's titles, and then action commences in Tunisia in 1943, with Patton a two-star general.

NOW SHOWING: American Gladiator

What a year for war movies 1970 was! *Catch-22*, *Cromwell*, *Kelly's Heroes*, *M*A*S*H*, *Tora! Tora! Tora!*, the international production *Waterloo*, even Jerry Lewis's *Which Way to the Front?* presented diverse attitudes and approaches to war-time stories. And we haven't even mentioned what is, with apologies to *The Deer Hunter* (1978) and *Apocalypse Now* (1979), the best war movie of the decade, and one of the best of all time.

It could be argued that *Patton* (1970) is a biographical movie first and a war movie second, but those are hairs that don't need to be split because the man the movie is about *is* war. As shown in this bold, powerful movie, General George Patton revels in the glories of war and is only truly alive on the battlefield: "I do this job because I've been trained to do it," his friend General Bradley (Karl Malden) tells him, "You do it because you love it." When he's temporarily sent to the sidelines, he can't wait to get back into the fray and begs for a new command; when he considers a future of push-button "wonder weapons" with "no troops, no generals," he says he's glad he "won't live to see it." He reads military books in bed, sometimes sleeps in his uniform, and whenever he imagines past incarnations of himself, it's always a military man he sees.

As Patton, the great George C. Scott becomes both a philosophical poet who reads the Bible every day and a dynamic man of action who enthusiastically leaps from

windows to fire his pistols at oncoming enemy planes. Scott's brilliance was that he could present all sides of this complex man so convincingly. He's charming and complimentary when he gives a humorous speech to British civilians, he's crude and formidable when he sternly addresses the troops, he's erudite when he orders fine cuisine in French, he's temperamental when his superiors put obstacles in his way, and he's believably humble when he acknowledges his long-time debt to General Bradley after Bradley scolds him as "a pain in the neck." Scott's portrayal is so iconic that for most people he is their idea of what Patton himself was really like, though there are some physical differences (unlike the gruff-voiced barrel-chested Scott, the real George Patton had a high-pitched voice and the wiry frame of the Olympic athlete he once was). It's a thrilling, fascinating performance that deservedly brought Scott the Best Actor Oscar, which he famously refused to accept because he detested the idea of acting competitions. Interestingly, while it's hard to imagine anyone but Scott in the role, he was supposedly not the first choice: actors said to have turned down the part include Burt Lancaster, Lee Marvin, Robert Mitchum, and Rod Steiger.

At almost three-hours long, *Patton* presents a detailed retelling of this warrior's World War Two life. The movie shows him at his confident best (planning strategy, leading his men), but it isn't hagiographic, so we also see Patton at his self-destructive worst—the notorious incident when he slaps an enlisted man, and his egotistical attempts to lift his own glory above that of his chief rival, Britain's Field Marshal Montgomery. Big spectacle fills this big movie, from the riveting opening speech in front of an immense flag to the panoramic tank battles to the final image of the maverick general walking alone among windmills like an idealistic Don Quixote. But there are plenty of quiet moments, too. We hear Patton's inner thoughts as he narrates scenes, he tells us a poem he's written, he composes a letter to the parents of his dead aide, he reads a prayer, he describes recent dreams, and he confesses his deepest fears and vulnerabilities.

Working from an Oscar-winning script co-written by Francis Ford Coppola, director Franklin Schaffner, who had previously made the influential *Planet of the Apes* (1968), strikes effective balances throughout *Patton*: volatile Patton with stable Bradley, vivid war scenes with private conversations, parade-worthy victories with bloody defeats, American officers with their German and Russian counterparts, military aggressiveness with diplomatic restraint, and lavish-living generals with ordinary soldiers. Perfectly complimenting the movie's themes is the instantly identifiable music by Jerry Goldsmith, who uses echoing trumpets to express Patton's belief in reincarnation, fifes to evoke the historical battles he mentions throughout, and a rousing fanfare to rally the troops and the audience (but not the Oscar voters, who were successfully courted by *Love Story* for the Best Music award).

"All glory is fleeting," is Patton's (and the movie's) last line. Maybe for heroes and champions, but not for *Patton*. A smash hit in 1970, if anything the movie's glory has only increased as less accomplished rivals have come and gone and history has nudged the general's stature into the realm of folk hero. Epic and intimate, *Patton* is the thinking-man's war movie.

ADDED ATTRACTION: Battlin' Patton

These are the major battles shown in the movie.

- **Battle of Kasserine Pass**, Tunisia, February 1943:
  Rommel's forces pummel the American army; Patton is not yet on the scene.
- **Battle of El Guettar, Tunisia**, March–April 1943:
  Patton leads America's first North African victory.

- **Invasion of Sicily**, Italy, July–August 1943:
  Patton charges across Sicily from Palermo to Messina.
- **Operation Cobra**, France, July–August 1944:
  After D-Day, Patton's Third Army makes "a sweeping end run right across France."
- **Battle of the Bulge**, France, December 1944–January 1945:
  Patton boldly relieves imperiled Allied forces at Bastogne.

Start the Revolution Without Me

Released: February 1970

Director: Bud Yorkin

Stars: Gene Wilder, Donald Sutherland, Hugh Griffith

Academy Awards: None

PREVIEW: In 1789 two sets of twins get mixed up with the royal court and the French Revolution.

NOW SHOWING: *Viva la Farce*

Ignored upon release, but later a cult favorite, *Start the Revolution Without Me* (1970) continues to split audiences. That some viewers laugh and others shrug is understandable—after all, even the beloved *Some Like It Hot* (1959) has detractors. Everyone, however, can agree that *Start the Revolution Without Me* is a significant link between past "costume comedies" like *Monsieur Beaucaire* (1946) and later farces, like Woody Allen's *Love and Death* (1975), Mel Brooks's *History of the World: Part I* (1981), and Cheech & Chong's *The Corsican Brothers* (1984) that all spoof earlier centuries. *Start the Revolution* isn't in Woody's league, but it's still fun, stylish entertainment.

The movie's direct ancestor is the great *Tom Jones* (1963), and indeed they share four actors and a composer (John Addison, whose lively music sprints through both films). The convoluted story involves two sets of identical twins (Gene Wilder and Donald Sutherland) that get switched at birth in 1759. Thirty years on, the two sets crisscross and assume opposite roles, so the peasant twins join the royal court and the aristocratic twins become peasant revolutionaries. Louis XVI and Marie Antoinette figure prominently, Alexandre Dumas's Man in the Iron Mask shows up, and one of the two narrators is modern-day Orson Welles, introducing this as "a color film, which I am not in."

The inspired silliness takes many forms: nutty wordplay, as when a royal is called "the scrounge of Corsica" ("*Scourge* of Corsica," he replies testily); goofy sight gags (Wilder rides around with a dead falcon on his arm); witty French names (Duke d'Escargot, Mimi Montage, Count Henri Manzini); clever recurring on-screen text (reminding us a dozen times that it's *still* 1789); hilarious extended scenes (a ridiculous costume mistakenly worn to a formal ball); and some bits slyly borrowed from other movies (the "patty-cake" fighting strategy from the Hope-and-Crosby *Road* movies). The last thirty minutes start to get tedious as the plot wraps up with frenetic chases, multiple pratfalls, and a chaotic battle, but a daring two-minute finale brings everything to an absurd halt (even Welles is abruptly killed off). The funniest performances are by Wilder, simmering and suddenly erupting as he will in *Young Frankenstein* (1974), and Hugh Griffith, playing the delightfully daft king. In addition, the dazzling costumes and opulent French settings are undeniably impressive. So, is *Start the Revolution Without Me* a timeless classic? *Non*. How about an underappreciated romp? *Oui*.

ADDED ATTRACTION: More Costume Dramas, Comedies, and Musicals

The 1970s did have other costume comedies besides *Start the Revolution Without Me*, and the decade had some costume dramas and costume musicals, too. Here are a dozen chronological examples of well-costumed movies set between 1600 and 1899. Not included are all of the many westerns and Sherlock Holmes movies released during the '70s, so there's no *Blazing Saddles* (1974) or *The Seven-Per-Cent Solution* (1976) on this list.

- *The Hawaiians* (1970)
- *1776* (1972)
- *Tom Sawyer* (1973)
- *The Three Musketeers* (1973)
- *The Arena* (1974)
- *Daisy Miller* (1974)
- *Love and Death* (1975)
- *Hester Street* (1975)
- *The Man Who Would Be King* (1975)
- *Barry Lyndon* (1975)
- *Swashbuckler* (1976)
- *The Prisoner of Zenda* (1979)

Zabriskie Point

Released: February 1970
Director: Michelangelo Antonioni
Stars: Mark Frechette, Daria Halprin, Rod Taylor
Academy Awards: None

PREVIEW: A defiant man flies a stolen plane to the desert, where he meets an independent girl.

NOW SHOWING: Please Tell Us the *Zabriskie Point*

Zabriskie Point (1970) invites parody titles: *Zabriskie Pointless*, *Zabriskie Disappoint*, etc. Slow and pretentious, it was a notorious bomb and often makes lists of all-time worst movies.

Following his successful *Blow-Up* (1966), which artfully captured swingin' mid-'60s London, director Michelangelo Antonioni seems to want *Zabriskie Point* to deliver a damning statement about late-'60s America. His thin plot starts with a charmless student (Mark Frechette) almost shooting a cop, running off, and effortlessly stealing a plane to fly from L.A. to the desert. There he meets a pretty girl (Daria Halprin) who's on a solo road trip to go meditate. She drives them to Death Valley's actual Zabriskie Point, where they run around and make sweet sweet love. "I wanna take risks," he declares, so he returns to the sound of sirens (he's a fugitive, remember) and is killed by policemen; she continues her desert journey, imagines she watches a magnificent house explode, and drives into the sunset.

Everything has a forced hipness, exemplified by the girl's oh-so-heavy statement, "It's not something I really dig to do, I just work when I need bread." Both main performers use their real first names in the movie, and both are total novices. Shaggy-haired Mark has a sullen non-conformist demeanor; natural-beauty Daria has more depth. Some viewers consider them refreshing, possibly a euphemism for "amateurish." Eventually, what could be philosophical and liberating about their time together becomes dumb and meaningless. When they have sex in the desert, dozens of naked couples inexplicably emerge nearby for an orgy in the sand and then vanish, maybe to go get some Zabriskie Ointment.

Audiences could legitimately respond to the startling visuals. The ugly, noisy city is dominated by corporate billboards, though they're rarely relevant (an exception comes when Mark, contemplating escape, stands by one that reads "Let's get away from it all"). In contrast, the vast desert is breathtaking and enhanced by cool rock music. The climax features five minutes of explosions from many different angles. The slow-motion shots of flying consumer products seem significant, though exactly how isn't clear. Perhaps this ending made more sense in 1970, when anti-establishment hippie attitudes were radical and right-on, especially after a Zabriskie Joint, so repeated detonations of an expensive house seemed like a Zabriskie Exclamation Point. Or maybe it's just Antonio saying, "You liked *Blow-Up*? Here, the house blows up nineteen times, go crazy!" Pondering this movie, you might.

ADDED ATTRACTION: Movie Explosions

At the end of *Zabriskie Point*, the serene desert is shockingly disrupted by a series of explosions. Here are a half-dozen other 1970s movies that have dramatic explosions at or right near the end.

- *Alien* (1979): The *Nostromo* explodes with slit-scan special effects similar to those in *2001: A Space Odyssey* (1968).
- *Apocalypse Now* (1979): Originally this movie ended quietly, but later versions added spectacular final shots of the jungle exploding after an air strike.
- *Beneath the Planet of the Apes* (1970): A doomsday weapon destroys Earth.
- *Jaws* (1975): After a satisfying explosion, for a few seconds it's raining shark.
- *Silent Running* (1972): As explosives are carefully activated, the camera pulls back through the window to show the entire spacecraft suddenly erupting.
- *Star Wars* (1977): The Death Star's explosion sends a shower of sparks into space.

Airport

(One of 1970's five **FAR-OUT** movies)

Released: March 1970

Director: George Seaton

Stars: Burt Lancaster, Dean Martin, Jacqueline Bisset

Academy Awards: One win (Best Supporting Actress—Helen Hayes), plus nine more nominations (Best Picture; Best Supporting Actress—Maureen Stapleton; Best Writing; Best Editing; Best Cinematography; Best Art Direction; Best Costume Design; Best Music; Best Sound)

PREVIEW: A commercial jetliner is threatened by a snow storm and a bomb-carrying passenger.

FINE LINE: "That's one nice thing about the 707. It can do everything but read." (Chief mechanic Joe Patroni, after he has successfully piloted the stranded jet out of the snow.)

CLOSE-UP: Joan, the beautiful blonde stewardess on the flight, is played by Patty Poulsen, an actual American Airlines flight attendant who appeared in numerous ads for the airline. Joan survives the *Airport* flight and is one of the first people off the damaged jet.

NOW SHOWING: *Airport*, the Disaster Game Changer

Airport (1970) basically created the disaster-movie template. There had been tragic-voyage movies in the past—*A Night to Remember* (1958)—and even some earlier airliner-disaster movies—*Zero Hour!* (1957)—but *Airport* revolutionized the entire genre. In a decade full of blockbusters, *Airport* was one of the first (it debuted in March 1970), one of the most acclaimed (ten Oscar nominations), and one of the most lucrative (*Love Story* was the only other 1970 movie to gross over $100 million). It was also the first of the major disaster movies about the four natural elements: *The Poseidon Adventure* (1972) was set in water, *Earthquake* (1974) moved the earth, and *The Towering Inferno* (1974) erupted in fire, but the airborne *Airport* was first. Not merely *ahead* of the curve, *Airport* instantly *became* the curve for disaster movies.

A "cold opening" jump-starts the revolution. Before there are any visuals or musical notes, the movie begins with thirty atmospheric seconds of crowd chatter, announcements, and jet engines from a busy airport terminal, immediately welcoming the audience, not just to a movie, but to a world. It's an effective technique: *Chitty Chitty Bang Bang* (1968) opened with dark-screen engine sounds, and later *Jaws* (1975) starts with eerie underwater noises before the main titles and grim theme music commence.

More significantly, *Airport* doesn't rush to its disaster. A weak predecessor, *Krakatoa, East of Java* (1969), reveals its major effects—erupting volcano, flowing lava, surging tsunami—in the *opening credits*. Similarly, the airliner in the disappointing *Skyjacked* (1972) is airborne in the first seven minutes and immediately reveals its bomb threat. The 136-minute *Airport* takes its time: sixty-nine minutes to get the jet airborne, and thirty-three additional minutes to explode the bomb. Most of this movie actually takes place on the ground, not in the air (the title, after all, is *Airport*, not *Airliner*). Borrowing this delaying tactic, the big one doesn't rumble into *Earthquake* (1974) until fifty minutes have passed.

Smartly, *Airport* suggests but doesn't completely divulge a specific thrill to anticipate. We see the suitcase bomb thirty-five minutes in, and we *know* it will explode. But then what? Will the jet explode, too? Could it fly with a ruptured fuselage? Chief mechanic Joe Patroni (George Kennedy) prepares us: "Sudden decompression at thirty-thousand feet is something you've gotta see to believe," he says as he quickly summarizes the horror of people and objects being sucked through the open hole. This, we know, is going to be good. A later disaster classic, *Titanic* (1997), similarly alerts viewers with an early showing of a computerized re-creation of the ship splitting in half. Everyone already knows an iceberg is looming, but this warning prepares us for an astonishing sequence that otherwise isn't explained in the movie.

Like the 1968 Arthur Hailey novel it was based on, *Airport* precedes its disaster story with interesting subplots. In the movie they include "the worst storm in six years" and a snow-bound jet blocking the main runway; a harried airport manager (Burt Lancaster) dealing with picketing protestors and an unhappy wife (Dana Wynter); and a married pilot (Dean Martin) with a pregnant girlfriend (Jacqueline Bisset) who's on the doomed flight. We also get an adorable elderly stowaway (Helen Hayes) for comic relief, some familiar TV faces—including Sandra Gould (*Bewitched*) and Pat Priest

Dean Martin and Jacqueline Bisset.

(*The Munsters*)—to root for, plus an obnoxious passenger (the annoying whiner in seat 21-D) who gets his comeuppance.

With feminism emerging as a hot topic at the turn of the decade, *Airport* stayed current by including a strong female character who wants her freedom. She's Tanya Livingston (Jean Seberg), an efficient, beautiful widower who helps run the airport and is ready to take a better job in San Francisco. Later disaster movies that will incorporate independent women include *The Towering Inferno* (1974) and *Airport '77* (1977), where Faye Dunaway and Brenda Vaccaro's characters, respectively, also declare their intentions to transfer to new cities for big promotions.

In almost every way, *Airport* presents polished entertainment. The cast sports four Oscar winners: Helen Hayes, Van Heflin, George Kennedy, and Burt Lancaster. In addition, the ten-million-dollar budget (epic for that time) is all on the screen, so the movie looks great and audiences feel like they're getting their money's worth. True, a few special effects are now easily mockable (especially the model of the jet among cottony clouds), but on the ground that's a genuine 707 lurching in the snow, and the airport interiors and exteriors are of an actual Minnesota airport. *Airport* puts on a real—and a realistic—show.

Revving up the intensity is the propulsive Oscar-nominated music by nine-time Oscar-winning composer Alfred Newman. *Airport* would be his last score (three weeks before *Airport* opened, Newman died at age sixty-eight), and it's among the decade's best. Later disaster movies took this exciting musical page from the *Airport* playbook, most notably when the legendary John Williams composed scores for *The Poseidon Adventure* (1972), *Earthquake* (1974), and *The Towering Inferno* (1974) before he started winning Oscars for his work with Steven Spielberg and George Lucas.

Modern audiences who deride the dated clichés, the sexist slang, or the 1970s costumes and hair styles are underestimating the movie's influence. Many later disaster movies made *Airport* connections, including three sequels and *Airplane!*, one of the greatest parodies ever. Like that awesome stack of jumbo shrimp wheeled through the 707's aisle, *Airport* is a satisfying spectacle.

ADDED ATTRACTION: *MAD* Magazine's Parodies of 1970 Movies

Airport got its own movie parody, "Airplot," in *MAD* magazine (the parody ran in December 1970). Below are nine other 1970 movies that were similarly honored, followed by the titles of the parodies. *MAD*'s parodies of 1971 movies are with the entry for *Willard* (1971).

- *Catch-22*: "Catch-All-22"
- *Five Easy Pieces*: "Five Easy Pages … and Two Hard Ones"
- *Joe*: "Shmoe"
- *Little Big Man*: "Little Dull Man"
- *Love Story*: "Lover's Story"
- *M*A*S*H*: "M*I*S*H M*O*S*H"
- *On a Clear Day You Can See Forever*: "On a Clear Day You Can See a Funny Girl Singing 'Hello Dolly' Forever"
- *The Owl and the Pussycat*: "The Foul and the Prissy Cats"
- *Patton*: "PUT*ON"

The Ballad of Cable Hogue

Released: March 1970
Director: Sam Peckinpah
Stars: Jason Robards, Stella Stevens, David Warner
Academy Awards: None

PREVIEW: Alone in the desert, a man finds a water hole and turns it into a successful business.

NOW SHOWING: Slow Music

The Ballad of Cable Hogue (1970) is aptly titled: "ballad" is the right word for this unhurried, poetic western. In 1908, Cable Hogue (Jason Robards) is abandoned in the desert by two partners. Wandering for four days, Cable talks to himself and to God. Then, near death, he miraculously uncovers a hidden water hole. Cable stakes his claim and develops his water hole into a successful business with a rudimentary restaurant. Joining him is a beautiful prostitute, Hildy (Stella Stevens), who's been run out of town. Entering the movie with a country twang, blonde hair, and an hour-glass figure, Hildy becomes Cable's loving ally, and for a while they share tender moments together. However, the movie gets dark two-thirds of the way through when Hildy leaves and Cable finally gets revenge on the villains who originally abandoned him. Ironically, Hildy returns in a new horseless carriage that runs over and kills Cable.

The surprise of this generally gentle movie is that it was directed by Sam Peckinpah. Known for screen violence, Peckinpah was between *The Wild Bunch* (1969) and *Straw Dogs* (1971). *The Ballad of Cable Hogue* does have some shootings and dead animals, but it's much tamer than either of those other two disturbing movies. Instead, Peckinpah tries for moments of mild comedy, though his clumsy efforts rely on gimmicks like fast-motion, drunken pratfalls, and a dopey animation on a five-dollar bill.

Underneath the few laughs there's a message about rugged self-reliance. Cable makes everything on his own: "Out here," he says, "what you gotta do is, you gotta work and make do." Hildy is equally determined to make good in the big city as "the ladyest damn lady you ever seen." The last shots blend the past (the horses, a stagecoach) and the future (a car, a motorcycle). Cable dies just as he's decided to leave the former and embrace the latter. Unfortunately for him, you can take the desert out of the desert rat, but you can't take the desert rat out of the desert.

ADDED ATTRACTION: Singing Actresses

As Cable gives Hildy a sexy bath, she sings a pretty ballad, "Butterfly Mornin's," for two minutes. Here are nine more actresses who crooned tunes in 1970–1974 movies.

- Karen Black, *Five Easy Pieces* (1970): During the long road trip she sings two songs a cappella.
- Ellen Burstyn, *Alice Doesn't Live Here Anymore* (1974): Burstyn gently sings "Where or When" and "I've Got a Crush on You."
- Faye Dunaway, *Little Big Man* (1970): "Bringing in the Sheaves," sung a cappella for thirty seconds.
- Jane Fonda, *Klute* (1971): The hymn "We Gather Together," sung a cappella for thirty seconds.
- Ruth Gordon, *Harold and Maude* (1971): She enthusiastically belts out a Cat Stevens song.
- Sophia Loren, *Man of La Mancha* (1972): As Aldonza/Dulcinea, Loren sings several numbers.
- Cybill Shepherd, *Daisy Miller* (1974): A confident ninety seconds of an old folk song, "When You and I Were Young, Maggie."
- Mae West, *Myra Breckinridge* (1970): West talk-sings two minutes of "Hard to Handle."
- Shelley Winters, *Bloody Mama* (1970): A rousing minute of "I Didn't Raise My Boy to Be a Soldier."

Bloody Mama

Released: March 1970
Director: Roger Corman
Stars: Shelley Winters, Don Stroud, Bruce Dern
Academy Awards: None

PREVIEW: During the Depression, Ma Barker leads her four crude sons on a violent crime spree.

NOW SHOWING: "Mama's Boys"

Roger Corman, the director of dozens of low-budget horror, gangster, and biker movies in the 1950s and '60s, got his 1970s off to an auspicious start with the violent *Bloody Mama* (1970). Most of his quick, cheap flicks starred unknowns, some of whom later became famous (notably Jack Nicholson), but *Bloody Mama* starred a two-time Oscar winner, Shelley Winters, alongside *two* future famous names, Bruce Dern and Robert De Niro.

Taking the style of *Bonnie and Clyde* (1967) to sleazy extremes, the movie loosely rushes through the Depression-era story of real-life criminal Ma Barker. In the opening scene she's a young girl in Arkansas, the victim of an incestuous rape who afterwards pledges to someday raise her own "mama's boys." Three decades later Winters plays her just as she's kicking her loser husband out the door. "You never did mount me proper," she tells him, but she's got four grown-up sons, so he must have been doing something right. Ma's not your typical mother: she spits, praises the boys' car theft, personally gives them baths, and even takes them to bed. Fiercely loyal to her lawless brood and determined to escape poverty, she brandishes a tommy gun and leads her gang in a bank robbery. Throughout the movie Ma narrates some black-and-white footage of 1920s and '30s events to give historical context to their exploits.

"None of us Barkers is people," says Lloyd (De Niro), which seems about right. There's little attempt to generate sympathy for these cruel, perverse hicks, especially when Ma drowns a helpless kidnap victim in a bathtub and later when two of the gang members disturbingly feed a live piglet to an alligator that they then shoot. At the end, Lloyd, a loopy glue-sniffing dope addict, dies of an overdose; another son intentionally (and graphically) shoots himself in the face; Ma kills a gang member who's trying to surrender; and everybody else gets gunned down in a violent police shoot-out. Winters over-emotes all her scenes and roars guttural screams in the blazing finale.

There's a twisted energy to the craziness, and while scornful viewers can dismiss *Bloody Mama* as a sordid curiosity, it was enough of a hit to lead Corman to produce more in this jugular vein. His even trashier *Big Bad Mama* (1974) offers similar themes and settings but adds more sex, notably a steamy bedroom scene between Angie Dickinson and William Shatner.

ADDED ATTRACTION: Corman Goes Airborne

After *Bloody Mama*, Roger Corman's next directorial effort was the ambitious World War One epic *Von Richthofen and Brown* (1971), a fictionalized retelling of events leading up to a climactic eight-minute aerial duel between Germany's Red Baron and Canada's Roy Brown. Instead of relying on campy sleaze or cheap horror, Corman goes for exciting biplane action above beautiful Irish countrysides (he generally achieves it) and serious drama (he misses once the planes land and the poorly dubbed characters take over). It's a watchable movie, but when it was indifferently received Corman abandoned directing for almost two decades so that he could focus on producing.

Woodstock

Released: March 1970

Director: Michael Wadleigh

Stars: The Who, Jimi Hendrix, Joan Baez

Academy Awards: One win (Best Documentary), plus two more nominations (Best Editing; Best Sound)

PREVIEW: Huge crowds come to the classic three-day music festival to see famous rock groups.

NOW SHOWING: "We Must Be in Heaven, Man!"

Appropriately, history's most famous rock concert was chronicled with one of Hollywood's greatest documentaries. *Woodstock* (1970) is the Oscar-winning record of the 1969 music festival advertised as "3 days of peace and music" and planned for about 200,000 attendees. A half-million people showed up.

Like that enormous throng, the movie is sprawling and spirited. Whereas other excellent concert films, such as *Ladies and Gentlemen: The Rolling Stones* (1974), focus exclusively on what's onstage, *Woodstock*'s three hours ambitiously cover preparations, jammed highways, arrivals, individual experiences, and the garbage-filled aftermath; we hear opinionated interviews with organizers, musicians, cops, townies, and hippies; and director Michael Wadleigh goes backstage, out to the ponds, and into the air to film, not merely a concert, but the entire world of "the Woodstock generation." The movie impressively presents it all.

Many unexpected events are shown or mentioned. With ticketless fans clambering over flattened fences, quickly the promoters declare it a free concert, though it will be "a financial disaster." When rain pours on the second day, the show stops, power is cut, and "the mud's a hassle," but everyone improvises their own entertainment, and a helicopter drops flowers and dry clothes. There are rumors of a traffic death and overdoses (lots of weed is smoked on camera), but there's also a yoga class, skinny-dipping, and a birth. We get two minutes with the guy cleaning out the portable toilets, blessings from kindly Max Yasgur ("the gentleman upon whose farm we are"), and groovy statements like, "I was rapping to the fuzz."

Most of the music rocks. Not all the invitees—the Beatles, Bob Dylan, Led Zeppelin—made the show, and not all the performers—the Band, Creedence Clearwater Revival, Janis Joplin—made the movie. About 106 minutes of songs (over 55% of the movie) are actually shown, ranging from the beautiful (Crosby, Stills & Nash's epic "Suite: Judy Blue Eyes") to the colossal (two anthems at dawn by the mighty Who, ending when Pete Townshend tosses his guitar into the crowd). Jimi Hendrix scorching his legendary "Star-Spangled Banner" solo, folkie John Sebastian forgetting his own lyrics and requesting help—so many memorable sights and sounds, so much hope, so much *hair*. Director Wadleigh and his editors (including Martin Scorsese) use creative split-screens, extreme close-ups, and multiple angles to capture the colorful artists. If you weren't at Woodstock, this important, often magical movie is the next-best thing.

ADDED ATTRACTION: Wordstock

During the festival, many announcements are made from the stage. Most of these come from the shirtless emcee, Chip Monck (John Sebastian introduces him two-thirds of the way into the movie). Here are five of the more interesting comments from Monck and his fellow announcers.

- "The brown acid that is circulating around us is not specifically too good."
- "Wherever you are, Marilyn Cohen, Greg wants you to meet him at the information booth 'cause he wants to marry you."
- "Sidney McGee, please come immediately to backstage right, I understand your wife is having a baby. Congratulations."
- "Good morning! What we have in mind is breakfast in bed for 400,000."
- "Keep feeding each other, and if you're too tired to chew, pass it on."

A Man Called Horse

Released: April 1970
Director: Elliot Silverstein
Stars: Richard Harris, Jean Gascon, Corinna Tsopei
Academy Awards: None

PREVIEW: Captured by the Sioux, an Englishman wins respect and becomes a member of the tribe.

NOW SHOWING: Sioux Me

Only see *A Man Called Horse* (1970) if you're sure you can live with a nightmarish vision for the rest of your life. There's a ghastly four-minute ceremony midway through this movie that is almost unwatchable and is thoroughly unforgettable. Be warned, it's not for kids or the squeamish.

The journey to that harrowing midway point is interesting. It's 1825, with Richard Harris as a rich Englishman hunting in the Dakota territory. He's bored and spoiled: "Everything I ever wanted in life I've bought," he declares, thanks to vast inheritances. Eight minutes into the movie his helpers are murdered and scalped by Sioux Indians, and Morgan is literally dragged back to their camp. There he's cruelly mocked, tormented, and treated like a workhorse. Morgan plans to escape until he gets a good look at Running Deer, a nicely manicured maiden played by 1964's Miss Universe, Corinna Tsopei. His eyes on this lovely prize, Morgan adopts the Sioux's ways and single-handedly kills two of their enemies. Marriage, though, requires the Sun Vow ritual so he can "be made sacred" by "tests of pain" ("if no pain, nothing good is born"). *Pain*? Excruciating agony is more like it. Pierced through the chest, hoisted aloft by the piercings, and spun in midair, he and probably many viewers hallucinate until it's over (psychedelic imagery does appear in this sequence). By enduring he earns respect and becomes a leader. Eventually Morgan commands the tribe in a successful defense against attack, though Running Deer sadly dies. Harris is convincing and committed throughout.

Like *Little Big Man* from later that year and *Dances with Wolves* (1990), *A Man Called Horse* respectfully shows Indian culture from the inside, not as some previous westerns did with nameless savages suddenly swooping in to attack stagecoaches. Prefatory text says that events have been historically "documented" by "eye witnesses," so the portrayal of the Sioux is, presumably, realistic (some experts challenge the authenticity, but the filmmakers have seemingly made sincere attempts at accuracy). There's beautiful nature photography, harsh violence, abundant drumming and chanting, and long periods of spoken Sioux language with no subtitles, essentially uniting the audience with Morgan as baffled outsiders. It's all strangely compelling. Since the last scene shows Morgan and a band of Indian brothers riding into the wilderness, the drama continued with *The Return of a Man Called Horse* (1976).

ADDED ATTRACTION: Movie Titles, Man

Besides *A Man Called Horse*, these English-language movies from the 1970s all have titles that start with "Man," "A Man," or "The Man." Listed chronologically.

- *A Man Called Sledge* (1970)
- *The Man Who Haunted Himself* (1970)
- *Man and Boy* (1971)

- *Man in the Wilderness* (1971)
- *The Man* (1972)
- *Man of La Mancha* (1972)
- *The Man Who Loved Cat Dancing* (1973)
- *Man on a Swing* (1974)
- *The Man with the Golden Gun* (1974)
- *Man in the Glass Booth* (1975)
- *The Man Who Would Be King* (1975)
- *Man Friday* (1975)
- *The Man Who Skied Down Everest* (1975)
- *The Man Who Fell to Earth* (1976)
- *A Man, a Woman, and a Bank* (1979)

Beneath the Planet of the Apes

Released: May 1970
Director: Ted Post
Stars: James Franciscus, Linda Harrison, Maurice Evans
Academy Awards: None

PREVIEW: Taylor and a newly arrived astronaut fight apes and mutants below Earth's surface.

NOW SHOWING: Monkey Business, Part One

After the enormous success of the Oscar-nominated *Planet of the Apes* (1968), four sequels swung into theaters in the early 1970s. None of them matched the impact of their classic predecessor, but they all advanced the story of a future Earth dominated by sophisticated talking apes.

Audaciously, the first sequel, *Beneath the Planet of the Apes* (1970), actually ends the entire saga. It is set two-thousand years in the future, like the original *POTA*, and begins with that movie's famous surprise ending where Taylor (Charlton Heston) and Nova (Linda Harrison) find the ruined Statue of Liberty, proving that they've been on Earth all along. Meanwhile, a new astronaut, Brent (James Franciscus), emerges nearby from a wrecked spacecraft. Nova, alone on horseback, mysteriously appears and takes Brent to the ape city in search of Taylor. There they see a militant ape general declaring, "The only good human is a dead human." (Later, young ape protestors advocate peace.) Nova and Brent are quickly captured but escape to an underground subway station, where Brent soon realizes that he's in New York.

Below the city they stumble upon a mutant race of telepathic humans who worship a "divine bomb" as "a holy weapon of peace." Taylor reappears, the apes attack the humans, and in the ensuing battle Taylor, Brent, and even Nova are, shockingly, all shot dead. In his death throes Taylor detonates the nuclear missile, incinerating the world. An epilogue informs us that Earth, a "green and insignificant planet, is now dead."

Though it ends with doomsday, *Beneath the POTA* actually seems less profound than *POTA*, and it is certainly less polished: many of the apes wear obvious Halloween-style

Linda Harrison and James Franciscus.

ape masks, not the full-fledged ape makeup that earned *POTA* an honorary Oscar. But there are some welcome sights and sounds for ape-addicted fans. For instance, familiar apes from the first movie—Zaius, Cornelius, and Zira—are seen again, and at last we hear mute Nova speak, though it's more of a grunt and it's just a single word ("Taylor!"). Weaker than its predecessor, the sequel was still a box-office hit. And you know what that means…

ADDED ATTRACTION: Planet of the Sequels

Planet of the Apes spawned four sequels in the 1970s. Other movie series also had three or more entries during the decade. Here are eight alphabetically listed series that *originated* and continued in the 1970s (thus the James Bond, Pink Panther, and Billy Jack movies, which all started in the 1960s, aren't included).

- *Adventures of the Wilderness Family* (1975)
  The Further Adventures of the Wilderness Family (1978)
  Mountain Family Robinson (1979)

- *Airport* (1970)
  Airport 1975 (1974)
  Airport '77 (1977)
  The Concorde … Airport '79 (1979)

- *The Bad News Bears* (1976)
  The Bad News Bears in Breaking Training (1977)
  The Bad News Bears Go to Japan (1978)

- *Dirty Harry* (1971)
  Magnum Force (1973)
  The Enforcer (1976)

- *The Doberman Gang* (1972)
  The Daring Dobermans (1973)
  The Amazing Dobermans (1976)

- *Shaft* (1971)
  Shaft's Big Score! (1972)
  Shaft in Africa (1973)

- *Uptown Saturday Night* (1974)
  Let's Do It Again (1975)
  A Piece of the Action (1977)

- *Walking Tall* (1973)
  Walking Tall Part 2 (1975)
  Walking Tall: Final Chapter (1977)

Two Mules for Sister Sara

Released: May 1970
Director: Don Siegel
Stars: Clint Eastwood, Shirley MacLaine, Manolo Fábregas
Academy Awards: None

PREVIEW: A rugged loner and a nun form an unlikely friendship as they ride through the desert.

NOW SHOWING: The Odd Couple

Two Mules for Sister Sara (1970) is a well-made, generally entertaining western variation on the tough-man-helping-a-polite-nun conceit in *Heaven Knows, Mr. Allison* (1957). Clint Eastwood's first 1970s film, *Two Mules* lightens up the "mysterious stranger" role from his 1960s "spaghetti westerns" and adds an attractive co-star, Shirley MacLaine (she gets top billing, though Eastwood is seen more).

Adorable and charismatic, MacLaine generates intrigue as a spirited, well-made-up nun with a secret. Hogan (Eastwood), a lone mercenary, finds her in the desert as a half-dressed damsel in distress surrounded by three assailants. He kills all three and agrees to escort her and her mule out of danger (twice she says he's as stubborn as the mule, and she even calls him "Mr. Mule," thus the movie's title). As they ride together and have adventures, the audience sees things that Hogan doesn't (she smokes, drinks, and swears), so we suspect that Sara isn't what she says she is.

Hogan, meanwhile, is chattier than the laconic gunslingers Eastwood usually played back then. He's also the guy you want along on a perilous desert trek because he can kill rattlesnakes with just a knife and improvise surgery when he's wounded. Somehow he's surprised by Sara's big reveal, even after she punches him in the face, calls him a "dirty bastard," and slugs whiskey from the bottle.

The two stars work together beautifully as they parry, bicker, and eventually get romantic. Their amusing relationship is the movie's strength, and it overcomes the movie's weakness, which is a violent massacre near the end. Suddenly this likeable movie turns into *The Wild Bunch* (1969) with men on fire, a machete slicing a face, and an arm being severed. Thankfully, a fun and sexy two-minute coda restores the movie's considerable charm.

After *Two Mules for Sister Sara* was a minor hit, Eastwood and director Don Siegel re-teamed for another unusual nineteenth-century tale, *The Beguiled* (1971). Atmospheric, slow, and suspenseful, the movie incorporates flashbacks, fantasy sequences, and a grisly amputation scene. Eastwood plays a wounded Civil War soldier who is cared for by the females at a girl's school. Though he's laid up, this manipulative liar enchants the girls (including a twelve-year-old he deems "old enough for kisses") until lust and dark psychological complications turn them against him. With Eastwood effective as a silver-tongued scoundrel, *The Beguiled* offers a compelling contrast to his typical movies with gruff gun-slinging heroes.

Shirley MacLaine and Clint Eastwood.

ADDED ATTRACTION: Eastwood's Directors

Besides *Two Mules* and *Beguiled*, Clint Eastwood starred in two other memorable '70s movies directed by Don Siegel, *Dirty Harry* (1971) and *Escape from Alcatraz* (1979). Eastwood considered Siegel an influential mentor: in the first movie Eastwood directed, *Play Misty for Me* (1971), he gave Siegel a role, and he mentions Siegel in his dedication at the end of his Oscar-winning western, *Unforgiven* (1992). But neither Siegel nor Eastwood directed *Joe Kidd* (1972), another of Eastwood's early-'70s westerns. This one was directed by John Sturges, who a decade earlier had made two classics, *The Magnificent Seven* (1960) and *The Great Escape* (1963). Despite having Eastwood in his familiar character of a squinty gunslinger (here with a touch of sardonic humor), Robert Duvall as a detestable villain, and a showpiece train-crash scene, the been-there-shot-that action gets routine, and *Joe Kidd* quickly fades as one of Eastwood's least-memorable '70s movies.

On a Clear Day You Can See Forever

Released: June 1970

Director: Vincente Minnelli

Stars: Barbra Streisand, Yves Montand, Larry Blyden

Academy Awards: None

PREVIEW: Under hypnosis a modern young woman recalls her elegant nineteenth-century life.

NOW SHOWING: Cloudy with a Chance of Decent Songs

On a Clear Day You Can See Forever (1970) is an average movie musical with some appealing moments. It's reminiscent of *Hello, Dolly!* (1969), another movie based on a mid-1960s Broadway hit that pairs a young, energetic Barbra Streisand with an older man (Walter Matthau).

Streisand's previous movie musicals (*Dolly* and 1968's *Funny Girl*) were set entirely in the past; *Clear Day* jumps repeatedly from the present to the past (1976's *A Star Is Born* is her one completely up-to-the-moment movie musical). Streisand plays modern-day Daisy, a chatty twenty-two-year-old New Yorker. To end her five-pack-a-day smoking habit, Daisy visits a psychiatry professor (the bland Yves Montand) for hypnosis. Putting her under, he discovers that she lived a past life in 1814. For these vivid re-enactments, Streisand becomes "Melinda," a gorgeous society lady with an English accent that is sometimes aristocratic ("We shahn't be togethah") and sometimes cockney ("cor blimey"). Predictably, the fascinated professor falls for this incarnation. Daisy

eventually quits her treatment, but she leaves saying "see you later" because she knows they'll be happily married in 2038. Never do the two stars have any chemistry together, making any past-present-or-future relationship implausible.

Written by Alan Jay Lerner, *Clear Day* shares some traits with *My Fair Lady* (1964), which Lerner also scripted: both open with beautiful flowers, present a young-woman-older-man relationship, and have lavish Cecil Beaton-designed costumes. Unfortunately, *Clear Day* has more clever lines ("man cannot live by bed alone") than memorable songs. Highlights include the theme, sung three times but only once with the full

Streisand treatment; her duet with a vision of herself, "Go to Sleep"; and the Manhattan vistas accompanying Montand's "Come Back to Me." Other amusements include non-musical scenes with Jack Nicholson as a sitar-playing hipster and Bob Newhart as a college president, but nobody connected with the movie will claim it as their best work. Note the thrice-repeated phrase "for Pete's sake"—the title of Streisand's kooky 1974 comedy.

Five months after *Clear Day*, Streisand's next movie opened. A contemporary urban comedy based on a successful play, *The Owl and the Pussycat* (1970) teams George Segal, a frustrated writer, with Streisand, a volatile, foul-mouthed prostitute (it's her first non-singing movie role). They're well-matched, the movie is loud but funny, and receptive audiences made it a substantial hit.

ADDED ATTRACTION: Classic Directors in the '70s

While young, creative directors like George Lucas, Martin Scorsese, and Steven Spielberg flourished in the 1970s, some legendary directors were still working. One was Vincente Minnelli, director of *On a Clear Day You Can See Forever* and already an Oscar winner for *Gigi* (1958). Here are other classic directors who made movies during the decade; each name is followed by the year he made his first feature and a '70s selection.

- George Cukor, 1930: *Travels with My Aunt* (1973)
- Stanley Donen, 1949: *Lucky Lady* (1975)
- Howard Hawks, 1926: *Rio Lobo* (1970)
- Alfred Hitchcock, 1925: *Frenzy* (1972)
- John Huston, 1941: *Fat City* (1972)
- Elia Kazan, 1945: *The Last Tycoon* (1976)
- Joseph L. Mankiewicz, 1946: *Sleuth* (1972)
- Otto Preminger, 1931: *Rosebud* (1975)
- Billy Wilder, 1942: *The Front Page* (1974)
- Robert Wise, 1944: *The Hindenburg* (1975)
- William Wyler, 1926: *The Liberation of L.B. Jones* (1970)
- Fred Zinnemann, 1936: *Julia* (1977)

Kelly's Heroes

Released: June 1970
Director: Brian G. Hutton
Stars: Clint Eastwood, Telly Savalas, Donald Sutherland
Academy Awards: None

PREVIEW: In World War Two, a group of American soldiers tries to rob a bank behind enemy lines.

NOW SHOWING: "Have a Little Faith, Baby"

Five months after the smash that was *M*A*S*H* (1970), another war comedy, *Kelly's Heroes* (1970), opened to positive reviews and good-sized audiences. Effectively balancing military drama with wry humor, *Kelly's Heroes* offers big, satisfying entertainment, and its influence extends to later war epics like *Saving Private Ryan* (1998), *Three Kings* (1999), and *Inglourious Basterds* (2009).

Director Brian G. Hutton had already made a long war movie with Clint Eastwood, *Where Eagles Dare* (1968). That excellent adventure was intricate and serious; *Kelly's Heroes*, while just as good, is much simpler and lighter. During a World War Two battle in France, a captured Nazi tells Private Kelly (Eastwood) about a bank that's holding $16 million in gold; unfortunately, the bank is thirty miles behind German lines and is heavily guarded. Realizing this could be "the perfect crime," for the first third of the movie Kelly organizes supplies, vehicles, and "a tight little unit" that will go for the gold. The movie's next third shows their dangerous journey to the town where the bank is located, and the last third has them trying to access the loot.

For the first seventy minutes everything is relatively amusing and injury-free (at least for the Americans), but the tone quickly gets melancholy when three of Kelly's soldiers die in a minefield. The jaunty heist suddenly feels solemn, and later there's real suspense when Kelly and two cohorts intentionally march toward a lethal Tiger tank, hoping their "private enterprise operation" can negotiate a business deal (the edgy music here cleverly echoes Eastwood's spaghetti westerns).

The lively cast energizes the movie. Eastwood plays straight man to an unlikely ensemble that includes an intense sergeant (Telly Savalas), a wise-guy comedian (Don Rickles), and, anachronistically for 1944, a groovy long-haired hippie (Donald Sutherland). They're all terrific, but the funniest is Sutherland as the "freak" who likes to sit "catching some rays" and says "negative waves" six times in the movie. All the G.I.s are resourceful and brave, and all the officers are uninformed nitwits.

Something that doesn't really work is the Mike Curb Congregation's easy-listening theme song, heard three times but never feeling relevant. There's also an obvious problem with the getaway. Kelly would need dozens of trucks, not just one, to cart

Donald Sutherland, Clint Eastwood, and Telly Savalas.

off 14,000 gold bars. Additionally, that slow-moving truck is uncovered, is laden with American soldiers, and is taking open roads across enemy-held territory. Kelly's heroes? Kelly's crazies.

ADDED ATTRACTION: Kings of Comedy

Comedian Don Rickles almost steals *Kelly's Heroes* from the movie's bigger stars. Here are twelve more comics, stand-ups, and otherwise funny people who were professional comedians before they played prominent roles in 1970–1974 movies.

- Woody Allen: *Play It Again, Sam* (1972)
- Mel Brooks: *Blazing Saddles* (1974)
- Bill Cosby: *Uptown Saturday Night* (1974)
- Marty Feldman: *Young Frankenstein* (1974)
- Henry Gibson: *The Long Goodbye* (1973)
- Bob Hope: *Cancel My Reservation* (1972)
- Alan King: *The Anderson Tapes* (1971)
- Robert Klein: *The Owl and the Pussycat* (1970)
- Jerry Lewis: *Which Way to the Front?* (1970)
- Jackie Mason: *The Stoolie* (1972)
- Bob Newhart: *Catch-22* (1970)
- Richard Pryor: *The Mack* (1973)

Catch-22

Released: June 1970
Director: Mike Nichols
Stars: Alan Arkin, Martin Balsam, Jon Voight
Academy Awards: None

PREVIEW: World War Two airmen try to maintain their sanity as they're sent on risky missions.

NOW SHOWING: "That's Some Catch"

In mid-1970 two very different war comedies, *Kelly's Heroes* and *Catch-22*, opened on the same weekend. *Kelly's Heroes* has dumbbell officers, one entertaining mission, and a catchy theme song; *Catch-22* has devious, dangerous officers, surreal situations instead of one storyline, and no music score. *Catch-22*'s real connection is with a smashing success from five months earlier, *M*A*S*H* (1970). Unfortunately, *Catch-22*, a box-office disappointment, suffers in comparison to that innovative masterpiece.

Whereas *M*A*S*H* generally maintains its comedic tone, *Catch-22* is bifurcated. The fast-paced first hour establishes the idiosyncratic World War Two flyers and outrageous activities—the paranoid protagonist, Yossarian (Alan Arkin), accepts a medal while totally naked—that make this an anarchic satire. However, the traumatic second hour starts with Yossarian's friend being sliced in half by a low-flying plane, and the mood instantly darkens. A funeral follows, then comes a serious discussion about America's destruction, Yossarian awkwardly impersonates a dying airman, he shoots at a colonel, the airfield explodes, he takes a dreadful walk through Rome at night, and comrades are dead or missing. Yossarian's ludicrous escape is tacked onto the end, but it's too late. Anti-war despair has replaced anti-war humor.

Squeezing Joseph Heller's massive novel into a two-hour movie, screenwriter Buck Henry eliminated some of the book's characters (Washington Irving is one) and sequences (unlike the book, the movie opens with Yossarian being stabbed, a disorienting scene replayed and understood 105 minutes later). Interestingly, the dreamlike segments with Snowden, the injured gunner, appear twice on the page but five times on-screen, most memorably in a horrifying death scene. Henry captures the book's spirit by supplementing its distinctive language with great lines of his own ("He died, you don't get any older than that"). Appropriately, a word used 115 times in the book—"crazy"—is spoken three-dozen times in the movie. But a classic book's elements don't guarantee a classic movie, and *Catch-22* ultimately feels like an assemblage of parts.

Those parts are impressive, though, especially the wonderful ensemble cast that includes Orson Welles, comedian Bob Newhart, singer Art Garfunkel, and scene-stealer Jon Voight. Director Mike Nichols orchestrates long, absorbing scenes and spectacular shots of the vintage planes. Note how scenes are often linked via a word, and how characters are usually alone or in twos on the airfield to emphasize their isolation. Even if isn't a flawless triumph, *Catch-22* is still a fascinating misfire that rewards careful study.

ADDED ATTRACTION:
Movies Based on Bestselling Novels, Part One

Like *Catch-22*, the following 1970–1972 movies were based on recent bestselling novels. See a similar list about 1973–1974 movies in the entry for *The Day of the Jackal* (1973).

Movie (Year)	Book's Author (Publication Year)
The Adventurers (1970)	Harold Robbins (1966)
Airport (1970)	Arthur Hailey (1968)
The Andromeda Strain (1971)	Michael Crichton (1969)
Catch-22 (1970)	Joseph Heller (1961)
A Clockwork Orange (1971)	Anthony Burgess (1962)
Deliverance (1972)	James Dickey (1970)
Diamonds Are Forever (1971)	Ian Fleming (1956)
The Gang That Couldn't Shoot Straight (1971)	Jimmy Breslin (1969)
The Getaway (1972)	Jim Thompson (1958)
The Godfather (1972)	Mario Puzo (1969)
The Love Machine (1971)	Jacqueline Susann (1969)
Love Story (1970)	Erich Segal (1970)
M*A*S*H (1970)	Richard Hooker (1968)
The Other (1972)	Tom Tryon (1971)
The Poseidon Adventure (1972)	Paul Gallico (1969)
Slaughterhouse-Five (1972)	Kurt Vonnegut (1969)

Where's Poppa?

Released: July 1970
Director: Carl Reiner
Stars: George Segal, Ruth Gordon, Trish Van Devere
Academy Awards: None

PREVIEW: A harried son, struggling to care for his senile mother, is helped by a lovely nurse.

NOW SHOWING: Hellzapoppin'

Ordinarily we're big fans of Carl Reiner, the brains behind TV's classic *The Dick Van Dyke Show* and the director of Steve Martin's *The Jerk* (1979). Unfortunately, Reiner's *Where's Poppa?* (1970) is a distasteful, unlikeable movie. Some fans may applaud its audacity or see some method to the madness, but many in the audience will be asking, where's the comedy?

George Segal, brandishing a big Sundance Kid moustache, plays the beleaguered son of his dotty old mother (Ruth Gordon), who shares his Manhattan apartment and gives the movie its title by constantly asking for her deceased husband. Unable to care for her (he calls her a "vegetable"), and having promised not to put her in a home, he hires a kind, beautiful nurse (Trish Van Devere) and quickly falls for her. Chaos at home, at work, and in the park ensues. Segal gives it his all and seems genuinely exhausted by the time he finally delivers Mom to a home.

It's a vulgar movie that strains mightily to be outrageous by including racial slurs, raw profanities, a disgusting wedding-night anecdote, and such surreal sights as a dog getting arrested and a man in a gorilla costume hailing a cab. Some viewers may be amused—fair enough, *de gustibus non est disputandum*. But do they also like the rape scene that is played for laughs? Or the football coach who kidnaps athletic children? Or the embarrassing scene the movie's poster actually brags about—"The tush scene alone is worth the price of admission"—that has Mom ardently and repeatedly kissing her adult son's bare butt? There's mild interest seeing Garrett Morris (a mugger), Rob Reiner (a defendant), and Penny Marshall (a courtroom observer). But much of the rest simply isn't funny. For a great black comedy with Ruth Gordon, see *Harold and Maude* (1971).

For a more subdued 1970 comedy with George Segal, see *Loving*, which arrived four months before *Where's Poppa?* Directed by Irvin Kershner, who would next make *Up the Sandbox* (1972) and eventually *The Empire Strikes Back* (1980), *Loving* positions Segal as a confused, unhappy man at a busy intersection in his life: he's a commercial artist with higher ambitions, he's juggling a wife (Eva Marie Saint) and a mistress (Janis Young), and he's got self-destructive impulses that lead to a disastrous fling with a neighbor. This small, intelligent movie drew generally positive notices from critics, especially for the performances.

ADDED ATTRACTION: All in the Family

Carl Reiner directs his son, Rob Reiner, in *Where's Poppa?* Here are other directors who put their own children in their 1970–1974 movies. Often these were uncredited background roles, but not always—Jeannie Berlin got an Oscar nomination in her mother's movie.

- Robert Altman
  Stephen Altman, *M*A*S*H* (1970)

- John Cassavetes
  Xan Cassavetes, *A Woman Under the Influence* (1974)
  Nick Cassavetes, *Husbands* (1970)
- Francis Ford Coppola
  Sofia Coppola and Roman Coppola, *The Godfather: Part II* (1974)
- Elaine May
  Jeannie Berlin, *The Heartbreak Kid* (1972)
- Paul Newman
  Nell Potts, *The Effect of Gamma Rays on Man-in-the-Moon Marigolds* (1972)
- Mark Rydell
  Christopher Rydell, *Cinderella Liberty* (1973)
- Mel Stuart
  Peter Stuart, *Willy Wonka & the Chocolate Factory* (1971)

Joe

Released: July 1970

Director: John G. Avildsen

Stars: Peter Boyle, Dennis Patrick, Susan Sarandon

Academy Awards: One nomination (Best Writing)

PREVIEW: A crude bigot counsels his affluent friend as they search for his runaway daughter.

NOW SHOWING: Regular *Joe*

The Greatest Generation meets the Pepsi Generation in *Joe* (1970), and nobody wins. Loud and antagonistic, this low-budget movie was a surprising hit then, though it seems like a dated relic now.

While Joe (Peter Boyle) is the title character and the star of the movie's "Keep America Beautiful" poster, he doesn't appear until twenty-six minutes have passed. That's because *Joe* is really the story of Bill (Dennis Patrick), a successful executive who learns a tragic lesson about living and dying by the sword (here, the gun). Early in the movie Bill beats his daughter's drug-dealing boyfriend to death. At the end, he unknowingly shoots his daughter during a rage-filled bloodbath that kills eight other youths. In between he gets encouragement from his blue-collar pal Joe, who enters the movie mouth-first. Joe's a beer-guzzling, gun-collecting bigot who spews hateful opinions about rich white kids, blacks, lazy hippies, Communists, modern music, and anything else in range. Joe *admires* how Bill handled the boyfriend; Bill, meanwhile, welcomes Joe as "a refreshing change" and agrees with him that the murder was "a humanitarian act" because he "saved the world from another lousy junkie."

When Bill's daughter (Susan Sarandon, in her movie debut) runs away, Joe and Bill conduct a search that leads to a psychedelic party. There they surprisingly smoke dope, sleep with younger women, and get robbed. Joe smacks a woman around until she reveals the location of a rural hideout. Joe and Bill, loaded with Joe's guns and Joe's venom, massacre the inhabitants.

Joe is dangerously unbalanced, but the kids in the movie aren't much better. These aren't the beautiful flower children from 1967's Summer of Love; they're more like the dirty scroungers from 1969's Manson Family. The early scenes spotlight the awful boyfriend (Patrick McDermott), who shoots up heroin, feeds his girlfriend pills, and spitefully insults Bill. At the tacky orgy, lowlife druggies conspire to steal Joe and Bill's wallets.

Boyle's committed performance is the movie's strength. Though Joe's attitudes and racist words are despicable, Boyle somehow makes this ignorant blowhard mildly comical, even sympathetic, before the violent climax fully exposes his ugly heart. It's not hard to connect the dots from Joe to Archie Bunker, who debuted in TV's *All in the Family* six months later. Five years after that, director John Avildsen would make a more inspiring movie about another uneducated protagonist in a pork-pie hat: *Rocky* (1976).

ADDED ATTRACTION: Student Cinema

After *Easy Rider* (1969) proved that there was a big audience for movies about disaffected young people, immediately a wave of movies flowed into theaters to show non-conforming college-age students in various degrees of rebellion. In addition to *Joe*, here are an additional seven from 1970 in chronological order. A few more would follow in 1971, including *Drive, He Said* (1971), a downbeat drama about student radicals and basketball players directed by Jack Nicholson.

- *Zabriskie Point* (1970)
- *Getting Straight* (1970)
- *The Magic Garden of Stanley Sweetheart* (1970)
- *The Strawberry Statement* (1970)
- *The Revolutionary* (1970)
- *R.P.M.* (1970)
- *Love Story* (1970)

Diary of a Mad Housewife

Released: August 1970
Director: Frank Perry
Stars: Carrie Snodgress, Richard Benjamin, Frank Langella
Academy Awards: One nomination (Best Actress—Carrie Snodgress)

PREVIEW: Ignored and berated by her husband, a wife has an affair that leads to more problems.

NOW SHOWING: Mad Love

In *Diary of a Mad Housewife* (1970), Carrie Snodgress gives a mesmerizing, career-defining performance as Tina, an intelligent well-to-do Manhattan woman who goes from mad/"loony" (her term) to mad/livid. Before the opening titles we see her smug, pretentious husband (Richard Benjamin) being so ludicrously cruel to her that the movie starts like a comical satire. He berates her body, "God-awful hair," habits, cooking, and general inability to meet his expectations, all in the first five minutes. Meek and accepting, Tina finally speaks her first words—"I'm sorry"—and then dutifully does the chores Jonathan has dictated. For most of the movie he's a narcissistic jerk, ignoring her, insulting restaurant workers, and talking about himself. Tina is so thoroughly defeated, even her two obnoxious daughters challenge her. She calls herself a "coward through and through."

Tina's backbone strengthens during her affair with George, a smoldering writer played by young Frank Langella in his movie debut. Indulging in a loveless "straight sex thing," she finds some temporary solace (the movie's quietest moment comes during their unhurried four-minute sex scene). Unfortunately, George turns out to be just another condescending jackass who insults and complains the way Jonathan does. Viewers waiting for her to react finally get some satisfaction when she flings a dinner plate at home and stands up to (and slaps) George. There's no fantasy escape, however, as there will be two years later for the unappreciated wife in *Up the Sandbox* (1972); Tina lands in therapy where, once again, there's no real support, just people who criticize her without understanding her. Still relatively early in the era's surging women's-lib movement, the filmmakers could show her frustrating situation, it seems, but couldn't yet resolve it.

Director Frank Perry, an Oscar nominee for *David and Lisa* (1962), keeps the focus on Tina. She's in virtually every scene, and everything is filtered through her perspective. For the tender confessional scene near the end, he has Tina and Jonathan take turns speaking directly into the camera, a technique that Mike Nichols will use effectively in *Carnal Knowledge* (1971). Then, with her therapy group (including Peter Boyle!) yelling chaotically, Perry presents a fascinating final close-up of Tina as her eyes drift around the room and settle on us before she smiles enigmatically. Viewers will have different interpretations of this allusive moment, but everyone can agree that *Diary of a Mad Housewife* is a significant, memorable movie.

ADDED ATTRACTION: Real Music Groups That Are Shown Performing in 1970–1974 Movies

Twelve minutes into *Diary of a Mad Housewife*, the Alice Cooper band, on the brink of stardom, performs live at a rowdy party. Below are six more early-'70s feature films (not documentaries or concert films, such as 1970's *Woodstock*) that show real rock bands performing.

- *American Graffiti* (1973)
  Flash Cadillac and the Continental Kids
- *C.C. & Company* (1970)
  Wayne Cochran and the C.C. Riders
- *The French Connection* (1971)
  The Three Degrees
- *Taking Off* (1971)
  Ike and Tina Turner
- *200 Motels* (1971)
  The Mothers of Invention
- *Zachariah* (1971)
  Country Joe and the Fish

Five Easy Pieces

Released: September 1970

Director: Bob Rafelson

Stars: Jack Nicholson, Karen Black, Susan Anspach

Academy Awards: Four nominations (Best Picture; Best Actor—Jack Nicholson; Best Supporting Actress—Karen Black; Best Writing)

PREVIEW: A dissatisfied man visits his family and confronts old feelings and frustrations.

NOW SHOWING: "Auspicious Beginnings"

Five Easy Pieces (1970) is a deceptive movie. The first half feels haphazard—a scruffy, irresponsible man goes bowling with trailer-park friends, impulsively quits his boring oil-rig job, and cheats on his adoring girlfriend—but in the second half the meandering plot coalesces into a deeply existential drama that accumulates power as it goes.

Alienation is the theme, symbolized by the disaffected Bobby (Jack Nicholson). Unlike the era's other anti-heroes who were hard-core murderers—*Bonnie and Clyde* (1967)—or anti-establishment lawbreakers—*Easy Rider* (1969)—this one is a gifted musician and frustrated working man whose main flaw is indecisiveness.

Bobby literally doesn't know what he wants to do and grapples with actions he thinks he *should* be doing. For instance, he walks away from his clinging, child-like girlfriend, Rayette (Karen Black), as she sulks, but he feels guilty and returns. He doesn't want to drive from California to Washington, but he feels he must because his father is ill. About to leave Rayette behind, he seethes but retrieves her. He reluctantly picks up two grouchy women on the highway because he can't leave them stranded. Nine times in the movie Bobby says, "I don't know."

After the most uncomfortable road trip ever, which includes the famous diner scene where Bobby tells a waitress where to hold the chicken, he reaches the family's lakeside house. The character study intensifies as Bobby's failings and personality are revealed.

Everyone there is a talented musician with more purpose than he has. He sleeps with his brother's fiancée and gets into a physical fight. Other characters call him "the moodiest man" and "strange," but we also see flashes of the rascally charisma that Nicholson will unleash in later movies. The most riveting scene comes when Bobby talks to his catatonic father. Bobby cries, apologizes, and admits that he runs away from "auspicious beginnings" before things "get bad."

Bobby's inner torment peaks in a gas-station restroom, where he stares silently into a mirror. He then goes outside and does precisely what he told Rayette he wouldn't do. He leaves her, and also his wallet, car, jacket, and family, by climbing into the nearest logging truck heading north. "I'm fine, I'm fine," he repeats to himself.

Is he? Has he finally found himself? Is he running away? Or running toward? The ambiguity leaves this important movie open to interpretation, which is what great art like this does.

Jack Nicholson.

ADDED ATTRACTION: Easy Pieces

Music is a key ingredient of *Five Easy Pieces*. As Bobby works in the oil fields during the opening credits, Tammy Wynette is on the soundtrack singing "Stand by Your Man." Bobby's girlfriend plays Wynette's records throughout the movie, and Wynette's "D-I-V-O-R-C-E" is on the phonograph as Bobby prepares to leave Rayette behind. Rayette sings two of Wynette's songs to Bobby on their long road trip. Later, one character plays a ukulele, and others play pianos (the movie's title is from a piano student's instruction book). Bobby plays piano twice—first on a piano being carried on a truck, and then in the family house. In the final shot, Bobby rides away with no music playing, only road noises; the absence of all music in the movie's last six minutes perhaps suggests that he is leaving his musical life behind.

Tora! Tora! Tora!

Released: September 1970

Director: Richard Fleischer, Kinji Fukasaku, Toshio Masuda

Stars: Martin Balsam, E.G. Marshall, Takahiro Tamura

Academy Awards: One win (Best Visual Effects), plus four more nominations (Best Editing; Best Cinematography; Best Art Direction; Best Sound)

PREVIEW: In 1941 Japan plans and unleashes a daring attack on American ships at Pearl Harbor.

NOW SHOWING: The *Tora! Tora! Tora!* Aura

Tora! Tora! Tora! (1970) is a long documentary-style epic that realistically presents all the dramatic events leading up to Japan's bold attack on Pearl Harbor, plus the historic air raid itself. Did we mention long? Bombs finally drop after 106 minutes, with about forty minutes still to go. Some critics, tranquilized by the slow, methodical build-up, thought the movie was "torable torable torable," but we applaud the ambitious film-makers who were trying to do justice to this important story by getting as many details as possible right. Audiences see all stages of the planning and preparations on the Japanese side (with subtitles), every lapse and miscalculation on the American side (see "Added Attraction"), every pre-attack negotiation between the two countries, every effort to decode messages that might be clues, and every major military figure who had any bearing on these momentous events. It's a noble effort.

Considering that everybody basically knows what happened on December 7, 1941, the movie still generates real suspense when those majestic Japanese aircraft carriers approach Hawaii and their torpedo bombers swoop to their targets. By the end we've seen bad luck on all sides: the Japanese arrive to find the important American aircraft carriers are absent, and American bombers fly into the middle of the air attack but happen to be unarmed and so can't fight back. Thankfully, there are no lame romantic subplots as there are in *Pearl Harbor* (2001), and there's only a touch of comic relief (for example, a Japanese pilot who misidentifies his own ship, and an American biplane instructor who finds herself surrounded by incoming Zeros). Instead, the focus is fixed on the main story, which is well-delivered by an all-star cast and Oscar-winning special effects.

ADDED ATTRACTION: America's Pre-Attack Lapses

Tora! Tora! Tora! shows the Americans making plenty of pre-attack mistakes, including these ten.

- 13 minutes into the movie:
  Col. Bratton notes that key leaders are not authorized to see the Navy's decoding system.

- 19 minutes:
  To prevent sabotage, Lt. General Short groups planes together at the airfield, unintentionally making them easier aerial targets.

- 24 minutes:
  Admiral Kimmel receives a detailed report about a possible attack but doesn't fully act on it.

- 42 minutes:
  The new radar operators aren't fully trained and have no phone.

- 50 minutes:
  Col. Bratton concludes, "We're going to be attacked on Sunday the 30th of November," but his superiors delay action.

- 66 minutes:
  Holding decoded messages that suggest war is imminent, Lt. Commander Kramer visits leaders in Washington who are either unavailable or unimpressed.

- 68 minutes:
  A Honolulu radio station broadcasts all night, helping Japanese pilots who are "riding that beam" to find Hawaii.

- 92 minutes:
  A Navy destroyer fires on a Japanese sub near Pearl Harbor, but the report is dismissed because the ship's captain is "a green kid."

- 97 minutes:
  Before the attack, radar operators detect "a large formation of planes," but their superiors assume those are incoming American planes.

- 100 minutes:
  A cablegram warning General Short to be on alert is mistakenly not marked "urgent," so he doesn't receive it until the attack is almost over.

C.C. & Company

Released: October 1970
Director: Seymour Robbie
Stars: Joe Namath, Ann-Margret, William Smith
Academy Awards: None

PREVIEW: A biker falls for a beautiful journalist and fights to get away from his outlaw gang.

NOW SHOWING: Broadway Joe & *C.C. & Company*

Following in the tire tracks of the amazingly successful *Easy Rider* (1969), numerous fast-and-cheap-and-mediocre movies kept the outlaw-biker genre alive and sick during the 1970s. The early '70s offered motorcycle movies with a nun (1971's *The Jesus Trip*), lycanthropy (1971's *Werewolves on Wheels*), and Jack Nicholson (1970's *The Rebel Rousers*). The highest-profile entry was probably *C.C. & Company* (1970), a dumb train wreck of a movie with no train. Or much of a screenplay, which was written by Ann-Margret's husband, Roger Smith.

Unlike other motorcycle movies with generally unknown actors, this one pairs two glamorous superstars. Joe Namath had won Super Bowl III in 1969 and was still in his football prime, unlike Jim Brown and other famous athletes who retired and then segued into movies. Namath plays C.C., a rogue member of the Heads biker gang (that's really Broadway Joe on the zebra-striped chopper). Delivering his lines with relaxed courtesy, Namath proves that as an actor he's an awesome quarterback. Twice C.C. saves Ann-Margret's character, a magazine journalist, from attacks by his own gang, so naturally they fall in love and split the scene, man.

It's not all awful. William Smith is a menacing villain, the desert scenery is impressive, the theme song rocks, and the two stars look fabulous. Namath is muscled and handsome, wearing long hair, tight jeans, and occasionally no shirt; Ann-Margret is ravishing despite some odd outfits and, briefly, an unflattering brunette wig. Together they dance, go riding (she's on a minibike), and share a sexy love scene. She even sings a tender love song. So there's all that. But too many flaws send this movie skidding off the road. The Heads are idiotic (someone says they "give motorcycling a bad name"), and some of their silly antics are accompanied by lightweight cartoon-style music with a slide whistle. The plot is so slight that the movie feels padded with three minutes at a concert, ten minutes of motocross racing (Namath competes as #12, his football number), and five minutes of a one-on-one race.

C.C. & Company didn't do much career damage. Namath continued with the New York Jets and quickly co-starred in an amiable comedy, *Norwood* (1970); Ann-Margret got an Oscar nomination for *Carnal Knowledge* (1971). Just a week after *C.C.* came out, the biker genre rumbled on with a slightly better movie, *Little Fauss and Big Halsy*.

ADDED ATTRACTION: From Music to Movies

In *Norwood*, Namath and singer Glen Campbell play Vietnam veterans; Namath chases girls and is gone for much of the movie, while Campbell chases his musical dream. Campbell was hot off *True Grit* (1969) and still had his own TV variety show, but he was a Grammy-winning musician first. Here are other music stars who had prominent roles in 1970–1974 feature films (not just documentaries or concert films).

- Harry Belafonte: *Buck and the Preacher* (1972)
- Johnny Cash: *A Gunfight* (1971)
- Bob Dylan: *Pat Garrett & Billy the Kid* (1973)
- Art Garfunkel: *Carnal Knowledge* (1971)
- Marvin Gaye: *Chrome and Hot Leather* (1971)
- Mick Jagger: *Ned Kelly* (1970)
- Kris Kristofferson: *Cisco Pike* (1972)
- Dean Martin: *Airport* (1970)
- Michelle Phillips: *Dillinger* (1973)
- Diana Ross: *Lady Sings the Blues* (1972)
- Frank Sinatra: *Dirty Dingus Magee* (1970)
- Barbra Streisand: *What's Up, Doc?* (1972)
- James Taylor: *Two-Lane Blacktop* (1971)

little Fauss and Big Halsy

Released: October 1970
Director: Sidney J. Furie
Stars: Robert Redford, Michael J. Pollard, Lauren Hutton
Academy Awards: None

PREVIEW: A shallow, womanizing motorcycle racer selfishly exploits everybody around him.

NOW SHOWING: Little-Seen and Big Problems

You're Robert Redford, and you've achieved sudden stardom with the wildly popular *Butch Cassidy and the Sundance Kid* (1969). So what's your first movie of the new decade? Daringly, Redford answered that question with *Little Fauss and Big Halsy* (1970), a low-budget drama about two struggling bikers on the motorcycle-racing circuit. Redford plays Halsy Knox, an arrogant, womanizing racer who exploits and betrays his one friend, steals from the two women he's just taken to bed simultaneously, and degrades all his sexual conquests as "pigs." This isn't our beloved Sundance, a charming audience-pleasing rogue; constantly looking for shady shortcuts, Halsy is a selfish, impulsive, rule-breaking manipulator who bums cigarettes, coffee, beer, donuts, and motorcycle parts from ordinary hard-working people and pays them back with the smooth talk of a cheap con artist. Symbolizing his inability to commit to anything, Halsy sports different hats throughout the movie.

He and Fauss (Michael J. Pollard), another small-timer who becomes Halsy's mechanic, strike up an odd partnership that turns when Halsy takes the woman that Fauss likes but is too bashful to pursue (Lauren Hutton, whose kooky, free-spirited character enters the movie naked). There's sweet justice at the end when Fauss, finally fed up with Halsy, confidently speeds ahead while the irresponsible Halsy is broken down along the track. Redford is surprisingly good as an unlikeable sleazeball, and he weaponizes his virile golden-boy looks and smiling charisma to maximum advantage (he spends half the movie impressively shirtless). Pollard, as amiable and goofy as he was in his Oscar-nominated role in *Bonnie and Clyde* (1967), provides an excellent contrast as the quirky introvert who overcomes his diffidence. Director Sidney J. Furie captures the dusty deserts and the down-and-dirty motorcycling world effectively, and Johnny Cash sings some rollicking songs that complement the action. Redford fans shouldn't miss this obscure but watchable curiosity.

Though *Little Fauss and Big Halsy* was a box-office disappointment, Redford rebounded just three months later with *The Hot Rock* (1972). More winning and sympathetic here than he was as the shallow loser Halsy, Redford plays a career criminal who is drawn into a complicated diamond heist. When the plan goes disastrously (and humorously) wrong, the inept gang is forced to repeatedly re-steal the hard-to-keep jewel. This offbeat crime caper is a nice, lightweight entertainment that helped reinvigorate Redford's career before two 1973 blockbusters, *The Way We Were* and *The Sting*, cemented his superstardom.

ADDED ATTRACTION: Models in Movies

Model Lauren Hutton makes one of her earliest movie appearances in *Little Fauss and Big Halsy*. Here are fifteen other actresses who were successful models *before* they made movies in the 1970s (a movie from the decade follows each name).

- Maud Adams: *The Man with the Golden Gun* (1974)
- Marisa Berenson: *Cabaret* (1972)
- Candice Bergen: *Carnal Knowledge* (1971)
- Lois Chiles: *The Great Gatsby* (1974)
- Tamara Dobson: *Cleopatra Jones* (1973)
- Britt Ekland: *The Wicker Man* (1973)
- Shelley Hack: *Annie Hall* (1977)
- Veronica Hamel: *Cannonball!* (1976)
- Margaux Hemingway: *Lipstick* (1976)
- Iman: *The Human Factor* (1979)
- Ali MacGraw: *Love Story* (1970)
- Charlotte Rampling: *Zardoz* (1974)
- Isabella Rossellini: *A Matter of Time* (1976)
- Cybill Shepherd: *The Last Picture Show* (1971)
- Twiggy: *The Boy Friend* (1971)

The Private Life of Sherlock Holmes

Released: October 1970
Director: Billy Wilder
Stars: Robert Stephens, Geneviève Page, Colin Blakely
Academy Awards: None

PREVIEW: Holmes and Watson look for a missing person and uncover a strange Loch Ness mystery.

NOW SHOWING: Wilder Goes Holmes

Nearly everything Sherlock Holmes fans could hope for is in director Billy Wilder's *The Private Life of Sherlock Holmes* (1970). Respected stage actors energetically portray Holmes (Robert Stephens) and Watson (Colin Blakely) to deliver sophisticated amusement; Holmes plays the violin and goes "on one of his cocaine binges"; familiar characters, like landlady Mrs. Hudson and Holmes' brother Mycroft, and shout-outs to other adventures further immerse us into Holmes' distinctive world; we even hear the famous declaration, "the game is afoot." The great Wilder and his long-time co-screenwriter I.A.L. Diamond also inject some titillating new developments, as when Holmes discusses a never-before-mentioned fiancée who died just before their wedding (proving to Holmes that "women are unreliable").

What Wilder and Diamond haven't done is give "the world's first, and undeniably most famous, consulting detective" a cohesive, masterful movie. Instead, they present two dissimilar stories. The first, an oddment lasting 33 minutes, has Holmes pretending to be gay so he can evade a ballerina's amorous invitation. This section does introduce the characters' idiosyncrasies and the elegant 1887 milieu, but it's awkwardly played for only mild laughs. By the end not even Watson can definitively specify Holmes' sexual preference.

The ninety-minute follow-up, touted by Watson as Holmes' "most outrageous case," is unrelated to the first story, except for "some missing midgets" who are mentioned early in the movie and turn up later when a missing-persons investigation takes Holmes to Scotland. There he digs up a grave, has a close encounter with the bug-eyed Loch Ness monster, and meets Queen Victoria. In one ten-second spurt Holmes almost solves the case by linking the midgets, the monster, canaries, chlorine, and submersibles, but then he's bamboozled by an unanticipated spy in his midst. It all sounds more complicated than it is. In a coda set a year later, sad news sends Holmes to his cocaine for comfort.

Interestingly, Wilder's fallible Holmes isn't always admirable. He can be moody and petulant; he harangues a grieving widow minutes after she's lost her husband; he helps murder seven German agents, watches their gruesome deaths, and quickly cracks a morbid joke. Even so, Wilder does have an obvious affection for the time and place. He photographs everything beautifully, shows off impressive sets, and tours Scotland's photogenic countryside and castles. Too bad the tale, as Holmes himself says, is a little closer to one of his, and Wilder's, "occasional failures."

ADDED ATTRACTION: Sherlock's '70s

The 1970s were busy years for the great detective. During the decade these six theatrical movies included either a serious or a comic portrayal of Sherlock Holmes (actors playing Holmes are identified).

- *The Private Life of Sherlock Holmes* (1970): Robert Stephens
- *They Might Be Giants* (1971): George C. Scott
- *The Adventure of Sherlock Holmes' Smarter Brother* (1975): Douglas Wilmer
- *The Seven-Per-Cent Solution* (1976): Nicol Williamson
- *The Hound of the Baskervilles* (1978): Peter Cook
- *Murder by Decree* (1979): Christopher Plummer

Dirty Dingus Magee

Released: November 1970
Director: Burt Kennedy
Stars: Frank Sinatra, George Kennedy, Michele Carey
Academy Awards: None

PREVIEW: An unsuccessful outlaw and a dumb sheriff battle for money and women in the Old West.

NOW SHOWING: Dingus the Kid

Imagine the pre-production strategizing that probably went into *Dirty Dingus Magee* (1970). *Butch Cassidy and the Sundance Kid* (1969) had been a popular Oscar-winning western just a year before; *Dingus* had two Oscar-winning stars, Frank Sinatra (coming off his well-received role in 1968's *The Detective*) and George Kennedy (coming off the early-1970 blockbuster *Airport*); director Burt Kennedy had just made another successful western comedy, *Support Your Local Sheriff!* (1969); and, amazingly, Joseph Heller (of *Catch-22* fame) was a co-writer. What could go wrong?

If history has taught us anything, it's taught us never to ask that question. *Dirty Dingus Magee* is a simple-minded amusement that's humorous in an adolescent sort of way. It's got juvenile jokes, forced double entendres, Indian stereotypes, and older men paired up with nubile young women. The women, actually, are the movie's best features. Michele Carey plays a sexy Indian maiden in suede go-go boots who constantly asks "Ding-goose" to "make bim bam" (though they're always experiencing *maidenus interruptus*), and pretty Lois Nettleton inverts her clichéd schoolmarm role by transitioning into a sweet nymphomaniac. The unruly plot has the outlaw Dingus (Sinatra) and Sheriff Hoke (Kennedy) double-crossing each other and bedding various women as they try to steal a strongbox full of money. Cartoony action with Indians, cavalry, and a reputable gunfighter ends with a wedding, a fire, and a chase.

Dingus was a nineteen-year-old kid in the book this movie was based on; consequently, the fifty-five-year-old Sinatra youths up his role with an awfully conspicuous (or just awful) black Beatles wig and a lithe girlfriend, Carey, who is literally half his age. Maybe it's no surprise that Sinatra went a full decade before he made another feature film, *The First Deadly Sin* (1980), and when he did return it was in a thriller, not a comedy. Kennedy, on the other hand, was in *nineteen* movies during the 1970s (almost two a year!), including three more in 1970: *...tick...tick...tick...* with Jim Brown, *Zig Zag* with Eli Wallach, and *Airport* with all those Oscar nominations. Typically Kennedy was a commanding presence, but in *Dirty Dingus Magee* he's the butt of jokes and seems to be practicing for his nitwit role in *The Naked Gun* (1988).

Critics didn't find much to like here, but they weren't the right audience. Lightweight and silly, with no real bloodshed or profanity, *Dirty Dingus Magee* is a comedy for your inner fourteen-year-old.

ADDED ATTRACTION: Cheyenne Social Comedy

Another slightly risqué western comedy that stampeded into theaters in 1970 was *The Cheyenne Social Club*. Like *Dirty Dingus Magee*, this one also had two stars who were already Oscar winners, James Stewart and Shirley Jones, plus Hollywood legend Henry Fonda and a name director, Gene Kelly. The formulaic story has a conservative cowpoke (Stewart) reluctantly inheriting a lively brothel headed by Jones' kind-hearted character. The stars' amusing banter, the spirited gals, and Henry Fonda's crooning during the opening credits are the highlights of this mildly entertaining movie. *The*

Michele Carey and Frank Sinatra.

Cheyenne Social Club and *Dirty Dingus Magee* were two of many western comedies that seemed to be trying to capitalize on the trailblazing success enjoyed by *Butch Cassidy* in 1969; other contenders from 1970 and 1971 include *The Ballad of Cable Hogue* (1970), *The Cockeyed Cowboys of Calico County* (1970), *Skin Game* (1971), *Something Big* (1971), and *Support Your Local Gunfighter* (1971).

Gimme Shelter

Released: December 1970
Director: Albert Maysles, David Maysles, Charlotte Zwerin
Stars: Mick Jagger, Melvin Belli, Grace Slick
Academy Awards: None

PREVIEW: Documentary footage shows the Rolling Stones at their infamous Altamont concert.

NOW SHOWING: "Everybody Be Cool Now"

Throw a free concert for 300,000 people, put in two days of rushed preparation, let people park cars anywhere "for experimental purposes," and hire the Hells Angels for stage security (with free beer as their payment). This recipe for disaster is served up in *Gimme Shelter* (1970), a remarkable documentary that, like the Oscar-winning *Woodstock* (1970) from nine months earlier, is more about the culture than the music. If *Woodstock* is a mid-summer celebration, *Gimme Shelter* is a winter death knell.

The movie divides neatly in two. First, the Rolling Stones play blistering versions of their classics at Madison Square Garden; this live footage is intercut with a hyper-sexual number by Ike and Tina Turner; scenes of the Stones on the road and in the studio; and administrative preliminaries for the California concert set for December 6, 1969 (Michael Lang, who co-organized the Woodstock festival, is seen providing assistance). The second half is at Altamont Speedway, a wide-open field where the concert takes place. The Flying Burrito Brothers start in the afternoon with the dancing, laughing crowd feeling good, though the set ends with a nearby scuffle.

The mood really turns ominous for the Jefferson Airplane. With fights continually breaking out, an Angel grabs a microphone to lecture the band. Night falls, and the Stones take the tiny stage, surrounded by Hells Angels. Playing "Sympathy for the Devil," the alarmed band watches the increasing violence in the audience. "Everybody be cool now," implores vocalist Mick Jagger, with the band temporarily stopped and the ugliness intensifying in front of them. "Why are we fighting," Jagger asks the crowd, but as doctors are summoned, and as Jagger seems to shrink in size and power, it's obvious that events are beyond his or anybody's control. After two more songs, the band immediately helicopters away.

What's fascinating is that we watch when Jagger later screens this disturbing movie on a monitor. As slow-motion replay immortalizes the chilling moment when an Angel kills someone with a knife, Jagger's face freezes in grim disbelief. Finally, "Gimme Shelter," the Stones' dark epic, plays while concertgoers trek to their cars at dawn (note the credits—George Lucas is listed as a cameraman). After the Altamont debacle, the Stones showed off their concert prowess, to the utter exclusion of any outside issues, in a happier documentary, *Ladies and Gentlemen: The Rolling Stones* (1974).

ADDED ATTRACTION: Mick's Movies

For Jagger, 1970 was a busy year for his movie career. Besides *Gimme Shelter*, he starred in two British dramas. In the surreal *Performance* (1970), a violent gangster movie, Jagger basically plays himself, a decadent rock star, and he performs the musical highlight, "Memo from Turner." Later that year, *Ned Kelly* (1970) presents Jagger as an actual character, the titular Australian outlaw/folk hero. This decent action movie has a good feel for the Victorian era, and it boasts songs by Waylon Jennings and Kris Kristofferson (Jagger sings a three-minute folk song). Unfortunately, Jagger's the reason viewers might not get satisfaction. This slender Stone is never convincing as a rough, bearded renegade who is "twice the man of any of us" and capable of winning a bare-knuckle boxing match, like he does in the movie. His most authentic moment is his last one, when he smiles and taunts the judge who has just sentenced him to death. That's our cheeky Mick.

Husbands

Released: December 1970
Director: John Cassavetes
Stars: Ben Gazzara, Peter Falk, John Cassavetes
Academy Awards: None

PREVIEW: After their friend dies, three disillusioned men take an impromptu trip to London.

NOW SHOWING: *Husbands* at Large

After John Cassavetes' *Faces* (1968) earned three Oscar nominations, and after *Life* magazine put his next movie, *Husbands* (1970), on its May 9, 1969, cover, audiences walked into *Husbands* with grand expectations. This nervy movie turned out to be difficult and polarizing. After unusual opening credits that pack all the names into two title cards, writer/director/actor Cassavetes tells a long, slow non-story. Three middle-aged friends attend a funeral in New York, talk, drink, fly to London, chase women, and then two of them return to their suburban families. They seemingly improvise dialogue while enjoying lots of "guy" stuff—shooting hoops, swimming, smoking, drinking, shouting, singing loudly, gambling badly, playing grab-ass with each other. Some scenes are uncomfortable, as when one husband gets into a physical fight with his wife.

Many viewers find the insights brave and penetrating as the men reveal their mid-life disillusionments. Others are turned off by these clumsy, drunken buffoons who aren't nearly as funny as they think they are (another character calls them "silly sniggering schoolboy friends," an apt description for these middle-aged juveniles). An early litmus test for viewers comes after the funeral when the guys participate in an excruciating twenty-one-minute bar-room singing contest in which they drunkenly bully the poor participants around them. This disturbing scene is followed by sixteen minutes that are spent mostly in the men's room, where intense vomiting ensues. Are these long scenes brilliant and honest? Or merely ugly and offensive? Cassavetes' *cinéma verité* approach is interesting, but frankly the three main men in the movie are not. They're embarrassing. The *Husbands* subtitle is, "A comedy about life death and freedom"; some viewers might be applauding at the end, but many others will feel like this tedious joke was on them.

Falk and Gazzara would both work in multiple Cassavetes movies later in the decade. Cassavetes, meanwhile, turned to his actual wife, Gena Rowlands, for his first movie after *Husbands*, the slightly more accessible *Minnie and Moskowitz* (1971). Rowlands plays an attractive middle-aged woman who's surrounded by angry men. Forty-seven minutes into the movie she's rescued from a fight by a defiantly unambitious parking-lot attendant (Seymour Cassel, wearing the decade's bushiest moustache). He too is aggressive and physical, but over four tumultuous days of talking, yelling, and hitting they somehow find love. This "romantic comedy" is either amusing and authentic or strident and irritating, depending on personal taste and tolerance.

ADDED ATTRACTION: John Cassavetes and Gena Rowlands Show *A Woman Under the Influence*

After *Minnie and Moskowitz*, Gena Rowlands next starred in her husband's *A Woman Under the Influence* (1974), the longest of these three early-'70s Cassavetes movies. Rowlands plays an emotionally unstable woman whose reckless behavior and extreme mood swings threaten to destroy her family. As her angry, sometimes violent working-class husband, Peter Falk struggles to deal with his wife's unnamed condition and eventually has her institutionalized. When she returns after six months, their lives are no simpler, their issues no more resolved. Spiked with threats, shouting, and intense, drawn-out scenes, it's a grueling drama that throws a harsh light on private pain and complicated situations. Many critics have recognized this as perhaps Cassavetes' best movie, and nearly everyone commends the leads' devastating performances. *A Woman Under the Influence*, however, still isn't a movie that all viewers will enjoy, especially for 155 minutes. Oscar voters were impressed and responded with nominations for Rowlands (Best Actress) and Cassavetes (Best Director).

Brewster McCloud

Released: December 1970
Director: Robert Altman
Stars: Bud Cort, Sally Kellerman, Shelley Duvall
Academy Awards: None

PREVIEW: An odd young man constructs wings so that he can fly inside of the Houston Astrodome.

NOW SHOWING: Astroboy

If you ever wondered who inspired Waldo's look in the popular *Where's Waldo?* children's books, check out Bud Cort in *Brewster McCloud* (1970). Playing the title character, he wears a red-and-white striped long-sleeve shirt and big round glasses the entire movie; all that's missing is Waldo's beanie and his ability to hide in a crowd.

Brewster McCloud was director Robert Altman's follow-up to *M*A*S*H* (1970), his mega-hit masterpiece. The two movies share actors and actresses, especially Cort, Sally Kellerman, Michael Murphy, John Schuck, and Rene Auberjonois. They both have the same kind of anarchic spirit, too, but whereas *M*A*S*H* was funny and compelling, *Brewster McCloud* settles for idiosyncratic and mildly interesting.

The strange story is about a peculiar young man (Cort) who lives inside the Houston Astrodome and dreams of flying. Not in a plane—literally flying. In his hidden room he constructs elaborate mechanical wings and converses with a mysterious angel (Kellerman). By the end he's fallen in love with sweet Shelley Duvall, confessed to some killings, and been described as a "really weird boy," "crazy," and "deranged." He finally breaks out the wings a hundred minutes into the movie and soars for three minutes inside the enormous cage-like stadium until he loses power and crashes onto the field. The poignant ending seems to deliver a murky message about our desire, and our inability, to break free from external limitations.

It's a challenging, at times baffling movie that will beguile some viewers, but others will think it's for the birds. (In fact, a seemingly mad scientist frequently interrupts the story to lecture about birds and eventually turns into a feathered, seed-gulping bird himself.) Audiences will get to see Duvall profusely vomit, Kellerman frolic topless, Jennifer Salt dressed like Dorothy in *The Wizard of Oz* (1939), and Stacy Keach under mean-old-man makeup. A beautifully photographed car chase with classic '70s cars—a Camaro Z28, a Road Runner, a Gremlin—includes a cool slow-motion scene where they all get airborne. And some songs by John Phillips (of the Mamas and the Papas) are on the soundtrack. With so many kooky, disparate elements, no wonder *Brewster McCloud* is such an odd duck.

Shelley Duvall and Bud Cort.

ADDED ATTRACTION: The Wicked Witch of the Astrodome

During the opening credits, Margaret Hamilton, the wicked witch in *The Wizard of Oz*, sings the national anthem inside the Houston Astrodome. Naturally, this quirky movie has to do something unusual: Hamilton stops mid-song, and when she restarts from the beginning, so do the credits. The end credits are equally bizarre. With Brewster dead on the field, all the other characters parade into the stadium dressed in circus costumes as rousing music plays and an announcer declares, "The greatest show on Earth proudly presents the cast of *Brewster McCloud*!"

The Aristocats

Released: December 1970
Director: Wolfgang Reitherman
Stars: Phil Harris, Eva Gabor, Sterling Holloway
Academy Awards: None

PREVIEW: Four city cats are stolen and taken to the country, where they meet a smart alley cat.

NOW SHOWING: The Cat's Meow

It's not *magnifique*, but *The Aristocats* (1970) was catnip to audiences, who made it an international box-office hit. Disney's twentieth animated feature is a pleasing, a humorous, and, at only seventy-eight minutes long, a short diversion that kids will adore and adults could easily admire.

The story is set in Paris in 1910, but fully a third of the movie takes place in the country. That's where a four-cat family has been dumped by a greedy butler, who is second in line behind the cats for the big inheritance left by a doting matron. Fortunately the abandoned foursome encounters Thomas O'Malley the alley cat, who leads them through some rural adventures, guides them back to Paris, and rallies some "swingin' hepcats" to help in the final showdown with the butler. O'Malley's evolution from carefree bachelor to caring father for the kittens is one of the movie's nicest developments.

The Aristocats borrows heavily from some earlier Disney classics. The street-wise male romancing a lovely socialite is similar to *Lady and the Tramp* (1955); the plot device of beloved pets being taken from the city to the country echoes *101 Dalmatians* (1961); and the bold use of hand-drawn "sketch" animation, which is not to every taste, is also a throwback to *101 Dalmatians*. What's not borrowed from a Disney classic is a great antagonist, because there isn't one. The "old pickle-puss" butler is a stupid, inept bumbler without any of Captain Hook's, Maleficent's, or Cruella De Vil's magnificent menace.

There's also an unusual mix of voices. For a movie set in Paris, hardly anyone has a French accent; Eva Gabor's aristocratic Duchess is Hungarian, and most of the other animals are either British or American (some speak with heavy southern accents). Even the money is in American dollars. The co-starring cat, O'Malley, is voiced by Phil Harris, a languid mid-westerner playing the second of three similar roles for Disney; previously he was the happy-go-lucky Baloo in *The Jungle Book* (1967), and next he'd be Little John in *Robin Hood* (1973).

Duchess and Thomas O'Malley.

Of the half-dozen new Disney songs, only the lively "Ev'rybody Wants to Be a Cat" is a keeper. However, those kittens are undeniably delightful, Paris looks lovely at times, and there are some funny animal antics (the scene with geese leading a march is a hoot). *The Aristocats* is an agreeable addition to the legendary line of Disney animation. *C'est bien.*

ADDED ATTRACTION: The Missing Song

Eagle-eyed viewers may notice an apparent error one hundred seconds into the movie's opening credits. Five songs and their composers are identified, but only four songs are in the movie. The third one on the list, "She Never Felt Alone," was written by Disney's staff songwriters, the brothers Richard M. and Robert B. Sherman. As Richard Sherman reveals on the DVD's special features, this slow ballad was recorded but "wasn't used, I don't know why"; had it stayed, it would have been sung early on by Madame (Hermione Baddeley) and then reprised later by Duchess (Robie Lester, singing for Eva Gabor).

Little Big Man

(One of 1970's five **FAR-OUT** movies)

Released: December 1970

Director: Arthur Penn

Stars: Dustin Hoffman, Faye Dunaway, Chief Dan George

Academy Awards: One nomination (Best Supporting Actor—Chief Dan George)

PREVIEW: The oldest white survivor of Custer's Last Stand recalls events before the battle.

FINE LINE: "There is an endless supply of white men. But there always has been a limited number of Human Beings. We won today. We won't win tomorrow." (Old Lodge Skins, lamenting his tribe's situation as he gets ready to die.)

CLOSE-UP: Two-thirds of the way into the movie, Wild Bill Hickok (Jeff Corey) is gunned down in a saloon, several months *before* Custer's Last Stand. Jack Crabb is rearranging history here as he narrates. On August 2, 1876, Hickok was shot and killed while holding a poker hand of two aces and two eights (the famed "dead man's hand"). However, his death came about five weeks *after* the Battle of Little Big Horn (June 25–26, 1876), not before.

NOW SHOWING: Wild Wild West

Fans could accept that Dustin Hoffman lost the Oscar for Best Actor in 1969 when his astonishing performance in *Midnight Cowboy* (1969) couldn't overcome the career-achievement respect for John Wayne, who had performed admirably in *True Grit* (1969). But a year later, Hoffman couldn't even get *nominated* for *Little Big Man* (1970)? That just felt wrong. Hoffman convincingly plays a teen, a 121-year-old man, a gunfighter, a drunk, a coward, a hero, a Cheyenne brave (and more), evoking laughter and sadness and sympathy (and more) in a sprawling western that is humorous, tragic, horrifying, intimate (and more). What an actor; what a movie.

And what an achievement for Arthur Penn. Just as he had revised the typical gangster movie with *Bonnie and Clyde* (1967), director Penn brashly inverts the traditional Hollywood western with *Little Big Man*. Here the sympathetic Cheyenne people (who call themselves Human Beings) try to live with tolerance and dignity, while the barbaric white men often act like impulsive, short-sighted savages, reversing the typical order shown in decades of westerns. With a scratchy voice and a severely wrinkled face, Hoffman narrates the long story as Jack Crabb, a 121-year-old man in a rest home who claims to be "the sole white survivor of the Battle of Little Big Horn." What Jack remembers about his nineteenth-century life isn't always factual, but it is believable and engrossing.

Jack starts the movie as a ten-year-old white child on the plains who is captured and raised by the Cheyenne. After making friends and enemies, he leaves the Cheyenne in his mid-teens when, now being played by Hoffman, he's recaptured by the U.S. Cavalry. Crabb then encounters various swindlers and hypocrites, discovers he's a "natural-born gunfighter," fails at shopkeeping, gets married, reunites with the Cheyenne, remarries, witnesses the massacre of his tribe by General Custer's soldiers, and joins the army so he can personally assassinate Custer. At Little Big Horn, he steers the insane Custer into catastrophe (and gets wounded himself) before reuniting with the Cheyenne.

If this brief summary sounds like a lot of adventure, it is, all of it packed into a 139-minute epic that skillfully contrasts humor (as when Jack becomes the gun-slingin' Soda Pop Kid) with horror (the army's bloody, merciless slaughter of Cheyenne women and children). Throughout, situations seem to show a world out of balance: a religious wife (Faye Dunaway) turns out to be a prostitute, one of the Human Beings intentionally does everything backwards, and Jack is saved by accident. "An enemy had saved my life by the violent murder of one of my best friends. The world was too ridiculous even to bother to live in," he decides after a cavalry soldier shoots one of the Cheyenne who mistakenly attacks Jack after Jack has been adopted into that same tribe.

A hit with audiences and critics, *Little Big Man* works as pure entertainment, as a sensitive study of a past culture, and as a beautifully photographed presentation of the American landscape. Some viewers suggest that there are even thematic parallels with modern times, especially between the cavalry destroying Cheyenne camps and American soldiers destroying Vietnamese villages. "Shooting rifles against bow and arrow, I never could understand how the white world could be so proud of winnin' with them kind of odds," Jack says, which may evoke thoughts of high-tech B-52 bombers flying over

Dustin Hoffman.

Vietnam in the 1960s and '70s. Perhaps such correlations are there to be made, but there's already enough profundity in the nineteenth-century drama that's shown on the screen.

Today this poignant, thoughtful movie still doesn't feel old or dated. Hoffman's virtuoso performance as the fascinating, multi-dimensional Jack Crabb is enabled by some great scene-stealers, especially Richard Mulligan as the insane Custer, Martin Balsam as an ever-optimistic but ever-shrinking salesman, and the Oscar-nominated Chief Dan George as Jack's wise "adopted grandpa." Grandpa says at the end that "sometimes the magic works, sometimes it doesn't." It sure does with *Little Big Man*.

ADDED ATTRACTION: How Old Are Those Teenagers?

In the first third of *Little Big Man*, seventeen-year-old Jack is played by thirty-three-year-old Dustin Hoffman (born 1937). Here are other 1970–1974 movies with teen characters played by grown-up stars; following each star's name is his/her age in the year the movie came out.

- *American Graffiti* (1973)
  High schoolers Debbie, Laurie, and recent-grad Curt: Candy Clark (26); Cindy Williams (26); Richard Dreyfuss (26)
- *Badlands* (1973)
  Holly (15): Sissy Spacek (24)
- *Bless the Beasts & Children* (1971)
  Cotton (16): Barry Robins (26)
- *Butterflies Are Free* (1972)
  Jill (19): Goldie Hawn (27)
- *Carnal Knowledge* (1971)
  College freshmen Jonathan and Sandy (both 18 or 19): Jack Nicholson (34); Art Garfunkel (30)

- *A Clockwork Orange* (1971)
  Alex, a teenager still in school: Malcolm McDowell (28)
- *Lady Sings the Blues* (1972)
  Young Billie Holiday (14): Diana Ross (28)
- *Made for Each Other* (1971)
  Pandora (19): Renée Taylor (38)

Love Story

(One of 1970's five **FAR-OUT** movies)

Released: December 1970

Director: Arthur Hiller

Stars: Ali MacGraw, Ryan O'Neal, Ray Milland

Academy Awards: One win (Best Music), plus six more nominations (Best Picture; Best Actress—Ali MacGraw; Best Actor—Ryan O'Neal; Best Supporting Actor—John Marley; Best Director; Best Writing)

PREVIEW: Two students meet, marry, and are struggling for success when one of them gets sick.

FINE LINE: "Would you please do something for me, Ollie? Would you please hold me? No, I mean really hold me. Next to me." (Jenny's last words.)

CLOSE-UP: Twenty-seven minutes into the movie, Oliver drives Jenny onto the magnificent grounds of his family's 160-acre estate. Audiences may recall seeing this imposing home before. These are the Old Westbury Gardens on Long Island, New York, built by the heir to the U.S. Steel fortune and used as a location in many movies. Six minutes into *North by Northwest* (1959), Cary Grant's character is abducted, driven here, and forced by his captors to get drunk.

NOW SHOWING: "Foul-Mouth Angel-Face"

What can you say about a movie that opens with the question, "What can you say about a twenty-five-year-old girl who died?" Literally one sentence into *Love Story* (1970), we already know the ending, which is a daring way to start any movie. But that's what is surprising about this straightforward tear-jerker. *Love Story* cleverly blends the traditional and the unconventional.

Perhaps the most unconventional thing about *Love Story* is its phenomenal success. Romantic movies about two young people, unless they are Jack and Rose in *Titanic* (1997), typically don't top year-end box-office charts, but *Love Story* did, surpassing epics like *Airport* and *Patton* as 1970's most popular movie. Additionally, it received seven Oscar nominations, including Best Picture; its elegant instrumental theme, and the subsequent version with lyrics and a new title—"(Where Do I Begin?) Love Story"—became hit records; and many important critics lauded it as terrific entertainment. Note also that *Love Story* was parodied on both *The Carol Burnett Show* and in *MAD* magazine, which only happens for movies that are prominent and significant. So why all the love for *Love Story*?

Some historical context might help. In 1970, the complex, exhausting Vietnam War was a constant topic, and radical new movies were shifting Hollywood toward the gritty counter-culture themes sparked by two 1969 hits, *Easy Rider* and *Midnight Cowboy*. *Love Story*'s jam-packed theaters suggested that many people were looking for a life-line back to the simpler, more traditional "good old days" represented by 1950s melodramas. What's more, movie violence was surging; following the leads of *Bonnie and Clyde* (1967) and *The Wild Bunch* (1969), even some of 1970's high-profile comedies—*M*A*S*H*, *Catch-22*—were gory. Compared to all these, *Love Story* was a perfectly timed throwback to a safe, romantic, nonviolent hit from 1957, *An Affair to Remember*. Finally, *Love Story* the movie was based on *Love Story* the book, which had been published earlier that year and was 1970's top-selling novel; there's nothing like ten months of advance publicity to get audiences excited about a movie's upcoming release.

True to form, *Love Story*'s affair to remember is indeed conventional, with a plot so thin that if it were an icy pond viewers would fall right through. In ten words or less, boy meets girl, boy and girl get married, girl dies. In some ways the presentation is also orthodox, starting with a bland male lead who evokes the 1950s' Troy Donahue. Unlike the nontraditional anti-heroes who were becoming popular (Jack Nicholson, Dustin Hoffman), *Love Story* stars the unadventurous Ryan O'Neal, who beat out edgier options like Christopher Walken and Jon Voight. O'Neal is Oliver Barrett IV, a rich Harvard student who falls for Jenny, a "smart and poor" Radcliffe student played by the striking Ali MacGraw, who in late 1970 was known more for a *Vogue* magazine cover (March 1970) than her one previous movie credit (1969's *Goodbye, Columbus*).

Jenny is the movie's most daring ingredient, its biggest departure from romantic stereotypes. As *MAD* magazine well illustrated (October 1971), she casually and profusely swears—to Oliver, to her father, to children—something Audrey Hepburn, Grace Kelly, Deborah Kerr, and similar Hollywood heroines never did. In addition, for much of their courtship she doesn't seem to *like* Oliver, much less love him. Relentlessly sarcastic, Jenny disdainfully calls him "preppie" nine times (even on her deathbed) and "stupid" three times (again, on her deathbed). After they're married she still addresses him by his last name. Before he's used to her, Oliver confronts her and calls her "the supreme Radcliffe smart-ass." One of his friends labels her "foul-mouth angel-face."

Oliver is so smitten he woos her anyway, even though it outrages his formal, intolerant father (Ray Milland, for once without a hairpiece). Oliver calls his father "sir," whereas Jenny lovingly calls hers "Phil," his first name. The family and religious differences are reminiscent of *Romeo and Juliet*, with star-crossed lovers Oliver and Jenny determined to get married on their own terms (pre-marital sex, an impromptu proposal, an informal wedding, creative vows) and live without outside help (while he's in law school she abandons her musical dreams and supports them both by teaching). There's a beguiling sweetness and purity to their efforts that makes it easy for audiences to root for them. By the time Jenny, looking more radiant than ever, dies of an unnamed disease (clearly leukemia in the book), she has won over the teary audience with hard work and sacrifice. Triumphing in the role, MacGraw ascended from unknown to icon with an immediate *Time* magazine cover (January 11, 1971) under the tagline, "The Return to Romance."

Not all viewers get choked up, however. *Love Story* is one of the most polarizing movies of the decade, generating equal amounts of unabashed adoration and derisive scorn. Is this uncomplicated movie direct, or simple-minded? Moving, or mawkish? Classic, or calculating? Do these attractive young stars truly have chemistry together, or are they in over their heads, smirking instead of sizzling? Is the dialogue natural and memorable, or artificial and clichéd? The movie's famous "Love means never having to say you're sorry" quote, which is spoken twice, is it meaningful or insipid? There are strong convictions on both sides. Millions of fans, and Oscar voters, found it to be engrossing and fashionable, though today's newcomers may think there's less to this pretty picture than meets the eye.

Ryan O'Neal and Ali MacGraw.

ADDED ATTRACTION: Star Debuts

Six minutes into *Love Story*, Tommy Lee Jones, a future Oscar winner, makes his big-screen debut as Oliver's poker-playing neighbor. Here are sixteen other movie stars and the 1970–1974 movies in which they debuted.

- F. Murray Abraham: *They Might Be Giants* (1971)
- Kathy Bates: *Taking Off* (1971)
- Keith Carradine: *McCabe & Mrs. Miller* (1971)
- Chevy Chase: *The Groove Tube* (1974)
- Candy Clark: *Fat City* (1972)
- Laura Dern: *Alice Doesn't Live Her Anymore* (1974)
- Jodie Foster: *Napoleon and Samantha* (1972)
- Jeff Goldblum: *Death Wish* (1974)
- Samuel L. Jackson: *Together for Days* (1973)
- Diane Keaton: *Lovers and Other Strangers* (1970)
- Madeline Kahn: *What's Up, Doc?* (1972)
- Tatum O'Neal: *Paper Moon* (1973)
- Randy Quaid: *The Last Picture Show* (1971)
- Susan Sarandon: *Joe* (1970)
- Sissy Spacek: *Prime Cut* (1972)
- Arnold Schwarzenegger: *Hercules in New York* (1970)

Rated
G
but may be too intense
for younger
children.

The picture
runs 130 minutes!...
The story
covers 96 of the most critical hours in man's history!...
The suspense
will last through your lifetime!

A **ROBERT WISE** PRODUCTION

From the Best Seller by
MICHAEL CRICHTON

THE **ANDROMEDA STRAIN**

STARRING
ARTHUR HILL · DAVID WAYNE · JAMES OLSON · KATE REID

Production Designed by **BORIS LEVEN** · Screenplay by **NELSON GIDDING** · From the Novel by **MICHAEL CRICHTON** · Directed by **ROBERT WISE** · Music by **GIL MELLÉ**

Soundtrack Album
exclusively on 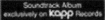 Records

G

A UNIVERSAL PICTURE
TECHNICOLOR® PANAVISION®

NOTE: *NO ONE WILL BE SEATED DURING THE LAST 10 MINUTES.*

In Film

- Oscar for Best Picture: *The French Connection.*
- Most Oscar wins (five): *The French Connection.*
- Most Oscar nominations (eight): *Fiddler on the Roof, The French Connection, The Last Picture Show.*

- Top-grossing movie: *The French Connection.*
- Top-grossing comedy: *Carnal Knowledge.*
- Top-grossing horror or sci-fi: *The Andromeda Strain.*
- *A Clockwork Orange, Dirty Harry,* and *Straw Dogs* generate controversy with their violence; *Sweet Sweetback's Baadasssss Song,* the year's top-grossing independent movie, is arguably the first entry in the blaxploitation genre.
- The first permanent IMAX theater debuts in Toronto, Canada.
- Five memorable actors: Clint Eastwood, Gene Hackman, Malcolm McDowell, Richard Roundtree, Gene Wilder.
- Five memorable actresses: Ann-Margret, Julie Christie, Jane Fonda, Cloris Leachman, Vanessa Redgrave.
- Movie debuts: F. Murray Abraham, Kathy Bates, directors Clint Eastwood, George Lucas, Elaine May.
- Deaths include silent-film star Harold Lloyd, composer Max Steiner.

In America

- The voting age is lowered from twenty-one to eighteen.
- The *New York Times* publishes the Pentagon Papers.
- Lieutenant William Calley is found guilty of the twenty-two murders known as the My Lai Massacre.
- Greenpeace is founded.
- President Nixon announces a new "war on drugs" campaign.
- The new Nasdaq index debuts on the stock market.
- Charles Manson and followers are convicted of murder and given the death penalty.
- Hijacker D.B. Cooper parachutes from an airliner and disappears.
- Now open: Amtrak, Southwest Airlines, Starbucks (Seattle), Walt Disney World (Orlando).
- The first aerobics dance classes are held, leading to a national fitness craze.
- Joe Frazier defeats Muhammad Ali in the "Fight of the Century."
- Veteran's Stadium, new home of baseball's Phillies and football's Eagles, opens in Philadelphia, and Texas Stadium, new home of the Dallas Cowboys, opens in Irving, Texas.
- First issue of *Ms.* magazine.
- Bestselling novel: *Wheels.*
- Music: The Carpenters' "Close to You," Led Zeppelin's "Stairway to Heaven," Don McLean's "American Pie," and Carole King's *Tapestry* album are released.
- TV debuts: *All in the Family, Masterpiece Theatre, The Sonny & Cher Comedy Hour.*
- Deaths include Duane Allman, Louis Armstrong, Jim Morrison.

Vanishing Point

Released: January 1971
Director: Richard C. Sarafian
Stars: Barry Newman, Cleavon Little, Dean Jagger
Academy Awards: None

PREVIEW: A bold driver eludes police as he speeds down highways from Denver to San Francisco.

NOW SHOWING: Running on Fumes

What makes *Vanishing Point* (1971) the quintessential '70s chase movie is the picturesque chase itself. Unlike other high-octane movies with long car chases—*Smokey and the Bandit* (1977), say—which have personality and purpose, this one never explains why its laconic, inscrutable driver starts and ends the chase like he does. Viewers have debated his existential decisions ever since *Vanishing Point* was a drive-in hit.

Most of the movie is presented in flashback. After we watch a roadblock being slowly assembled in California, the scene shifts to "two days earlier." Now midnight in Denver, a car-delivery driver named simply Kowalski (cool, rugged-looking Barry Newman) revs up a pristine Dodge Challenger for delivery in San Francisco in about sixty hours. For some unexplained reason Kowalski impulsively bets he'll cover that 1,200 miles in only *fifteen* hours. "You're gonna kill yourself someday," his boss warns him.

Gulping Benzedrine, he freely speeds along until he runs a motorcycle cop off a highway. From here on the police are in avid pursuit, but Kowalski always escapes with daring maneuvers. These scenes are accompanied by flashbacks to Kowalski's own racing disasters on a motorcycle and in a stock car (for a pro, he sure crashes a lot). Continuing across Nevada's desert he fixes a flat, endures meandering conversations with a drifter (Dean Jagger), listens to musical faith healers, and has a ridiculous confrontation with gay bandits. More flashbacks: Kowalski as a cop, his surfer girlfriend before she drowns. The police also reveal some of his biographical details—a Medal of Honor, a dishonorable discharge—as they track him. In the last perplexing scene, Kowalski enigmatically smiles as he self-destructively accelerates into that California roadblock we saw earlier.

During the chase, Kowalski gets coaching over the radio from Super Soul (Cleavon Little), an energetic DJ who seems to communicate telepathically. Super Soul magnifies Kowalski into a celebrity, calling him "the last American hero" and a "soul hero in his soul-mobile" being pursued by "blue meanies" in "Nazi cars." Nazis, really? Super Soul's anti-establishment point vanishes behind overexcited hyperbole. Also needing a tune-up is an encounter with a naked girl on a motorcycle, her slow-motion arrival suggesting a hallucination. Like some of Kowalski's other road experiences, it's watchable, mildly interesting, and insignificant. Just enjoy the movie's compelling chase—the smokin'-hot car, stunning scenery, and rock music—because the rest of *Vanishing Point* aims for myth but misses.

ADDED ATTRACTION: *Two-Lane Blacktop* to Enigmatown

Six months after *Vanishing Point* premiered, an even more oblique road movie hit the highway. In *Two-Lane Blacktop* (1971), an unnamed driver (James Taylor) and mechanic (Dennis Wilson) cruise the Southwest in their souped-up '55 Chevy. These two rock stars play sullen, car-focused characters who seemingly represent alienated youth. Given minimal dialogue, they never reveal anything about themselves, and when a cute, flighty girl (Laurie Bird) spontaneously jumps in the car and rides along, they barely even acknowledge her. Most of the movie is their cross-country duel against a shiny 1970 GTO and its older driver (Warren Oates), a lively teller of tall tales. It's a frustrating race: the racers help each other, take meandering side trips, stop for a driving lesson, pick up hitchhikers, etc. Capped by a unique, self-destructive ending that still startles, *Two-Lane Blacktop* is a possibly profound, definitely artistic cult movie that, like *Vanishing Point*, offers more questions than answers.

The Andromeda Strain

Released: March 1971

Director: Robert Wise

Stars: James Olson, Arthur Hill, David Wayne

Academy Awards: Two nominations (Best Editing; Best Art Direction)

PREVIEW: Scientists in an underground lab try to control a deadly micro-organism from space.

NOW SHOWING: Believing *The Andromeda Strain*

What makes *The Andromeda Strain* (1971) so great—and it *is* great, one of the decade's best science-fiction movies—is its realism. This long, fascinating movie dares to challenge the audience with scientific complexity and detail without dumbing anything down. There are no big movie stars to pre-condition our expectations, and there's no sappy love story to deflect our attention. Instead, director Robert Wise, the four-time Oscar winner behind an earlier sci-fi classic, *The Day the Earth Stood Still* (1951), creates a totally plausible scientific world and keeps the focus directly on the immediate emergency. It is all so believable, *The Andromeda Strain* feels closer to science fact than science fiction.

The movie is based on the bestselling 1969 novel by Michael Crichton (fifteen minutes into the movie, he's shown wearing hospital scrubs and sitting in an operating room). While the screen story closely follows the book's suspenseful plot, it adds a tough, sarcastic female microbiologist (Kate Reid) to the main cast. The opening credits begin documentary-style, with official-sounding acknowledgements and real-looking classified documents, maps, and graphics establishing authenticity before we're quickly plunged into the tense drama. Spanning five days in February 1971, the action revolves around a crashed satellite carrying the Andromeda Strain, a lethal "space germ" that instantly kills anyone nearby. A team of scientific experts assembles at a top-secret underground facility to try to isolate, identify, and control whatever it is the satellite has brought back. Most of the movie is confined to this impressive subterranean structure, where the scientists have to solve various puzzles to avert a national catastrophe. Director Wise uses micro-photography, split-screen, innovative computer graphics, and realistic labs to show the scientists at work. Throughout the crisis, mistakes and bad luck impede the team's progress, and at one point a broken seal threatens fatal contamination. The last ten minutes are genuinely suspenseful as a nuclear self-destruct device counts down and a team member has to battle past laser defenses to deactivate it.

Ordinarily, the complicated scientific issues would confuse the layman, but *The Andromeda Strain* tells its story clearly and effectively. Interestingly, the germ mutates by itself and drifts to extinction over the ocean, so that nature, not the team, does the heavy lifting in killing it. However, the last shot through an electron microscope suggests that similar situations are inevitable, thus making this excellent, cerebral movie more like an actual warning than mere entertainment.

ADDED ATTRACTION: The Crichton Connection

What a decade it was for Michael Crichton. Here are the movies this prolific writer was involved in during the 1970s.

Movie (Year)	Crichton Connection
The Andromeda Strain (1971)	Based on his novel, and a cameo role
Dealing (1972)	Based on his novel
The Carey Treatment (1972)	Based on his novel
Extreme Close-Up (1973)	His screenplay
Westworld (1973)	Director, and his screenplay
The Terminal Man (1974)	Based on his novel
Coma (1978)	Director, and his screenplay
The Great Train Robbery (1978)	Director, and his screenplay based on his novel

The Barefoot Executive

Released: March 1971

Director: Robert Butler

Stars: Kurt Russell, Joe Flynn, Harry Morgan

Academy Awards: None

PREVIEW: Aided by a chimp that predicts hit shows, the mail boy at a TV network rises to the top.

NOW SHOWING: Two Opposable Thumbs Up

The '70s got off to a wobbly start for live-action Disney movies. The studio's first three offerings of 1970—*King of the Grizzlies*, *The Boatniks*, and *The Wild Country*—were either run-of-the-mill wilderness movies or, in the case of *The Boatniks*, an inane "comedy" that critics promptly sank. Fortunately, seven months after that sailboat silliness, Walt Disney Productions released *The Barefoot Executive* (1971). It's a deceptively clever movie, because though it's ostensibly a nice comedy with a lightweight premise built for buoyant family fun, hiding inside is a sly satire.

Stuck in the mail room at a TV network is twenty-one-year-old Steven (Kurt Russell), who is struggling to come up with "one good program idea." Fortunately, his girlfriend's pet chimp is a programming genius. The chimp watches TV, freaks out at bad shows, changes channels, and even grabs beers during commercials. Steven notes the chimp's preferences, submits them to the network like they're his own, and then vaults to a V.P. position when all those suggestions become hits. Rival executives spy on the "boy wonder" to figure out his technique; once the chimp is exposed as the true programmer, and after some overlong slapstick escapades conclude, the execs buy the chimp from Steven and fly him off to the jungle so they can all go back to business as usual. This being Disney, naturally the bad guys are foiled, Steven and the chimp are reunited, and Steven even marries his girlfriend.

The movie's argument—today's TV programming is so haphazard that it must be the work of a chimp—is pretty audacious, especially for a conservative media giant like Disney. One of the movie's best scenes involves a frustrated viewer who loudly complains about the network's dumb decisions ("maybe a chimp *is* behind this mess," she reasons hilariously).

Russell is appealing as a "crazy movin' groovin' kid who just won't stop" (according to the theme song), and that's really him riding a motorcycle around L.A. streets (and with no helmet!). Some reliable veterans join the fun, especially an irritated Joe Flynn, a cranky Harry Morgan, and a scene-stealing Wally Cox. For Cox it's his final movie before his untimely death; meanwhile, making his movie debut as a smug preppy is young John Ritter. Children won't know any of these names, of course, but they'll be kept amused by the well-timed expressions of Raffles, the brainy chimp.

ADDED ATTRACTION: The Chimp's Choices

Steven's lame idea for a new show is *Abraham Lincoln's Doctor's Dog*, based on research that audiences love Lincoln, doctors, and dogs. Fortunately the chimp makes selections for him. The chimp prefers old Disney movies—*The Shaggy Dog* (1959), *Babes in Toyland* (1961)—plus TV series with familiar-sounding titles. Here are twelve shows and one movie mentioned in *The Barefoot Executive* with titles that parody actual productions.

The Movie's Fictional Titles	The Real Shows (Years)
Beverly Mutineers	*The Beverly Hillbillies* (1962-1971)
The Fastest Gun	*The Restless Gun* (1957-1959)
High Spy	*I Spy* (1965-1968)
I Love Ruthie	*I Love Lucy* (1951-1957)
Laugh Out	*Laugh-In* (1967-1973)
Love Calif. Style	*Love, American Style* (1969-1974)
The Mad Squad	*The Mod Squad* (1968-1973)
Mission Improbable	*Mission: Impossible* (1966-1973)
Pistol Smoke	*Gunsmoke* (1955-1975)
Rock Stones	*The Flintstones* (1960-1966)
Star Journeys	*Star Trek* (1966-1969)
Then Came Johnson	*Then Came Bronson* (1969-1970)
Thoroughly Modern Billie	*Thoroughly Modern Millie* (movie, 1967)

Summer of '42

Released: April 1971

Director: Robert Mulligan

Stars: Jennifer O'Neill, Gary Grimes, Jerry Houser

Academy Awards: One win (Best Music), plus three more nominations (Best Writing; Best Editing; Best Cinematography)

PREVIEW: A teenage boy falls for a beautiful older woman whose husband is fighting in the war.

NOW SHOWING: The One Who Got Away

With the Vietnam War raging, Americans in the early 1970s seemed ready for something old-fashioned at the movies. Consider: 1970's biggest blockbuster was a teary melodrama, *Love Story*. Four months after that movie's debut, another popular hit, *Summer of '42* (1971) delivered similar nonviolent, escapist entertainment, this time sending viewers to a tastefully nostalgic past when times, and wars, were simpler.

Like *Love Story*, *Summer of '42* is narrated by a 1970s man (voiced by director Robert Mulligan) who is warmly remembering his lost love. Long ago he was Hermie (Gary Grimes), a sensitive fifteen-year-old boy summering on an unnamed East Coast island (northern California provides the locations). Hermie and his two friends talk about girls, drool over the sex pages in a medical manual, goof around on the beach, and go to movies. Amused audiences will surely identify with their youthful, uninformed conversations: "I *hope* I'm not in love with her," worries Hermie's pal Oscy (Jerry Hauser), "I *hate* her!"

Complicating Hermie's life is Dorothy (Jennifer O'Neill), a lovely married woman in her twenties. She's presented as a daydream—occasionally in slow motion, always sunny, naturally radiant. When her husband goes off to war, Dorothy is left alone and becomes

Jennifer O'Neill and Gary Grimes.

the object of Hermie's obsession. He is nervous and overly polite around her, blurting out "mature" comments like, "Laughter becomes you." Three-fourths of the way through the movie everything changes when Dorothy learns of her husband's death; when Hermie visits that evening, she tenderly, wordlessly, and inexplicably takes him to bed.

Here's where the movie gets problematic. Her response to heartbreaking loss may seem illogical, but screenwriter Herman Raucher says the movie is autobiographical, so we'll accept her actions without judgment. Also overlook Hermie's status as a minor, which has serious implications. The bigger issue is their obvious lack of chemistry: before the bedroom scene, they'd been together for only nineteen minutes, most of them awkward. Dorothy doesn't reveal her name until just before the tragedy, and she offers zero explanations in the note she leaves before departing the next day. The narrator concludes by saying he "lost Hermie forever," a poignant but vague statement. Perhaps it's better not to over-think the ending and to focus instead on what's undeniably wonderful about the movie—the exquisite cinematography, the evocative details, the gorgeous Oscar-winning music. *Summer of '42* is indeed haunting and beautiful, but it's not convincing.

ADDED ATTRACTION: May/December Relationships

Younger-men-with-older-women romances are in the following 1970s movies (with ages of the actors and actresses in the years when the movies premiered). For movies pairing May-actresses/December-actors, see the entry for *The Poseidon Adventure* (1972).

- *Animal House* (1978): Tim Matheson, 31; Verna Bloom, 39
- *The Beguiled* (1971): Clint Eastwood, 41; Geraldine Page, 47
- *Bloody Mama* (1970): Bruce Dern, 34; Shelley Winters, 50
- *Butterflies Are Free* (1972): Edward Albert, 21; Goldie Hawn, 27
- *40 Carats* (1973): Edward Albert, 22; Liv Ullmann, 35
- *Harold and Maude* (1971): Bud Cort, 23; Ruth Gordon, 75
- *The Last Picture Show* (1971): Timothy Bottoms, 20; Cloris Leachman, 45
- *Moment to Moment* (1978): John Travolta, 24; Lily Tomlin, 39
- *Nashville* (1975): Keith Carradine, 26; Lily Tomlin, 36
- *Sextette* (1978): Timothy Dalton, 32; Mae West, 85
- *Summer of '42* (1971): Gary Grimes, 16; Jennifer O'Neill, 23

Sweet Sweetback's Baadasssss Song

Released: April 1971
Director: Melvin Van Peebles
Stars: Melvin Van Peebles, Hubert Scales, John Dullaghan
Academy Awards: None

PREVIEW: A black man retaliates against racist white cops, hides in L.A., and runs to Mexico.

NOW SHOWING: Sour Notes

After the crime-comedy *Cotton Comes to Harlem* (1970) and the bizarro-comedy *Watermelon Man* (1970) lit the fuse, the militant *Sweet Sweetback's Baadasssss Song* (1971) set off the black-cinema explosion. Confrontational, daring, and relentless, it's a howling response to what the movie calls "the overdose of black misery" in America. When it became one of the highest-grossing independent movies *ever*, major studios started targeting urban black audiences, and the blaxploitation revolution was underway.

Working with a miniscule budget, Melvin Van Peebles (director of *Watermelon Man*) basically did everything himself on *Sweet Sweetback*. Not only does he star in the movie, he produced, wrote, directed, and edited it, and he even composed the soundtrack's Earth, Wind & Fire songs. Van Peebles experiments with psychedelic and split-screen effects, incorporates radical jump-cuts to speed the action, and repeats some lines over and over again for emphasis. Most of all, he shoves angry black themes right into viewers' faces. Those themes are packed into the story of Sweetback, an expressionless, almost wordless man who retaliates violently when he watches racist white cops beat up a helpless black youth. Leaving the cops unconscious, Sweetback runs across L.A. and into numerous encounters. After killing two aggressive deputies, he makes a desperate try for the Mexican border.

It's a difficult movie to enjoy. Originally rated X, *Sweet Sweetback* opens with a controversial scene of a young boy and a much older woman having graphic sex (the adult Sweetback is in explicit sex scenes later). The movie's language gets rough, especially for 1971 when extreme profanity was still rare in movies. Additionally, much of *Sweet Sweetback* is either filmed at night or severely underlit, and often the sound quality is poor, making entire scenes hard to follow. And for some reason Van Peebles insists on showing things many people would rather not see: thirty seconds of an almost-naked fat man doing his business on the toilet are thirty seconds too many, and nobody needs a man-eating-a-raw-lizard close-up. Audiences might also be perplexed by the extremely abrupt ending that suggests Van Peebles simply ran out of film.

Modern viewers may think it amateurish or incoherent, but *Sweet Sweetback*'s importance as a cultural groundbreaker is undeniable. Without it, there might have been no *Super Fly* (1972), no *Coffy* (1973), maybe no Richard Pryor or Spike Lee. Rebellious and unruly, *Sweet Sweetback's Baadasssss Song* is hard to watch, but harder to ignore.

ADDED ATTRACTION: "Watch Out"

Director Melvin Van Peebles literally puts written words where his movie is. He starts off with a printed quote that implies the "song" in the title is "a hymn from the mouth of reality." Then comes a dedication "to all the Brothers and Sisters who had enough of the Man." The opening credits say that *Sweet Sweetback* stars "The Black Community"; the closing credits use the N-word, warn the audience to "watch out," and possibly suggest a sequel (that never came) with Sweetback "coming back to collect some dues." Van Peebles did make one more movie in the '70s, a spirited, rough-edged oddity called *Don't Play Us Cheap* (1973). Based on his Broadway musical (with his own songs) that ran for four-and-a-half months in 1972, this avant-garde movie is filmed like a presentation of that show and tells the story of two bat-winged devils who visit a lively Harlem party. Later in the decade Van Peebles was also one of the writers of *Greased Lightning* (1977), the entertaining biographical movie about Wendell Scott. Scott, played by Richard Pryor (with Pam Grier playing his wife), was a black bootlegger in Virginia who switched to racing stock cars and in the 1960s became the first black driver to win a major NASCAR race.

Banana**ſ**

Released: April 1971
Director: Woody Allen
Stars: Woody Allen, Louise Lasser, Howard Cosell
Academy Awards: None

PREVIEW: To impress a girl, a clumsy New Yorker aids a revolution in a Latin American country.

NOW SHOWING: Appealing *Bananas*

To follow Woody Allen's career in the 1970s is to witness his progression from an eager, amateurish filmmaker into a confident, Oscar-winning filmmaster. The journey that peaks with *Annie Hall* (1977) and *Manhattan* (1979) was underway early in the decade with *Bananas* (1971).

When long-time fans reminisce about Allen's "early funny ones," *Bananas* is one they're remembering. It's no masterpiece, but it shows remarkable growth from the previous movie Allen wrote, directed, and starred in, *Take the Money and Run* (1969). That faux documentary strung together funny, scattershot sequences that occasionally seemed unrelated to the plot. *Bananas* changes that. It tells a laugh-filled story about Fielding Mellish (Allen), a nebbish New Yorker who tries to impress a politically minded girl (Louise Lasser) by flying to a Latin American country (the fictional San Marcos, representing Cuba) and joining a revolution against a corrupt dictator.

This anarchic, fast-moving comedy has far more hits than misses. Before the opening credits, sportscaster Howard Cosell announces a presidential assassination ("You've heard it with your own eyes," he says); he finishes the movie by delivering play-by-play of Mellish's wedding night ("the bride wore the traditional virginal white, as did Mellish"). There are wacky slapstick scenes (Mellish the product tester), terrific

Woody Allen and Louise Lasser.

one-liners ("Why did I quit college? ... I was in the Black Studies program, by now I could have been black"), and a classic sequence (lunch for a thousand rebels). Not everything works. Semi-smutty jokes, an out-of-left-field fake commercial, and a prolonged courtroom scene with jurors sharing a joint all feel forced.

Throughout, Allen moves toward what will become his familiar style. Foreshadowing future movies like *Sleeper* (1973) and *Zelig* (1983), *Bananas* has his first one-word title. At only eighty-two minutes, *Bananas* is short, as most of his later movies will be. It's the first time he films in New York and plays a New Yorker, just like in *Annie Hall* and many subsequent movies. He includes homages to the greats (see "Added Attraction"). He's got a soon-to-be famous actor in the cast (young Sylvester Stallone, appearing eleven minutes into the movie as a subway thug). And as with most of his movies, this one underwent major surgery in editing (the original title was *El Weirdo*, and an awkward finale that had Fielding in blackface after a bomb explosion was abandoned). With *Bananas*, Woody Allen wasn't there yet, but he was on his way.

ADDED ATTRACTION: Allen's Homages

Many of Woody Allen's later movies include scenes and themes derived from past classics. *Manhattan Murder Mystery* (1993), to name just one example, borrows the mirror-maze ending, and some of the exact lines, from *The Lady from Shanghai* (1947). In *Bananas*, Allen includes the following references to earlier famous movies.

- The fast-moving Execusizor machine = Charlie Chaplin's hyper-efficient feeding machine in *Modern Times* (1936).

- Guards torture a rebel by repeatedly playing the operetta *Naughty Marietta* = a similar scene with "Itsy Bitsy Teenie Weenie Yellow Polka Dot Bikini" in Billy Wilder's *One, Two, Three* (1961).

- Mellish silently seduces a sexy rebel at a picnic lunch = the famous dining-room seduction scene in *Tom Jones* (1963).

- Fifty-seven minutes into *Bananas*, a baby carriage slowly moves down some steps = an iconic scene in *Battleship Potemkin* (1925).

Plaza Suite

Released: May 1971
Director: Arthur Hiller
Stars: Walter Matthau, Maureen Stapleton, Barbara Harris
Academy Awards: None

PREVIEW: This anthology movie tells three humorous stories set in a single Plaza Hotel room.

NOW SHOWING: The Simon Hotel

Writer Neil Simon would triumph later in the decade with *The Sunshine Boys* (1975), *The Goodbye Girl* (1977), and other hits, but his initial screenplays of the '70s were slight disappointments compared to his final screenplay of the '60s, *The Odd Couple* (1968). *The Out-of-Towners* (1970), his first movie that was not based on one of his earlier Broadway plays, presents intermittently funny answers to a single question:

what could go wrong for a small-town couple visiting Manhattan for the weekend? The nightmarish possibilities include delayed flights, lost luggage, a transit strike, canceled hotel reservations, a night in Central Park, an exploding manhole cover, robbery, mugging, kidnapping, a chipped tooth, a bloody foot, even a hijacking. A determined Jack Lemmon tries to bull his way through endless adversity, but as the stereotypical city problems pile up, the movie gets wearying.

For his next movie, Simon returned to adapting one of his hit plays, this one a 1968 Tony Award winner. *Plaza Suite* (1971) is a mildly amusing anthology movie that occasionally feels like a TV sitcom. Every segment offers Simon's patented one-liners and relationship musings, but none of the segments is hilarious. In a bravura display of acting versatility, Walter Matthau plays three different characters in three different segments set in the same Plaza Hotel room. In the first (and least funny) segment, he's a heel meeting his needy wife in the room; Maureen Stapleton steals their scenes with her subtlety and believability. There are some humorous moments, but a hurtful revelation darkens this segment.

Next, Matthau is miscast as a sex-minded Hollywood producer in a ridiculous blond wig who's trying to recruit women. Barbara Harris, as his ex-girlfriend, lightens up what might otherwise be a creepy encounter. Matthau isn't convincing or funny in what is the weakest of the three segments.

Finally, Matthau and Lee Grant play the beleaguered parents of a reluctant bride who's locked herself in the bathroom before the big wedding that's being held downstairs. This is the only segment that actually goes outside the room, which Matthau does when he walks on the window ledge. There's more slapstick in this segment than in the other two, and it's also the best of the three. Though it's uneven, the movie was successful enough to warrant another try at the same concept, resulting in *California Suite* (1978), a four-segment anthology movie set in the Beverly Hills Hotel.

ADDED ATTRACTION: Subsequent Simon

Plaza Suite is one of Neil Simon's 1970s movies that were later remade. Here's a list of his chronologically ordered '70s movies and remakes.

Original Movie (Year), Starring …	Remake Year, Starring …
The Out-of-Towners (1970): Jack Lemmon, Sandy Dennis	1999: Steve Martin, Goldie Hawn
Plaza Suite (1971): Walter Matthau, Barbara Harris	1987 TV movie: Carol Burnett, Dabney Coleman
The Heartbreak Kid (1972): Charles Grodin, Cybill Shepherd	2007: Ben Stiller, Michelle Monaghan
The Sunshine Boys (1975): George Burns, Walter Matthau	1996 TV movie: Woody Allen, Peter Falk
The Goodbye Girl (1977): Richard Dreyfuss, Marsha Mason	2004 TV movie: Jeff Daniels, Patricia Heaton

Escape from the Planet of the Apes

Released: May 1971
Director: Don Taylor
Stars: Roddy McDowall, Kim Hunter, Bradford Dillman
Academy Awards: None

PREVIEW: Two apes who fly from the future back to 1973 might cause Earth's later destruction.

NOW SHOWING: Monkey Business, Part Two

In some ways *Escape from the Planet of the Apes* (1971) is the best of the 1970s sequels to the classic *Planet of the Apes* (1968). *Escape from the POTA* makes a daring choice by scaling down from big battles to tell a more intimate human ... uh, simian ... story. This time apes, not human astronauts, are the immigrants who have come to a strange place (maybe the title should've been *Planet of the People*).

Unlike the original *POTA* and its first sequel, *Beneath the Planet of the Apes* (1970), which are both set in the distant future, this second sequel flashes back to Earth in 1973. The spaceship that sank in a lake in the original *POTA* has been salvaged and now crashes in the ocean near Los Angeles. Inside are three "ape-o-nauts," including the familiar Cornelius (Roddy McDowall) and Zira (Kim Hunter), plus Dr. Milo (Sal Mineo), who is quickly killed off. How these future apes, who have come from a low-tech society with no cars or planes, are able to repair and launch the soggy rocket is never explained.

The movie's tone in the first half is often light, especially when Cornelius and Zira check into the Beverly Wilshire Hotel, go clothes shopping, and hit some L.A. hot spots. But everything darkens once Zira becomes pregnant. Immediately the implications are

Kim Hunter and Roddy McDowall.

clear to Dr. Hasslein (Eric Braeden), the "senior scientific advisor at the White House" whose time-travel hypothesis was discussed in both previous movies: if that talking ape baby survives, Earth will be destroyed in twenty centuries. Imprisoning Cornelius and Zira, Hasslein plans to kill their unborn baby, but the apes escape and Zira delivers baby Milo at a small traveling circus. Tragically, Cornelius, Zira, and what is apparently her baby are all gunned down in a heartbreaking confrontation, but the last scene reveals they've pulled off the ol' baby switcheroo, with Milo alive and talking as the circus heads to Florida. Thus is Earth's future sealed.

While it's not equal to the original *POTA* (few sci-fi movies are), *Escape* is much better than the messy, noisy first sequel. Fans will welcome back composer Jerry Goldsmith, who was Oscar-nominated for *POTA* and returns for his last *Apes* movie with another atmospheric score. As with the previous sequel, this movie was also a number-one hit at the box-office, which naturally meant a follow-up was only a year away.

ADDED ATTRACTION: Aldo of the *Apes*

Fifty-two minutes into *Escape from the Planet of the Apes*, Cornelius recounts in detail "how apes arose" over man. In the future, he says, after a plague takes all human house pets, primitive apes are brought inside to take their place. "Twenty times more intelligent than dogs or cats," the apes eventually become articulate servants who resent their slave-like treatment. An ape named Aldo is the first to say "no" aloud, sparking the revolution. Aldo does appear in the next two sequels, but he's not the leader of the revolution, which makes Cornelius' future-history lesson somewhat confusing. Or maybe not: perhaps Cornelius is wisely trying to deflect attention away from the true instigator of the apes' uprising, his son, Caesar. Played by Roddy McDowall, Caesar will be the star of the next two movies in the *POTA* series.

Support Your Local Gunfighter

Released: May 1971
Director: Burt Kennedy
Stars: James Garner, Suzanne Pleshette, Jack Elam
Academy Awards: None

PREVIEW: Mayhem in the Old West results when a con man is mistaken for a dangerous gunfighter.

NOW SHOWING: Frontier Fun

Something Hollywood likes more than a new idea is a proven formula. With *Support Your Local Sheriff!* (1969) a surprising hit, director Burt Kennedy reunited a dozen members of that cast for another low-budget western parody, *Support Your Local Gunfighter* (1971). The second movie is not really a sequel (there's no mention of its predecessor), and nobody plays the same character, but the family-friendly tone and setting are similar, making *Local Gunfighter* a worthy follow-up.

Mistaken identity pushes the plot. James Garner plays Latigo, a sly rogue who escapes his imminent wedding by hiding in a strange town. The locals confuse him with the dangerous Swifty Morgan simply because he's got the look of "the best gunman in the whole Southwest." Latigo shifts that identity onto a nitwit cowpoke (Jack Elam) and instead becomes the nitwit's agent as they get involved with two rival mining companies.

Naturally the real Swifty (menacing Chuck Connors) shows up for a final confrontation. The amusing dialogue gets some laughs by recycling old clichés, and many scenes invert standard western situations: Latigo is a con artist but a terrible gambler, women start and finish a two-minute bar-room brawl, and Patience (Suzanne Pleshette) is anything *but* patient and "just likes to shoot people" (fortunately she's a terrible shot).

Slightly departing from his previous role as the likeable sheriff, here Garner's confident, opportunistic character is occasionally a little prickly. Co-star Pleshette is an energetic new addition, looking beautiful even when she's an ornery spitfire for the first two-thirds of the movie. Elam adds his usual terrific comic support, and one of his lines—"Don't ever come up on my blind side like that"—pokes fun at his sightless left eye. As he did in *Support Your Local Sheriff!*, Elam wraps things up by directly addressing the audience and giving updates (he says he'll become "a big star in Italian westerns"). It's not as fresh as *Local Sheriff*, but *Local Gunfighter* is still an amiable improvement over director Kennedy's raunchy western parody *Dirty Dingus Magee* (1970). For Garner, *Local Gunfighter*, sandwiched in between *A Man Called Sledge* (1970) and *Skin Game* (1971), was his second of three consecutive western-themed movies.

ADDED ATTRACTION: Garner's *Game*

Four months after *Support Your Local Gunfighter*, Garner returned to the frontier in a more adventurous comedy, *Skin Game* (1971). Garner plays an easy-going pre-Civil War conman partnered with a black man (Lou Gossett) who poses as a slave so the conman can sell him. Each night the slave escapes to reteam for another sale in another town (the towns all have humorous names—Dirty Shame, Rough Deal, etc.). It's never laugh-out-loud funny, but the movie has some good lines: when the men joke about trading places, Garner's character says, "You're the color they're buyin' this year." The movie's first half is more amusing than its second, when a harsh slave owner takes possession, leprosy becomes a running joke, and both main characters get whipped. The two stars have excellent chemistry together, Susan Clark plays an attractive thief, and Ed Asner is a bigoted villain. The busy Garner wasn't done with western comedies; just down the trail were two for Disney: *One Little Indian* (1973), featuring camels and young Jodie Foster in a small role, and *The Castaway Cowboy* (1974), with Hawaii as the exotic setting for cattle-ranching action.

Willard

Released: June 1971
Director: Daniel Mann
Stars: Bruce Davison, Sondra Locke, Ernest Borgnine
Academy Awards: None

PREVIEW: A meek young man befriends rats and trains them so he can get revenge on his mean boss.

NOW SHOWING: Oh, *Rats*

The surprise about *Willard* (1971) isn't that this interesting little horror movie was a big box-office hit; the real surprise is that there's not much horror until the end. There's creepiness, sure, but the first two-thirds of *Willard* are more of a psychological study of a timid, over-worked, twenty-seven-year old "sweet boy" with a doting mother and an overbearing boss.

Seven minutes into the movie friendless Willard (Bruce Davison) feeds a solitary rat outside his house, and soon he's supporting an entire rat family, giving them names, training them, and setting them up in the garage with little structures. Willard gets so close to the quickly multiplying rodents that he carries them on his shoulders and takes them to work because he's "lonely" for them. In a darkly humorous scene, Willard gets some payback by unleashing the rats at his boss's anniversary party.

Once mom (Elsa Lanchester) dies, Willard's weirdness intensifies. Alone in the big house, he moves his beloved rats, now numbering into the hundreds, into the cellar. Willard also talks to the rats in complete sentences, and he suspects that one of them, Ben, is becoming a defiant "troublemaking" leader.

Seeing his boss, Martin (Ernest Borgnine), violently kill a rat drives Willard over the edge. The scares accelerate in the last twenty minutes as Willard and his four-legged friends confront Martin in the office: "We've come to talk to you," Willard announces, and soon Martin is dead. Willard's triumph is short-lived, however, as Ben mobilizes his rat army to get the last word. That the animals win is an ending reminiscent of *The Birds* (1963) and a forecast of *Frogs* (1972).

The performances makes *Willard* special. Slender, meek, and a little clumsy, Bruce Davison's Willard is a pitiable character before his madness is fully ratified. Ernest Borgnine is a harsh, intimidating antagonist, and Sondra Locke, wearing short skirts throughout, is a beautiful, sympathetic co-worker. Even Ben gives a good performance; shot repeatedly in close-up, Ben actually looks like he's calculating his next move—which, evidently, was to prep for the sequel, *Ben* (1972). This weak, sometimes absurd movie picks up from the ending of *Willard* and introduces an even younger human friend for Ben and his rat pack. Though it has some touching boy/rat interaction and bloody rat attacks, the most notable thing here is the gentle Oscar-nominated theme song, sung by Michael Jackson, about the murderous rodent.

ADDED ATTRACTION: *MAD* Magazine's Parodies of 1971 Movies

Willard got its own movie parody, "Willies," in *MAD* magazine (the parody ran in March 1972). Here are eight other 1971 movies that were similarly honored, followed by the titles of the parodies. *MAD*'s parodies of 1972 movies are with the entry for *The Godfather* (1972).

- *Billy Jack*: "Billy Jock"
- *Carnal Knowledge*: "Carnival Knowledge"
- *A Clockwork Orange*: "A Crockwork Lemon"
- *Diamonds Are Forever*: "Dollars Are Forever"
- *Dirty Harry*: "Dirty Larry"
- *The French Connection*: "What's the Connection?"
- *Fiddler on the Roof*: "Antenna on the Roof"
- *Summer of '42*: "The Trauma of '42"

Klute

Released: June 1971
Director: Alan J. Pakula
Stars: Jane Fonda, Donald Sutherland, Charles Cioffi
Academy Awards: One win (Best Actress—Jane Fonda), plus one more nomination (Best Writing)

PREVIEW: Looking for a missing person, a private investigator protects a Manhattan hooker.

NOW SHOWING: Working Girl

Klute (1971) is a stylish, if simplistic thriller that showcases two exceptional performances. The title is the last name of a small-town private investigator (Donald Sutherland) who's looking for a missing person in New York City. There he connects with Bree (Jane Fonda), a cool call girl who is such a dominating character that the movie could easily have been named after her. Klute finds himself on a murder case, but unfor-

tunately much of the suspense has already drained away because the perpetrator's identity is tipped off early and then gets blatantly announced with a half-hour still to go. While there are some chilling scenes, especially a tense fourteen-minute sequence near the end when Bree is alone in a dark garment factory and suddenly comes upon the murderer, *Klute* isn't a serpentine mystery that keeps viewers guessing; even the killer himself says, "It's just an ordinary matter."

Where the movie excels is in its depiction of Bree's unusual world, which includes wild parties and strung-out junkies. She seduces a client and then checks her watch as she fakes some rapturous moans; she lists the kinky preferences of "freaks" and explains why she complies ("When you're a call girl you control it. ... For an hour I'm the best actress in the world"); we even learn about her finances ("six- or seven-hundred tricks a year" at $50-$200 each). Braless, wearing a groovy shag haircut and thigh-high boots, at times confident and composed and at other times vulnerable and raw, Fonda is utterly convincing in a complicated role that earned her a well-deserved Oscar. In her most riveting scene, she silently weeps as she listens for three minutes to a tape recording of her friend being killed. Sutherland matches her with his own distinctive performance as a persistent by-the-book investigator.

Unlike Humphrey Bogart's fast-talking city-wise private eyes, Sutherland's Klute is a restrained, emotionless outsider who makes no quips and literally says nothing right after he sleeps with Bree midway through the movie.

Every other facet of the movie adds interest or intrigue. The stellar supporting cast features Roy Scheider as a pimp and, briefly, Jean Stapleton (from TV's *All in the Family*) as a secretary. Director Alan J. Pakula and cinematographer Gordon Willis make rooms and hallways shadowy and claustrophobic to intensify the menacing atmosphere, and the creepy music could support a horror movie. *Klute* isn't undeniably great, but it's undeniably effective.

ADDED ATTRACTION: Two Acting Oscars in the 1970s

Many actors and actresses earned more than one Oscar nomination for their performance in movies that were released in the 1970s. Al Pacino, for instance, got nominated five times during the decade (with zero wins); Jack Nicholson got nominated four times (one win); Ellen Burstyn got nominated four times (one win); and Jane Alexander, Lee Grant, and Marsha Mason all got nominated three times (zero wins, one win, and zero wins, respectively). However, only three actors or actresses actually *won* two acting Oscars during the '70s. Here is that trio, listed alphabetically.

- Jane Fonda
  Best Actress: *Klute* (1971); *Coming Home* (1978)
- Glenda Jackson
  Best Actress: *Women in Love* (released in the U.S. in 1970); *A Touch of Class* (1973)
- Jason Robards
  Best Supporting Actor: *All the President's Men* (1976); *Julia* (1977)

Le Mans

Released: June 1971

Director: Lee H. Katzin

Stars: Steve McQueen, Siegfried Rauch, Elga Andersen

Academy Awards: None

PREVIEW: A driver attempts to win the grueling Le Mans road race a year after he crashed there.

NOW SHOWING: Car Wars

Cars are the stars in *Le Mans* (1971), a high-octane racing movie with exhilarating track action. Viewers who endure some low-revving personal drama will be rewarded with a thrilling sprint to the finish line.

A notoriously troubled production that lost its original director, *Le Mans* still manages to showcase amazing images. The movie opens with a flashback to a fiery accident the year before and then presents the long build-up to the "the supreme test of speed and stamina," a two-day French road race that totals 3,000 miles of driving. After shots of fans arriving, the quiet town filling up with traffic, drivers suiting up, and cars being readied, the race finally starts twenty-eight minutes into the movie. Fifty-five drivers in six classes of cars are on the eight-mile track simultaneously, which means powerful, beautiful race cars going 230 mph zoom past normal production sports cars. With cameras down on the road and up in the cockpits, the actual race footage, accompanied by thunderous engine sounds, generates plenty of adrenaline. Highlights include two awesome crashes where cars disintegrate in silence and in slow-motion, and dangerous maneuvers near the checkered flag as a tight trio of cars heads to "the most closely contested finish in the history of Le Mans." Fans will love it, and even non-fans will be impressed.

The energetic visuals matter much more than the dialogue, which is where the movie goes off the road. Virtually nothing is revealed about the drivers to make us want to root for any one of them in particular. There's one famous actor, Steve McQueen, iconically handsome and cool as a skilled driver who temporarily falls out of the competition, returns to position his team for victory, and seems to win the pretty girl at the end even if he himself doesn't win the race. But his dialogue, what little there is, seems improvised. He briefly philosophizes about racing—"it's life," the rest is "just waiting"—and in the entire movie he speaks, by our count, only 344 words, an average of just three per minute (the track announcer speaks 344 words before the *eighteenth* minute, and this *Le Mans* essay before these parentheses totals exactly 344 words). Characters constantly make lingering, meaningful eye contact, and McQueen's last ninety seconds are a wordless staring contest. As a fictional narrative, *Le Mans* crashes and burns; as a pure racing movie, it's a champion.

ADDED ATTRACTION: 1970s Racing Movies

What makes *Le Mans* so good is its authenticity, something that racing devotee McQueen demanded (the credits list him as one of the drivers). Here are additional movies from the 1970s that show, as *Le Mans* does, organized races with pros in motorized vehicles. Some are comedic, but all are usually entertaining. We're not including informal cross-country endurance challenges, like in *Vanishing Point* (1971), or spontaneous street sprints, like in *American Graffiti* (1973).

- *Bobby Deerfield* (1977): Formula One race cars
- *Checkered Flag or Crash* (1977): Off-road vehicles
- *Death Race 2000* (1975): Futuristic sports cars
- *Greased Lightning* (1977): Stock cars
- *Herbie Goes to Monte Carlo* (1977): European sports cars
- *The Last American Hero* (1973): Stock cars
- *Little Fauss and Big Halsy* (1970): Motorcycles
- *More American Graffiti* (1979): Dragsters
- *On Any Sunday* (1971): Motorcycles (documentary)
- *One by One* (1975): Formula One race cars (documentary)

McCabe & Mrs. Miller

Released: June 1971

Director: Robert Altman

Stars: Warren Beatty, Julie Christie, Rene Auberjonois

Academy Awards: One nomination (Best Actress—Julie Christie)

PREVIEW: A gambler partners with a businesswoman and faces hired killers in a frontier town.

NOW SHOWING: Western Poetry

McCabe & Mrs. Miller (1971) improves each time you see it. Underappreciated upon release, it's now regarded as one of the great westerns and, for many critics, director Robert Altman's finest and most atmospheric work.

Viewers who struggle with *McCabe & Mrs. Miller* generally disparage three aspects—the story (the conflict isn't clear until midway through), the mumbled conversations (especially the early ones, when viewers are trying to get their bearings), and the dark, shadowy visuals (dim lamps and candles light many scenes, and the entire movie has the brownish hue of vintage photographs). What nobody derides are the soundtrack's poignant songs. Leonard Cohen's soft ballads parallel the movie's slow action, which starts when a mysterious gambler (possibly a gunfighter with "a big rep") rides into a tiny mountain town. McCabe (Warren Beatty) establishes his poker game in the saloon and then buys three "chippies" to work as whores out of ramshackle tents. After some success, he partners with Constance Miller (Julie Christie), a tough businesswoman who expands his modest operation into "a proper sporting house, with class girls and clean linen."

McCabe does so well that a monopolistic company tries to buy him out. When he arrogantly rejects its offer, the company sends bounty hunters to terminate discussions. Mrs. Miller instantly recognizes the threat: "They'll get you," she warns McCabe, "and they'll do something awful to you." As if to prove her point, one of the gunmen shoots a harmless victim in cold blood. The last twenty minutes pit McCabe against the killers in a suspenseful cat-and-mouse chase through town.

Altman incorporates many western conventions into his movie—guns, horses, etc.—but he upends all expectations. The frontier setting isn't hot and dusty, it's cold and muddy. The only actual cowboy is a callow youth who's inept with firearms (Keith Carradine, in his movie debut). The awkward final shoot-out kills every participant and concludes quietly and pathetically in snowdrifts, not dramatically and valiantly in the center of town. McCabe is a flawed, foolish hero—his lover charges him for sex, he's a poor businessman who can't do rudimentary arithmetic, and he badly underestimates the opposition. There's no happy ending, naturally; McCabe dies ignored, and Mrs. Miller is alone, anesthetizing herself with opium and holding a delicate object. The closer she stares at it, the more beauty it reveals—a sad, appropriately poetic coda for this sublime, enigmatic movie.

ADDED ATTRACTION: Interesting *Images*

Robert Altman's thirteen 1970s movies range from the brilliant (1970's *M*A*S*H*) to the incomprehensible (1979's *Quintet*). His next movie after *McCabe & Mrs. Miller*, *Images* (1972), falls somewhere in between. *Images* is unusual because, unlike Altman's other '70s movies, he filmed it overseas (in the Irish countryside) with a small cast. It's an ambiguous psychological thriller about a schizophrenic young woman (Susannah York) who seems to be losing her mind. Throughout, she and the audience are never sure if what she's seeing and hearing are real: a phone call has multiple voices, a dead lover appears, she kisses a man who morphs into someone else, she sees her doppelgänger walking on a road, and more. She apparently kills off the apparitions with a gun, a knife, and a car, but her last victim turns out to be a surprise. John Williams's Oscar-nominated music enhances this eerie, challenging movie.

Shaft

(One of 1971's five **FAR-OUT** movies)

Released: June 1971

Director: Gordon Parks

Stars: Richard Roundtree, Moses Gunn, Charles Cioffi

Academy Awards: One win (Best Song), plus one more nomination (Best Music)

PREVIEW: A tough, hip private detective is hired to rescue a gangster's kidnapped daughter.

FINE LINE: "Party's over. You have to split. Some other time, huh? Same feeling. Same place. Right now, I've got to take care of some business." (Shaft, dismissing the girl he's just spent the night with.)

CLOSE-UP: Eighty minutes into the movie, Shaft is hit with a machine-gun bullet in the shoulder, gets "a bad sprain on that right wrist," and is kicked in the face until he's unconscious. After getting some fast medical attention from his friend a few minutes later, that very same night Shaft is able to swing on ropes and finish his violent mission (because, as the theme song states, he's "the cat that won't cop out when there's danger all about"). Late that night, with no scars, blood, or bruises on his face, Shaft is even able to laugh uproariously in the last shot.

NOW SHOWING: Just Talkin' 'Bout *Shaft*

Shaft (1971) is a triumph of ultra-cool style over average substance. The ultra-cool is the detective; the average is the meandering plot, which covers lots of territory and expands from a tight story about a single crime into an impending gang war.

In 1970s New York, John Shaft is a tough private detective who is hired to find a gangster's kidnapped daughter. Shaft diligently pursues the case and soon learns that a rival gang is responsible. He locates the girl, but he gets shot before he can rescue her. Quickly patched up, Shaft leads a stealthy mission that involves a diversionary explosion and disguises for his team. After an improbable but successful rescue, Shaft walks away, though a city-wide gang war is looming. The movie includes some good action scenes as it explores New York City's gritty, sinister side, but it leaves some hanging threads.

Hanging threads don't really matter, and they definitely aren't part of the detective's stylish wardrobe. He is what makes this movie so daring and important. Originally written for a white actor, the part of John Shaft was cast with Richard Roundtree, a handsome, rugged black actor who exudes strength and self-assurance. Sidney Poitier, of course, had already broken through as an Oscar-winning star of significant dramas like *Lilies of the Field* (1963) and *In the Heat of the Night* (1967), but it's Roundtree who created the template for black men and women playing the conquering heroes of violent action movies in modern urban settings.

Richard Roundtree.

Roundtree doesn't just star in the movie; he dominates it. No matter whom he's talking to—a cabbie who almost runs into him, white cops, powerful gangsters, petty thieves, beautiful women—Shaft is always in command. We do see other sides of this tough guy—he's kind to old newsies and street kids—but mostly he is all bad-ass attitude. He's got the right look for the job, too, with his intimidating moustache/sideburns combo. As if to make sure we see that he is like a black version of the smoothest detective of the 1960s, Steve McQueen in *Bullitt* (1968), Shaft sports the suave turtlenecks that McQueen wore. So is it any surprise that Shaft has both a gorgeous girlfriend and additional sex in the shower with a woman he meets in a bar? The man is indeed "a sex machine to all the chicks," as the theme song accurately describes him.

It's the theme song that made *Shaft* an Oscar winner. Instantly recognizable, it's the highlight of the movie. When Shaft walks near Times Square for four-and-a-half minutes during the opening credits, confidently weaving through car traffic and cruising the sidewalks, Isaac Hayes' funktastic song accompanies him, describes him, and glorifies him. Sure the lyrics are blunt and insipid, and the stylishly arranged music may seem of its time to today's audiences, but the whole sequence perfectly summarizes the defiant tone of the man and the movie.

To appreciate how effective *Shaft* is, check out the decade's two Shaft sequels, which are relatively underwhelming compared to the original movie. In *Shaft's Big Score!* (1972), Isaac Hayes contributes just one song, and the novelty of the first movie has worn off. Roundtree returns and gets between two mobsters who are both looking for a missing $250,000 and control of the numbers rackets. Along the way Shaft is beaten up in slow-motion and literally tossed into a dumpster. Veering into James Bond's territory, the climactic sixteen-minute chase scene involves a muscle car, a speedboat, and a helicopter for an exciting if implausible finish that leaves Shaft with all the loot.

It's not in *Shaft*'s league, but *Shaft's Big Score!* has enough style and suspense to be a watchable crime drama worthy of its exclamation mark.

The second sequel, *Shaft in Africa* (1973), is the longest, most vulgar, most violent, and least compelling of the three movies. Isaac Hayes is long gone, but Roundtree is back. Unfortunately, he's out of his element when he's kidnapped, put through some brutal physical tests, and then sent to Africa to bust up a European slavery ring ("I'm *not* James Bond," Shaft protests). Dressed in dirty robes, our "uptown dude" crosses the Ethiopian desert by camel. He's then transported across the Mediterranean by boat, but even when he's masquerading as an impoverished slave Shaft still manages to sleep with the one sexy girl on board. Arriving in Paris, he escapes and single-handedly vanquishes the crime kingpin, a far-fetched ending that actually does seem very Bond-like. This movie also introduces a new social issue, the African tradition of clitoridectomy, to the conversation. And these two sequels do show us two Shaftmobiles: Shaft didn't drive in *Shaft*, but in *Shaft's Big Score!* he has a two-tone 1972 Plymouth Sebring, and in *Shaft in Africa* he drives an orange 1972 Alfa Romeo. But again, this sequel is no *Shaft*.

Evaluated solely as a movie, the original *Shaft* is decent entertainment (*Dirty Harry*, another hard-boiled detective thriller released in 1971, was much more compelling). And evaluated strictly on a financial basis, *Shaft* was indeed a popular hit, though *Super Fly* (1972), about a stylish drug dealer, was even more successful. But evaluated as a cultural milestone with a revolutionary protagonist, a cutting-edge soundtrack, two '70s sequels, a 1973–1974 TV series, and numerous copycats, *Shaft* has to be considered as one of the decade's most influential movies. Can you dig it?

ADDED ATTRACTION: The Empire Looks Back

Forty-eight minutes into *Shaft*, John Shaft talks on the phone to his girlfriend. "I love you," she says. "Yeah, I know," he replies. Sound familiar? At the end of *Gator* (1976), Burt Reynolds' character says "I love you" to Lauren Hutton's character, who responds, "I know, I know." Mia Farrow and Rock Hudson in *Avalanche* (1978), and John Heard and Mary Beth Hurt in *Head Over Heels* (1979), are more movie couples that have the same I-love-you-I-know exchange. Harrison Ford and Carrie Fisher famously repeat the bit in *The Empire Strikes Back* (1980) and then reverse it in *Return of the Jedi* (1983) so she gets to answer, "I know."

The Hellstrom Chronicle

Released: June 1971
Director: Walon Green
Stars: Lawrence Pressman
Academy Awards: One win (Best Documentary)

PREVIEW: A scientist presents dramatic evidence to show brutal and relentless insects are.

NOW SHOWING: A Bug's Life

You know a movie is truly terrifying when just the *memories* of its scenes are still scary decades later. That's the case with *The Hellstrom Chronicle* (1971), a powerful documentary about insects. Seen today, it's just as impressive, and disturbing, as it ever was.

Incredible microphotography won this movie an Oscar. Viewers can legitimately wonder how the filmmakers captured such astonishing close-up footage of insects chewing or laying tiny eggs. Slow-motion bugs in flight, a fast-motion spider rapidly constructing its web, camouflaged insects hiding in plain sight, and a caterpillar-to-butterfly metamorphosis are among the nicer highlights. Fascinating facts are woven into the narration (see "Added Attraction"), and the expressive music by Lalo Schifrin makes a perfect marriage with the spectacular imagery.

The Hellstrom Chronicle, however, isn't a gentle, child-friendly nature documentary. It's got a disturbing agenda, which is to convince viewers of a compelling theory. The movie is framed as a presentation by an authoritative narrator, Dr. Nils Hellstrom, who believes that hardy, predatory insects, which can overcome anything, even pesticides and radiation, will inevitably "overrun" the world.

He tries to prove it with alarming sequences that illustrate "one single and ugly truth: life must take life, in the interest of life itself." Thus we see grotesque close-ups of bugs devouring other living bugs, a hideous ant war that leaves severed but still-moving ant heads, and the death throes of a lab mouse that's been bitten by a lethal mosquito. Imagine this close-up visual of a black widow: "puncturing his head, she sucks his body dry." Or this view of wasps, "bizarre killing machines" that "yank the defenders from the hive and crush them in their huge jaws." And that's before the hellish finale in which a mile-long army of twenty-million driver ants ferociously slaughters everything in its path. Watching these "mindless, unstoppable" monsters eat the eyes of living lizards and frogs is a repulsive sight that is, unfortunately, unforgettable. Maybe it's no surprise that *The Hellstrom Chronicle* was written by David Seltzer, who would soon write a successful horror movie, *The Omen* (1976).

The real surprise comes at the end when it's revealed that, while Hellstrom's facts are true, he himself is false and is a character being played by actor Lawrence Pressman. That doesn't stop the nightmares, though. This is an easy movie to admire on technical grounds, but it might scare the Hellstrom out of you.

ADDED ATTRACTION: Insect Info

While some of Dr. Hellstrom's narration sounds like exaggerated opinion, he does include some startling facts about man and insects. Here are six examples, listed in their chronological order in the movie.

- "Today as most other animal species are diminishing in population, only two are definitely on the increase: man and insect."
- An insect "can pull an object a hundred times his weight" and "jump a distance fifty times his size."
- "Great, throbbing masses of energy," termite queens "may live a half-century" and produce eggs "at the rate of 10,000 per day."
- "Each year more of the world's population is killed by insect-borne diseases than by any other single cause. More than wars, highway deaths, old age."
- "To support his own life," an insect "will consume as much as a hundred times his own weight each day, which to each of us would be like eating an entire cow, a herd of thirty each month."
- A locust plague can cover 400 miles and "consume 80,000 tons of food each day; in a single week it will devour what could have fed one million people for an entire year."

Carnal Knowledge

Released: June 1971

Director: Mike Nichols

Stars: Jack Nicholson, Art Garfunkel, Ann-Margret

Academy Awards: One nomination (Best Supporting Actress—Ann-Margret)

PREVIEW: For twenty years, two male friends discuss, and pursue, relationships with women.

NOW SHOWING: "Hormones Were Flying All Over the Screen"

On *All in the Family* (September 25, 1971), Archie complains that "hormones were flying all over the screen" in *Carnal Knowledge* (1971). He's overreacting. True, sex is this provocative movie's topic ("carnal" is even in the title), and the language gets rough, but the few sex scenes in *Carnal Knowledge* are either dark or obscured. This smart, insightful, wry movie makes adult audiences think about sex without graphically showing it.

Divided into three parts separated by brief "white outs," *Carnal Knowledge* presents two decades in the lives of two male friends who eternally discuss and pursue women. For the first thirty-eight minutes Jonathan (Jack Nicholson) and Sandy (Art Garfunkel) are Amherst students in the late 1940s. Jonathan is strong, confident, and focused on breast size; Sandy is "sensitive," "vulnerable," and "helpless." A relationship triangle with the same girl shows how they handle relationships (Jonathan aggressively, Sandy cautiously).

The movie then jumps ahead about fifteen years, when both men are successful Manhattan professionals. Sandy, as expected, has married his college crush. Jonathan, meanwhile, claims he would've "settled" for a recent girl if she'd had a slightly better figure. In this middle section, scene-stealing Ann-Margret plays

Jack Nicholson and Ann-Margret.

Jonathan's latest conquest, the voluptuous, insecure Bobbie. "Looks are everything," Jonathan declares, but their lust devolves into a long, remarkable argument that exposes her sadness and his selfishness.

The last twenty minutes shift to around 1970, both men now forty. Sandy wears a groovy moustache and dates an eighteen-year-old "love teacher." Jonathan, cynically misogynistic, is virtually impotent, needing rehearsed rituals with a prostitute to achieve satisfaction. In different ways, they're both pathetic, both depressing.

Some viewers critique the slow pace, and indeed it is a talky, serious movie with little action, no music score, and no special effects. But that's why *Carnal Knowledge* is great. Working with a small, perfect cast (of the seven, Carol Kane doesn't even speak, while Oscar-winner Rita Moreno is seen for only five minutes), director Mike Nichols arguably does his best work outside of *The Graduate* (1967). Note how characters converse but look directly into the camera, thus fully engaging the audience (an idea exploited in 1991's *The Silence of the Lambs*); at times we study a silent character as others talk out of frame; at the end, the wallpaper pattern rises like red corpuscles behind the kneeling hooker. Brilliant. It's not for everyone, but *Carnal Knowledge* is a masterful movie.

ADDED ATTRACTION: Familiar Actresses Who Dared to Bare

It's surprising when Ann-Margret, who had been playfully sexy on-screen without being explicit, is naked for a shower scene in *Carnal Knowledge*. That's the Daring Decade for you. Similarly, the following twenty actresses—some already famous, some about to be famous—all went topless (at least) in movies released between 1970 and 1974.

- Jenny Agutter: *Walkabout* (1971)
- Jacqueline Bisset: *Secrets* (1971)
- Julie Christie: *Don't Look Now* (1973)
- Angie Dickinson: *Big Bad Mama* (1974)
- Shelley Duvall: *Thieves Like Us* (1974)
- Britt Eklund: *The Wicker Man* (1973)
- Susan George: *Straw Dogs* (1971)
- Pam Grier: *Coffy* (1973)
- Barbara Hershey: *Boxcar Bertha* (1972)
- Sally Kellerman: *Brewster McCloud* (1970)
- Margot Kidder: *Sisters* (1972)
- Kay Lenz: *Breezy* (1973)
- Marsha Mason: *Cinderella Liberty* (1973)
- Helen Mirren: *Savage Messiah* (1972)
- Valerie Perrine: *Slaughterhouse-Five* (1972)
- Victoria Principal: *The Naked Ape* (1973)
- Charlotte Rampling: *The Night Porter* (1974)
- Cybill Shepherd: *The Last Picture Show* (1971)
- Stella Stevens: *Slaughter* (1972)
- Susannah York: *Images* (1972)

The Million Dollar Duck

Released: June 1971
Director: Vincent McEveety
Stars: Dean Jones, Sandy Duncan, Joe Flynn
Academy Awards: None

PREVIEW: When an irradiated duck lays gold eggs, its owners try to cash in but problems ensue.

NOW SHOWING: Laying an Egg

The last week of June 1971 welcomed two underwhelming live-action Disney movies. First came *Scandalous John*, a little-seen comedy/drama. With a delusional old coot (Brian Keith) undertaking a misguided mission, it's a decent modern-day Don Quixote story for kids.

Then came some fowl play. *The Million Dollar Duck* (1971) is a much-maligned Disney comedy that critics quickly shot down. Its reputation was so bad that it seemed like Disney was daring to see how low the bar was set for "family entertainment," as if undemanding kids and parents would watch *anything*. Something this audaciously awful ... as a Disney-loving kid in 1971, we had to check it out; as the writer of *The Daring Decade* in 2019, we had to get it in.

We can now safely say that *The Million Dollar Duck* is easily the best movie *ever* about irradiated waterfowl. After gamma rays accidentally bombard a laboratory duck, Albert (Dean Jones) brings the unwanted bird home, where it lays eggs with small solid-gold yolks. Albert's wife, Katie (Sandy Duncan), cashes in the gold, drawing the attention of treasury officials who suspect Katie's a "bagwoman" for a "nefarious gang." Men in suits, led by the always-exasperated Joe Flynn, decide the duck is a "valuable asset," and, as often happens in formulaic Disney comedies, a long wacky chase commences. This one involves a Stingray bike, a washing machine, a hot rod, and, naturally, inept cops. Everyone, including the duck, winds up in court, but the yolk's on the treasury, and Dad learns a family-values lesson.

To its credit, the movie tries to fit into the energetic era. Jones's brushed-back hair in *The Love Bug* (1968) now flows forward into short groovy bangs, and the adorable Duncan sports a kicky hairdo and colorful outfits. The movie mentions "the generation gap" and incorporates timely vocabulary words like "outta sight" and "hip." A Richard Nixon soundalike even says, "Now just let me say this about that."

But in other ways *The Million Dollar Duck* was already passé. Though the feminist movement was intensifying, Katie is an old-fashioned ding-a-ling who botches recipes and phraseology (her "20/20 hearing" line comes directly from 1961's *West Side Story*). Too much of the humor relies on dopey pratfalls, and only children will think the chase scene with Albert on a truck's extended ladder is a new idea. Adults will know that *The Million Dollar Duck* is basically bankrupt.

ADDED ATTRACTION: That's Snow Business!

After *The Million Dollar Duck*, Dean Jones's next live-action Disney movie was *Snowball Express* (1972). In this inoffensive charmer, Jones again brings the bangs as an amiable New Yorker who inherits an empty, cob-webbed Colorado hotel. He and his family (including Disney's go-to kid, Johnny Whitaker) move in, struggle to transform it into a thriving ski lodge, and then fend off an unscrupulous banker who covets the property. Snowy slapstick (especially Jones' wacky skiing debut) and a rollicking ten-minute snowmobile race should amuse kids, while adults will enjoy the pretty mountain scenery and the welcome presence of Hollywood veterans like Harry Morgan and Mary Wickes. This movie was a resounding box-office success and led Jones to *The Shaggy D.A.* (1976) and *Herbie Goes to Monte Carlo* (1977). Duncan, meanwhile, later starred in another lightweight comedy, *The Cat from Outer Space* (1978). Thus she and Jones spanned virtually the entire Disney decade. Way to represent!

Willy Wonka & the Chocolate Factory

Released: June 1971
Director: Mel Stuart
Stars: Gene Wilder, Jack Albertson, Peter Ostrum
Academy Awards: One nomination (Best Music)

PREVIEW: Eccentric Willy Wonka invites five children into his colorful chocolate factory.

NOW SHOWING: Sugar Rush

Willy Wonka & the Chocolate Factory (1971) is a movie we *want* to like more than we actually do. The premise is promising—an unorthodox genius invites contest winners inside his phantasmagorical chocolate factory, with the always-appealing Gene Wilder as the star. Unfortunately, the ensuing cruelty is too disturbing to dismiss.

After a long, slow build-up involving an international search for five elusive Golden Tickets, Willy Wonka (Wilder) finally arrives forty-four minutes into the movie via an inspired entrance that cleverly reveals his unpredictability. Soon everyone is in his fabled Chocolate Room, a sugary equivalent of Munchkin City. It's a nice moment: kids happily explore the colorful, imaginative interior where most everything is edible, and Wonka blissfully sings "Pure Imagination," one of two memorable songs in this musical ("The Candy Man," sung by a candy-shop owner, is the other).

But from here on, four of the kids become screechy, spoiled brats, misbehaving so badly that they get themselves kicked out of the increasingly dark story. Wonka maliciously induces real hysteria among the parents accompanying their obnoxious kids, making the parents *truly believe* that their disobedient sons and daughters could die. Later Wonka says nobody got hurt, but he declares this *after* he's generated genuine terror.

Even worse, the dreadful two-minute boat ride through a horrible tunnel is inexcusable for a family movie. Among the grisly sights are close-ups of a bug crawling on a man's face and a chicken getting decapitated, all while Wonka shouts hellish rhymes to his terrified guests. What's his message, "Hold on and suffer through life's ugliest moments (which, incidentally, I myself am inflicting upon you)"? By the end of the movie one parent has fainted, and the others have screamed at Wonka: "You terrible man!" "What a nightmare!" "I'll break you for this!" "You're … an inhuman monster!"

Viewers may have fond recollections of *Willy Wonka*, but they might be remembering the *idea* of it, or the creative sets, rather than the actual movie. Somehow, in the last scene Charlie (Peter Ostrum), forgetting what he and his grandpa have endured (including furious reprimands from Wonka), says he thinks the factory is "the most wonderful place in the whole world." Maybe the most unusual, surreal, or frightening place, but wonderful? What factory was *he* in?

ADDED ATTRACTION: Singing Actors

Besides Gene Wilder, these actors were not afraid to croon a tune in 1970–1974 movies.

- Edward Albert, *Butterflies Are Free* (1972)
  He sings excerpts of songs, including "Take Me Home, Country Roads."
- Richard Benjamin, *Westworld* (1973)
  Thirty seconds of "Home on the Range" with a western twang.
- Art Carney, *Harry and Tonto* (1974)
  Fragments of old songs.
- Clint Eastwood, *The Beguiled* (1971)
  His ballad opens and closes the movie.
- Henry Fonda, *The Cheyenne Social Club* (1970)
  "Rolling Stone" during the opening credits.
- Harrison Ford, *American Graffiti* (1973)
  "Some Enchanted Evening," sung a cappella.
- James Garner, *Skin Game* (1971)
  A minute in the bathtub singing "Wait for the Wagon."
- Charles Grodin, *The Heartbreak Kid* (1972)
  He and his bride sing while driving to Florida.
- Paul Newman, *The Life and Times of Judge Roy Bean* (1972)
  Twenty seconds of "The Yellow Rose of Texas."
- Jason Robards, *The War Between Men and Women* (1972)
  Thirty seconds of "You and Me."

On Any Sunday

Released: July 1971
Director: Bruce Brown
Stars: Steve McQueen, Mert Lawwill, Malcolm Smith
Academy Awards: One nomination (Best Documentary)

PREVIEW: Rousing footage of various races captures the world of competitive motorcycling.

NOW SHOWING: "The Ultimate Test of Man and Machine"

Viewers having nightmares after seeing 1971's terrifying Oscar winner for Best Documentary, *The Hellstrom Chronicle*, should immediately see one of that year's other documentary nominees, *On Any Sunday* (1971). This exhilarating classic is filled with fun.

You don't have to be a motorcycle fan to enjoy this movie, just as you didn't have to be a surfer to appreciate *The Endless Summer* (1966), director Bruce Brown's previous hit documentary. Again Brown and his crew travel extensively to capture the full spectrum of a particular sport. This time he goes across America and to different countries to showcase various motorcycling races and competitions, ranging from rough-and-tumble hill climbs to formal international trials that are "the Olympic Games of motorcycle sport." Fantastic aerial footage tracks individual riders as they slalom through race traffic, helmet cams give exciting first-person views from inside the races, and delightful music keeps most of the movie light.

Three riders get spotlighted—two racing legends and actor Steve McQueen, a terrific amateur who puts on his "race face" and competes in real races (he's on-screen for about fifteen minutes). All three riders move their high-powered machines with confidence and grace, making the different events look easy. Motorcycling *isn't* easy, obviously—it's "a violent world," and during races there's "no such thing as a small mistake." We see plenty of slow-motion crashes, a montage of "flying W's," and real injuries to prove it.

The movie slightly runs out of gas when some of the racing sequences go on too long. Also, Brown himself delivers the relaxed narration, which is mostly entertaining but sometimes pretty corny, and the fast-motion humor and silly sound effects are fairly juvenile. Unfortunately, we rarely hear anything from the riders themselves, although McQueen does briefly explain why he races.

Previous motorcycle movies—Marlon Brando's *The Wild One* (1953), for example—typically showed rowdy biker gangs. *On Any Sunday* has no gangs, no fights. The hard-working riders are dedicated to their sport simply for the thrills and the fun. While few viewers would want to compete in the dangerous races or spend "over a thousand hours a year" getting a motorcycle ready, as one of the racers does, who wouldn't want to playfully zoom around the beach like the friends do at the end? Let's go!

ADDED ATTRACTION: Motorcycle Mania

Various motorcycle activities and competitions are shown in *On Any Sunday*. Here are ten different segments, with quotes from the narration.

- Dirt-track racing at 100 mph: "One of the most dangerous sports in which man participates."
- Road racing at 160 mph: "A graceful and beautiful thing to watch."

- Motocross: "A motocross track is uphill, downhill, jumps, bumps, mud, rocks, and dust, the rougher the better."
- Off-road races: "Like riding from San Francisco to Los Angeles through the roughest imaginable terrain and averaging fifty mph."
- International Six-Day Trials, in El Escorial, Spain: "The ultimate test of man and machine."
- Sidecar racing: "Only about 200 people do it in the United States."
- Ice racing at ten degrees below zero: "Two-inch spikes in the tires for traction on the ice."
- Trials riders: "The magicians of the motorcycle world."
- Desert racers: "A cross between a race and a war."
- "Cow trailing" with friends: "A feeling of freedom, a feeling of joy, that really can't be put into words."

Bless the Beasts & Children

Released: August 1971
Director: Stanley Kramer
Stars: Bill Mumy, Barry Robins, Ken Swofford
Academy Awards: One nomination (Best Song)

PREVIEW: Six misfit kids leave their summer camp to try to rescue a buffalo herd from hunters.

NOW SHOWING: Rebels with a Cause

For years *Bless the Beasts & Children* (1971) was shown in schools, perhaps to provoke or inspire students. It may also have slightly confused them with its multiple-choice messages.

Stanley Kramer, who directed the anti-nuclear *On the Beach* (1959), often made thoughtful movies with a conscience. In *Bless the Beasts* he shows six oddball kids at an Arizona summer camp who are labeled as "bedwetters" by the "normal" campers, and as "psychos" by their own counselor. These misfits undertake a rebellious mission to liberate penned-up buffalo that are helpless hunting targets. The kids steal a truck and have various adventures across beautifully photographed countryside before they reach the preserve, where they hope to help the buffalo live "happily ever after." But this movie is no fairy tale, and a kid gets killed. Gunfire sends the buffalo stampeding into the wild, just like the kids wanted.

Throughout the movie, flashbacks interrupt the action to reveal the kids' problematic backgrounds with their neglectful parents. The most horrifying flashback shows the naïve kids making their first visit to the preserve. This disturbing seven-minute sequence shows hunters with high-powered rifles slaughtering motionless, unaware animals. How many students in school were crying as they witnessed this carnage?

Four of the kid actors are making their movie debuts. The most annoying is one who mistakenly thinks he's hilarious. The two leaders are the tough-talking, lock-picking Lawrence (Billy Mumy, far from his *Lost in Space* days), and military-minded Cotton (Barry Robins, a young Freddie Mercury lookalike). Wearing an army helmet, Cotton barks orders and reprimands. At the end, he seems to go insane with determination and pays dearly for his actions.

So what's Kramer's message? That underdogs can accomplish something if they put their minds to it? Maybe, but their mission leads to the death of their friend. That the misfit kids were preyed on back in camp just like the misfit buffalo that are being shot, and both groups need to be free? Youthful idealism is destroyed by harsh adult realities? Parental neglect produces troubled nonconformists? Students, please write an essay with your own interpretations.

ADDED ATTRACTION: Movie Marquees, Part One

Bless the Beasts & Children shows theaters where *The Grasshopper* (1970), *King of the Grizzlies* (1970), and *Blackbeard's Ghost* (1968) are playing. Here are other 1971–1972 movies where a marquee, or an actual clip, announces another movie. For more movie marquees, see the entry for *Mean Streets* (1973).

- *A Clockwork Orange* (1971): The disturbing Ludovico Technique includes scenes from *Triumph of the Will* (1935).
- *Dirty Harry* (1971): Clint Eastwood walks near a marquee displaying *Play Misty for Me* (1971), a movie he directed.
- *The Godfather* (1972): Radio City Music Hall's marquee displays *The Bells of St. Mary's* (1945).
- *The Last Picture Show* (1971): In the theater, clips from *The Father of the Bride* (1950) and *Red River* (1948).
- *Minnie and Moskowitz* (1971): Early on, clips from *The Maltese Falcon* (1941) and *Casablanca* (1942), plus a marquee displaying *Get Carter* (1971) and *Marlowe* (1969).
- *The Omega Man* (1971): Charlton Heston watches *Woodstock* (1970) in a theater.
- *Play It Again, Sam* (1972): The opening scene includes *Casablanca* (1942).
- *Shaft* (1971): The opening-credits marquees include *Little Fauss and Big Halsy* (1970).
- *Summer of '42* (1971): *Now, Voyager* (1942) plays in the local theater.

The Omega Man

Released: August 1971
Director: Boris Sagal
Stars: Charlton Heston, Anthony Zerbe, Rosalind Cash
Academy Awards: None

PREVIEW: After a global plague, a man aids other survivors while fighting infected mutants.

NOW SHOWING: "Now I'm the Only Game in Town"

Earth's last civilized human in *Planet of the Apes* (1968), Charlton Heston is alone again for much of *The Omega Man* (1971). Taking its title from the Greek alphabet's last letter and its inspiration from Richard Matheson's 1954 novel *I Am Legend*, this movie combines an intriguing premise with suspenseful action to deliver solid science-fiction entertainment.

The movie's first half, which lays the sole-survivor foundation, is more compelling than the second, which almost becomes *The Slowmega Man*. A 1975 "Sino-Russian border war," we learn, escalated into "global conflict" that unleashed "the horror long-feared, germ warfare." Heston plays Neville, a scientist who immunized himself at the last minute with an experimental vaccine. Humanity dies, Neville lives, and according to his journal it's now August 1977. Neville drives around unpopulated Los Angeles, listening to eight-track tapes, visiting unattended stores to take whatever he wants, and making wry observations to himself about his bizarre situation. Except for occasional moving vehicles in the far-distant background, the city streets really are lifeless, quite a visual accomplishment considering there were no digital effects back then.

Unfortunately for Neville, he's not really alone. Creepy plague-infected mutants with white hair, scarred faces, and sickly blue eyes attack his penthouse fortress nightly. Even with surprise, numbers, and a forceful leader on their side, their simplistic assaults can't overcome his resourceful defenses.

Everything changes when Neville encounters an attractive woman who's one of the "normal" survivors hiding outside of town. Black, fifteen years his junior, and spunky, Lisa (Rosalind Cash) adds a hip wrinkle to the story when she and Neville become lovers. Later her naïve kid brother walks right into the mutants' lair, leading to a heavy-handed finale that leaves Neville in an unsubtle crucifixion pose.

Heston has abundant gravitas for epic movies— at thirty-three-years old he played the intense, silvery Moses in *The Ten Commandments* (1956). At forty-eight, he looks fit in his safari jacket, zip-up track outfit, and military flight suit (he also goes shirtless several times, something he did so often in movies it must've been in his contract). Though his exciting motorcycle escape is obviously performed by a stuntman, Heston is a credible action hero, especially when it comes to handling machine guns. But more impressive is his loneliness as "the only game in town," which is what makes *The Omega Man* a meaningful, thought-provoking movie.

Rosalind Cash and Charlton Heston.

ADDED ATTRACTION: Tasty *Soylent Green*

Two years after *The Omega Man*, Charlton Heston, the go-to hero of early-'70s sci-fi movies, starred in another impressive futuristic hit, *Soylent Green* (1973). Playing a detective in the year 2022 when New York City has forty-million residents, he's investigating the source of a new artificial food, though viewers will solve the mystery long before he makes his dramatic declarations in the last scene. As usual in his movies, Heston's character is a hero who removes his shirt at some point. His much-younger companion is well-played by gorgeous Leigh Taylor-Young. What's best about *Soylent Green* is its bleak environment. A "greenhouse effect" has created "a heat wave all year long," overpopulation forces crowds to sleep in stairwells, and bulldozer-like trucks scoop paths through desperate multitudes. Director Richard Fleischer uglifies daytime in the depressing metropolis with a dirty brownish haze, sort of like the poisonous atmosphere coming later in *Blade Runner* (1982). Edward G. Robinson, in his last role, is a wise elder who opts out via a magnificent assisted suicide.

The Last Picture Show

(One of 1971's five **FAR-OUT** movies)

Released: September 1971

Director: Peter Bogdanovich

Stars: Timothy Bottoms, Jeff Bridges, Ben Johnson

Academy Awards: Two wins (Best Supporting Actor—Ben Johnson; Best Supporting Actress—Cloris Leachman), plus six more nominations (Best Picture; Best Supporting Actor—Jeff Bridges; Best Supporting Actress—Ellen Burstyn; Best Director; Best Writing; Best Cinematography)

PREVIEW: In the 1950s, lost dreams and loneliness bring heartaches to people in a Texas town.

FINE LINE: "Being crazy about a woman like her is always the right thing to do. Being a decrepit old bag of bones, that's what's ridiculous. Gettin' old." (Sam the Lion, reminiscing with Sonny.)

CLOSE-UP: Playing sad, sensitive Ruth Popper, Cloris Leachman is spell-binding. Her memorable last scene, when she finally unloads her feelings in her little kitchen and flings cups and coffee as she scornfully rebukes Sonny (Timothy Bottoms), is raw and powerful. But the most profound part of the scene is the hundred seconds of near-total silence as her anger shifts to sorrow and then to sweetness. The most tender moment in the movie comes when they gently hold hands and Ruth lovingly says, "Never you mind, honey, never you mind."

NOW SHOWING: Taking in *The Last Picture Show*

Peter Bogdanovich would direct two more 1970s hits—*What's Up, Doc?* (1972) and *Paper Moon* (1973)—and his career would continue into the twenty-first century. However, he'd never make a better movie—indeed, few '70s directors would—than his heartfelt masterpiece, *The Last Picture Show* (1971).

Spanning the two high school football seasons from 1951 to 1952, the melancholy story is set in a dusty Texas town called Anarene, population 1131. Everything seems dead at first sight: howling winds blow a tumbleweed through desolate streets, their dreary dullness underscored by harsh, unromantic black-and-white photography (a daring choice, but clearly the right one). Different characters say discouraging words about life in this forsaken place: "You ain't ever gonna amount to nuthin'," "everything is flat and empty here, and nothing to do," "I'm sick and tired of this town!" The glamorous, adventurous worlds we see in two movie clips with grand Hollywood stars (Elizabeth Taylor, John Wayne) feel like they're a million miles away and completely unattainable.

Though there are two sudden deaths (an old man, a young boy) and a creepy child abduction, the movie is almost plotless and is more of a meditative character study. What those characters themselves want to study is sex. With businesses failing, money scarce, the high school football team losing, and nothing much to do, sex is the main activity. Couples rearrange and desperate partners cheat on each other in a futile search for something positive, or at least something temporarily entertaining, to combat the harsh, hopeless realities of their unhappy lives. Most of the spouses desire someone else, and infidelity is common; even the movie's most beloved, most venerable character, Sam (Ben Johnson), recalls a nostalgic memory about his "pretty wild" time with another man's wife. The young males are so obsessed they'll pay $1.50 to an obese hooker for a back-seat quickie, and two guys seriously discuss having sex with a cow as a viable alternative to being alone ("Why the hell not? I say a heifer beats nothing."). We see nudity, passionless fondling in a car, a couple having passionless sex on a pool table, and inept attempts in a cheap motel, but no love. Ultimately all the "romantic" experiences are as sad and empty as the bleak landscape.

The performers express their characters' confusion and loneliness with such authenticity that it feels like they're not even acting. It's as if the actors and actresses truly *are* these desperate, aching people who are transitioning from youth to adulthood, or from hope to despair. In a stellar cast that includes Timothy Bottoms, Eileen Brennan, Jeff Bridges, Ellen Burstyn, Ben Johnson, Randy Quaid (his movie debut), and Cloris Leachman, the real surprise is Cybill Shepherd, who almost steals the movie from

Cybill Shepherd.

everybody else. She plays Jacy, a cunning blonde beauty who is selfish, manipulative, and hurtful to everyone around her. "Jacy's just the kind of girl that brings out the meanness in a man," we're told, and she proves it by talking a young guy into briefly eloping with her just because it'll upset her parents and "the whole town will be knocked for a loop." For Shepherd, who was already famous as a model, it's her first movie role ever, and it's still the highlight of her long career.

Throughout the movie everyone listens to country-western music; just as *American Graffiti* (1973) will later do, *The Last Picture Show* plays old songs by original artists through scratchy car radios, phonographs, and jukeboxes for its soundtrack. Thus it's fitting that Hank Williams gets the last word: after a lingering shot of the closed movie theater, the final song is "Why Don't You Love Me (Like You Used to Do)?" It's a sad question most of the despondent characters could pose at the end.

ADDED ATTRACTION: Black-and-White Movies, Part One

It's easy to remember the 1970s as a decade of neon colors and disco lights, but the following 1970–1971 movies are either in black and white, or they feature some black-and-white images. For more black-and-white movies, see the entry for *Lady Sings the Blues* (1972).

Black-and-White Movies

- *The Honeymoon Killers* (1970)
- *Johnny Got His Gun* (1971)
- *The Last Picture Show* (1971)

Color Movies with Short Black-and-White Segments or Photo Montages

- *The Beguiled* (1971): The movie begins with a black-and-white photo montage and then gradually shifts to color; the effect is reversed for the closing credits.
- *Bloody Mama* (1970): Black-and-white montages interrupt the color action to show historical 1920s-1930s events.
- *Hi, Mom!* (1970): One segment is like a grainy black-and-white documentary.
- *Made for Each Other* (1971): The first five minutes, set in 1935 and 1936, are in black and white.
- *Ned Kelly* (1970): The first three black-and-white minutes are set in the actual Australian prison where the convicted outlaw was held, and they even show the real scaffold where he was hanged.

The French Connection

(One of 1971's five **FAR-OUT** movies)

Released: October 1971

Director: William Friedkin

Stars: Gene Hackman, Roy Scheider, Fernando Rey

Academy Awards: Five wins (Best Picture; Best Actor—Gene Hackman; Best Director; Best Writing; Best Editing), plus three more nominations (Best Supporting Actor—Roy Scheider; Best Cinematography; Best Sound)

PREVIEW: Two tough New York detectives investigate an international drug-smuggling ring.

FINE LINE: "I got a man in Poughkeepsie wants to talk to you. You ever been to Poughkeepsie? Huh? Have you ever been in Poughkeepsie?" (Popeye Doyle, intentionally confusing a suspect during interrogation.)

CLOSE-UP: Eleven minutes into the movie, the glamorous nightclub trio singing Jimmy Webb's "Everybody Gets to Go to the Moon" is an actual group from Philadelphia called the Three Degrees. Their hit records included 1974's "When Will I See You Again."

NOW SHOWING: Connecting with *The French Connection*

The granddaddy of intense, gritty police movies, *The French Connection* (1971) dominated that year's Oscars and still regularly turns up on "greatest movies" lists. Modern audiences inured to its vulgarities, violence, and revolutionary documentary-style technique might not appreciate what a groundbreaker this riveting movie was back in the early '70s. But it was, it really was, and decades of brutal police dramas in theaters and on TV can trace their ancestry to *The French Connection*.

The movie begins its visceral assault on viewers immediately as pounding music, seemingly already underway, accompanies the in-your-face credits (director William Friedkin does something similar in 1973's *The Exorcist*, establishing a slow rhythm in the opening credits and then blasting the title at the viewer). In *The French Connection*'s very first sequence we immediately understand what makes this movie so startling: a guy in Marseilles is shot in the face. Next, in cold, unglamorous New York, two rough detectives chase down a petty crook and beat information out of him. Soon those cops stumble onto another criminal, and, completely obsessed with fighting crime, they follow their hunch and tail him overnight *on their own time*, gradually building the real case that will lead to the biggest drug bust in U.S. history. The police procedures are plausible, the locations, lighting, and language seem accurate, and some of the non-actors involved in the actual events are on-screen (the garage mechanic who searches the impounded Lincoln, for instance, and even the two main cops, though not as themselves). That's even genuine heroin being tested by the hip chemist.

Throughout, the thirty-two-year-old Friedkin, whose Oscar win made him the youngest Best Director ever, puts the audience right alongside the cops. We follow suspects on sidewalks, listen in on wiretaps, and are inside the car during the famous high-speed chase. Friedkin adds to the realism by often using a handheld camera and relying on urban noises instead of a music soundtrack. There's nothing romanticized about this police work. It's grueling, dangerous, and dirty.

Meanwhile, the criminals live the good life. We see the main villains relaxing, laughing, and conspiring in France, so we know where their crime is heading and can sense how easy they think it will be. They live well in New York, are formally polite to each other, shop for fancy gifts, and wear beautiful clothes. The main Frenchman's casual, elegant manner contrasts the manic urgency of the good guys. "Good guys" is a relative term, because the two hard-working detectives, Popeye Doyle (Gene Hackman) and Cloudy (Roy Scheider) are maniacal, impure heroes, especially Popeye, who reveals himself to be a hot-tempered racist who refuses to go by the book. But they're incredibly determined and rugged. It's fascinating to see the differences between the sophisticated villains and the street-wise cops, a distinction underscored when the French godfather leisurely savors an extravagant meal in an elegant Manhattan restaurant while Popeye watches from across the street, standing outside in the freezing cold and gulping bad coffee. The composed villains have seaside estates, sleep in fancy hotels with hookers, and treat conspirators like dignified friends; the exhausted cops live in functional cement-block rooms, grab catnaps in cars, and yell at each other.

Hackman and Scheider are perfect for their roles, and both got Oscar nominations (Hackman won as Best Actor). Popeye is all fury and vulgarity, the angry, violent "bad cop" to Cloudy's more reasonable, more restrained "good cop." Doyle insults and pushes anybody to get what he wants, so it's not really a surprise when he commandeers a citizen's car for the frantic chase scene and then destroys it in his headlong pursuit. Near the end, he accidentally kills an FBI man, he barely stops to acknowledge the mistake, and he quickly reloads his gun so he can continue the relentless hunt for his elusive quarry. Hackman drives the movie, impelling it toward its powerful conclusion. Instantly the role elevated him from supporting parts, like those he had in *Bonnie and Clyde* (1967) and *Marooned* (1969), to major stardom. Scheider, meanwhile, jumped to a starring role as another tough New York cop in *The Seven-Ups* (1973), a taut action

Gene Hackman and Marcel Bozzuffi.

movie that almost feels like *The French Reconnection*. It's got the first movie's gray New York setting, several of the same supporting actors, similarly tense music from *Connection* composer Don Ellis, and an equally thrilling car chase.

As great as *The French Connection* is, it isn't flawless. Looking for drugs, the police completely rip apart a luxury car's engine and interior, and the one place they *don't* search is precisely where the cache of heroin is hidden. Then they rapidly reassemble the car back to its immaculate pre-shredded condition, which seems literally impossible. At the end, the cops set up a huge roadblock with dozens of vehicles, all to trap a single car that drives right up to them in broad daylight, yet that car simply turns around and the key culprit slips away. Some viewers may also be frustrated by that ambiguous final gunshot as Popeye tracks the elusive Charnier (Fernando Rey) through the shadowy building: who shoots? And how does Charnier escape the scene and then the country? That last question isn't answered until the potent sequel, *French Connection II* (1975).

That previous paragraph of French Disconnections doesn't at all diminish the electrifying thrills in *The French Connection*. Friedkin's masterpiece, dominated by Hackman's career-making performance, is a doozy.

ADDED ATTRACTION: Marvelous Movie Chases

The six 1970–1974 movies listed below tell stories that *include* a fantastic chase, but they're not stories *about* a chase, which means we haven't included movies that are essentially one continuous pursuit, like *Vanishing Point* (1971).

- *The French Connection* (1971)
  Popeye weaves a Pontiac LeMans through traffic while chasing a train.
- *Dirty Mary Crazy Larry* (1974)
  Near the end, a Dodge Charger races through orchards with cops close behind.
- *The Seven-Ups* (1973)
  Two Pontiacs compete as detective chases bad guys for nine screeching minutes.
- *Westworld* (1973)
  This relentless chase is on foot as a murderous robot tracks a guest through the theme park.
- *What's Up, Doc?* (1972)
  The nutty nine-minute chase, using a stolen bike and a stolen Volkswagen, ends up in San Francisco Bay.
- *White Lightning* (1973)
  At the end, it's cops vs. Burt Reynold's Ford Galaxie through rural Arkansas.

Play Misty for Me

Released: October 1971
Director: Clint Eastwood
Stars: Clint Eastwood, Jessica Walter, Donna Mills
Academy Awards: None

PREVIEW: A disc jockey has an affair with a devoted fan who turns out to be a deranged murderer.

NOW SHOWING: Death by Request

Play Misty for Me (1971) was one of Clint Eastwood's boldest career moves. The first movie he ever directed, it's a tense modern thriller, a radical departure from the westerns and war movies that had made him a successful actor. Furthermore, Eastwood's starring role veers dramatically from his decade-long image as a laconic, indestructible tough guy. Playing a jazz-loving, poetry-reciting DJ, he wears sneakers and colorful shirts, not cowboy boots and ponchos, and the only horsepower is in his vintage Jaguar. It was a risky role: he'd played a mild, singing frontiersman in *Paint Your Wagon* (1969), and that movie had bombed. But Eastwood pulls it off, and *Play Misty for Me* initiated his long career of directorial hits.

Anyone who's seen *Fatal Attraction* (1987) will recognize *Misty* as the obvious inspiration. Eastwood's character is Dave Garver, whose groovy lifestyle is so casually libidinous that his cleaning lady calls his bed his "workbench." Garver has a fling with Evelyn (Jessica Walter), a beautiful fan with one song request (the phrase "play 'Misty' for me" is spoken four times in the movie). Immediately he finds himself in a serious relationship, despite their mutual "no strings" declarations. She starts showing up unannounced and causing public scenes to get attention, but he's not an entirely sympathetic victim; after all, he picked *her* up in a bar, and he continues to sleep with her despite the red flags when she vulgarly screams at strangers. The suspense and violence build steadily as Evelyn goes from being an obsessed groupie to a neurotic stalker to a deranged killer with a knife. The final ten-minute pursuit through a dark house is as scary as Alfred Hitchcock's most terrifying scenes.

The movie decelerates when Garver romances a pretty girl, Tobie (Donna Mills). They share a six-minute montage that includes sex outdoors and a lovely pop song, followed by five minutes of concert footage. Both open-air sequences are nice contrasts

Donna Mills and Clint Eastwood.

to the claustrophobic scenes with Evelyn, but coming back-to-back they interrupt this otherwise straightforward story. Elsewhere, however, there's plenty to enjoy, especially Jessica Walter as the villainess who's both coquettish and maniacal, with virtually no back story to soften or explain her. In addition, Carmel is a picturesque backdrop (aerial shots open and close the movie), the women sport awesome early-1970s shag hairstyles, and at one point Garver hunts his assailant while wearing only his tightie-whities. Now *that's* daring.

ADDED ATTRACTION: It's the Real Thing

Three times in *Play Misty for Me* Evelyn asks for a Coke. That soda is not the only "real thing" in the movie.

- Garver works at KRML, an actual Carmel radio station.
- Garver introduces a record of "the big band sounds of Dee Barton"; Barton composed the movie's original music.
- Garver meets Evelyn in the Sardine Factory, a real Monterey restaurant.
- Don Siegel plays the bartender; Siegel had previously directed three of Eastwood's movies.
- Garver's disastrous business meeting is at another Monterey restaurant, the Windjammer.
- Garver sends a package to "Mal Paso TV Productions"; Eastwood's actual production company is the Malpaso Company.
- The unique house where Garver lives is a real home (it's not Eastwood's, though).
- The concert scenes were shot during the actual Monterey Jazz Festival.
- In the last shot, that's really Jessica Walter, not a stunt double, floating in the water.

Bedknobs and Broomsticks

(One of 1971's five **FAR-OUT** movies)

Released: November 1971

Director: Robert Stevenson

Stars: Angela Lansbury, David Tomlinson, Roddy McDowall

Academy Awards: One win (Best Visual Effects), plus four more nominations (Best Art Direction; Best Costume Design; Best Song; Best Music)

PREVIEW: A witch learns a vital spell that she uses to save her village from a military attack.

FINE LINE: "We live in a world of fakery and false images. It is not what things *are*. It is what they *seem* to be." (Emelius Browne, chatting up his customers as he tries to impress them with cheap magic tricks.)

CLOSE-UP: The opening credits are styled like the Bayeux Tapestry, the famous 230-foot-long eleventh-century embroidery that depicts historical events in the Middle Ages. In the movie, the tapestry panels tip off the upcoming plot by showing a flying witch, other main characters, the ghostly army, and the arrival of gun-firing Nazis.

NOW SHOWING: *Mary Poppins* 2.0

In the early 1960s, Walt Disney, battling with author P.L. Travers over her stories for the movie that would become *Mary Poppins* (1964), purchased the rights to some 1940s books by Mary Norton as a back-up in case his *Poppins* plan collapsed. Norton's stories finally became a movie, *Bedknobs and Broomsticks* (1971), seven years after Disney's *Mary Poppins* and five years after Walt's death.

There are obviously many overlaps between the two movies. They share the same director (Robert Stevenson), screenwriters (Bill Walsh and Don DaGradi), composers (Richard M. Sherman and Robert B. Sherman), and co-star (David Tomlinson). Both are 139 minutes long, both show a singing, flying woman taking care of someone else's children, and both drop live-action actors into animated settings with animated characters. *Bedknobs* inevitably suffers in comparison with its multiple-Oscar-winning predecessor; judged on its own, however, it's by far the best, and easily the most financially successful, of the twenty live-action Disney movies released from 1970 to 1974. And while it may seem an unlikely recipient of our "FAR-OUT" designation, the masterful Oscar-winning special effects make *Bedknobs and Broomsticks* Disney's most advanced movie of the early '70s.

Different versions of *Bedknobs* try to cope with the long 139-minute runtime by shaving off scenes and songs. The full-version movie divides into three sections that go from rural England to London (with a side trip to a fantasy island) and then back to the English countryside. The year is 1940, "a time for valor" and "whispered events." The unorthodox Eglantine Price (Angela Lansbury) enters riding a motorcycle and reluctantly takes in three young orphans evacuated from London. They quickly figure out that she's an "apprentice witch" and travel with her to London so she can learn an "exceptionally important" spell. The forty-second trip is made via a magical bed that flies past flashing stars and over unnaturally colored landscapes, an effective sequence reminiscent of the famous Star Gate ending to *2001: A Space Odyssey* (1968).

In London the co-star, David Tomlinson, shows up as "The Great Emelius Browne," a self-described "fraud" and "fake" sidewalk magician. Another classic 1968 movie is echoed when entertainers and merchants perform the "Portobello Road" dance number that's a close cousin of the energetic "Consider Yourself" street frolic in *Oliver!* Unfortunately, the spell that Eglantine wants is missing five key words, and the only way to get them is to fly the bed to the animated island of Naboombu. There she and the others have an underwater animated adventure that moves to land for a wild soccer match played by various animated animals. When Eglantine acquires the missing words, her live-action group zooms back to the English coast. It was a daring decision to interrupt the main live action with a twenty-two minute animated side trip, but this clever sequence emerges as the movie's highlight. However, it too is a little derivative: some of those animals seem like they're straight out of *Fantasia* (1940), and visually the bear is a dead-ringer for Baloo in *The Jungle Book* (1967).

The last section brings on the Nazis, who slink in from their U-boat "to spread a little mischief," as Nazis were wont to do in World War Two. Eglantine takes to her broomstick and orchestrates a novel defense of her village. Her last spell, "substitutiary locomotion," causes "objects to take on a life force of their own" and brings hundreds of suits of armor to life so they can ride on ghostly steeds for a one-sided battle against the overmatched invaders. Conman Emelius Browne musters some bravery at the end, gives Eglantine a real smooch, and joins the army, leaving her with the kids and the war.

Given all the songs, spells and Disney flourishes, what could go wrong? The almost two-and-a-half-hour length, for one thing. Scenes that enchant some viewers will seem lumbering to others (the ten-minute long "Portobello Road" is a prime example). The casting might also be a concern. As endearing and tuneful as Angela Lansbury is, she's no Julie Andrews, one of the century's truly great singers. Andrews gave her *Mary Poppins* songs personality and polish; Lansbury gets through hers like a pro but without Andrews' elevated artistry. What's more, the *Bedknobs* kids have an uneven appeal: the oldest, an eleven-year-old boy, does most of the talking and is borderline obnoxious. Third-billed Roddy McDowall is barely in the movie at all.

The songs are also vulnerable to criticism. None of them is consequential, not even the Oscar-nominated "The Age of Not Believing," which is pretty but unmemorable (in contrast, *Mary Poppins* boasts several songs, such as "Chim Chim Cher-ee" and "Supercalifragilisticexpialidocious," that most people recognize, even if they haven't seen the movie). Some critics also take issue with the presence of Nazis in a children's fantasy movie; certainly the close-ups of realistic machine guns blasting point-blank at oncoming knights might be unsettling.

Despite these drawbacks, there's still plenty to recommend. The movie boasts lovely live-action backgrounds and impressive interiors. The wonderful Naboombu interlude was created with help from some of the legendary animators Walt called his "nine old men." And the superlative climactic battle with the empty suits of armor is the kind of creative sequence that Disney's special-effects wizards do best (even the head Nazi calls this remarkable scene a "pretty good trick"). As is often the case, it's Disney magic that makes *Bedknobs and Broomsticks* a bewitching experience.

Angela Lansbury.

ADDED ATTRACTION: And Moreover ...

Three months after its imaginative *Bedknobs and Broomsticks*, Disney returned to the reliable kids-and-dogs formula it had been using successfully since the days of *Old Yeller* (1957). In *The Biscuit Eater* (1972), bushy-haired Johnny Whitaker is the boy, Lonnie, who swaps for a raggedy "no-account" pooch that's a "suck-egg biscuit eater." Lonnie thinks Moreover (named after a word picked from the Bible) could be a champion pointer, if only he had some love and the right kind of training. George Spell plays Lonnie's best friend, who has a modern-sounding name, Text (where oh where are the folksy neighbors named Doc and JPeggy Sue?). Together the boys train Moreover on the family farm, with humorous mishaps, a little drama, and some life lessons along the way. This amiable, unpretentious movie is populated with warm, smiling characters, especially comedian Godfrey Cambridge as a lively cigar-chompin' "tradin' fool."

Diamonds Are Forever

Released: December 1971

Director: Guy Hamilton

Stars: Sean Connery, Jill St. John, Charles Gray

Academy Awards: One nomination (Best Sound)

PREVIEW: Agent James Bond goes to Amsterdam and Las Vegas to investigate diamond smugglers.

NOW SHOWING: My Name Is Connery, Sean Connery

After George Lazenby's unconvincing attempt to fill 007's tuxedo in *On Her Majesty's Secret Service* (1969), producers threw mountains of money at Sean Connery to return for his sixth movie as the charismatic British agent. They also surrounded him with recurring allies—M, Q, Moneypenny, Felix Leiter—plus a familiar villain and strong behind-the-scenes support, especially director Guy Hamilton and singer Shirley Bassey, both from the glorious *Goldfinger* (1964). The result was *Diamonds Are Forever* (1971), Connery's only Bond movie in the 1970s. Audiences, immediately reassured when he confidently announces, "My name is Bond, James Bond" before the opening credits, eagerly welcomed Connery back and made this robust movie a financial success.

Unfortunately, this glittering diamond has flaws. For a movie with an extremely complicated international plot—a megalomaniac smuggles diamonds for his satellite and a global ransom scheme—Bond spends most of his time in one city, Las Vegas; by contrast, *Moonraker* (1979) takes Bond to three continents and into outer space. In addition, Blofeld, an evil bald genius previously played by Donald Pleasence and Telly Savalas, is portrayed here by yet another actor, Charles Gray. His aristocratic Blofeld has hair and wit, but he embarrassingly dresses in drag for one scene. (Improbably, Bond converses politely with Blofeld several times in *Diamonds Are Forever* and never mentions that Blofeld had killed Bond's wife on their wedding day in the previous movie.) Even worse are Blofeld's two well-mannered assassins: the men finish their assignments by exchanging unfunny remarks and holding hands.

As usual, there are lusty women on view throughout Bond's adventures, especially slinky Jill St. John (initially a formidable challenge, but eventually a "stupid twit" in a bikini) and helium-chested Lana Wood (her murder is unnecessary, since she's not involved with any crimes). In addition, Bond survives his normal quota of dangerous dilemmas, including a two-minute elevator fight, a cremation, two vehicular chases (see "Added Attraction"), and an explosive assault on an oil rig. Connery is relaxed and charming, and the movie is generally entertaining, but the humor often falls flat, some special effects aren't, and the tone seems closer to lightweight comic books than serious adult thrillers. Ultimately, *Diamonds Are Forever* is the shortest of the decade's five Bond movies, but it feels like one of the longest.

ADDED ATTRACTION: Bondmobiles

The man gets around. Here are memorable Bondcar and Bondboat scenes in the decade's five 007 movies.

- *Diamonds Are Forever* (1971)
  Bond escapes a desert lab in an experimental moon buggy.
  In Las Vegas, Bond drives a Mustang Mach 1 that's tipped onto two wheels through an alley.

- *Live and Let Die* (1973)
  Bond jumps a speedboat over a car and back into the water.
  Bond steals a double-decker bus, does a 180-degree spin, and drives under a low bridge to slice off the vehicle's upper-half.

- *The Man with the Golden Gun* (1974)
  Bond speeds an AMC Hornet Hatchback across a ramp and does a midair barrel roll to clear a river.

- *The Spy Who Loved Me* (1977)
  Bond's car, a Lotus Esprit S1, converts into a missile-launching mini-submarine.
  His unique ocean-going Wetbike is a precursor to the popular WaveRunner.

- *Moonraker* (1979)
  A Venetian gondola becomes a land-crossing hovercraft.
  Bond's sleek speedboat transforms into a hang glider.

A Clockwork Orange

Released: December 1971

Director: Stanley Kubrick

Stars: Malcolm McDowell, Patrick Magee, Michael Bates

Academy Awards: Four nominations (Best Picture; Best Director; Best Writing; Best Editing)

PREVIEW: In the near future, officials try a new way to change a violent teenager's behavior.

NOW SHOWING: *Orange* Zest

Screenwriter/director Stanley Kubrick devoted four intense years to *2001: A Space Odyssey* (1968), his landmark reinvention of the science-fiction genre. After the studio quashed his next project, a mammoth epic about Napoleon, Kubrick made a leaner movie based on a 1962 novel by Anthony Burgess.

Completed relatively quickly, *A Clockwork Orange* (1971) was a radical departure for Kubrick. For one thing, unlike his previous two movies, *Dr. Strangelove* (1964) and *2001*, it was originally rated X and generated so much controversy that Kubrick himself pulled it from British theaters for the rest of the century. Blending a near-future dystopia with wicked satire, *A Clockwork Orange* tells the story of Alex (Malcolm McDowell), a savage teenage hooligan who merrily runs wild for the first third of the movie. His sadistic fun ends in the second third when he's captured and "conditioned" by a disturbing medical procedure. Released into society in the last third, he becomes a political liability, so the government restores him to his natural violent self.

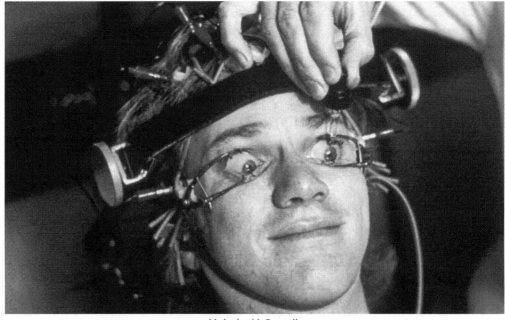

Malcolm McDowell.

Alex is an amazing character who can be deferential, charming, or vicious as occasion demands, and McDowell gives an energetic, career-defining performance. But it's the *telling* of Alex's story that makes *A Clockwork Orange* an unforgettable triumph. Kubrick controlled every facet of the movie, even wielding the camera for handheld scenes (he'd probably hammer nails into the sets if given the time). With its innovative costumes, makeup, and color scheme, its futuristic synthesizer music, and its creative mix of cinematic techniques ranging from fast motion to slow motion to distorted close-ups to high-speed editing, it's a monumental spectacle that illustrates what a consummate craftsman in full command of his powers can achieve.

However, *A Clockwork Orange*, like a movie released almost concurrently, *Straw Dogs*, is difficult for many viewers to watch. "Ultra-violence" is treated with ultra-black humor: graphic bloodshed is backed with whimsical light opera, and a rape is prefaced by a vigorous rendition of "Singin' in the Rain." (Imagine the outcry if Kubrick hadn't slightly softened the novel: the voluptuous woman under attack in Kubrick's casino is only ten years old in the book, and Kubrick doesn't have Alex running over animals in a stolen car, as Burgess does.) But Kubrick isn't trying to please viewers; he's provoking them with a dazzling artwork that is audacious, nightmarish, and utterly mesmerizing. Even if viewers want to condemn *A Clockwork Orange*, they still can't ignore it.

ADDED ATTRACTION: 1970s Quantity

After *A Clockwork Orange*, Stanley Kubrick made only one other 1970s movie, *Barry Lyndon* (1975). Both got Oscar nominations for Best Picture and Best Director (Kubrick didn't make mere movies, he made *worlds*, so his projects often took a long time). Here are three-dozen prominent directors and the number of feature-length movies they made during the decade. Including Kubrick, this august group earned seven Best Director Oscars and twenty-three additional Best Director nominations in the 1970s.

Movies	Directors(s)
13	Robert Altman
11	Arthur Hiller, Sidney Lumet
10	Herbert Ross
9	John G. Avildsen, Sam Peckinpah
8	Martin Ritt, Michael Schultz, Don Siegel
7	Woody Allen, Hal Ashby, Peter Bogdanovich
6	Clint Eastwood, John Guillermin, Robert Mulligan, Alan J. Pakula, Sydney Pollack, Martin Scorsese
5	Mel Brooks, John Cassavetes, William Friedkin, George Roy Hill, John Huston, Norman Jewison, Paul Mazursky, Franklin J. Schaffner, Robert Wise
4	Francis Ford Coppola, Gordon Parks, Steven Spielberg
3	Bob Fosse, Milos Forman, George Lucas, Arthur Penn, Elaine May, Joan Micklin Silver
2	Alfred Hitchcock

Harold and Maude

(One of 1971's five **FAR-OUT** movies)

Released: December 1971

Director: Hal Ashby

Stars: Bud Cort, Ruth Gordon, Vivian Pickles

Academy Awards: None

PREVIEW: Young Harold, who is preoccupied with death, falls for elderly, optimistic Maude.

FINE LINE: "Vice, virtue, it's best not to be too moral. You cheat yourself out of too much life. Aim above morality. If you apply that to life, then you're bound to live it fully." (Maude advising Harold as they share a hookah.)

CLOSE-UP: Seven minutes into the movie, Harold talks to a psychiatrist in his office. Note that they are wearing identical blazers, pants, shirts, ties, socks, and shoes. When they speak again seven and then fourteen minutes later, they've both changed into new clothes that are again identical.

NOW SHOWING: Sing Out

Many critics sternly rejected *Harold and Maude* (1971) when it first came out, and audiences were mostly unenthusiastic. However, over time this quirky movie has been acclaimed as one of the great black comedies (or even *romantic* comedies), and for many people it is now cherished like a personal treasure. This evolution is probably not surprising; after all, *Harold and Maude* was created to defy expectations.

Defying expectations was something director Hal Ashby had already done in his first movie, *The Landlord* (1970). In this underappreciated social comedy, Beau Bridges plays a twenty-nine-year-old man who still lives with his rich parents. "To gain territory" he buys a Brooklyn tenement so he can kick everybody out and remodel the building into his own private residence. Early in the movie Bridges' character talks directly to the camera from a lawn chair while a black servant brings him a drink, a scene that reveals how spoiled and self-indulgent he is, but to his credit he eventually becomes sympathetic to the plight of the poor tenants. He even has relationships with two black women, and when he gets one of them pregnant, he takes on the baby and moves in with the other woman. For 1970 these are all provocative topics, obviously, but Ashby handles them with humor and sensitivity.

Ashby brings the same touch to *Harold and Maude*. When we first meet young, pale Harold (Bud Cort), he's attempting the first of eight fake suicides in the movie (see "Added Attraction"). Rich, bored, and dominated by his socialite mother (Vivian Pickles), Harold likes to attend funerals for strangers and watch buildings get demolished. Early in the movie he meets seventy-nine-year-old Maude (Ruth Gordon) inside a church; when they step outside, their different approaches to life are perfectly symbolized by the casket being lifted into the hearse (that's morbid Harold) while an upbeat marching band plays in the background (there's optimistic Maude). The rest of the movie covers the single week they spend together.

Maude is the perfect tonic for everything that ails Harold. She's a feisty, rascally old dame (literally—she introduces herself as Dame Marjorie Chardin). Joyfully chattering about life's possibilities, always quick to sing and launch out on a new escapade, she encourages Harold to be spontaneous, to make music and dance, and to "try something new each day." He starts to loosen up, goes on adventures with her, and eventually

Bud Cort and Ruth Gordon.

falls in love with her, even as his mother tries to run his life by arranging a series of imperfect computer dates for him and steering him toward the army. But the fake death Harold has embraced arrives full force at the end. Throughout the movie Maude has hinted that she's going to die on her eightieth birthday (it's "a good time to move on," she tells Harold, and "it's all going to be over after Saturday," clues he doesn't recognize). Shockingly, she does finally commit suicide, leaving him to grieve and dance alone on a cliff overlooking the sea.

It's likely that Maude is the reason why so many people regularly re-watch this movie to refresh their attitudes. Seemingly a Holocaust survivor (we glimpse a number tattooed on her arm), she inspires and motivates, she rallies for good causes, and she connects spiritually with Harold in a way that is believable and convincing. Not everything she does is endearing, though: she's a serial car thief (even stealing a police motorcycle at one point), she endangers everyone around her with her extremely reckless driving, and when Harold gives her a special present she immediately bewilders him and the audience by casting it into the Monterey Bay "so I'll know where it is." Frustratingly, for someone who argues so passionately about living life to the fullest, she kills herself because it simply feels like the right time, no matter what her actions will do to Harold.

Some viewers may also think that the movie takes some cheap shots at easy targets. Everyone not named Harold or Maude is basically a caricature (the controlling mother, the military uncle, the wanna-be actress on the third computer date, the ineffectual psychiatrist, the embarrassingly inept motorcycle cop). Harold himself is so self-absorbed and spoiled that he quit boarding school early and hasn't had to do anything since, it seems. As his mother says, he is living "the life of a child" and is free to indulge in his "little eccentric moments." It's hard to truly sympathize with someone so completely withdrawn and pampered (in a way he's a younger version of the privileged, unaware character Beau Bridges plays in *The Landlord*).

Still, *Harold and Maude* is a brave, poetic, and occasionally hilarious movie. The inter-generational love affair, which includes a scene in bed together, might have been uncomfortable (at least) or disgusting (at most), but director Ashby treats the material respectfully. Like *The Graduate* (1967), another movie about an affluent, alienated young man who falls for an older woman, *Harold and Maude* is blessed with a soundtrack of perfect pop songs (here by Cat Stevens) that beautifully express moods and meanings. It all adds up to an uplifting experience that has affected how some people live and think. You know who loves *Harold and Maude*? Mary. In *There's Something About Mary* (1998), Mary (Cameron Diaz) calls it her "all-time favorite movie" and one of the greatest love stories of our time." Many fans would agree.

ADDED ATTRACTION: Harold's Fake Suicides

Fourteen minutes into *Harold and Maude*, Harold tells the psychiatrist that he has attempted fifteen suicides ("that's a rough estimate," he adds). We see eight apparent attempts in the movie, though they're staged so that Harold survives all of them.

- 3 minutes into the movie:
  Harold hangs himself inside the house.
- 6 minutes:
  Slits his throat and wrists in the bathtub.
- 12 minutes:
  Drowns himself in the pool.
- 20 minutes:
  Shoots himself in the forehead.
- 29 minutes:
  Immolates himself in the garden.
- 60 minutes:
  Chops his hand off with a butcher's knife.
- 74 minutes:
  Commits hara-kiri with a knife.
- 88 minutes:
  Drives his Jaguar off a cliff.

Dirty Harry

Released: December 1971
Director: Don Siegel
Stars: Clint Eastwood, Andrew Robinson, Reni Santoni
Academy Awards: None

PREVIEW: A renegade police inspector disregards laws as he tries to catch a demented killer.

NOW SHOWING: "The Law Is Crazy"

In the 1960s, Clint Eastwood was a western star; with *Dirty Harry* (1971), he was an urban icon. Eastwood plays a rogue police inspector, Harry Callahan, and he makes it look easy. He wears cool shades, has longish hair, and calmly eats lunch as he strolls through an in-progress bank heist and shoots the robbers. Never yelling, his quiet delivery of droll lines enhances their humor, and the first time he points his .44 Magnum and asks a criminal if he feels lucky, he's smiling. Not that Harry is entirely

admirable. He flings a racial slur at his Hispanic partner; someone says he earned his nickname because "Harry hates everybody"; he shoots a suspect whose hands are clearly raised, then tortures him for information.

That torture scene inspired loud arguments about the victim's-rights-vs.-criminal's-rights issue. The movie does seem like propaganda rigged to make the audience root for this macho gunslinger. It opens with a tribute to fallen cops; Scorpio (Andy Robinson) is an over-the-top cackling psychopath who cruelly murders innocent women and children (a ten-year-old is "shot in the face"); and there's sympathy for Harry as he discusses his wife's death, suffers physical pain, and challenges his superiors to act ("the law is crazy," Harry says in frustration). With spineless leaders capitulating to the deranged killer, Harry is the only one willing to do whatever's necessary to stop him, even if that means disobeying orders, breaking laws, and ignoring the Bill of Rights ("I shoot the bastard," he says, "that's my policy.").

Politics aside, *Dirty Harry* is one well-made, effective, and brutal thriller. Beginning with a close-up of a rifle barrel, director Don Siegel doesn't waste time with lame romantic side stories or unimportant events. Supported by Lalo Schifrin's jazzy score, scenes often play out with little or no dialogue, and visuals underscore meanings, as when Harry boards a bus blatantly advertising a Maverick, the Ford car (possibly we're even supposed to consider Harry a savior, thanks to heavy-handed religious imagery like the Jesus Saves sign above his stakeout, the giant cross he faces in the park, and his first word in the movie, "Jesus").

Fans so fully welcomed Siegel's gritty, unrelenting style and Eastwood's violent justice-seeking hero that four sequels followed, as did urban-vigilante movies like *Death Wish* (1974) and later action stars. Viewers don't have to be wild about Harry, but they can't deny his importance.

ADDED ATTRACTION: Magnum Sequel

In *Dirty Harry*'s last scene, Harry disgustedly throws his badge into the water, an action similar to the dropping-the-badge-into-the-street conclusion to *High Noon*

(1952). Though he's quit the department, Harry is back on the job for *Magnum Force* (1973), with no explanations (his former partner gets a mention, though). In this strong sequel directed by Ted Post, Harry seemingly renounces his own code of self-imposed justice as he pursues vigilante cops who have gone too far by brazenly killing villains. "When police start becoming their own executioners, where's it gonna end … pretty soon you start executing people for jaywalking," he declares. Like *Dirty Harry*, *Magnum Force* takes place in San Francisco, but this time the city is the setting for a thrilling vehicle chase a la *Bullitt* (1968). And whereas Harry previously had no private life, he now has a girlfriend. He also has a new repeated line: "A man's got to know his limitations."

Straw Dogs

Released: December 1971
Director: Sam Peckinpah
Stars: Dustin Hoffman, Susan George, Del Henney
Academy Awards: One nomination (Best Music)

PREVIEW: A timid man and his wife defend themselves against a group that attacks their house.

NOW SHOWING: Beware of *Straw Dogs*

A single three-day period in December 1971 welcomed three important new movies that incorporated extreme violence into their stories. Released after *A Clockwork Orange* and *Dirty Harry*, *Straw Dogs* quickly became a lightning rod for controversy. Disturbing and incendiary, it seems to use gratuitous sex and violence to illustrate some sociological truth about human nature, but for many viewers several harrowing scenes obliterate whatever lesson this ferocious movie hopes to teach.

Straw Dogs isn't some simple-minded independent movie made by raw unknowns. It was nominated for an Oscar, stars a brilliant actor, and was directed and co-written by a major filmmaker. There's artistry at work here. Events begin with David (Dustin Hoffman), a timid mathematician, moving to the quiet English countryside with his sexy wife Amy (Susan George), who's symbolically introduced alongside a jaggedly dangerous contraption called a mantrap. They enjoy playful, intimate moments but bicker over his need for solitude and her need for attention. "You act like you're fourteen," David scolds; Amy counters by challenging his masculinity and resolve. Defiantly she goes braless and topless in front of the local men. To prove how vulnerable David and Amy are, these ruffians sneak in and strangle Amy's cat. Emboldened when David doesn't respond, they lure him away, and two of them rape Amy. Later, five men assault the house at night, killing a cop in the process. For twenty-five minutes David becomes a resourceful hero and defends his home with shockingly violent actions.

The graphic nine-minute rape scene drew the most criticism. Though she's struck hard, Amy comes to enjoy the first encounter, eventually kissing her attacker and smiling afterwards. What is director Sam Peckinpah's message here? The same question applies to the intense siege. That David feels strongly about repelling the invaders is clear; that this pacifist is suddenly able to seems improbable. He brutally beats one man to death, kills another with the mantrap, flings boiling oil, and more. Is Peckinpah saying we're all capable of violence? That aggression is unavoidable, and peace must be earned? That it takes brawn, not brains, to survive? Ultimately, is this hard-to-watch movie toxic or tenable?

Like the title, which is never mentioned (it possibly refers to disposable ceremonial statues), definitive explanations are elusive. *Straw Dogs* raises difficult ethical questions that viewers must answer for themselves, if they've got the stomach for it.

ADDED ATTRACTION: Bring Me the Head of Sam Peckinpah

It seems impossible to believe, but *Straw Dogs* might not have been Sam Peckinpah's most disturbing movie of the early 1970s. In *Bring Me the Head of Alfredo Garcia* (1974), a furious Mexican *jefe* offers to pay anyone who delivers *la cabeza de Garcia*. An American played by Warren Oates becomes obsessed during his long, slow search and, after murdering several rivals, finally takes possession of the severed head in rural Mexico. He then talks to it, ices it to keep flies away, drives back for the reward, and eventually … loses everything. Dark, daring, and ugly, the movie represents Peckinpah unbound: many people are killed, prostitutes get hit, a father breaks his daughter's arm, and there's nobody in Peckinpah's wretched world to root for. Widely lambasted as an offensive disaster (several countries banned it) even while some critics declared it a haunting masterpiece, this movie is unforgettable, though not always in a good way.

The Legend of Boggy Creek

A TRUE STORY

A HOWCO INTERNATIONAL PICTURES RELEASE

A PIERCE-LEDWELL PRODUCTION

Produced and Directed by CHARLES PIERCE · Written by EARL E. SMITH · Music by JAMIE MENDOZA-NAVA · Executive Producers L.W. LEDWELL/CHARLES PIERCE
Color by TECHNICOLOR® · Filmed in TECHNISCOPE

In Film

- Oscar for Best Picture: *The Godfather*.
- Most Oscar wins (eight): *Cabaret*.
- Most Oscar nominations (ten): *Cabaret* and *The Godfather*.

- Top-grossing movie: *The Godfather*.
- Top-grossing comedy: *What's Up, Doc?*
- Top-grossing horror or sci-fi: *The Legend of Boggy Creek*.
- *The Godfather* supplants *Gone with the Wind* as the highest-grossing movie of all time.
- *The Last House on the Left* is considered the decade's first "slasher" movie.
- Five memorable actors: Marlon Brando, Michael Caine, Joel Grey, Al Pacino, Jon Voight.
- Five memorable actresses: Goldie Hawn, Liza Minnelli, Diana Ross, Maggie Smith, Cicely Tyson.
- Movie debuts: Jodie Foster, Samuel L. Jackson, Sissy Spacek, director Robert Benton.
- Deaths include George Sanders, columnist Louella Parsons.

In America

- February: President Nixon makes an unprecedented visit to Communist China. June: White House operatives are arrested while burglarizing the Watergate complex, setting the famous political scandal in motion. November: Nixon is re-elected in a landslide; among those who ran against him were Senator George McGovern, Governor George Wallace (who was shot and paralyzed in May), and Shirley Chisholm, the first black congresswoman.
- The Dow Jones Industrial Average breaks 1000 for the first time ever.
- At the Winter Olympics in Sapporo, Japan, America sends the largest delegation (103 athletes) and wins eight medals (the fifth-highest total among competing nations).
- At the Summer Olympics in Munich, Germany, America wins ninety-four medals (the second-highest total), including a then-record seven gold medals by swimmer Mark Spitz. Events are overshadowed by the "Munich massacre"; during the Games, Palestinian terrorists take hostages at the Olympic Village and kill eleven Israeli athletes and coaches.
- Football's Miami Dolphins go undefeated.
- After Howard Hughes conducts a phone interview with journalists to debunk claims by author Clifford Irving, Irving acknowledges that his Howard Hughes biography is a hoax.
- Two major NASA missions: *Apollo 16*, featuring the lunar rover, and *Apollo 17*, the last manned lunar mission.
- New cars: Chevy LUV truck, Honda Civic.
- Bobby Fischer becomes the first American world chess champion when he defeats Russia's Boris Spassky.
- Atari releases the Pong video game.
- Women compete in the Boston Marathon for the first time.
- *Life* magazine ceases weekly publication.
- Burt Reynolds poses nude for *Cosmopolitan* magazine.
- Music: debut albums by Jackson Browne, the Eagles, Peter Frampton, Michael Jackson, and Steely Dan are released.
- TV debuts: HBO; *M*A*S*H*, *The Price Is Right*, *The Waltons*.
- Deaths include Charles Atlas, Roberto Clemente, J. Edgar Hoover, Jackie Robinson, Harry Truman.

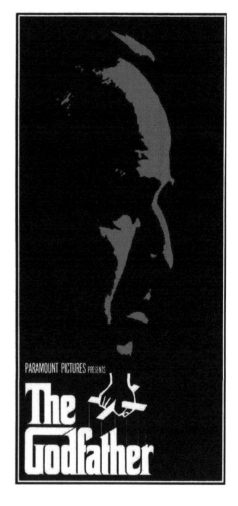

PARAMOUNT PICTURES presents

The Godfather

The Cowboys

Released: January 1972
Director: Mark Rydell
Stars: John Wayne, Roscoe Lee Browne, Bruce Dern
Academy Awards: None

PREVIEW: A desperate rancher recruits a team of boys to assist on his dangerous cattle drive.

NOW SHOWING: Boys 2 Men

John Wayne started out his 1970s with three traditional westerns: *Chisum* (1970), *Rio Lobo* (1970), and *Big Jake* (1971). All three are solid, typical Wayne westerns where he plays a sturdy hero (a rancher, an army colonel, and a gunfighter, respectively) who's givin' the bad guys hell, and in all three he survives. That's what makes his fourth '70s movie, *The Cowboys* (1972), unique. For the first time in a western since *The Alamo* (1960), where he portrayed the doomed Davy Crockett, viewers see the Duke's demise. It wouldn't be the last time during the decade, either, as Wayne would later be gunned down in *The Shootist* (1976). The times were changing, even for John Wayne.

A gem in Wayne's legendary career, *The Cowboys* puts him in the dual role of swaggering western hero and wise father figure. When his hired hands unexpectedly abandon him, Wil Anderson (Wayne), an aging rancher, is "cornered"; desperate to drive his fifteen-hundred cattle across "four-hundred miles of the meanest country in the West," he hires ten kids that put the "boy" in "cowboy" (one more joins in later). It's a bold choice. They can all ride horses, but they're totally inexperienced, so out on the trail is where "school really begins" (at this "school" the boys get drunk and one gets killed). Unfortunately, a vicious rustler (Bruce Dern) and his gang want the herd and stalk the cattle drive. After he loses a bloody fistfight with Wil, the rustler then repeatedly shoots the unarmed Duke in one of the decade's most cowardly and most notorious killings. The distraught kids regroup and decide they're "gonna finish a job." They make a daring plan, miraculously massacre the rustlers, and then successfully deliver the herd.

Admittedly that all seems a bit implausible. And at 134 minutes, including an overture, intermission, and exit music, the movie is too long (it takes fifty-one minutes just to start the cattle drive). But we do get beautiful outdoor photography, a rousing score by John Williams (later of *Jaws* and *Star Wars* fame), good performances by the young actors, and a memorably creepy one by Dern. It's John Wayne's movie, however, as he skillfully shifts from being a boss ("We're burnin' daylight!" is his signature command) to a mentor ("Tryin' don't get it done," he cautions the boys). It's a different kind of western for Wayne, but it's one of his best.

ADDED ATTRACTION: From Big Screen to Small Screen

The Cowboys was quickly made into a short-lived 1974 TV series starring Jim Davis. Here are other 1970–1974 movies that became shows during the 1970s; movies that became shows decades later, like *Westworld* (1973) and its TV series (2016), aren't included.

1970–1974 Movie (Year), Starring...	1970s TV Show (Years), Starring...
Alice Doesn't Live Here Anymore (1974), Ellen Burstyn	*Alice* (1976–1985), Linda Lavin
The Life and Times of Grizzly Adams (1974), Dan Haggerty	*The Life and Times of Grizzly Adams* (1977–1978), Dan Haggerty
The Lords of Flatbush (1974), Sylvester Stallone	*Flatbush* (1979), Joseph Cali
Love Story (1970), Ali MacGraw	*Love Story* (1973–1974), Bonnie Bedelia
*M*A*S*H* (1970), Donald Sutherland	*M*A*S*H* (1972–1983), Alan Alda
The Paper Chase (1973), Timothy Bottoms	*The Paper Chase* (1978–1986), James Stephens
Paper Moon (1973), Tatum O'Neal	*Paper Moon* (1974–1975), Jodie Foster
Serpico (1973), Al Pacino	*Serpico* (1976–1977), David Birney
Shaft (1971), Richard Roundtree	*Shaft* (1973–1974), Richard Roundtree

Cabaret

(One of 1972's five **FAR-OUT** movies)

Released: February 1972

Director: Bob Fosse

Stars: Liza Minnelli, Joel Grey, Michael York

Academy Awards: Eight wins (Best Actress—Liza Minnelli; Best Supporting Actor—Joel Grey; Best Director; Best Editing; Best Cinematography; Best Art Direction; Best Music; Best Sound), plus two more nominations (Best Picture; Best Writing)

PREVIEW: A quiet Englishman is befriended by a brassy singer in a decadent Berlin nightclub.

FINE LINE: "Behaving like some ludicrous little underage femme fatale! You're about as fatale as an after-dinner mint!" (Brian, scolding Sally.)

CLOSE-UP: Seventy-four minutes into the movie, Sally and Brian (who are already a couple) and Maximilian join together in a close dance at Maximilian's estate. As the dance begins they're all laughing, but even with no dialogue it becomes obvious that new alliances have been formed. After the music stops, the next fifteen seconds pass in an awkward silence as Brian realizes he has become the odd man out.

NOW SHOWING: Divine Decadence

In any other year, *Cabaret* (1972) probably would have been the runaway winner of the Best Picture Oscar. After all, it won for Best Director (Bob Fosse), for Best Actress (Liza Minnelli), and in six more categories (*Cabaret* is still the record-holder for most Oscar wins by a movie that *didn't* win the Best Picture award). Unfortunately for *Cabaret*, *The Godfather*, one of the all-time great movies, came out the same year, and though that classic won far fewer awards (three) than *Cabaret* did, one of them was, deservedly, for Best Picture.

Doesn't matter. *Cabaret* is today what it was in 1972—a timeless, superbly crafted entertainment from artists all doing the best work of their careers. The movie still holds up beautifully, unlike another musical that actually won the Best Picture award, *The Sound of Music* (1965), which remains charming but now seems saccharine and old-fashioned (and please don't even mention bloated late-'60s musicals like *Doctor Dolittle*; *Hello, Dolly!*; and *Paint Your Wagon*, which aren't in *Cabaret*'s league). *Cabaret* is deep and daring; it fearlessly tackles fascism, anti-Semitism, abortion, and bisexuality, not to mention the references it makes to cross-dressing, sexual threesomes, venereal disease, and drug abuse (the movie was briefly rated X in the United Kingdom). The tone and themes are constantly shifting as Fosse boldly crosscuts scenes of supreme musical artistry with savage violence; for every quiet romantic scene there's another showing triumphant Nazis acting with brazen impunity. And like another powerful musical, *West Side Story* (1961), it doesn't have a stereotypical happy ending. As pure musical entertainment, as personal drama, and as commentary on the political world outside the club, *Cabaret* succeeds on all levels.

Based on Christopher Isherwood's stories, John Van Druten's play, and the 1966 Tony Award-winning Broadway musical (which was directed by Harold Prince, not Fosse), *Cabaret* was reinvented for the big screen. It was filmed entirely in Germany, for one thing, opening up the visuals to various homes, shops, streets, and rural locations. The movie also changes some of the characters: Sally (Liza Minnelli) is British in the original stories, but American in the movie. In addition, several songs from the Broadway musical are not performed on-screen and were relegated instead to background music heard on gramophones, while several new songs (including the show-stopping "Money, Money" number) were added to the movie.

On Broadway, Joel Grey had already won a Tony in the role of the Master of Ceremonies, and he successfully carried over to the movie, beating Al Pacino and two other *Godfather* actors for the Best Supporting Actor Oscar. Welcoming, personable, hilarious, and mocking, with no lines other than what he says onstage, the garishly made-up emcee is one of the few characters who seems to understand the implications of the advancing Nazis. Set in Berlin in 1931, the movie doesn't show Nazis in the opening shot of the distorting mirror; however, after we've witnessed Nazis gathering strength all movie long, they're conspicuous in the closing shot of the same mirror (Hitler himself is never mentioned in the movie). That mirror brackets the movie, but it's the emcee who is the first and last character from the nightclub that we see.

New to the role of Sally was the electrifying Liza Minnelli. She is exciting, irresistible, and in complete command when she's performing in the Kit Kat Klub, making it hard to believe that all her previous starring screen roles had been in non-musicals (her prior movie was 1970's *Tell Me That You Love Me, Junie Moon*, a poignant but unpopular drama from director Otto Preminger; Minnelli's character goes through most of the movie with half her face terribly scarred after her angry boyfriend flings acid at her). In *Cabaret*, Minnelli balances the dynamic musical numbers with scenes outside the club that prove she's nothing if not a versatile actress—she's funny, captivating, impulsive, self-centered, sympathetic, vulnerable, heartbreaking, and ultimately totally convincing as a fully realized three-dimensional character.

Director Fosse is endlessly inventive as he stages the razzle-dazzle musical performances. You could watch these scenes with the sound turned off and they'd still be fascinating. The John Kander/Fred Ebb songs are not separate from the plot, instead arriving at key moments to enhance or express the story. For instance, "Maybe This Time" is Sally's onstage song as she and Brian (Michael York) begin their relationship; "Money, Money" accompanies her introduction to the handsome rich aristocrat who will seduce her (and Brian, too); as all three head off for the weekend, the emcee launches into the comical "Two Ladies." All the songs are performed inside the club, except one. The sinister "Tomorrow Belongs to Me" Nazi anthem, begun by a blond Nazi youth but finished by almost everyone in attendance, is sung at a countryside inn. It's a disturbing moment as we watch proud people enthusiastically invite catastrophe into their lives.

Prophetic and haunting, stunning and sublime, a major success with audiences and critics: *Cabaret*, still one of the half-dozen greatest musicals ever made, is the best musical of the 1970s.

Liza Minnelli and Joel Grey.

ADDED ATTRACTION: The Kit Kat Klub's Acts

Early on, the Master of Ceremonies (Joel Grey) introduces "the charming *chanteuse* from America, *Fräulein* Sally Bowles"; she is the star of the show, but she's not the *whole* show. Six minutes in, the emcee names some of the other performers to come, including a contortionist called the "Pretzel Woman," "the Huber Sisters," and "*die Spielknaben*, the Toy Boys!" None of these three acts perform, but others do, as shown below (we're not including Sally's numbers in this list).

- 17 minutes into the movie:
  Two women mud-wrestle in a "ring" as the emcee sprays them with seltzer.
- 23 minutes:
  A dance number by the emcee and the Kit Kat Klub's dancers.

- 60 minutes:
  A man plays a musical saw as a shadow-pantomime is performed behind him.
- 65 minutes:
  The emcee and two "cabaret girls" sing "Two Ladies."
- 89 minutes:
  The emcee, the dancers, and an instrumental called "Tiller Girls."
- 101 minutes:
  The emcee sings "If You Could See Her" to a gorilla.
- 109 minutes:
  The dancers briefly perform the high-kicking "can-can."

What's Up, Doc?

Released: March 1972
Director: Peter Bogdanovich
Stars: Barbra Streisand, Ryan O'Neal, Madeline Kahn
Academy Awards: None

PREVIEW: Four identical suitcases get switched, leading to crazy mix-ups in San Francisco.

NOW SHOWING: What's Not to Like, Doc?

Just six months after *The Last Picture Show* (1971) premiered, Peter Bogdanovich followed up his Oscar-winning drama with a terrific comedy. How could *What's Up, Doc?* (1972) *not* be terrific? Bogdanovich and his screenwriters—Buck Henry, David Newman, and Robert Benton—had all earned Oscar nominations for earlier screenplays. Both stars also had Oscar history—Barbra Streisand had won for *Funny Girl* (1968), and Ryan O'Neal had been nominated for *Love Story* (1970). Additionally, the supporting cast is sweetened with hilarious scene-stealers, especially Madeline Kahn (making her movie debut). Mix in photogenic San Francisco, serve this light confection with first-class style, and you've got the recipe for a scrumptious hit.

Movie buffs adore *What's Up, Doc?* because this nostalgic movie, though it's set in July 1972, is filled with allusions to classics from yesteryear. For instance, the opening credits arrive via a time-tested technique, a book's turning pages. The zany impossible-to-summarize plot about four identical overnight bags—including one with jewels, another with secret documents—that get switched among their owners evokes the screwiest of the great screwball comedies from Hollywood's Golden Age. Streisand, here at her most appealing and attractive, is reminiscent of the wonderful Carole Lombard. O'Neal is a distracted, bespectacled scientist a la Cary Grant in *Monkey Business* (1952), his jacket gets torn the way Grant's tuxedo is ripped in *Bringing Up Baby* (1938), and O'Neal even says "Judy Judy," an allusion to a phrase associated (incorrectly) with Grant. There are beloved old songs—Streisand sings "You're the Top" twice and a minute of "As Time Goes By"—and she delivers a famous line from *Casablanca* (1942). A fun snippet of an old Bugs Bunny cartoon, *What's Up, Doc?* (1950), adds a joyous touch to the ending.

Most of the first hour takes place in one night in one hotel; like some nutty Marx Brothers movie, this section includes a madcap dinner and a torched room. Then, after a wild party with a pie fight, the movie sprints through a fabulous Keystone Kops-style chase up and down San Francisco's hills, finally dumping everyone into the bay and into court. Even with all the broad slapstick and Buster Keatonish pratfalls, there's lots of subtle humor to appreciate: in the Chinatown section of the nine-minute chase, the Chinese parade is playing "La Cucaracha." Of course. With so much to like, only a curmudgeon couldn't savor this movie's daffy delights.

Barbra Streisand and Ryan O'Neal.

ADDED ATTRACTION: What Decade, Doc?

While *What's Up, Doc?* does look back to movies of past decades, it also includes some references to some current events from the late '60s and early '70s.

- The bag with secret government documents is reminiscent of 1971's Pentagon Papers.
- Eunice reads a bestselling sex manual, *The Sensuous Woman* (1969) by "J."
- A minute into the long chase through city streets, a speeding car loses a hubcap, as in the famous chase in *Bullitt* (1968).
- That chase ends with a Volkswagen floating in San Francisco Bay, a scene parodying current TV commercials and ads that showed the same car afloat.
- The judge calls the confusing proceedings a "horror show," a term from *A Clockwork Orange* (1971).
- Judy's last line is from *Love Story* (1970): "Love means never having to say you're sorry."

Silent Running

Released: March 1972
Director: Douglas Trumbull
Stars: Bruce Dern, Cliff Potts, Ron Rifkin
Academy Awards: None

PREVIEW: The astronaut protecting Earth's last trees on a spaceship is told to destroy them.

NOW SHOWING: Loudly Praising *Silent Running*

Ingenious and passionate, *Silent Running* (1972) is one of the decade's better science-fiction movies. It sure has a sterling pedigree. Director Douglas Trumbull was the special-effects wizard behind the remarkable visuals in *2001: A Space Odyssey* (1968); two of the co-writers, Michael Cimino and Deric Washburn, would later collaborate on *The Deer Hunter* (1978); and the third co-writer, Steven Bochco, would win multiple Emmy Awards for his hit TV shows. Bruce Dern plays an emotional lead character trying to save the last of Earth's forests, Joan Baez sings two sensitive songs, and the movie's perfectly timed ecological message is powerfully delivered. Unfortunately, even though most critics responded favorably to the movie's charms, audiences stayed away.

The straightforward story has a renegade space botanist (Bruce Dern), disgusted by a deforested Earth where there's "no beauty, no imagination" and "nobody cares," sacrificing his colleagues and even himself to save the beloved greenhouse he's preserving in space. He rationalizes his dramatic actions with a conservationist's zeal: "What's gonna happen if these forests and all this incredible beauty is lost for all time?" While the plot is simple, the *presentation* is brilliant, especially given the movie's small budget. Trumbull used the interiors of an actual aircraft carrier as the sets for his vast spaceship (both the aircraft carrier and the spaceship are named the *Valley Forge*, and both have an unglamorous industrial look that's the opposite of the clean, white styles of the vessels in *2001*). The filmmakers modified ski outfits and wetsuits into believable spacesuits, they invented cool little carts for the astronauts (see "Added Attraction"), and they created an intense sequence when the ship flies through Saturn's rings. Most impressive are the drones, the small helpful robots that assist the crew. Inside each machine is a double-amputee maneuvering the drone, working the "arms" to perform tasks (even performing surgery and playing poker!), and conveying so much personality that the heartbreaking destruction of one of them is more affecting than the human deaths.

Granted, there are some flaws. The audience guesses before the veteran botanist does that the dying forest isn't getting adequate sunlight. After the botanist kills the crew, the movie has little dialogue and tends to drag. And just how long will that final forest last under the care of a single drone using exhaustible supplies? Overlook these problems, however, and you'll find an impressive movie filled with sweetness and meaning.

ADDED ATTRACTION: The ATV of the Future

The movie's astronauts playfully zoom through their immense spaceship on bouncy four-wheel all-terrain vehicles. According to the DVD's special features, these fast, mobile little carts were built by the filmmakers using lawn-mower engines, big tires, plywood, and plastic. There was nothing like these on the market yet, so to 1972 audiences they looked totally revolutionary and totally fun. Within a decade Honda,

Suzuki, and other companies would start selling four-wheeled single-seat ATVs to the public. A similar movie-to-market transition occurred five years later with the unique ocean-going Wetbike prototype that James Bond rides in *The Spy Who Loved Me* (1977). Within a few years Yamaha released a more powerful personal water craft, the popular WaveRunner. Another 1977 movie, *Demon Seed*, anticipated today's voice-activated smart-home technology. In this bizarre horror movie, the Proteus IV computer controls locks, alarms, lights, and various devices via vocal command (the computer's own voice is provided by Robert Vaughn).

The Godfather

(One of 1972's five **FAR-OUT** movies)

Released: March 1972

Director: Francis Ford Coppola

Stars: Marlon Brando, Al Pacino, James Caan

Academy Awards: Three wins (Best Picture; Best Actor—Marlon Brando; Best Writing), plus seven more nominations (three for Best Supporting Actor—James Caan, Robert Duvall, Al Pacino; Best Director; Best Editing; Best Costume Design; Best Sound)

PREVIEW: A New York crime family with an aging leader faces daunting challenges from rivals.

FINE LINE: "Leave the gun, take the cannoli." (Peter Clemenza to Rocco, getting ready to leave the car with Paulie's dead body slumped over the steering wheel.)

CLOSE-UP: Is "I'm with you" the turning point of the movie? At the sixty-six-minute mark, Michael whispers these words twice to his wounded father in the hospital, causing the Don to smile and cry. It's in these hospital scenes that Michael, who so far has rejected the family business, asserts himself as his father's protector. Soon he'll implement his own idea to be his father's avenger, and eventually he'll become his father's true heir. "I'm with you" could be interpreted as the precise moment when Michael finally faces his destiny.

NOW SHOWING: The Grand *Godfather*

If there's an unassailable 1970s movie, *The Godfather* (1972) is it. It's the decade's most universally acclaimed film and regularly tops lists of the *all-time* greats. Interestingly, it didn't sweep that year's Academy Awards, winning three to *Cabaret*'s eight. But in the hearts of moviegoers, even moviegoers from different generations, *The Godfather* is indisputably *il capo di tutti capi*.

The brilliance of this epic movie is that it shows vicious gangsters facing business challenges and family problems. Though they murder, bribe, and steal, they also run what is essentially a large company, not some small-time neighborhood operation, and they have disloyal employees impeding the company's progress. In addition, the family itself includes a dim-witted black sheep (Fredo), a violent hot head (Sonny), an uninvolved youngest son (Michael), an adopted sibling (Tom), a kid sister (Connie) with an abusive husband (Carlo), and a wise, aging patriarch who's like a corporate CEO (Don Corleone). Their situations involve infidelities and sibling squabbles, just like any family might have.

Complicated but never confusing, the long story is brought to vivid life by some of Hollywood's best: *The Godfather*'s cast and crew earned twenty-nine Oscar wins and seventy-six additional Oscar nominations during their combined careers. The movie's got the perfect ensemble cast, masterful images by the great cinematographer Gordon Willis (dimly lit interiors—even during daytime!—evoke the family's dark, shadowy world), and a haunting, instantly identifiable score. No wonder audiences don't merely *watch* this movie; they get fully engrossed in it like they're visiting a fascinating country and want to learn its language, observe its customs, and understand the citizens.

Surprisingly, the movie's most famous name and that year's Best Actor winner, Marlon Brando, is an active character for only about one-third of the movie's running time, though he's always an influential presence and is frequently referenced by everyone else. Though he often speaks in raspy whispers, Brando is able to convey the Don's awesome strength. Of his many memorable scenes, his last one is especially effective: moments before his death, the Don plays with his grandson and cuts an orange peel to create terrifying "fangs," reminding viewers that despite all his dignity and poise he has been a monstrous villain.

Mario Puzo's book discussed the Don's boyhood in Sicily and rise to power in New York, but Coppola saves all that for the sequel, *The Godfather: Part II* (1974). Among many other changes, Coppola also jettisoned the book's long section about singer Johnny Fontane and his tawdry Hollywood life, and he ends the movie with Kay (Diane Keaton) sadly being shut out of her husband's life; the book has an additional chapter that puts Kay and her kids in New Hampshire, with Tom Hagen (Robert Duvall) bringing her back to New York.

The result of Coppola's streamlining is a towering masterpiece that became the year's biggest moneymaker. Additionally, *The Godfather* is probably the decade's most-studied movie, so instead of an unnecessary plot summary we're going to pose some questions that have occurred to us after many, many viewings. For instance, how did gangsters get that severed horse's head into the Hollywood producer's house, up the stairs, and into his bed without waking him or anyone else up? There's no suggestion that the producer was drugged; he just wakes up with this

Al Pacino and Marlon Brando.

huge gory thing under the bloody sheets. The Don can get things done, sure, but this is more like a stupendous magic trick.

At the fifty-seven-minute mark, Clemenza, Rocco, and Paulie drive to Manhattan. For Paulie, it's a one-way trip. After he's executed, Clemenza and Rocco abandon the car with the bloody body still in it. They don't seem to be anywhere near a bus stop or a cab, and "that fat Clemenza" doesn't seem like someone up for a long walk. No colleagues have followed them way out to the Jersey weeds. So how do they get home?

Exiled in Italy, Michael sees young Apollonia for literally twenty-five seconds, and they never even speak; immediately he goes into town, talks to her father, and announces his intention to marry the girl. Okay, it's a three-hour movie, and there isn't time for a lengthy courtship, but twenty-five seconds? "The thunderbolt" hits and Michael's getting engaged? Wonder what Kay, his long-time girlfriend back home, will think.

Why isn't Fabrizio hunted and killed? He's the Sicilian traitor who helps car-bomb Michael's bride; the Corleones are usually quick to get revenge, and in the book he's indeed gunned down, but we don't see Fabrizio's death in the original *Godfather* (he finally get car-bombed in *The Godfather Saga*, Coppola's 1977 seven-hour re-edit of the first two *Godfather* films with extra footage).

Why isn't Fredo at Don Corleone's funeral? The Don's enemies are there, but his oldest surviving son couldn't leave Las Vegas?

Near the end, Michael attends the baptism while the heads of the other four crime families are being killed. It's an amazing sequence as Coppola crosscuts between Michael's solemn words and the savage assassinations he's ordered. Won't these deaths unite those angry families against the heavily outnumbered Corleones? Michael is making a statement, but is it the *right* statement?

Obviously we're being facetious, but it's out of deep respect for what is one of the true masterpieces of Hollywood history. No gentle teasing, no amount of nit-picking, and no academic critique could diminish this movie's lasting, monumental power. In every way, it's a triumph.

ADDED ATTRACTION: *MAD* Magazine's Parodies of 1972 Movies

The Godfather got its own movie parody, "The Oddfather," in *MAD* magazine (the parody ran in December 1972). Below are five other 1972 movies that were similarly honored, followed by the titles of the parodies. *MAD*'s parodies of 1973 movies are with the entry for *Serpico* (1973).

- *The Cowboys*: "The Cowkids"
- *The Heartbreak Kid*: "The Heartburn Kid"
- *The Hot Rock*: "The Cute Rook"
- *The New Centurions*: "The New Comedians"
- *The Poseidon Adventure*: "The Poopsidedown Adventure"

Slaughterhouse-Five

Released: March 1972
Director: George Roy Hill
Stars: Michael Sacks, Ron Liebman, Valerie Perrine
Academy Awards: None

PREVIEW: A time-traveler jumps to various events in his life, chiefly those in World War Two.

NOW SHOWING: So It Goes

Viewers unfamiliar with the title might wonder what this movie is about. A really good basketball team? Animal friends escaping from a meat-packing plant? Is it the fifth in a series of slasher movies? Once the movie ends, some viewers might still be puzzled. *Slaughterhouse-Five* (1972) is a quirky, challenging, sometimes disorienting, occasionally dazzling movie, just like the celebrated 1969 Kurt Vonnegut novel it closely follows.

Anyone who's read the book might be surprised that Vonnegut's oft-repeated "so it goes" phrase, which he uses 106 times, isn't in the movie at all. That aside, the movie is generally faithful to Vonnegut's book. The time-traveling main character, Billy Pilgrim (Michael Sacks), has "come unstuck in time," zigging and zagging uncontrollably through six different eras of his life, but not in chronological order, and sometimes only momentarily. We see Billy as a child (for a minute); as a naïve soldier in World War Two (almost half the movie); as a post-war newlywed (about ten minutes); as a successful optometrist, circa 1968 (a half-hour); again around 1968, but on an alien planet (twelve minutes); and as an old man getting assassinated (one minute). Sometimes his jumps happen randomly, but occasionally a transitional image or sound bridges a gap: a question to the aliens immediately cuts to a past answer from a Nazi commander, for instance. Occasionally the different periods overlap, as when the sounds of Billy's 1968 surgery are heard during a 1945 war scene. This nonlinear approach is a daring way to tell a story, though what enthralls some viewers might confuse others.

Some of Billy's experiences are amusing, but late in the movie the tone darkens when the lovely city of Dresden, Germany, where Billy is a POW, is demolished and his best friend is mercilessly executed. Earlier, the fatal accident with Billy's wife was handled with black humor, but this death feels sad and meaningful. Billy's then whisked 423-billion miles away to a zoo-like exhibit on the planet Tralfamadore, where he's joined by the erotic actress Montana Wildhack (Valerie Perrine). Eventually he realizes that "life has no beginning, no middle, and no end" and it is just "a collection of moments all strung together." "Ignore the bad times," the unseen Tralfamadorians tell him, "and concentrate on the good." Billy underscores this last lesson by paraphrasing those very words. It's a simple and profound takeaway from a special and thought-provoking movie.

ADDED ATTRACTION: Strange Ages

Michael Sacks makes his movie debut as Billy Pilgrim in *Slaughterhouse-Five*. Thanks to remarkable make-up, Sacks ages about fifty years in the movie, and at one point he's father to the son played by Perry King, even though Sacks and King are approximately the same age in real life. Here are other 1970s movies that have unlikely age disparities between movie parents (some of them artificially aged with wigs and make-up) and their movie children.

Movie (Year)	"Parent," Star's True Age at the Time "Child," Star's True Age at the Time
Barry Lyndon (1975)	Marisa Bersenson, 28 Leon Vitali, 27
Earthquake (1974)	Lorne Green, 59 Ava Gardner, 52
The Godfather (1972)	Marlon Brando, 48 John Cazale, 37
Harry and Tonto (1974)	Art Carney, 56 Larry Hagman, 43
The Heartbreak Kid (1972)	Doris Roberts, 47 Charles Grodin, 37
The Reincarnation of Peter Proud (1975)	Margot Kidder, 27 Jennifer O'Neill, 27
Tommy (1975)	Ann-Margret, 34 Roger Daltrey, 31

Play It Again, Sam

Released: April 1972

Director: Herbert Ross

Stars: Woody Allen, Diane Keaton, Tony Roberts

Academy Awards: None

PREVIEW: Helped by an imaginary Humphrey Bogart, a recently divorced man tries to get dates.

NOW SHOWING: You Must Remember This

With *Play It Again, Sam* (1972), Woody Allen took a break from directing and handed over the reins to Herbert Ross. But it's still Allen's movie. It's based on his 1969 hit Broadway play, which starred Allen, Diane Keaton, and Tony Roberts (Keaton and Roberts are both in this movie and will later star in other Allen hits). For Allen, *Sam* is the first movie where he seems to be playing himself, displaying the casual urban look and humorously neurotic behavior he'll perfect in *Annie Hall* (1977). The clumsiness, difficulty with mechanical objects, alcohol intolerance, and affinity for jazz that are all in *Sam* become hallmarks of his later movies. Keeping it personal, this is the only movie where Allen uses his real first name (he was born Allan Konigsberg), and he even mentions his actual high school, Brooklyn's Midwood High.

Like the play, the movie presents Allan Felix (Woody Allen), an insecure, recently divorced writer who's ineptly trying to date. Helped by an imaginary Humphrey Bogart (Jerry Lacy), he romances his best friend's wife (Keaton). Eventually she returns to her husband (Roberts), but by then Allan has gained some style and confidence.

Unlike the play, which was set entirely inside a Manhattan apartment, the movie relocates to San Francisco and uses various outdoor settings, including a cable car and a Marin County beach. Most of the jokes, which are generally terrific, come straight from the play (and some of those are taken almost verbatim from Allen's earlier stand-up act: prolonging sex by thinking about baseball comes directly from his "Second Marriage" routine, and the line "When I go to the beach, I don't tan, I stroke" is

Woody Allen and Diane Keaton.

copied from a bit called "Brooklyn"). *Play It Again, Sam* also showcases Allen as a gifted physical comedian; his blind-date preparations could be watched with no sound and would still generate huge laughs.

Modern audiences may not laugh at everything, however. It's hard to believe the play's uncomfortable rape jokes lasted thirteen months on Broadway, but they're repeated in the movie. And this movie's many references to *Casablanca* may not resonate now as they did in the '70s, when there was renewed interest in Bogart. But there's so much sweetness and romance (especially at the end when Allan recites *Casablanca*'s famous "you're getting on that plane" monologue) that ultimately *Play It Again, Sam* is more than merely funny; it's adorable.

ADDED ATTRACTION: Replay It Again, Sam

The 1972 movie *Play It Again, Sam* makes changes to the original 1969 play. Some are noted here, in the order the changes appear.

Play	Movie
Setting: New York.	Setting: San Francisco.
Opening scene: *The Maltese Falcon* (1941) on TV.	Opening scene: *Casablanca* (1942) in a theater.
Allan plays a Thelonius Monk record.	Allan plays an Oscar Peterson record.
Allan mentions a Franz Kline painting.	Allan mentions a Jackson Pollock painting.
Allan daydreams about dating Gina.	No Gina; Allan dates Julie and fights bikers.
Allan fantasizes about Linda; she sprays tear gas.	Allen tries to seduce Linda; screams, but no tear gas.
Allan says "Play it again, Sam" to end Act Two.	These words aren't spoken in the movie.
Allan imagines rejecting his ex-wife should she return to him.	His ex-wife does return—to New York.
Final scene: Allan discusses Bogart with a cute new neighbor.	Final scene: Allan walks into the fog alone.

Skyjacked

Released: May 1972
Director: John Guillermin
Stars: Charlton Heston, James Brolin, Yvette Mimieux
Academy Awards: None

PREVIEW: A disturbed passenger with weapons demands that an airliner be rerouted to Moscow.

NOW SHOWING: "My Aircraft, My Crew, Mine!"

Skyjacked (1972) isn't a great disaster movie, but it's a good bridge between more famous movies in the genre. The plot involves a bomb-carrying passenger on a 707, like in *Airport* (1970), and a near-collision between an airliner and a small plane, something that actually happens in *Airport 1975* (1974). As in *Airport* and *Airport 1975*, *Skyjacked*'s flight includes a medical emergency, a romantic connection between a pilot and a younger stewardess, and a Hollywood legend as a passenger (see "Added Attraction"). Significantly, *Skyjacked* gives Charlton Heston his first starring role in a 1970s disaster movie; he'll later play stalwart heroes in *Airport 1975*, *Earthquake* (1974), *Two-Minute Warning* (1976), and *Gray Lady Down* (1978). It's also the first disaster movie for director John Guillermin, who will guide *The Towering Inferno* (1974) to an Oscar nomination for Best Picture.

Skyjacked differs from its unhurried predecessor, *Airport*, by speeding everything up: the jet is airborne in only seven minutes, and the hippie passenger played by Susan Dey (making her movie debut) discovers the bomb threat six minutes later. Another passenger correctly identifies the bomber just a third of the way into the movie (the suspect has been lying, drinking, taking pills, and "bugging out"), and at the movie's mid-point the bomber is fully revealed when he stands up with a hand grenade. Soon he's using racist language, ranting about "my aircraft," and directing the flight toward Moscow. Suspense builds as the crew deals with this violent lunatic who gets more unstable by the minute. Everything really intensifies when the jet lands and the bomber realizes he may not get a welcome reception. Throughout the movie, five short fantasy sequences try to flesh out the two main characters, but these superficial scenes add little.

Modern viewers will undoubtedly notice the dated behavior. Amazingly, the bomber saunters aboard with a bag full of weapons. The about-to-deliver pregnant woman rejects milk for alcohol, passengers smoke during the flight (the pilot lights a pipe, like Barry Nelson's character did in *Airport*), and the navigator mentions a "menopausal broad." The pregnant woman goes into labor, takes five minutes to deliver her pristine baby, and thirteen minutes later walks off the plane. Impressive.

Though it's not as magnificent as the Oscar-winning *Airport*, audiences made *Skyjacked* a hit, ensuring that airline-disaster movies would fly on. In two years, Helen Reddy will sing to Linda Blair in *Airport 1975*.

ADDED ATTRACTION: Hollywood Legends in 1970–1974 Disaster Movies

A screen legend from Hollywood's Golden Age is a key ingredient in the recipe for a successful disaster movie. *Skyjacked* boasts two classic Oscar-nominated stars on its passenger list: Jeanne Crain and Walter Pidgeon (in the movie, both survive). Here are eight more Hollywood legends in 1970–1974 disaster movies, plus their movie outcomes.

- Fred Astaire
  The Towering Inferno (1974): He's trapped in the building, but survives.
- Ava Gardner
  Earthquake (1974): Gardner drowns in a storm drain.
- Helen Hayes
  Airport (1970): She survives and earns lifetime airline passes.
- Van Heflin
  Airport (1970): He blows himself up aboard the jet.
- Jennifer Jones
  The Towering Inferno (1974): She falls to her death from the scenic elevator.
- Myrna Loy
  Airport 1975 (1974): Drinking steadily, she survives.
- Gloria Swanson
  Airport 1975 (1974): Swanson survives and delivers the last line.
- Shelley Winters
  The Poseidon Adventure (1972): Winters drowns making her underwater swim.

Boxcar Bertha

Released: June 1972
Director: Martin Scorsese
Stars: Barbara Hershey, David Carradine, Barry Primus
Academy Awards: None

PREVIEW: In the Depression, a young woman rides trains and falls into a life of violent crime.

NOW SHOWING: Train in Vain

When is a low-budget B-movie not a typical low-budget B-movie? When it's directed by young Martin Scorsese. Though it's got extreme violence and gratuitous sex for the drive-in crowd, *Boxcar Bertha* (1972) was made with flair and passion. It's much closer to a thoughtful crime classic like *Bonnie and Clyde* (1967) than it is to an unpolished cheapie like *The Honeymoon Killers* (1970).

Only Scorsese's second movie, *Boxcar Bertha* shares some traits with his later masterworks. According to the opening text, it's based on a true story, as *Raging Bull* (1980) will be; like *Casino* (1995), it's got a strong, personable female lead; Scorsese puts blues music on the soundtrack, as he will in many movies; he captures an era (here the Depression) with convincing period detail, one of his obvious strengths; his overhead camera observes action below, as it will for the bloodbath in *Taxi Driver* (1976); there's abundant carnage, a la *Goodfellas* (1990); and the quote from *The Wizard of Oz* (1939) foreshadows *Oz* references in *Alice Doesn't Live Here Anymore* (1974).

The plot follows Bertha, a young, innocent woman (Barbara Hershey), who's called "very pretty" with "a remarkable figure." She attaches to Bill (David Carradine), a "notorious Bolshevik." Unfortunately, his outspoken union views lead to arrest, an escape, and a life of crime, with Bertha his gun-toting bank-robbing accomplice. She's often on the run: eight different times Bertha, true to her nickname, runs alongside trains.

The most powerful of these scenes is the last one, where she tries to keep up with the crucified corpse nailed to the side of a train. This religious symbolism ties a thread running through the movie: there are Bible quotes, a religious mural, and a movie poster for *The Man Who Could Work Miracles* (1936), plus Bertha poses as a missionary for the chain-gang break-out.

Sex and violence made this movie controversial. Tame by today's standards, the two erotic scenes got extra attention when the stars later said the sex was real, not simulated. The shotgun violence that peppers the movie comes to a blood-soaked crescendo with the final shoot-out. This over-the-top scene is not for the squeamish, but it's not what makes this movie interesting. Scorsese's staging and editing of the train/car collision, his unusual camera work (the artsy walk through a corridor at forty-three minutes)—these lift *Boxcar Bertha* above the ordinary and show Scorsese's budding talents starting to bloom.

ADDED ATTRACTION: Movies Set During the Depression

After *Bonnie and Clyde* (1967) and *They Shoot Horses, Don't They?* (1969) achieved critical and commercial success, numerous '70 movies, including *Boxcar Bertha*, were set during America's Great Depression. Here are sixteen more examples, listed chronologically (stars are noted).

- *Bloody Mama* (1970): Shelley Winters
- *A Bullet for Pretty Boy* (1970): Fabian
- *The Moonshine War* (1970): Patrick McGoohan
- *Fools' Parade* (1971): James Stewart
- *Sounder* (1972): Cicely Tyson
- *Charley and the Angel* (1973): Fred MacMurray
- *Paper Moon* (1973): Ryan O'Neal
- *Emperor of the North* (1973): Lee Marvin
- *Dillinger* (1973): Warren Oates
- *The Sting* (1973): Paul Newman
- *Thieves Like Us* (1974): Keith Carradine
- *Big Bad Mama* (1974): Angie Dickinson
- *Brother Can You Spare a Dime?* (1975): Documentary
- *Hard Times* (1975): Charles Bronson
- *Bound for Glory* (1976): David Carradine
- *The Prize Fighter* (1979): Don Knotts

Conquest of the Planet of the Apes

Released: June 1972

Director: J. Lee Thompson

Stars: Roddy McDowall, Don Murray, Ricardo Montalban

Academy Awards: None

PREVIEW: In 1991, Caesar leads a bloody revolt to free the apes enslaved in a futuristic city.

NOW SHOWING: Monkey Business, Part Three

Many *Apes* aficionados rank *Conquest of the Planet of the Apes* (1972) uppermost on the series' sequel list. It's definitely the most violent *Apes* movie and was the first one to warrant a PG, not a G, rating. After the original *Planet of the Apes* (1968) and two sequels, *Beneath the POTA* (1970) and *Escape from the POTA* (1971), there's lots of non-sequential back story to remember, so in *Conquest* Armando (Ricardo Montalban), the circus leader from the previous movie, briefly recaps everything.

Conquest of the POTA continues the *Escape from the POTA* story but jumps eighteen years ahead to 1991, when apes have become docile, silent servants in a futuristic city. Milo, the baby ape who survived *Escape*, is now an adult named Caesar, for some reason (perhaps to conceal his identity); like his father Cornelius, he's played by the same excellent actor, Roddy McDowall. Alarmed at the "monstrous" way humans treat apes, Caesar leads an insurrection that quickly escalates from petty disobedience to bloody revolution. In his climactic victory speech, Caesar dramatically announces "the birth of the planet of the apes!"

Ricardo Montalban and Roddy McDowall.

It's not as monumental as the original *POTA*, as scattered as *Beneath the POTA*, or as whimsical and heartfelt as *Escape from the POTA*, but this third sequel is packed with action. It also implies some bold parallels with American history: there are chain-shackled ape slaves, slave auctions, masters with whips, and a fiery city riot. Significantly, a black man who calls himself "a descendent of slaves" is Caesar's sole human ally.

Fans went ape for *Conquest* and made it a number-one box-office hit, so naturally another *Apes* movie followed. Last but unfortunately least of the decade's sequels, *Battle for the Planet of the Apes* (1973) briefly zooms forward to 2670 A.D. but then flashes back to the early twenty-first century (clips from the previous two movies bring everyone up to date). "The vilest war in human history" has returned Earth to an uncivilized state and sent apes into treehouses, where singer/songwriter Paul Williams has joined the cast as the resident intellectual. The titular "battle" is actually fought on two fronts against mutant humans and rebellious gorillas. Director Thompson returns from *Conquest* and pulls back on that movie's PG violence to regain a G rating. Despite having big battle scenes, this chaotic, low-budget movie feels tedious, and it dragged the 1968–1973 *Apes* saga to a tired close.

ADDED ATTRACTION: The *POTA* Timeline

The zig-zagging main events, in chronological order, of the first five *Planet of the Apes* movies (with abbreviated titles). In the list, note the fifth and sixth items: inexplicably, the first and second *POTA* movies don't agree on the year and thus show events on Earth *after* it's been destroyed.

- 1972: This is the year when Taylor's rocket leaves Earth (the date is shown in the first movie, *POTA*).
- 1973: Two future apes return to this year in Taylor's rocket (third movie, *Escape*).
- 1991: The ape baby from the third movie is now eighteen (fourth movie, *Conquest*).
- 2670: From here to a flashback to the twenty-first century (fifth movie, *Battle*).
- 3955: An astronaut follows Taylor to Earth; Earth is destroyed in the last scene (second movie, *Beneath*, with this year clearly given).
- 3978: Taylor lands on a planet that turns out to be Earth with a ruined Statue of Liberty (first movie, *POTA*, with this year clearly given).

frenzy

Released: June 1972
Director: Alfred Hitchcock
Stars: Jon Finch, Barry Foster, Alec McCowen
Academy Awards: None

PREVIEW: A Londoner being hunted as a serial killer hides out as he looks for the true culprit.

NOW SHOWING: Masterfeast Theater

After ending the 1960s with the underwhelming *Torn Curtain* (1966) and *Topaz* (1969), Alfred Hitchcock stepped boldly into the 1970s with *Frenzy* (1972). Like *North by Northwest* (1959) and other Hitchcock classics, *Frenzy* shows an innocent man trying to wriggle free of false accusations (wriggling, naturally, only worsens his situation). *Frenzy* removes the international espionage of Hitchcock's previous two movies and focuses instead on British serial killings. It's not a byzantine story twisting with red herrings: the inspector's dippy wife intuitively solves the case, and the movie abruptly ends without a chase or complications. Nevertheless, Hitchcock's cinematic storytelling is so delicious that audiences and critics ate it up.

"Ate it up" is appropriate here, because food is frequently present. The charming killer, who's revealed early, is named after food, is introduced eating, and owns a fruit shop. In the one brutal murder we actually witness, he eats immediately before and after his crime (his victim is having lunch). Later, he hides a body among potato sacks. Scenes in pubs, at breakfast, and, in a recurring joke, at a dinner table where inedible meals are served almost make this movie *Feeding Frenzy*.

In some ways, *Frenzy* is an unusual Hitchcock movie. For one thing, it's R-rated. The seventy-three-year-old director takes advantage of the decade's new permissions to show nude women and corpses (starting with the first scene, as if announcing his intentions). In addition, *Frenzy* lacks the famous names that energize Hitchcock's more glamorous movies. From 1958 to 1966 he cast high-powered legends like James Stewart, Cary Grant, Sean Connery, and Paul Newman; *Frenzy*'s leads are Jon Finch and Barry Foster, two skilled actors but not luminous stars (imagine the wattage if dynamos like Michael Caine or Anthony Hopkins had lit up this movie).

While *Frenzy* may be different for Hitchcock, it still has the master's virtuoso touch. Sixty-five minutes in, Hitchcock lets the killer's repeated declaration, "You're my type of woman," indicate what is about to occur behind closed doors. The camera then slowly retreats down the stairs, to the sidewalk, and across the street, building suspense and sadness for a full minute. Later, a thrilling hunt for evidence in the back of a moving truck is punctuated with Hitchcock's morbid humor. Entertaining stuff, that. *Frenzy* isn't a masterpiece, but good Hitchcock is better than no Hitchcock at all.

ADDED ATTRACTION: Go Direct Yourself, Part One

As with other Alfred Hitchcock movies, *Frenzy* includes a brief appearance by Hitchcock himself (see below). Here are 1970–1972 movies in which directors gave themselves cameos. We're not including leading roles, like when Woody Allen starred in his own movies. For director cameos in 1973–1974 movies, see the entry for *Charley Varrick* (1973).

- *Boxcar Bertha* (1972): Seventy-three minutes into the movie, director Martin Scorsese is in a whorehouse asking if he can spend the night.
- *A Clockwork Orange* (1971): Many viewers claim that the bearded man standing in the record shop as Alex walks by is director Stanley Kubrick.
- *Drive, He Said* (1971): Bearded director Jack Nicholson is seen twice in the induction center.
- *Frenzy* (1972): Wearing a bowler hat, Alfred Hitchcock stands by the river in two different shots within the movie's first three minutes.
- *Harold and Maude* (1971): Seventy-six minutes into the movie, director Hal Ashby is the bearded man briefly standing between the two leads as they all watch the model trains inside the arcade at the Santa Cruz Beach Boardwalk.
- *The Landlord* (1970): In the five-second opening shot of a wedding, director Hal Ashby is the white-suited groom.
- *The Life and Times of Judge Roy Bean* (1972): Director John Huston briefly appears as fur-covered Grizzly Adams.
- *Minnie and Moskowitz* (1971): Director John Cassavetes has a small role as Minnie's violent lover.
- *Shaft* (1971): Director Gordon Parks is briefly seen as the Harlem landlord twenty-seven minutes into the movie.
- *Watermelon Man* (1970): Director Melvin Van Peebles is wearing a hat and a smock as the painter lettering the insurance-office door.

Napoleon and Samantha

Released: July 1972
Director: Bernard McEveety
Stars: Johnny Whitaker, Jodie Foster, Michael Douglas
Academy Awards: One nomination (Best Music)

PREVIEW: Two kids and a lion have adventures as they search for their friend in the mountains.

NOW SHOWING: Lion Around

A high school nerd hopes to take a sexy cheerleader to the prom in this hilarious sequel to *Napoleon Dynamite* (2004) … oops, wrong story. *Napoleon and Samantha* (1972) is a charming Disney adventure about two kids and a lion. For director Bernard McEveety, it's the first (and best) of three outdoor adventures that will continue with *One Little Indian* (1973) and *The Bears and I* (1974). Additionally, *Napoleon and Samantha* was written by Stewart Raffill, writer and director of another outdoor hit, *Adventures of the Wilderness Family* (1975).

Michael Douglas, soon to star in TV's *The Streets of San Francisco*, is on hand for thirty-five minutes, but it's the kids who make *Napoleon and Samantha* successful. This is Jodie Foster's first movie *ever*, following dozens of TV appearances. She was only nine years old when *Napoleon and Samantha* came out, and co-star Johnny Whitaker was twelve. Much of the movie is left to them, yet they pull it off.

Napoleon (Whitaker) and Samantha (Foster) are two mischievous friends in an Oregon town. Somehow Napoleon inherits Major, "an old milk-drinking lion," as a big, slow pet. Realizing they need to relocate, Napoleon launches off to find Danny (Michael Douglas), a charismatic loner who's got a cabin somewhere in the picturesque mountains. Samantha tags along and proves to be a plucky companion. Unfortunately, not only have they left without any food and only a vague sense of where they're going, the rugged terrain confronts them with a precarious slip off a cliff, a cougar attack, and a scary bear.

That may sound like a lot of action, but the movie is leisurely paced. Until, that is, the kids reach Danny's cabin, where the story speeds up and turns dark. Leaving a creepy guy to babysit, Danny goes into town to find Samantha's parents (the kids are out of the movie until the final scenes). Quickly Danny's arrested, and the creepy guy is revealed to be an escaped mental patient who's a "psycho" and a "lulu." Danny busts out of the police station and steals a motorcycle (Douglas looks like he's actually riding) with police cars and a chopper in pursuit. Napoleon and Samantha reappear for the requisite happy ending that sends everyone, even Major, to appropriate destinations. Danny delivereth the lesson: "Nobody can make it alone. We all need people to help us." Nice message, nice movie.

ADDED ATTRACTION: Jaws and Claws

"Sure is a nice lion," says Samantha when she first meets Major. She seems to be right: both kids, and even a live chicken, happily ride him. However, Jodie Foster later told a different story about this movie in the special features of the *Freaky Friday* DVD: "I was mauled by a lion. He picked me up by my hip after shooting, and he turned me around and shook me a whole bunch of times. I saw the whole world shake a lot in a horizontal position. As I was watching everybody run away from me, one of the trainers said, 'Drop it," and the lion ... just dropped me out of its mouth, and I went rolling down the hill. ... The lion came running after me and gave me a big swat on my behind and stopped me from going over a cliff. ... I still have a few scars to prove it."

Butterflies Are Free

Released: July 1972

Director: Milton Katselas

Stars: Goldie Hawn, Edward Albert, Eileen Heckart

Academy Awards: One win (Best Supporting Actress—Eileen Heckart), plus two more nominations (Best Cinematography; Best Sound)

PREVIEW: A domineering mother disapproves of her blind son's love for a free-spirited girl.

NOW SHOWING: Love Is Blind, Part One

In the 1960s and '70s, blind characters were usually put in dramatic or scary situations, as with *A Patch of Blue* (1965), *Wait Until Dark* (1967), *See No Evil* (1971), and *Ice Castles* (1978). *Butterflies Are Free* (1972) is distinctive in that a character's blindness propels a nice romantic comedy. Two attractive young singles—blind soft-rock guitarist Don (Edward Albert) and quirky wannabe-actress Jill (Goldie Hawn)—meet when she moves in next door. The movie's first fifty-two minutes are casually entertaining: the kids banter easily, discuss his blindness, and seem like two charming modern youths (she's nineteen, he's close). As per the free-lovin' era, she invites him to bed long before they discuss any shared romantic feelings.

Paradise found is quickly lost when Don's disapproving mother (Eileen Heckart) unexpectedly arrives. She tangles with both kids together, and with each separately, hoping to bring her son home. While the movie's tone suddenly gets more serious, the sarcasm still generates some mild amusement. Things really get grim when Jill shockingly announces that she's leaving for another guy. The last twenty minutes with an emotional break-up and make-up are virtually humorless.

Butterflies Are Free is based on a hit Broadway play that was set in New York, but the movie's city is San Francisco, with all the hippie beads and funky fashions that this ultra-groovy location implies. Hawn is adorable, playfully parading around in her underwear and constantly eating. Like Hawn's characters on TV's *Laugh-In*, Jill is a little nutty, and she spends eight minutes with Don before she realizes that he's blind, something the audience perceives almost immediately. Then when she recites her memorized "favorite quotation," she gets it wrong (she attributes a line containing "butterflies are free" to Mark Twain, but it's actually Dickens, and she admits she's never read either author).

Albert, in his movie debut, is sensitive and convincing. Heckart is so good as a woman who's both commanding and sympathetic that she won an Oscar (her confrontations with Jill are especially impressive). Not a lot happens in this occasionally clichéd chatfest that has few characters and basically one set, but the warm sentiments glow like a hand-dipped scented candle.

Edward Albert and Goldie Hawn.

ADDED ATTRACTION: Love Is Blind, Part Two

Vision problems are central to another New York-based comedy released in the summer of 1972. Based on James Thurber's work, *The War Between Men and Women* is a mildly amusing romantic comedy that matches a grouchy cartoonist (Jack Lemmon), author of an "anti-child, anti-dog, anti-female" book that has the movie's title, with a lovely divorcée (Barbara Harris), who of course has children and a dog. After literally bumping into each other in an ophthalmologist's office, they overcome his cynicism, get married, and then deal with her aggressive ex-husband, the problematic children, a sudden operation, and a melodramatic death. The worsening eyesight of Lemmon's character is used for comical mishaps until the more serious last act, when he's virtually blind. Both leads are strong (especially the always-appealing Harris, despite her unwieldy coiffure), the kids are actually effective actors, and Dr. Joyce Brothers gets a line at a party. Some unusual touches add flair: at times the cartoonist directly addresses the audience, Thurber-style drawings occasionally come to life, and near the end characters walk into a four-minute cartoon.

Now You See Him, Now You Don't

Released: July 1972

Director: Robert Butler

Stars: Kurt Russell, Joe Flynn, Cesar Romero

Academy Awards: None

PREVIEW: A student invents an invisibility spray and uses it to save his college from crooks.

NOW SHOWING: The Invisible Kid

The team from *The Computer Wore Tennis Shoes* (1969), including the director, screenwriter, stars, and many supporting players, reunited three years later for another lightweight sci-fi romp. Not only does *Now You See Him, Now You Don't* (1972) successfully use the same characters and settings from that earlier hit, it even makes reference to the previous movie when the jail-bound crook A.J. Arno (Cesar Romero) turns up, now somehow free; "that was a mistake" is his brief explanation, and the plot is underway.

Arno returns as the new mortgage-holder on Medfield College, ready to foreclose and transform the entire campus into Arno Town with a giant casino and a dog track. Meanwhile, Medfield student Dexter (Kurt Russell) inadvertently invents an invisibility spray, thanks to a stray bolt of lightning that electrifies his chemistry experiment. Dexter and a pal spray themselves invisible and sneak into Arno's offices to uncover his nefarious scheme. However, Arno learns of the spray and steals it so he can commit the perfect crime: invisible robbers sauntering out of a bank with invisible money and escaping in an invisible car. After a wacky thirteen-minute chase that has cops crashing around in confusion, everything resolves when the crooks accidentally plunge into a swimming pool, washing off the spray and returning them to easy-to-apprehend visibility.

Russell, the charismatic, confident leader of a group of "crazy kids," continually reinvents new plans and urges everyone on with "let's go!" It's nice seeing him still in his innocent Disney phase, sporting around in a nifty dune buggy and wearing colorful collegiate clothes; a year later he'd be in two more Disney comedies, the lightly regarded *Charley and the Angel* and *Superdad*, but before long he'd be starring as the violent Snake in *Escape from New York* (1981).

Throughout *Now You See Him*, the invisibility effects are top-notch (for the era), the sight gags are funny, and the mesmerizing round of golf involving two actual golfers (Billy Casper and Dave Hill) and an invisible Russell is a riot. The movie doesn't have the wit or the clever subtext of *The Barefoot Executive* (1971), the previous collaboration between director Robert Butler and Russell, but both movies have the entertaining Joe Flynn, here playing the exasperated dean. This movie also has some fascinating costumes, especially men in the wildly patterned pants that were a mercifully short fashion trend. Now you see them, now you don't.

ADDED ATTRACTION: School Daze

In *Now You See Him*, Dexter attends fictional Medfield College (the movie's buildings are actually located at the Disney studio in Burbank). Medfield first appeared in *The Absent-Minded Professor* (1961) and was used again in *The Strongest Man in the World* (1975). Here are thirteen other fictional schools shown in '70s movies.

- Bates High School: *Carrie* (1976)
- Cadwallader University: *Fast Break* (1979)
- Central High School: *Massacre at Central High* (1976)
- Dewey High School: *American Graffiti* (1973)
- Faber College: *Animal House* (1978)
- Freedom School: *Billy Jack* (1971)
- Haddonfield High School: *Halloween* (1978)

- Harper Valley High School: *Harper Valley P.T.A.* (1978)
- The Marion Hadley School: *No Deposit No Return* (1976)
- Merrivale College: *The World's Greatest Athlete* (1973)
- Puckerbush Union High School: *Eat My Dust!* (1976)
- Rydell High School: *Grease* (1978)
- Vince Lombardi High School: *Rock 'n' Roll High School* (1979)

Fat City

Released: July 1972
Director: John Huston
Stars: Stacy Keach, Jeff Bridges, Susan Tyrrell
Academy Awards: One nomination (Best Supporting Actress—Susan Tyrrell)

PREVIEW: A young fighter and his older mentor struggle to find success in the ring and in life.

NOW SHOWING: The Other Side of *Rocky*

Whereas *Rocky* (1976) spotlights an unknown but heroic boxer who eventually rises up to boxing's big-leagues, *Fat City* (1972) is John Huston's dark, depressing character study of unknown, unheroic pugs who never overcome their sad, dilapidated lives. *Rocky* is a rousing look at boxing, and it makes audiences cheer at the end; *Fat City* is grim and discouraging, and movie audiences are probably sitting in numbed silence after the last pathetic scene.

As despairing as it is, *Fat City* was generally praised upon its release, and its stature has only grown over the decades. It's also notable as one of the first starring roles for future Oscar-winner Jeff Bridges, who was just coming off an Oscar-nominated supporting role in *The Last Picture Show* (1971). *Fat City* is also the movie in which Candy Clark makes her big-screen debut, playing the girlfriend (later the wife) of Bridges' character (a year later she'll be a memorable part of the ensemble cast of a Best Picture nominee, *American Graffiti*). Fans of TV's *Cheers* will recognize Nicholas Colasanto as a boxing manager, and fans of boxing will recognize the names of several former champs in the cast.

This bleak movie doesn't give the audience much to cheer for. Living in the ugliest parts of Stockton, California, everyone in *Fat City* seems to hang out in shabby bars and stay in flea-bag rooms. An older boxer (Stacy Keach) mentors a young up-and-comer (Jeff Bridges), but neither emerges as a very admirable man. There's a six-minute boxing match near the end when Keach's character wins his big comeback bout, but the fight is so brutal and punishing that he doesn't even know he won.

It seems impossible, but the old boxer's life actually gets *worse* after his victory. Somehow he loses his girl, played by the Oscar-nominated scene-stealer Susan Tyrrell, and his life "makes a beeline for the drain." He winds up a hopeless drunken bum who has nothing to say to his younger friend when they eat together in a cheap diner in the final scene. All he has are vague recollections of some small past glories. It's a dismal sight but a memorable finish to a tough movie that is light-years from Huston's early classics like the fast-talking *The Maltese Falcon* (1941) and the romantic adventure *The African Queen* (1951). A revealing and realistic look at life's losers, *Fat City* packs a powerful punch.

ADDED ATTRACTION: Fat City Flying

Fat City is one of the decade's movies with a mysterious title. The words "fat city" are never mentioned by any character or explained in the movie in any way. "Fat city" is a slang term, probably from the 1950s or 1960s, that means "prosperity" or "a good situation." A different 1970s movie helps clarify the meaning. Forty-two minutes into *Skyjacked* (1972), a smiling, confident air-traffic controller uses the term to calm down an anxious airline pilot who is flying his jet at night through a howling storm: "No sweat, sir, you're in fat city." Another movie from this era with a mysterious title is *A Clockwork Orange* (1971), which incorporates that color without ever using the actual words; however, they're included in Anthony Burgess' 1962 novel when Alex reads from a book with that "fair gloopy title" and later refers to it several times.

Deliverance

(One of 1972's five **FAR-OUT** movies)

Released: July 1972

Director: John Boorman

Stars: Jon Voight, Burt Reynolds, Ned Beatty

Academy Awards: Three nominations (Best Picture; Best Director; Best Editing)

PREVIEW: Friends take a canoe trip into the backcountry and find life-threatening dangers.

FINE LINE: "Sometimes you have to lose yourself before you can find anything." (Lewis, giving Ed his first look at the river.)

CLOSE-UP: The song in the energetic four-minute banjo scene is called "Duelling Banjos," though only the boy plays a banjo (Drew plays guitar). All the characters enjoy the moment, and one local even improvises a playful jig. Significantly, the scene shows how out-of-place the city slickers are. Drew can't keep up, and once the song concludes he offers his hand to the boy, who refuses to shake it. Bobby's condescending response is to "give him a coupla bucks."

NOW SHOWING: "You Don't Beat This River"

In the early 1970s, several important developments spurred the ecology movement in America. Among these were the first Earth Day, the Clear Air Act, and the formation of the Environmental Protection Agency in 1970; the creation of Greenpeace in 1971; the Clean Water Act, and even John Denver's hit song "Rocky Mountain High," in 1972. With the environment a major national concern, in 1972 Hollywood responded with a run of nature-themed movies in various genres, including westerns (*Jeremiah Johnson*), horror (*Frogs*), and science-fiction (*Silent Running*). But the best nature-themed movie of the year—perhaps of the decade—was *Deliverance* (1972).

An Oscar nominee for Best Picture, this gripping, well-crafted thriller still packs a powerful wallop. Nature is beautiful and worth exploring with respect, *Deliverance* tells us, but it's also unpredictable and hostile. As the movie transitions from a happy-go-lucky weekend getaway into a terrifying fight for survival, we realize that in a man-vs.-nature confrontation the best anyone can hope for is a tie.

Deliverance opens with five seconds of laughter as four guys yak about a casual Friday-Sunday canoe trip. They're heading into a "vanishing wilderness" with vague plans to cruise the last "wild, untamed, unpolluted" major river in Georgia before it's dammed up into a huge lake. Of the four guys, only one, Lewis (Burt Reynolds, in one of his signature roles), has any river experience. Muscular and macho, wearing a conspicuous "Survival" patch on his jacket, Lewis arrogantly brags, "I don't believe in insurance, there's no risk." Meanwhile, total novices Ed (Jon Voight), Bobby (Ned Beatty), and Drew (Ronny Cox) share nervous laughter as they cautiously negotiate rippling water that they mistakenly think qualifies as rapids. They'll soon learn what rapids are.

Early on, there are some edgy signs that trouble lurks ahead. The guys say things like "those woods are real deep," "the river's inaccessible," and "no one can find us up here." An old-timer tells Bobby, "You don't know nuthin'," another local warns them about the trip, and even Lewis concedes, "You don't beat this river." Ed gets spooked and suggests they "go back to town and play golf," but Lewis won't retreat from a challenge.

Saturday starts out bucolic and calm, with quiet music accompanying peaceful scenes along the river. Then, a third of the way into the movie, two gun-toting hillbillies arrive, and everything changes. In an infamous scene, one of them savagely rapes Bobby. Lewis slays Bobby's attacker with a bow and arrow, and Ed chases off the second hillbilly.

This nine-minute sequence is shocking and unforgettable. But it's the next seven minutes that are truly fascinating. With the dead victim of the "center shot" propped up, the four men debate their moral dilemma and the question, "What we gonna do with him?" Drew wants to turn the body in because, he shouts, "it is a matter of the law!" "What law!? Where's the law," argues Lewis, defiantly. He and the others contemplate a possible "murder trial" and a "trial by jury" with the dead man's "mama and his daddy sittin' in the jury box." With their passionate beliefs intensifying into face-to-face shouting matches, eventually they decide to sink the corpse deep in the river.

The next harrowing half-hour is filled with dramatic adventure. The escaped hillbilly shoots and kills Drew in an exciting four-minute career down churning white water that leaves the canoes capsized and Lewis with a hideously broken leg. A suspenseful twelve-minute sequence sends Ed up a sheer cliff so he can kill the hillbilly who's hunting them; Ed somehow manages to run himself through with an arrow in the process, but this mild-mannered suburban businessman finds an inner strength he didn't know he had. Eventually the three survivors get off the river, concoct lies to explain Drew's death and to cover their actions, and run into an inquisitive sheriff (James Dickey, the author of the 1970 novel) who starts exposing contradictions in their clumsy story.

All viewers seem to acknowledge how effective the stars and the rustic supporting players are. The scenery looks exquisite, and the action sequences are believable because in many cases the actors are doing their own stunts. However, some viewers register legitimate complaints about the movie. The sordid rape scene, for instance, is so over-the-top that it does seem extreme—we would understand that the hillbillies are demented and deadly without having to witness what happens to Bobby.

It's also possible to call the last fifteen minutes anti-climactic, since visceral action fades into subdued talk. But this ending reinforces one of the movie's themes. Survival in wild nature requires the canoers to kill two men and push themselves to their physical limits, but the safe return to their civilized lives requires cover-ups (disposal of their murder weapon and three corpses, one of them their friend), conspiracy, and equivocation. Nature, civilization—the two worlds are incompatible and require different skills. As if to remind us of the horror that's gone before, one last startling scene at the very end yanks Ed from the security of his own bed. His physical wounds will heal, but the psychological scars may not, and the movie that started with laughter ends, appropriately enough, with a chilling nightmare.

Jon Voight.

ADDED ATTRACTION: Dream Endings

Deliverance ends with Ed's ten-second nightmare that shows a gruesome hand rising from the dark river. Concluding a movie with a dream sequence or vision is a time-honored Hollywood technique. Earlier examples include *Wuthering Heights* (1939), where ghostly lovers walk off together, and *Seconds* (1966), which ends with a patient's blissful reverie as a cranial drill bores into his skull. Later movies with dream-sequence finales include *Titanic* (1997) and *Gladiator* (2000). As for the 1970s, here are six great movies that end with dreams or visions.

- *All That Jazz* (1979): Dying in the hospital, Joe Gideon hallucinates an eleven-minute musical number that ends with his corpse being zipped into a body bag.
- *Carnal Knowledge* (1971): With a hooker kneeling in front of him, Jonathan has a fifteen-second vision of a beautiful, unattainable ice skater.
- *Carrie* (1976): When a friend leans down to put flowers on Carrie's grave, a bloody arm suddenly reaches up from the ground, causing the friend to instantly wake up from her nightmare.
- *A Clockwork Orange* (1971): Recuperating in the hospital, Alex imagines himself romping with a naked girl in front of a politely applauding audience.
- *The Godfather: Part II* (1974): Sitting alone outside his Nevada compound, Michael thinks back to 1941 and the moment when he announced that he had joined the Marines.
- *Love and Death* (1975): Sonja has a final vision in which she converses with Boris, who has just been executed.

Super Fly

Released: August 1972
Director: Gordon Parks Jr.
Stars: Ron O'Neal, Carl Lee, Sheila Frazier
Academy Awards: None

PREVIEW: A Harlem drug pusher tries to make one last score so he can quit the business for good.

NOW SHOWING: "The American Dream"

A year after *Shaft* (1971) proved that audiences were ready for urban action movies with confident, handsome black stars, *Super Fly* (1972) lifted that concept to bigger financial heights. These two successful movies have much in common: both are set on New York's grittiest street, their black heroes are tough and violent, they've got black girlfriends but also sleep with white women, both have hip soundtracks (*Super Fly*'s Curtis Mayfield even performs live in one scene), and both directors are named Gordon Parks (Parks directed *Shaft*, and his son, Parks Jr., directed *Super Fly*).

The biggest difference between the two movies is their hero's profession. John Shaft is a slick private detective who solves crimes; Priest (Ron O'Neal) is an outlaw drug pusher who *creates* crimes. Employing a "family" of about fifty dealers, Priest makes a fortune and leads a glitzy life that includes a gigantic Cadillac, flashy suits with breathtaking lapels, maxi-coats, fedoras, and all the coke he can snort. Priest, we're told, is living "the American dream." Nevertheless, he wants out, "before I have to kill somebody," he says, "before somebody ices me." He just needs one last million-dollar deal, "the big one," to "be free." Other characters try to talk him out of quitting because he's so good at this job, and the options are limited: "I know it's a rotten game," he's advised, "it's the only one the Man left us to play." As Priest starts to execute his plan, his allies turn against him, forcing Priest to improvise his final getaway.

As expected, the cops are white, harsh, and corrupt, but interestingly Priest himself isn't very sympathetic. His defiant determination is admirable, but we don't feel sorry for him or laugh with him, he doesn't support the black militants who approach him, and he doesn't make any anti-drug speeches. Since the movie doesn't moralize or advocate for anything, many viewers back then felt it perpetuated black stereotypes and glamorized the drug lifestyle, but they forgot that Priest is trying desperately to leave that world.

What the movie is actually doing is preserving a convincing sociological record of a raw, rough subculture. Not helping this cause are extended scenes that feel like padding, the chaotic handheld camera, and the ludicrous slow-motion brawl at the end where Priest vanquishes four cops simultaneously. Even so, there's enough realism and relevance to make *Super Fly* an important, super-cool diversion.

ADDED ATTRACTION: Not-So-Super Sequels

Both *Shaft* and *Super Fly* generated immediate sequels, but *Super Fly T.N.T.* (1973), with Ron O'Neal now directing as well as starring, with his character Priest living in Italy, and with Curtis Mayfield absent, was so unsatisfying that the series temporarily stalled. *The Return of Superfly* (1990) tried to revive the series with Nathan Purdee as Priest and with new music from Mayfield, but the movie disappeared quickly. In the twenty-first century, both original titles were re-used for new movies. *Shaft* (2000 and 2019) continues the saga with Samuel L. Jackson first playing the nephew, and then the son, of John Shaft (the original Shaft, Richard Roundtree, is in both movies). The one-word *Superfly* (2018) remakes the 1972 movie with Trevor Jackson as the drug-dealing Priest. The relative merits of the original *Shaft* and *Super Fly* (plus other blaxploitation movies of the '70s) are briefly debated in Spike Lee's *BlacKkKlansman* (2018).

Everything You Always Wanted to Know About Sex * But Were Afraid to Ask

Released: August 1972
Director: Woody Allen
Stars: Woody Allen, Gene Wilder, Louise Lasser
Academy Awards: None

PREVIEW: Seven short films, four starring Woody Allen, that answer sex-related questions.

NOW SHOWING: Too Much Information

After *Bananas* (1971), the work of an exuberant still-learning beginner, Woody Allen created an anthology movie that enabled him to experiment with different styles and genres. *Everything You Always Wanted to Know About Sex * But Were Afraid to Ask* (1972) is uneven as far as delivering laughs, but it's generally enjoyable and is an interesting career development.

Allen's first R-rated movie, *Everything* was inspired by Dr. David Reubens' 1969 sex manual. But besides the title and format, there's little similarity between the two (Reubens himself didn't like the movie). Allen uses seven questions—"Do aphrodisiacs work?" "Are transvestites homosexuals?" etc.—as springboards for cinematic flights that soar to varying altitudes. The funniest four are those he's actually in. For the opening segment, he's a medieval court fool who acquires an aphrodisiac so he can seduce the queen (Lynn Redgrave); he urges haste because "soon it will be the Renaissance and we'll all be painting." Later he and ex-wife Louise Lasser speak Italian in a terrific send-up of hip Italian movies. The excellent final segments parody old horror movies (Allen visits a mad scientist's laboratory, scene of bizarre sexual experiments) and modern science-fiction movies (Allen plays a sperm to show what happens inside the human body during sex).

The Allen-less segments are inconsistent. In the best one, Gene Wilder plays a married Manhattan doctor who falls for a sheep and takes her for romantic trysts. A weak segment with Lou Jacobi prancing around as a transvestite goes on too long for its slim joke, but worse is the tasteless "What's My Perversion?" segment, which is shot to resemble an old black-and-white TV game show. A dark sequence that Allen worked on for weeks—he as a spider trying not to be killed by Lasser, a big black widow—was cut from the final movie.

In the early 1970s, Woody Allen's directorial skills improved dramatically from movie to movie, aiming him toward his breakthrough masterpiece, *Annie Hall* (1977). *Everything* continues that advance and shows him working to achieve his signature style; indeed, it's his first movie to start and end with an old song (Cole Porter's "Let's

Gene Wilder.

Misbehave") over the credits, and it even has a line ("more fun than laughing") that will transfer into *Annie Hall*, where it will be rephrased as "the most fun I've ever had without laughing." *Everything* was a smash hit, and for Allen another step forward.

ADDED ATTRACTION: Unusual Movie Titles

*Everything You Always Wanted to Know About Sex * But Were Afraid to Ask* has the longest title in Woody Allen's oeuvre. Here are other unique titles of alphabetically listed movies from the early 1970s, with some of their stars listed.

- *$* (1971): Warren Beatty, Goldie Hawn
- *Gas-s-s-s* (1970): Bob Corff, Elaine Giftos
- *M*A*S*H* (1970): Donald Sutherland, Elliott Gould
- *McQ* (1974): John Wayne, Eddie Albert
- *R.P.M.* (1970): Anthony Quinn, Ann-Margret
- *Sssssss* (1973): Strother Martin, Dirk Benedict
- *Sweet Sweetback's Baadasssss Song* (1971): Melvin Van Peebles, Simon Chuckster
- *THX 1138* (1971): Robert Duvall, Maggie McOmie
- *...tick...tick...tick...* (1970): James Brown, George Kennedy
- *Tora! Tora! Tora!* (1970): Martin Balsam, Jason Robards
- *W* (1974): Twiggy, Michael Witney
- *WUSA* (1970): Paul Newman, Joanne Woodward
- *X, Y and Zee* (1972): Elizabeth Taylor, Michael Caine
- *ZPG* (1972): Oliver Reed, Geraldine Chaplin

The Last House on the Left

Released: August 1972
Director: Wes Craven
Stars: Sandra Peabody, Lucy Grantham, David Hess
Academy Awards: None

PREVIEW: Four thugs drive two teenage girls to the woods and proceed to torture and kill them.

NOW SHOWING: "It's Only a Movie ... Only a Movie"

Slasher movies got jump-started in the 1970s by *The Last House on the Left* (1972). To name a few connections with later '70s horror movies: there's opening "true story" text, as in *The Texas Chain Saw Massacre* (1974); teenage girls get violently killed, like in *Halloween* (1978); bloody revenge scenes presage *I Spit on Your Grave* (1978). The minimal budget, no-name cast, rejection by disgusted critics, and embrace by enthusiastic fans also became slasher hallmarks.

Surprisingly, the movie isn't as graphic as the "it's only a movie" promo suggests. Depravity is mostly implied, not shown, the sickest sight being a glimpse of a victim's entrails. The movie starts with jokey banter and nature shots, but soon four psychos kidnap two teenage girls and humiliate, rape, and murder them, all with thirty-five minutes still to go. In the last act, parents mercilessly avenge their daughters' deaths, showing that everyone is capable of bloodlust. Attempts at humor (e.g., hapless police) and incongruously bouncy music don't alleviate the atrocities. Nearly everything in director Wes Craven's first movie is amateurish and ugly, but *Last House* has a vitality that makes it both hard to watch and hard to look away. Oh yeah, it ends with a chainsaw.

The decade's most famous chainsaw, of course, rips through *The Texas Chain Saw Massacre* (1974), a scarier and more stylish movie than *Last House*. Working with a micro-budget, unknown actors, and a simple plot, director Tobe Hooper skillfully marshals effective settings, sounds, and camerawork to create a dark, nightmarish world of savage anarchy. After some creepy images, radio reports, and encounters, five young people arrive at a decrepit house that "looks like the birthplace of Bela Lugosi." From here on, unrelenting suspense, punctuated by sudden shocking violence, dominates the movie as Leatherface (Gunnar Hansen), a grunting, demented assailant with a necktie, a crude mask, and bad teeth, periodically leaps out with a sledgehammer and a chainsaw. The final forty minutes of primal terror begin with his frenzied pursuit of the last survivor, an epic screamer with photogenic eyeballs (Marilyn Burns). To her horror, a temporary sanctuary only worsens her situation and intensifies the sadistic cruelty. As with *Last House*, *Chain Saw Massacre* suggests more gore than it shows, but it was still briefly rated X and banned from some theaters. Decades of prequels, sequels, remakes, and copycats have ensured its place as an influential horror classic.

ADDED ATTRACTION: The Slashin' '70s

The Last House on the Left and *The Texas Chain Saw Massacre* are two examples of American slasher (or "splatter") films. Typically these violent, low-budget horror movies show graphic gore produced by various implements (knives, hammers, hooks) and machines (engine propellers, power drills, chainsaws), usually against young people. A dozen chronological examples (with their stars) follow.

- *The Wizard of Gore* (1970): Ray Sager
- *Blood and Lace* (1971): Gloria Grahame
- *Scream Bloody Murder* (1973): Fred Holbert
- *Black Christmas* (1974): Olivia Hussey
- *Alice, Sweet Alice* (1976): Linda Miller
- *The Town That Dreaded Sundown* (1976): Ben Johnson
- *The Hills Have Eyes* (1977): Suze Lanier-Bramlett
- *The Toolbox Murders* (1978): Cameron Mitchell
- *The Redeemer: Son of Satan* (1978): Damien Knight
- *Halloween* (1978): Jamie Lee Curtis
- *I Spit on Your Grave* (1978): Camille Keaton
- *Tourist Trap* (1979): Chuck Connors

Sounder

(One of 1972's five **FAR-OUT** movies)

Released: September 1972

Director: Martin Ritt

Stars: Cicely Tyson, Paul Winfield, Kevin Hooks

Academy Awards: Four nominations (Best Picture; Best Actress—Cicely Tyson; Best Actor—Paul Winfield; Best Writing)

PREVIEW: In 1933, a black sharecropping family faces hardships when the father goes to jail.

FINE LINE: "You lose some of the time what you always go after, but you lose *all* the time what you don't go after." (Young David Lee, reciting his father's oft-said words early in the movie.)

CLOSE-UP: Seventy-three minutes into the movie, young David walks into the house of the kindly teacher. She hands him two volumes about Harriet Tubman and Crispus Attucks from her bookcase, and then she reads an inspiring passage about education from W.E.B. Du Bois's *The Souls of Black Folk*. It's a moving scene, for David and the audience; the next time he's here, he asks if he can "study school with the other children."

NOW SHOWING: "Like Good Air to Breathe"

What's nice about movies set in the past is that they usually don't date the way movies set in the present sometimes do, if only because the fashions, music, and attitudes of contemporary films can quickly go out of style. Consider 1970s movies about 1970s black characters—*Super Fly* (1972), for instance—that look embarrassingly cartoony now. In contrast, *Sounder* (1972), a beautiful, unpretentious movie about a black family in the 1930s, is as emotional and impressive today as it ever was.

In some ways, *Sounder* must be considered an extremely influential movie. It's not a blaxploitation knockoff filled with gratuitous violence, outrageous characters, and funky music, which back then seemed to be requirements for any movie aimed at black audiences. Instead, *Sounder* is classy and intelligent. It was directed by Martin Ritt, who had already been nominated for an Oscar (1963's *Hud*), and it would earn four Oscar nominations, including one for Best Picture and, for the first time ever, two for black performers (Paul Winfield, Cicely Tyson) as Best Actor and Best Actress. *Sounder* proved that a sensitive, well-made drama about black characters could succeed.

Ritt was a director with issues on his mind, as evidenced by two of his other 1970s movies, *The Molly Maguires* (1970) and *Norma Rae* (1979), both of which used appalling work-place conditions as catalysts for powerful social commentary. In *Sounder*, Ritt goes to authentic southern locations to tell a deliberate, low-key story about a poor black family struggling during the Great Depression. There's not much action, nor are there any complicated, unexpected twists. Ritt keeps everything simple to make the movie understandable and affecting to viewers of all ages (unsurprisingly, *Sounder* has been shown in schools for decades).

Though *Sounder* is named after the family's hound dog, the story is really about the teenage boy, David (Kevin Hooks). He speaks the movie's first line, raises his younger siblings, searches for his father, and ultimately embarks on a new life in a new school (the movie makes it clear how vital education is). Early on, David's sharecropping family is devastated when the father, Nathan (Paul Winfield), is arrested for doing "what he had to do," stealing "some food and stuff" for his hungry kids. As Nathan is being taken away, Sounder is shot and wounded, and he runs off into the woods to heal himself. The mother, Rebecca (Cicely Tyson), tries to stay optimistic, but Nathan is sentenced to a year of hard labor. David and his family struggle to run the farm without him, and the only good news is the return of Sounder.

Midway through the movie, David and Sounder journey on foot to find his father. They sleep under bridges, endure heavy rains, and cross several counties, only to get no help once they reach the prison camp. During his trip, though, David meets a kindly teacher who offers him a chance to return to her schoolhouse as a full-time student. The conflict between his family's needs and David's school opportunity fills the last act.

The movie has three major reunions. Sounder's return is fairly subdued, and David's return after his journey is joyous but frustrating, since he was never able to contact his father. But when Nathan finally limps home, there's not a dry eye in the family (or in the theater). He emerges in the distance like Ashley returning from the war in *Gone with the Wind* (1939), a tiny, injured figure overwhelmed by the world around him. Wounded though Nathan is, he's not beaten, and this proud, dignified man knows what's best for his son: "School is something you need, something that's good for you, like good air to breathe." Near the end Nathan tells David, "I want you to beat the life they got all laid out for you in this place 'cause there ain't nothin' here." David does indeed leave, but the movie's last shot puts the family back together, arm in arm.

That Sounder is barely in the last third of the movie, and isn't in the final freeze frame of the family, raises questions about the title. The dog's resilience is symbolic of the family's determination, but possibly there's a different meaning intended. A sounder is someone who makes a noise—is that David, heading to school where his voice will be heard? A sounder is also something that gauges the depth of water— Nathan, perhaps, revealing the depths of southern racism by his desperate actions.

There are indeed racist attitudes in the movie, but thankfully there's no ugly racist language or raw violence. Director's Ritt's presentation of black life seems like a Disney version of what was probably happening in rural Louisiana back then (Disney actually remade this story in 2003, with Winfield as the teacher and Hooks as the director). Instead, Ritt keeps quietly focused on the warm feelings and the hope and strength everyone needs to endure hardships. Also, by keeping Nathan and Sounder alive, he softens the sad ending of the book that the movie is based on. Lovely cinematography captures the fields and forest in all their beauty, and Taj Mahal's light blues music evokes the times and the situations (Mahal plays a family friend in the movie). Something of a landmark, *Sounder* is something of a perfect family film.

ADDED ATTRACTION: Black, But Not Blaxploitation

Though there had been previous movies primarily about black characters—notably *A Raisin in the Sun* (1961)—in the early 1970s blaxploitation movies like *Shaft* (1971) and *Blacula* (1972) were being aimed at black audiences. But when *Sounder* became successful, the tone of black-oriented movies started to shift toward a wider range of dramas and comedies with mainstream stars, as shown by these ten chronologically listed 1970s titles (stars noted).

- *Lady Sings the Blues* (1972): Diana Ross
- *Claudine* (1974): Diahann Carroll
- *Uptown Saturday Night* (1974): Sidney Poitier
- *Cooley High* (1975): Glynn Turman
- *Let's Do It Again* (1975): Sidney Poitier
- *Sparkle* (1976): Irene Cara
- *The Bingo Long Traveling All-Stars & Motor Kings* (1976): Billy Dee Williams
- *Norman ... Is That You?* (1976): Redd Foxx
- *A Piece of the Action* (1977): Bill Cosby
- *The Wiz* (1978): Diana Ross

Lady Sings the Blues

Released: October 1972

Director: Sidney J. Furie

Stars: Diana Ross, Billy Dee Williams, Richard Pryor

Academy Awards: Five nominations (Best Actress—Diana Ross; Best Writing; Best Art Direction; Best Costume Design; Best Music)

PREVIEW: The troubled and tragic life of the self-destructive music legend Billie Holiday.

NOW SHOWING: Supreme Music

It's unfair to complain, as some have, that in *Lady Sings the Blues* (1972) pop super-star Diana Ross doesn't sound like jazz legend Billie Holiday. Nobody does. Do those same critics reject George C. Scott in *Patton* (1970) because his growl doesn't match Patton's high, thin voice? Or Peter O'Toole in *Man of La Mancha* (1972) because he gives Cervantes an English accent? Some viewers also denigrate the way *Lady* distorts Holiday's turbulent life (the movie omits major collaborators and gives her just one husband instead of three); note, however, that *Amadeus* (1984) won Oscars while taking liberties with Mozart's biography. All these movies present dramatic interpretations, not literal impersonations, of famous people. *Lady Sings the Blues* is well-made mainstream entertainment, not hyperfactual nonfiction. If anyone insists on finding fault with this satisfying, if flawed movie, there are other areas to examine.

Diana Ross.

One is the extreme 144-minute length, which would've been longer if not for several photo montages that skip through years. The movie opens in 1936 with Holiday, a twenty-one-year-old junkie, in jail. A long flashback then shows how she got there. Raped at fourteen, she goes on to support herself as a cleaning lady, a prostitute, and a nightclub singer. On tour Holiday experiences racial tension (she sees a lynching and a Klan march) and starts using needle drugs. Eventually she becomes a mainlining addict, gets arrested, quits singing, and rallies for her triumphant Carnegie Hall concert. Two closing minutes of newspaper headlines skim through events leading to her early death.

Ross completely dominates the movie and plays every stage of Holiday's life—pigtailed teen, profane KKK foe, drowsy-eyed druggie, dazzling star in Bob Mackie's glitzy gowns—with total commitment. Daringly, she lets herself be shown appallingly deglamorized, something that didn't happen with Liza Minnelli in *Cabaret* (1972). She's well-supported by Billy Dee Williams as the loyal husband (he and Ross share genuine chemistry) and Richard Pryor as the comical piano man (he adrenalizes the movie anytime he appears).

The songs are supreme. Ross confidently knocks out excerpts from eighteen Holiday classics (the soundtrack album became a number-one hit) and gets the emotions right. Viewers may be inspired to seek out more about Holiday, but there's already plenty of music and spirit to celebrate in *Lady Sings the Blues*.

ADDED ATTRACTION: Black-and-White Movies, Part Two

These 1972-1974 movies are either in black and white or include black-and-white scenes, as *Lady Sings the Blues* does with its first two minutes of jail images. For more black-and-white movies, see the entry for *The Last Picture Show* (1971).

Black-and-White Movies

- *Lenny* (1974)
- *Paper Moon* (1973)
- *Tomorrow* (1972)
- *Young Frankenstein* (1974)

Color Movies with Short Black-and-White Segments or Photo Montages

- *Boxcar Bertha* (1972): Opening credits.
- *Dillinger* (1973): Opening credits, plus later montages.
- *Everything You Always Wanted to Know About Sex * But Were Afraid to Ask* (1972): One segment is like old black-and-white TV shows.
- *The Life and Times of Judge Roy Bean* (1972): A twentieth-century montage.
- *Pat Garrett & Billy the Kid* (1973): Color, and set in 1881, but black-and-white opening and closing scenes are in 1909.
- *Sisters* (1972): Some black-and-white documentary and hypnosis scenes.
- *Soylent Green* (1973): Opening black-and-white photos show life before 2022.

The Unholy Rollers

Released: November 1972

Director: Vernon Zimmerman

Stars: Claudia Jennings, Betty Anne Rees, Jay Varela

Academy Awards: None

PREVIEW: A harassed young woman quits her day job and becomes a rebellious roller-derby star.

NOW SHOWING: Heck on Wheels

The poster for *The Unholy Rollers* (1972) reads, "A locker room look at the toughest broads in the world." That summarizes the gritty appeal of director Vernon Zimmerman's down-and-dirty movie about the seedy world of roller derby. Manufactured on Roger Corman's high-speed production line, this non-P.C. movie is jam-packed with everything a drive-in audience could want, including ribald language, girls fighting like "mad dogs off the leash," and casual gunplay.

Fed up with the blatant sexual harassment at her factory job, Karen (former *Playboy* Playmate Claudia Jennings, in her first starring role) abruptly quits and joins the roller-derby circuit. She's beaten up by opponents, her own teammates, and her lover, but she eventually emerges as the sport's most popular and rebellious skater. As a celebrity she endorses products on TV, gets a bold tattoo, and unapologetically bashes around in a customized muscle car called "Karen's 'Lil Monster." The defiant, beautiful heroine is all attitude and sex appeal, the supporting characters are colorful and raunchy, and the scenes of derby competition are energetic and authentic, thanks to immersive hand-held tracking shots and brisk editing supervised by pre-*Mean Streets* Martin Scorsese.

In Jennings' next movie, *Group Marriage* (1973), she ditches skates for a suit, playing a gorgeous lawyer who teams with five other hip young singles in a six-way marriage because, as one of them says, "the group that plays together stays together."

Claudia Jennings.

This unconventional little comedy builds on the era's sexual revolution and includes a *Bob & Carol & Ted & Alice* (1969) moment when four people get in bed together. Contrasting the many dumb double entendres are some serious complications that arise from the unusual arrangement: angry neighbors, a pregnancy, and a new wife who decides she's "gotta be free." Jennings has the movie's most erotic scene, three other ladies with *Playboy* connections co-star, and folk-singer John Sebastian provides the amiable theme song.

For Jennings, 1974 brought two drive-in movies that helped crown her as one of the decade's B-movie queens. Jennings plays a robber and a prostitute in *Truck Stop Women* (1974), a simple-minded action movie with lots of topless scenes, several truck chases, and an unexpected bullet-riddled ending; in *'Gator Bait* (1974), she's a barefoot Cajun wildcat who gets revenge on the sleazy swamp rats who brutally killed her sister. Additional low-budget movies would follow until Jennings' tragic death at age twenty-nine in a 1979 car accident.

ADDED ATTRACTION: Roller Movies

In the 1970s, roller derby became the subject of several sports movies; roller-derby scenes even get slipped into the Disney comedy *The Shaggy D.A.* (1976). In addition, with roller skating becoming a popular fad, some non-skating movies managed to sneak in a little roller action: *Switchblade Sisters* (1975) includes a bloody shoot-out inside a roller rink, *The Buddy Holly Story* (1978) shows Holly and his band performing live in front of roller skaters, and *Promises in the Dark* (1979) lets Marsha Mason hit the rink for a couple of fun minutes. Here are six of the decade's movies that don't merely include a few skating scenes—they're dominated by roller derby or roller skating (stars are noted).

- *Derby* (1971): Documentary
- *Kansas City Bomber* (1972): Raquel Welch
- *The Unholy Rollers* (1972): Claudia Jennings
- *Rollerball* (1975): James Caan
- *Skatetown, U.S.A.* (1979): Patrick Swayze
- *Roller Boogie* (1979): Linda Blair

Sisters

Released: November 1972
Director: Brian De Palma
Stars: Margot Kidder, Jennifer Salt, Charles Durning
Academy Awards: None

PREVIEW: A woman witnesses a murder in a nearby apartment and investigates it on her own.

NOW SHOWING: "Morbid Fascination"

After *Get to Know Your Rabbit* (1972), a failed attempt at satirical comedy, director Brian De Palma rebounded strongly with *Sisters* (also 1972, but widely released in 1973). This low-budget-but-stylish thriller set De Palma on a sinister path that led to a run of violent, chilling successes.

Sisters opens with shots of a scary-looking fetus and then keeps the audience off balance with a four-minute game-show spoof called *Peeping Toms*. Next we follow "sweet," "normal" Danielle (Margot Kidder), who has a hideous hip scar from the operation that separated her from Dominique, the "truly disturbed" conjoined twin who died during surgery. Danielle, however, is schizophrenic and imagines conversations with this dead twin. Seemingly "possessed" by Dominique, Danielle brutally slays her own lover. This murder is witnessed from a neighbor's window, and when that neighbor, Grace (Jennifer Salt), can't convince skeptical policemen to believe her, she takes over the movie by investigating on her own. In a dark twist, the blood-soaked ending leaves Grace defiantly insisting she never saw any murder at all.

Most fans of Alfred Hitchcock's movies love *Sisters*, because De Palma deliberately draws on numerous Hitchcock classics. For instance, in *Sisters* nobody believes a woman's assertions about a possible crime, just like in Hitchcock's *The Lady Vanishes* (1938); people talk while they're unaware of the body hidden in the room, as in *Rope* (1948); from across the courtyard someone apparently sees a murder and later watches an accomplice search the crime scene, two situations in *Rear Window* (1954); the close-ups of Grace's eyes during hypnosis parallel the opening moments of *Vertigo* (1958); a creepy gardener, and Grace's approach to an imposing house so she can look through windows, are scenes reminiscent of *North by Northwest* (1959); a schizophrenic character "becomes" a knife-wielding dead relative, evoking *Psycho* (1960); and *Sisters'* jagged music is by Hitchcock's frequent collaborator, Bernard Herrmann.

De Palma's original touches include extra gore, five minutes of well-matched split-screen scenes, a documentary about a subject that generates "morbid fascination," and a surreal black-and-white hypnosis sequence near the end that gets terrifying once a meat cleaver appears. Eerie and effective, *Sisters* is the movie that establishes Brian De Palma as a budding master of suspense. From here he went on to a nifty horror spoof, *Phantom of the Paradise* (1974) starring William Finley (the weird ex-husband in *Sisters*), with the great *Carrie* (1976) lurking just over the horizon.

ADDED ATTRACTION: Splitting *Sisters*

Sisters makes good use of its two split-screen sequences. This storytelling technique that divides the screen into separate sections may have seemed innovative in 1972, but actually it had already been incorporated into short films dating back to the late

1800s. In the 1960s, audiences saw memorable split-screen scenes in *Grand Prix* (1966), *The Thomas Crown Affair* (1968), and *The Boston Strangler* (1968). During the '70s, the following thirteen movies all utilized split-screens at some point (*Wicked, Wicked* even tells its entire story via split-screen). Brian De Palma directed two on the list, *Carrie* and *Phantom of the Paradise*.

- *Airport* (1970)
- *The Andromeda Strain* (1971)
- *Annie Hall* (1977)
- *The Betsy* (1978)
- *Carrie* (1976)
- *Freaky Friday* (1976)
- *The Longest Yard* (1974)
- *More American Graffiti* (1979)
- *Phantom of the Paradise* (1974)
- *Sweet Sweetback's Baadasssss Song* (1971)
- *Twilight's Last Gleaming* (1977)
- *Wicked, Wicked* (1973)
- *Woodstock* (1970)

Jeremiah Johnson

Released: December 1972
Director: Sydney Pollack
Stars: Robert Redford, Will Geer, Delle Bolton
Academy Awards: None

PREVIEW: In the mid-1800s, a loner becomes a mountain man in the Rockies and faces hardships.

NOW SHOWING: Into the Wild

With a back-to-nature movement flourishing in the early 1970s, several movies placed lone men in remote wildernesses. Between the tense *Man in the Wilderness* (1971) and the family-friendly *The Life and Times of Grizzly Adams* (1974) came the best movie in this subgenre, *Jeremiah Johnson* (1972). Beautiful cinematography, haunting songs, and Robert Redford's controlled, often silent performance make it more like cinematic poetry than a western adventure.

That Redford plays a physical, rough-hewn mountain man so believably may be a surprise. Earlier that year he had been the golden-boy star of two hit movies with modern urban settings, *The Hot Rock* and *The Candidate*. In *Jeremiah Johnson* Redford goes to the mid-nineteenth century, roams the Rocky Mountains, grows a shaggy beard, and engages in violent hand-to-hand combat. He does it all with barely a hint of his big smile.

"Nobody knows where he came from," says the narrator: the mystery of Johnson's past, and the closing line that "he's up there still," suggest we're watching a legend, though Johnson's actions are rooted in facts about a real person. Disillusioned with civilization and seemingly a Mexican War veteran, Johnson arrives in Montana to live as a solitary mountain man. For the first seventy-one minutes we watch his struggles in a series of measured episodes that form the most satisfying part of the movie. Starting out as a cold, "starving pilgrim," he acquires basic tricks of the trade from another trapper, but mostly he learns survival skills the hard way. Eventually he builds a cabin, he gets a wife and child, and he finds happiness.

Everything changes in the movie's final thirty-five minutes. The story gets grim when Johnson helps some stranded settlers and returns home to find his family killed by arrows. Taking revenge by slaughtering a band of Indians, he then becomes the target of warriors who want to test themselves against him. Terrifying surprise attacks result before a peaceful détente is reached in the last scene. Throughout, Redford effectively underplays his character's emotions, even during moments of extreme grief.

If less is more as far as the movie's dialogue goes (a frustration to some viewers), more is more when it comes to the scenery. Director Sydney Pollack often presents characters as small figures in vast landscapes, emphasizing their isolation and their puny stature against the majestic mountains. Nature, not Redford, is the true star of this profound movie.

ADDED ATTRACTION: Vote for Redford

With starring roles in three good movies, 1972 was a big year for Robert Redford. Released midway between January's *The Hot Rock* and December's *Jeremiah Johnson*, *The Candidate* is a sharp political satire that showcases Redford's smiling, intelligent appeal. Wry and insightful (it won the Oscar for Best Writing), and still relevant

Robert Redford.

today, this realistic movie almost feels like an actual documentary as it goes inside the political campaign of an idealistic novice who is running for senator against a smug, old-school incumbent. In addition to the numerous real-life politicians and journalists glimpsed in the movie, at the thirty-five-minute mark Natalie Wood, playing herself, has a one-minute conversation about yogurt with the dashing young candidate.

Sleuth

Released: December 1972

Director: Joseph L. Mankiewicz

Stars: Laurence Olivier, Michael Caine

Academy Awards: Four nominations (two for Best Actor—Michael Caine, Laurence Olivier; Best Director; Best Music)

PREVIEW: Two cunning Englishmen engage in an intellectual contest to win a beautiful woman.

NOW SHOWING: The Plot Thickens

Like *Chinatown* (1974), *Sleuth* (1972) is a beautifully intricate movie you must see twice to fully understand. It's a stylish, challenging whodunit for observant adults willing to pay close attention for 138 minutes in order to experience marvelous entertainment.

While *Sleuth* is thoroughly intellectual, it also takes daring chances. Without revealing too much, the story presents two different days in and around a single setting (fortunately this particular English country estate is so fascinating—the interior resembles an amusement museum, the garden has a fabulous hedge maze—that the audience stays enthralled). Next, there are only two actors, the venerable Laurence Olivier and the younger Michael Caine, two masters at the top of their game. Yes, the opening credits list four more names, but they're all fictional to keep the story's delightful second-act twist a surprise (perceptive viewers might recognize a familiar name in those credits—Eve Channing, an Eve Harrington/Margot Channing composite taken from director Joseph L. Mankiewicz's 1950 classic, *All About Eve*). There had been earlier movies with only two actors—*Hell in the Pacific* (1968), for example—but this was the first one to bring both men, and thus the entire cast, Oscar nominations for Best Actor.

Intriguingly, half of that cast is apparently killed before the midway point. Olivier plays Andrew, a renowned mystery writer; Caine plays Milo, the handsome middle-class lover of Andrew's elegant wife. Andrew invites Milo to his magnificent home for "a little chat" that soon turns into a series of cunning deceptions and eventually becomes a suspenseful murder mystery that *ends* with a real murder. The two characters constantly engage in sharp verbal duels, batting clever words back and forth like expert tennis players. Screenwriter Anthony Shaffer, who wrote the Tony Award-winning play, has given both actors plenty to work with: they both dress up in costumes and affect accents, and the crackling dialogue is full of sly jokes, double meanings, and contemptuous put-downs. Notice some of the subtle detective-story details in the rooms, such as Agatha Christie's photo on the wall fifty-two minutes into the movie, and the Baker Street sign in the cellar.

Critics were rapturous in their praise of both the hit play and this riveting, rewarding movie. *Sleuth* was the last movie the literate, lauded Mankiewicz directed; fittingly, it is, as Andrew says in the movie about one of his own books, "an absolute corker."

ADDED ATTRACTION: Surprise Endings

Spoiler alert: here come summaries of surprise endings. Last-minute surprises have ended many movies, obviously, including *Citizen Kane* (1941) with its Rosebud reveal, *The Bad Seed* (1956) with its lightning zap, and *Planet of the Apes* (1968) with its startling statue. Like *Sleuth*, the following 1970–1974 movies have didn't-see-that-coming endings.

- *Dirty Mary Crazy Larry* (1974): Car meets train.
- *Electra Glide in Blue* (1973): Cop meets shotgun.
- *Escape from the Planet of the Apes* (1971): The ape baby survives.
- *A Gunfight* (1971): Each gunfighter is shown winning the final duel.
- *Soylent Green* (1973): "Soylent Green is people!"
- *Start the Revolution Without Me* (1970): A jump from 1789 to 1970.
- *The Taking of Pelham One Two Three* (1974): A revealing sneeze.
- *Two-Lane Blacktop* (1971): The film literally disintegrates.
- *Vanishing Point* (1971): Car meets roadblock.

Man of La Mancha

Released: December 1972

Director: Arthur Hiller

Stars: Peter O'Toole, Sophia Loren, James Coco

Academy Awards: One nomination (Best Music)

PREVIEW: In Don Quixote's musical fantasy, he sees himself as a chivalrous knight on a quest.

NOW SHOWING: *El Sueño Imposible*

From late 1971 to late 1972, four movies based on award-winning Broadway musicals arrived in theaters (see "Added Attraction"). Movie-to-original-musical comparisons are rarely enlightening, as the media are naturally different. Movie-to-other-movie comparisons are fair game, though, and in nearly every way *Man of La Mancha* (1972) suffers.

Peter O'Toole would eventually climb out of the crater left by this infamous bomb. In a framing device, O'Toole starts as author Miguel de Cervantes and transforms into Don Quixote for a series of random imaginary episodes. He's terribly miscast: not only is O'Toole's aristocratic English accent vocalizing a renowned *Spanish* character, he constantly shouts lines like someone enthralled with his own magnificent voice. Then, when the first song finally arrives after nineteen tedious minutes, it's clearly not O'Toole singing. Dubbing isn't new, obviously—check both leads in *West Side Story* (1961)—but bad dubbing distracts. By making a movie star, not a musical star, its lead, *Man of La*

Mancha foreshadows the mediocre *Mame* (1974) with raspy-voiced Lucille Ball; the strategy of choosing name recognition over musical expertise backfires on both movies. Alternatively, *Fiddler on the Roof* (1971) and *Cabaret* (1972), two extremely popular Best Picture nominees, perfectly marry stars to material.

Ravishing Sophia Loren, playing the "tigress" Aldonza (the whore Quixote idealistically venerates), capably sings her own songs and is the movie's best asset. Disappointments, however, accumulate around her. Instead of impressive dancing, there's choreographed brawling. Visually, nearly everything is uglified with a brownish tint. The movie tries to broaden the theatrical experience by journeying into the countryside, but whereas *Fiddler* epically expands to give viewers bang for their bucks, *Man of La Mancha* seems to diminish when it goes outdoors for the silly windmill fight (since it's a movie, viewers get to ride the windmill's vanes).

In *Fiddler*, dignified, upstanding Tevye struggles to sustain specific Old World traditions during the historical transition into modern times, a definable, realistic goal. In contrast, everyone in *Man of La Mancha* indulges a "ridiculous" "crack-brain" lunatic who recommends seeing life "as it should be" and making "a world of iron" into "a world of gold," which are vague, metaphorical ambitions. Devoted fans may be inspired, and certainly "The Impossible Dream" (spoken or sung four times) is moving. But after 132 unmagical minutes, most audiences will probably be too bored or exhausted by this awkward, plodding movie to be anything but relieved that it's over.

ADDED ATTRACTION: From Broadway to Hollywood

Fifteen '70s movies based on Broadway musicals, listed chronologically. Not included are movies based on off-Broadway productions like *Godspell* (the 1973 movie based on the 1971 musical).

Movie (Year)	Year of Broadway Opening (Tony Award for Best Musical)
On a Clear Day You Can See Forever (1970)	1965
Song of Norway (1970)	1944
The Boy Friend (1971)	1954
Fiddler on the Roof (1971)	1964 (Winner)
Cabaret (1972)	1966 (Winner)
1776 (1972)	1969 (Winner)
Man of La Mancha (1972)	1965 (Winner)
Jesus Christ Superstar (1973)	1971
Mame (1974)	1966 (Nominee)
Lost in the Stars (1974)	1949
The Rocky Horror Picture Show (1975)	1975
A Little Night Music (1977)	1973 (Winner)
Grease (1978)	1972 (Winner)
The Wiz (1978)	1975 (Winner)
Hair (1979)	1968 (Nominee)

The Poseidon Adventure

(One of 1972's five **FAR-OUT** movies)

Released: December 1972

Director: Ronald Neame

Stars: Gene Hackman, Ernest Borgnine, Shelley Winters

Academy Awards: Two wins (Best Song; Special Achievement Award for Visual Effects), plus seven more nominations (Best Supporting Actress—Shelley Winters; Best Editing; Best Cinematography; Best Art Direction; Best Costume Design; Best Music; Best Sound)

PREVIEW: When a ship capsizes, ten survivors try to escape by climbing through the interior.

FINE LINE: "God wants brave souls. He wants winners, not quitters. If you can't win, at least try to win! God loves triers!" (From Reverend Scott's afternoon sermon before that night's disaster.)

CLOSE-UP: Fifty-five minutes into the movie, Detective Rogo refers to the most famous sea disaster of all time when he sarcastically suggests that survivors should "break out their hymn books and start singing 'Nearer My God to Thee'." This is the song supposedly played on deck just before the *Titanic* sank in 1912.

NOW SHOWING: Ship Trip Flip

What *Airport* (1970) sowed, *The Poseidon Adventure* (1972) reaped. Key elements of the first important disaster movie of the 1970s were repurposed into the titanic drama of the S.S. *Poseidon*, and the result is one of the decade's most watchable movies.

At the time, critical praise for *The Poseidon Adventure* tended to be reluctant and conditional, as if highbrow reviewers couldn't believe they were actually enjoying a guilty pleasure they felt they ought to despise. Oscar voters had no problems, however, and nominated the movie in eight categories. But it's the general public that fully embraced *The Poseidon Adventure* and lifted it right behind *The Godfather* (1972) on the year-end box-office charts. Audiences recognized the movie for what it is: supreme, if imperfect entertainment.

Airport, of course, set the bar high for disaster movies and established an early template: gather various interesting people together, create a potential hazard for them to face, unleash that hazard, and see who survives. Briefly, *The Poseidon Adventure*'s now-familiar hazard is a tsunami that flips the ship upside-down so that ten survivors must climb up through the interior toward the thin hull, which is exposed at the surface. How these ten maneuver past a litany of dangerous obstacles and distractions—flooded compartments, fiery passageways, scalding steam, Ernest Borgnine's scenery-chewing outrage, Stella Stevens' jaw-dropping cleavage—is the core of the story.

The Poseidon Adventure takes a major departure from the *Airport* formula by speeding everything up. In *Airport*, the jet's bomb takes 102 minutes to explode; the temblor in *Earthquake* (1974) rumbles through at the fifty-minute mark. In contrast, the "mountainous" wave that capsizes the *Poseidon* arrives just twenty-six minutes into the movie. By then we've read a prologue summarizing the upcoming catastrophe, and we've been warned about this luxury liner's various problems: faulty pumps (three minutes into the movie), instability (four minutes), and the ship's "dangerous" speed for its advanced age (ten minutes). We've also seen a model of the *Poseidon* tip over (twelve minutes), learned that Poseidon is the "god of storms, tempests, earthquakes, and other miscellaneous natural disasters" (twenty minutes), and seen a radar screen's "frightening target." What's more, we've met ten crew members and passengers who will have to overcome personal fears and injuries to survive; we've sampled the great score by John Williams (yes, *that* John Williams) and heard two renditions of "The Morning After" theme song; and we've received news about a "subsea earthquake" and an "enormous wall of water." A lot happens in those first twenty-six minutes.

The movie is just cranking up. For the next ninety-one minutes hundreds of passengers are whittled down to ten and then to the final six who reach the rescue helicopter. Most of the passengers are killed when the ship initially overturns, an impressive, music-less sequence that lasts almost two minutes. Another large group drowns after an underwater explosion, and later about twenty misguided passengers insist on walking the wrong way to their doom. The movie follows the remaining ten survivors, commanded by Reverend Scott (Gene Hackman). He battles with an obstinate detective (Ernest Borgnine) as much as he does with the ruined ship, and their loud, nose-to-nose arguments intensify the already-dramatic events.

The main cast goes *Airport* one better by showcasing *five* Academy Award winners. Hackman was fresh off his Best Actor triumph in *The French Connection* (1971), Ernest Borgnine had won that award in 1955, Shelley Winters had twice been named Best Supporting Actress, and Jack Albertson and Red Buttons had each won as Best Supporting Actor. The remaining five of the ten-person group includes a smarty-pants kid, his teenage sister in hot pants, and a pretty singer in hot pants. Thankfully, the cast is spared some of the unsavory aspects of Paul Gallico's novel, which preceded the movie. In the book, Stella Stevens' character is a foul-mouthed racist, the smarty-pants kid dies, and his sister is raped by a deckhand.

The movie's real star is the ship itself. Some ship-board scenes were shot on the RMS *Queen Mary*, which was berthed in Long Beach, California. The dark, damp, labyrinthine sets of the interior, which present realistic perils down every hallway, earned an Oscar nomination. Footage of the full ship at sea, or rolling over, or exploding when it's underwater, used a detailed twenty-foot-long model.

While the movie seems like pure, suspenseful entertainment, it does deliver some messages. One is the lesson learned in every *Titanic* movie, where the greed for speed raced that ship into an iceberg. Here, to save time and money, a demanding company representative recklessly orders the unstable *Poseidon* "full ahead!" Hubris like this has got to be punished, obviously. Another message is the one embodied by Reverend Scott, who argues throughout for decisive action over quiet prayer. Scott dies, but his shouted encouragements drive the others to safety.

Boosted by *The Poseidon Adventure*'s phenomenal success, producer Irwin Allen moved on to the best of the decade's disaster movies, *The Towering Inferno* (1974). The *Poseidon* legacy extended to a 1979 sequel and a 2000 remake, but both sink next to the original, which sails on as a timeless highlight of the '70s.

ADDED ATTRACTION: May/December Relationships

In *The Poseidon Adventure*, there's a twenty-one year age difference between the two stars who are playing Linda and Mike Rogo (Stella Stevens is 34, Ernest Borgnine 55). Similarly, the following 1970–1974 movies present romantic relationships between younger actresses and actors who are at least twenty years older (their real ages follow their names). For movies pairing May-actors with December-actresses, see the entry for *Summer of '42* (1971).

- *Airport* (1970): Jacqueline Bisset, 26; Dean Martin, 53
- *Breezy* (1973): Kay Lenz, 20; William Holden, 55
- *Dirty Dingus Magee* (1970): Michele Carey, 27; Frank Sinatra, 55
- *The Front Page* (1974): Susan Sarandon, 28; Jack Lemmon, 49
- *The Life and Times of Judge Roy Bean* (1972): Victoria Principal, 22; Paul Newman, 47
- *Live and Let Die* (1973): Jane Seymour, 22; Roger Moore, 46
- *Lost Horizon* (1973): Liv Ullmann, 35; Peter Finch, 57
- *On a Clear Day You Can See Forever* (1970): Barbra Streisand, 28; Yves Montand, 49
- *Save the Tiger* (1973): Laurie Heineman, 25; Jack Lemmon, 48
- *Soylent Green* (1973): Leigh Taylor-Young, 28; Charlton Heston, 50

The Heartbreak Kid

Released: December 1972

Director: Elaine May

Stars: Charles Grodin, Cybill Shepherd, Eddie Albert

Academy Awards: Two nominations (Best Supporting Actor—Eddie Albert; Best Supporting Actress—Jeannie Berlin)

PREVIEW: A newlywed on his honeymoon woos a beautiful rich girl and must win over her father.

NOW SHOWING: Growing Up with *The Heartbreak Kid*

Wildly patterned polyester shirts for men were big in the '70s, and so was *The Heartbreak Kid* (1972). Neither has aged very well. At the time, audiences were won over by this comedy that's propelled by a smart, hard-working guy who's bubbling with enthusiasm, ideas, and charm. But seen again in this century, the movie, while still smoothly polished and well-acted, seems much crueler now. That cad Lenny isn't cute and fun; he's a selfish, manipulative liar.

The unusual comic predicament is touted in the first forty seconds of the movie's *trailer*. Boy meets girl, marries girl, meets better girl on his honeymoon, breaks up with first girl, pursues and marries second girl. Lenny (Charles Grodin) and Lila (Oscar-nominated Jeannie Berlin) date during the opening credits and have a small family wedding in the movie's first four minutes. Then, for all his declarations about his steely determination, Lenny quickly gives up on his new bride during the drive down the Atlantic Coast to their honeymoon destination. He's turned off by the way she eats (what, he's never seen her eat before?), and by her need for reassurance in bed (he knew she was a virgin, didn't he expect her to ask questions?). Once he gets "one good look" at blonde, perfect Kelly (Cybill Shepherd) in Miami, he then tortures Lila with preposterous lies that (a) make her genuinely worry, and (b) confine her to their hotel room, so (c) he can go out and romance Kelly. After getting out of his first marriage, Lenny follows Kelly to Minnesota, battles her openly hostile father (Oscar-nominated Eddie Albert) for her hand, and eventually marries Kelly in a majestic church wedding.

To our adult eyes, it seems totally implausible that Kelly would fall for Lenny, and in fact she never really seems to. She acts superior, distant, and uninvolved throughout their entire courtship, even after he completely upends his life and moves from

New York to Minnesota for her (she's "flattered" but has to get to class). In the final scene at the wedding, the camera focuses on him as he sits alone and stares, blankly lost in thought, humming the "Close to You" song played at both his weddings. Is he exhausted? Relieved? Regretful? Already dissatisfied, like the fun is the chase, not the actual conquest? It's an ambiguous ending, but we ask you: does anybody really think this couple will stay together?

ADDED ATTRACTION: Getting "Close to You"

"(They Long to Be) Close to You" was a Grammy-winning number-one hit for the Carpenters in 1970. The Carpenters' version isn't played in *The Heartbreak Kid*, but other versions of this Burt Bacharach/Hal David song are heard throughout the movie, as shown below. "(They Long to Be) Close to You," by the way, also appears in the documentary *Save the Children* (1973), where it's performed by Jerry Butler and Brenda Lee Eager.

- Played on piano at Lenny and Lila's wedding.
- Lenny and Lila sing it as they drive to Florida.
- A lush orchestral version is heard on the soundtrack as Lila returns to New York on a bus.
- Played on piano and violin at Lenny and Kelly's wedding.
- Lenny hums the song to himself as he sits alone in the last shot.

The Getaway

Released: December 1972
Director: Sam Peckinpah
Stars: Steve McQueen, Ali MacGraw, Sally Struthers
Academy Awards: None

PREVIEW: A married couple robs a bank in Texas and heads to Mexico with pursuers close behind.

NOW SHOWING: Stars and Cars

Good but not great, *The Getaway* (1972) is about a bank heist that goes wrong (don't they all?). After they're double-crossed, the married couple in the gang of thieves takes the money and races to Mexico with their ruthless colleagues in pursuit. There's a dramatic final shoot-out in El Paso before the couple finally crosses a border checkpoint in broad daylight, which seems a little too easy for these well-publicized criminals. Still, impressed audiences made this movie a huge hit.

Undoubtedly the magnetic star power pulled in the majority of those viewers. Steve McQueen plays Doc, a tough, laconic con who starts the movie already in prison for armed robbery. Released early, he plans the detailed heist and engineers the flight to Mexico. He wears glasses for the early action, so we know he's smart, but Doc is also an unsympathetic hero. He slaps his wife around in one disturbing scene, later grabs a child's arm and threatens to break it, and he punches a woman in the face. McQueen's a long way from the charming rascal he played in *The Reivers* (1969). He's ultra-cool, though, and his conservative black suit survives for Quentin Tarantino's *Reservoir Dogs* (1992).

Steve McQueen and Ali MacGraw.

The bigger surprise is McQueen's real-life love, Ali MacGraw, who's far from her college-girl role in her previous movie, *Love Story* (1970). Now in a violent thriller, she sleeps with the villain to spring Doc from prison, drives a robbery vehicle, kills two people with gunshots, gets packed into a dumpster, and suffers a facial cut (ironically, she swears way more in *Love Story*). Somehow, after successfully playing this pistol-packin' mama, MacGraw wouldn't make another movie until *Convoy* (1978).

Director Sam Peckinpah includes the trademark bloodshed he incorporated into the notorious *Straw Dogs* (1971). *The Getaway* starts slowly, though there's some interesting editing for the early prison scenes and on Doc's first day out. Once the heist is finally underway, however, there are many exciting shoot-outs and car crashes, plus a terrific train sequence. A sordid, unnecessary side story features Sally Struthers, Archie's little girl on TV's *All in the Family*, as a trashy sexpot. Peckinpah makes good use of the authentic Texas locations and Quincy Jones' harmonica-driven music. Wisely he jettisons the surreal conclusion to Jim Thompson's 1958 novel for a more amiable wrap-up with Slim Pickens; the ending provides one of the only nice scenes in this otherwise merciless movie.

ADDED ATTRACTION: Rodeo Roundup

The Getaway was not the first collaboration between Steve McQueen and Sam Peckinpah. Earlier that same year they made *Junior Bonner* (1972), a low-key rodeo-themed drama. It's an interesting departure from the typical McQueen or Peckinpah action movie, because there are no guns, and the most violent scene is a lively (but not deadly) four-minute barroom brawl. Unfortunately, *Junior Bonner* was a box-office flop, perhaps because it got lost amidst other 1971–1973 rodeo movies, which are listed here chronologically with their stars.

- *J.W. Coop* (1971): Cliff Robertson
- *Black Rodeo* (1972): Documentary
- *The Honkers* (1972): James Coburn
- *Junior Bonner* (1972): Steve McQueen
- *When the Legends Die* (1972): Richard Widmark
- *The Great American Cowboy* (1973): Documentary

Up the Sandbox

Released: December 1972
Director: Irvin Kershner
Stars: Barbra Streisand, David Selby, Ariane Heller
Academy Awards: None

PREVIEW: A frustrated housewife fantasizes about being in funny and dangerous situations.

NOW SHOWING: Fantasy Girl

A minor feminist landmark, *Up the Sandbox* (1972) is one of the first movies to show a 1970s housewife being liberated by the energy of the women's movement. The movie is smart, it's funny, and it's got Barbra Streisand in one of her most appealing non-singing roles. Irvin Kershner, who would later direct *The Empire Strikes Back* (1980), was at the helm, and Gordon Willis, the brilliant cinematographer, was behind the camera. Unfortunately, audiences didn't embrace this gem, though most critics did.

Streisand plays Margaret, a bored, underappreciated New York housewife whose daily routine is frequently interrupted by her rich fantasy life. Some of these fantasies arrive as she's doing something during the day and are then followed by the actual event that really does happen (as when she imagines a friendly conversation with a beautiful woman who may be her husband's mistress, followed by the real scene that shows the woman but includes no conversation). She also dreams in her sleep about imaginary characters and bizarre situations (in one dream a Castro-style Cuban leader reveals to her that he's actually a woman, in another she helps revolutionaries plant bombs under the Statue of Liberty). Some fantasies are funny (she inflates herself with bigger breasts), some are destructive (an argument with her husband that ends with self-defenestration), and some are exotic (a five-minute sequence where she goes to Africa to learn the "cherished secret of painless childbirth"). At times the audience isn't even sure if it's watching a scene that's fantasy or reality, but Margaret's frustrations are always clear.

After she declares "I'd like a day off," Margaret imagines a long ending that, according to Streisand's commentary on the DVD, is all in her head, though it blends fantasy and reality: saved from getting an abortion, she wheels into a park on a hospital gurney, smiles at happy children, gets catapulted into an actual sandbox (where she momentarily sits, alone and perplexed, in her hospital gown), goes back to her apartment, and returns to the park to confidently announce to her husband that she's pregnant. In the last shot she leaves in a cab for an unknown destination, and her supportive husband tends the kids. If most of this is real (the pregnancy, the politically correct husband, the new-found confidence to pursue her own goals in addition to motherhood), then Margaret really does seem to have it all at last.

ADDED ATTRACTION: More Women of 1972

Two more end-of-the-year movies presented women in domestic dramas. Based on a play, *Black Girl* shows a black teen living in an L.A. house that's packed with complications. She struggles to fulfill her dream of going to college and becoming a ballet dancer, but Cinderella-like family resentments are in her way (one sister even pulls a switchblade on a family member). Ossie Davis directed this modest melodrama that feels like it accurately evokes the issues, styles, and vocabulary of the early '70s; Louise Stubbs and Peggy Pettit head the strong ensemble cast. Meanwhile, *Pete 'n' Tillie* pairs a wise-cracking Walter Matthau and a cautious Carol Burnett in a witty romantic story of a mismatched San Francisco couple that dates, marries, and goes through turbulent experiences, including his infidelities and a tragic death that splits them apart. Burnett is impressive in her first starring role after years on TV. Co-star Geraldine Page and the screenplay both got Oscar nominations.

In Film

- Oscar for Best Picture: *The Sting*.
- Most Oscar wins (seven): *The Sting*.
- Most Oscar nominations (ten): *The Exorcist*, *The Sting*.
- Top-grossing movie: *The Sting*.
- Top-grossing horror or sci-fi: *The Exorcist*.
- Top-grossing comedy: *American Graffiti*.
- Hong Kong's *Five Fingers of Death* is a surprise hit in America and inspires a rush of kung fu movies.
- *Westworld* introduces sophisticated computer-generated graphics.
- Five memorable actors: Richard Dreyfuss, John Houseman, Jack Lemmon, Steve McQueen, Robert Redford.
- Five memorable actresses: Linda Blair, Pam Grier, Madeline Kahn, Marsha Mason, Barbra Streisand.
- Movie debuts: Tatum O'Neal, director Terrence Malick.
- Deaths include Betty Grable, Veronica Lake, Bruce Lee, director John Ford.

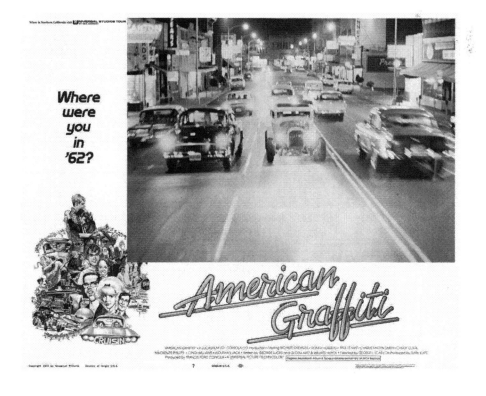

In America

- A peace agreement ends America's official involvement in the Vietnam War, bringing home most American soldiers and POWs.
- Televised Watergate hearings and related resignations.
- Tax-evasion charges lead to Vice President Spiro Agnew's resignation; Gerald Ford replaces him.
- The landmark Roe v. Wade decision overturns state bans on abortions; the Drug Enforcement Agency is founded; the Endangered Species Act is passed.
- The Twin Towers of the World Trade Center open; the Sears Tower in Chicago is finished and becomes the world's tallest building.
- The space station *Skylab* is launched.
- First call using a handheld cellular phone; first use of barcodes on grocery items; first Federal Express deliveries.
- Bestselling novel: *Jonathan Livingston Seagull*.
- George Steinbrenner leads a group that buys the New York Yankees from CBS.
- George Foreman defeats Joe Frazier to take boxing's heavyweight crown.
- Billie Jean King defeats Bobby Riggs; Secretariat wins horse racing's Triple Crown.
- Music: Pink Floyd's *Dark Side of the Moon*, Elton John's *Goodbye Yellow Brick Road*, and debut albums from Aerosmith, Bruce Springsteen, and Queen are released.
- TV debuts: *Kojak*, *The Midnight Special*, *The Young and the Restless*.
- Deaths include Pearl Buck, Jim Croce, Bobby Darin, William Inge, Gene Krupa, Lyndon Johnson.

Black Caesar

Released: February 1973
Director: Larry Cohen
Stars: Fred Williamson, Gloria Hendry, Art Lund
Academy Awards: None

PREVIEW: The rags-to-riches rise and the fall of New York City's violent "black godfather."

NOW SHOWING: Harlem Hellion

Many 1970s blaxploitation movies—*Shaft* (1971) and *Coffy* (1973), for instance—end with strong black actors and actresses triumphing. The rough-but-exciting *Black Caesar* (1973) is different in that its powerful protagonist suffers a final humiliating, possibly fatal beating at the hands of teenagers. The movie opens in 1953 with a Harlem shoeshine kid getting clobbered by a racist white cop. Cut to 1965, and young Tommy is now a handsome hood (Fred Williamson). The rest of the movie covers the next seven years of Tommy's life as he gets some political leverage and kills off rivals to become a top criminal; some Old World Italian music and *The Godfather* (1972) on a theater marquee remind us of familiar mobsters. He gets payback on that original racist cop, smearing him in blackface and making him sing "Mammy" before cathartically beating him to death. Wounded, Tommy then staggers to the dismal demise that was briefly shown in previews and is now on the DVD (according to the DVD's commentary, in 1973 theaters played an audience-pleasing ending that keeps Tommy alive). Williamson is a confident, charismatic presence who looks good in suits, and James Brown's funky songs propel the at-times bloody events.

When *Black Caesar* turned out to be a surprise hit, American International Pictures rushed out *Hell Up in Harlem* (1973); to reinforce the connection, this follow-up was possibly going to be called *Black Caesar's Sweet Revenge*. Picking up as if the near-fatal beating that ended the first movie had never happened, the action-packed sequel continues his saga with some unexpected developments. In the first movie, Williamson, an ex-football star, didn't get to show off his athleticism, but in the sequel we see him sprint and hurdle fences. As before, Tommy steals some important ledgers, and he shoots various villains. He also romances a nun (huh?) and takes her and their kid to Beverly Hills, where they live large until Tommy survives a mansion assassination attempt that foreshadows the bloody shoot-out that concludes *Scarface* (1983).

Tommy goes home, hoping to "make New York a decent place to live" by eliminating his enemies there. His wife disappears and his son is taken hostage, but Tommy eventually rescues him and vows to "start over." According to closing text, "Tommy Gibbs and his son vanished that night ... to this date they have not been heard of again." Movie-wise, that's true.

ADDED ATTRACTION:
Blaxploitation Versions of Earlier Movies

With its rise-and-fall gangster story and related title, *Black Caesar* obviously echoes *Little Caesar*, Edward G. Robinson's 1931 crime classic. Other entries in the blaxploitation genre similarly evoke earlier movies and modify the white characters into black ones. While the derivation is sometimes subtle—private-eye John Shaft dresses like Lt. Frank

Bullitt and is just as cool, but their stories are vastly different—the next eleven 1970s movies were aimed at black audiences and pointed to some previous movie.

Blaxploitation Movie (Year)	Earlier Related Movie (Year)
Abby (1974)	*The Exorcist* (1973)
Black Angels (1970)	*Hells Angels on Wheels* (1967)
Black Belt Jones (1974)	*Enter the Dragon* (1973)
Blackenstein, aka *Black Frankenstein* (1973)	*Frankenstein* (1931)
The Black Godfather (1974)	*The Godfather* (1972)
Black Mama White Mama (1973)	*The Defiant Ones* (1958)
Black Shampoo (1976)	*Shampoo* (1975)
Blacula (1972)	*Dracula* (1931)
Cooley High (1975)	*American Graffiti* (1973)
Dr. Black, Mr. Hyde (1976)	*Dr. Jekyll and Mr. Hyde* (1931)
Shaft (1971)	*Bullitt* (1968)

Save the Tiger

Released: February 1973

Director: John G. Avildsen

Stars: Jack Lemmon, Jack Gilford, Laurie Heineman

Academy Awards: One win (Best Actor—Jack Lemmon), plus two more nominations (Best Supporting Actor—Jack Gilford; Best Writing)

PREVIEW: A desperate, disillusioned businessman decides he must burn down his own factory.

NOW SHOWING: "Remembered Beauty"

Save the Tiger (1973) is a small low-budget movie that delivers powerful emotions. That it resonates in the memory long after it's over is a testament to Jack Lemmon, whose Oscar-winning tour-de-force performance is the movie's *raison d'être* (he's in virtually every scene). No longer the humorously flustered Lemmon of *The Odd Couple* (1968), this is a versatile, utterly convincing actor at his dramatic best.

The movie covers about thirty-six hours in the life of a successful but troubled businessman, Harry Stone (Lemmon). He wakes up screaming from a nightmare and endures further nightmarish experiences at work, including a client's near-death and a war hallucination that hits him while he's giving a major speech. His only rewarding experiences come when he twice picks up a young hitchhiker. She invites him to get high and spend the night; he does both.

Harry's the president of Capri Casuals, a clothing manufacturer in L.A.'s garment district. Despite "a little ballet with the books," bankruptcy looms. Harry will do anything to save his business and the jobs of about a hundred employees, whether that means arranging prostitutes for clients or paying an arsonist to torch his Long Beach factory for the insurance money. For half the movie he wrestles with the arson solution: is it wrong, he rationalizes, "to keep people working? ... Is it a criminal act to try to hang on to fifteen years of hard work?" Jaded and desperate, he finally decides "there are no more rules."

Harry's anguished, but he's not shallow. Valuing the past more than the present or future, he cherishes his poetic memories of the great big-band jazzmen and baseball players he admired long ago. Midway through the movie he signs a petition to "save the tiger" because there are so few left; later he's told that tigers "always return to a place of remembered beauty." Harry's like the tiger, endangered and easily drifting into the golden memories of his own "remembered beauty" (when he passes a tiger poster late in the movie, the sound from a passing vehicle makes the poster "growl" at him, as if in recognition).

The unresolved ending leaves Harry still searching. "I want to be in love with something, anything," he says, mourning the lost dreams and simpler times of his youth. An insightful, serious character study, *Save the Tiger* exposes Harry's flaws, but it also makes him sympathetic and unforgettable.

ADDED ATTRACTION: Later Lemmon

Jack Lemmon had other early-'70s successes, including the only movie he directed, *Kotch* (1971), a nice little comedy that brought Walter Matthau an Oscar nomination for playing a kindly old man. Lemmon then followed *Save the Tiger* with *The Front Page* (1974), his first on-screen reteaming with Matthau since *The Odd Couple* (1968). Here they seem slightly more desperate than delightful, and the movie is unfortunately more vulgar than previous versions of the giddy 1928 play about a newspaper editor and his ace reporter. Billy Wilder directed, and the cast includes Susan Sarandon (as Lemmon's young fiancée) and Carol Burnett (entirely wrong as a streetwalker). Though the movie looks terrific, what could've been a deliriously funny hit is only an above-average diversion that inevitably suffers in comparison to *His Girl Friday* (1940), Howard Hawks' rapid-fire screwball classic with Rosalind Russell as Lemmon's character.

The Long Goodbye

Released: March 1973
Director: Robert Altman
Stars: Elliott Gould, Nina van Pallandt, Sterling Hayden
Academy Awards: None

PREVIEW: While investigating a suicide, a private eye uncovers a maze of murders and deceit.

NOW SHOWING: "It's Okay with Me"

Jack-of-all-genres Robert Altman tackles detective stories in *The Long Goodbye* (1973). It's a hard movie to like, and initially many viewers (especially loyal Raymond Chandler fans) didn't. However, it has gained cult stature and is now frequently ranked among Altman's better works.

We admire Altman, a prolific, adventurous director, but can't rate *The Long Goodbye* a major triumph. Like he did in *M*A*S*H* (1970) and *McCabe & Mrs. Miller* (1971), Altman tells a meandering story—here an apparent suicide leads to a convoluted tangle of lies, infidelities, gangsters, missing money, and deaths—and he seems content to simply observe quirky characters and lifestyles. Elliott Gould plays Philip Marlowe, the private eye that Humphrey Bogart iconically defined in *The Big Sleep* (1946). That abstruse film noir masterpiece was co-written by Leigh Brackett, screenwriter of *The Long Goodbye*; she updates Chandler's 1953 novel with stronger language, a new ending, and an early-'70s setting. Marlowe is now a disheveled out-of-place relic with his 1948 Lincoln, one dark suit, and non-stop chain-smoking, all anachronisms in laid-back L.A. where topless girls practice yoga next door. In Gould's shambling, soft-boiled interpretation of the character, he mumbles smart-aleck remarks, hums, and mutters "it's okay with me" a dozen times. The movie's best line actually comes from someone else, a gangster who shockingly smashes a bottle across his girlfriend's face and then confronts Marlowe: "That's someone I love, and you I don't even like."

Altman being Altman, he experiments with imagery, here using a constantly mov-ing-and-zooming camera for ever-changing perspectives. Also unusual is the music, which presents various renditions (by vocalists, mariachis, pianos, even a doorbell) of the movie's theme song. The cast is typical Altman, so it features distinctive people like newsmaker Nina van Pallandt and ex-ballplayer Jim Bouton (plus David Carradine and mustachioed Arnold Schwarzenegger in tiny roles). Regrettably, the sum of all these interesting parts is a curiosity, not a classic.

Altman and Gould hit the jackpot with their next movie together, *California Split* (1974). In this satisfying, unpredictable comedy, Altman again probes with his agile camera, and Gould plays a charismatic chatterbox who turns the movie into his own stream-of-consciousness riff. He and George Segal are well matched as two compulsive gamblers who'll bet on anything—cards, horses, dogs, fistfights, the Seven Dwarfs' names, etc. Segal sells everything for one last stand in Reno, a twenty-seven-minute challenge that's as fascinating as it is entertaining.

ADDED ATTRACTION: The Sad Goodbye

In *The Long Goodbye*, David Arkin plays an inept hood; Arkin (1941–1991) died at age forty-nine. In *California Split*, Gwen Welles plays a pretty, soft-spoken escort who likes George Segal's character; Welles (1951–1993) died at age forty-two. Here are other stars of 1970s movies who died before turning fifty (a prominent '70s movie follows each name). Not included are Jimi Hendrix and other musicians who appeared in doc-umentaries and also died too soon.

- John Belushi, 1949–1982: *Animal House* (1978)
- Barry Brown, 1951–1978: *Daisy Miller* (1974)
- John Candy, 1950–1994: *1941* (1979)
- John Cazale, 1935–1978: *The Godfather* (1972)
- Brad Davis, 1949–1991: *Midnight Express* (1978)
- Marty Feldman, 1934–1982: *Young Frankenstein* (1974)
- Claudia Jennings, 1949–1979: *'Gator Bait* (1974)
- Bruce Lee, 1940–1973: *Enter the Dragon* (1973)
- Keith Moon, 1946–1978: *Tommy* (1975)
- Jean Seberg, 1938–1979: *Airport* (1970)
- Dennis Wilson, 1944–1983: *Two-Lane Blacktop* (1971)
- Natalie Wood, 1938–1981: *Meteor* (1979)

Lost Horizon

Released: March 1973
Director: Charles Jarrott
Stars: Peter Finch, Liv Ullmann, Sally Kellerman
Academy Awards: None

PREVIEW: After a plane crash, the survivors make it to a wondrous lamasery where nobody ages.

NOW SHOWING: Lost Potential

What makes *Lost Horizon* (1973) so disappointing is that this musical conceivably had potential. Producer Ross Hunter's previous movie was an entertaining Oscar-nominated blockbuster, *Airport* (1970); *Lost Horizon* had a big budget and a star-studded cast that boasted actors who already were or soon would be Oscar winners (Peter Finch, John Gielgud, George Kennedy); and the songs were by Burt Bacharach and Hal David, the Oscar-winning team behind *Butch Cassidy and the Sundance Kid* (1969). So how did *Lost Horizon* become one of Hollywood's most expensive and notorious debacles?

The running time is one answer. Considering that it's based on a short novel, somehow the musical becomes *Lost Two-and-a-Half Hours*. Movie musicals can be both long and great—the four Best Picture-winning musicals from *West Side Story* (1961) to *Oliver!* (1968) are all longer than *Lost Horizon*. Alas, forty minutes elapse before the audience even *knows* it's watching a musical. Once Olivia Hussey finally "sings" the first number (few of the cast members are singers, so nearly all the singing voices are dubbed), the movie lurches along from one forgettable song to another. Liv Ullmann's amateurish "The World Is a Circle," Bobby Van's silly "Question Me an Answer," and the six-minute Festival of the Family are lowlights reminiscent of well-meaning high school productions. Sally Kellerman bravely gives the music a go, while George Kennedy and Michael York wisely don't even try.

Remove the songs and the lumbering choreography, and what's left is the good adventure story familiar from James Hilton's 1933 bestseller and Frank Capra's 1937 movie: a plane is hijacked into the Himalayas, the passengers are escorted to the paradisiacal Shangri-La where nobody ages, some of the cast falls in love, others want to leave, etc. English thespian John Gielgud is an inscrutable Oriental, and Frenchman Charles Boyer is the High Lama delivering "one simple rule: be kind." Shangri-La itself seems to be played by a big bland hotel with pools out front (it's actually an enormous Burbank set).

More fun than the movie are the print reviews that followed its release. Esteemed critics rose (or, more accurately, *lowered* themselves) to the occasion with creative put-downs (*Least Horizon* was the *MAD* magazine parody, December 1973). "I can't wait to get back," says Michael York forty-seven minutes into the tedium. With another hundred minutes still to go, viewers are probably looking at their watches and thinking the same thing.

ADDED ATTRACTION: Musical Misfires

Between Bob Fosse's two awesome Best Picture nominees, *Cabaret* (1972) and *All That Jazz* (1979), Hollywood unleashed some musicals that were, at *best*, mildly disappointing. There were a few keepers in those years, like *The Rocky Horror Picture Show* (1975), *Saturday Night Fever* (1977), and *Grease* (1978), but the motley group of 1972–1979 musicals included more misses than hits, as evidenced by these ten chronologically listed selections (stars are noted). These didn't kill the movie-musical genre, but some of them wounded it a little.

- *Man of La Mancha* (1972): Peter O'Toole
- *Lost Horizon* (1973): Peter Finch
- *Mame* (1974): Lucille Ball
- *Huckleberry Finn* (1974): Jeff East
- *At Long Last Love* (1975): Burt Reynolds
- *New York, New York* (1977): Robert De Niro
- *A Little Night Music* (1977): Elizabeth Taylor
- *The Magic of Lassie* (1978): Mickey Rooney
- *Sgt. Pepper's Lonely Hearts Club Band* (1978): Peter Frampton
- *The Wiz* (1978): Diana Ross

Paper Moon

Released: April 1973

Director: Peter Bogdanovich

Stars: Ryan O'Neal, Tatum O'Neal, Madeline Kahn

Academy Awards: One win (Best Supporting Actress—Tatum O'Neal), plus three more nominations (Best Supporting Actress—Madeline Kahn; Best Writing; Best Sound)

PREVIEW: A con man and a precocious child have adventures as they drive across Kansas in 1935.

NOW SHOWING: Child's Play

In the early 1970s, director Peter Bogdanovich enjoyed a remarkable eighteen-month run of hits. He started with a sad drama (1971's *The Last Picture Show*), continued with a zany farce (1972's *What's Up, Doc?*), and ended with a nostalgic comedy about two con artists (1973's *Paper Moon*). There had been other recent movies about con artists—e.g., *The Producers* (1967) and *Skin Game* (1971)—but *Paper Moon* introduces the novel twist of pairing a con man with a con child (albeit one who smokes, swears, and manipulates). The results are marvelously entertaining.

Making her movie debut, nine-year-old Tatum O'Neal confidently creates a defiant character who is so riveting you can't *not* watch her. Often relying on subtle, silent reactions, O'Neal gives what is possibly the best performance ever by a child star (her Oscar made her the youngest winner of all time). O'Neal plays Addie, a truculent waif who is reluctantly driven to distant relatives by Moses, a slightly sleazy grifter. He's played by O'Neal's real father, Ryan O'Neal, the *Love Story* (1970) heartthrob who by this time had become a skillful comedic actor. The scenes of the two O'Neals clashing as well-matched adversaries are both hilarious and mesmerizing.

The fascinating evolution of their relationship propels this episodic movie. Addie and Moses continually bicker as they transition from wary co-travelers to strategic partners and finally into a family unit during their long road trip. Crisscrossing Kansas in 1935, they execute various scams, many that are small and successful, but one that is big and disastrous. They also pick up two passengers, a twenty-two-minute section of the movie that is stolen by the great Madeline Kahn as a buxom carnival dancer and sixteen-year-old P.J. Johnson as her cynical maid. Addie's masterful maneuvering so she can "innocently" jettison their two riders from the car is a thing of beauty.

Director Peter Bogdanovich brings off this sweet, sensitive movie by combining an effortless comedic touch with a poignant evocation of the Depression. Relocating the bestselling book from the Deep South to the vast, treeless Midwest, using rich black-and-white photography and authentic visual details, and setting the mood with scratchy music and radio shows from the era, Bogdanovich flawlessly captures a time when everyone is reminded to "keep your sunny side up" and places where sadness and poverty are always lurking. Warm, smart, and frisky, *Paper Moon* is one of the decade's timeless treasures.

Tatum O'Neal and Ryan O'Neal.

ADDED ATTRACTION: Take-Your-Kid-to-Work Day

While *Paper Moon* represents the decade's most famous pairing of a parent and a child in the same movie, it isn't the only one. Here are twelve more examples.

Movie (Year)	Parent	Child/Children
Alice Doesn't Live Here Anymore (1974)	Diane Ladd	Laura Dern (uncredited)
Big Jake (1971)	John Wayne	Patrick Wayne, Ethan Wayne
Boxcar Bertha (1972)	John Carradine	David Carradine
The Fifth Musketeer (1979)	Lloyd Bridges	Jeff Bridges
Grand Theft Auto (1977)	Rance Howard	Ron Howard, Clint Howard
Opening Night (1977)	Katherine Cassavetes	John Cassavetes
Rocky (1976)	Frank Stallone, Sr.	Sylvester Stallone
Saturday Night Fever (1977)	Helen Travolta	John Travolta

Movie (Year)	Parent	Child/Children
Sisters (1972)	Mary Davenport	Jennifer Salt
Sweet Sweetback's Baadasssss Song (1971)	Melvin Van Peebles	Mario Van Peebles
Wanda Nevada (1979)	Henry Fonda	Peter Fonda
A Woman Under the Influence (1974)	Gena Rowlands	Xan Cassavetes

Scarecrow

Released: April 1973
Director: Jerry Schatzberg
Stars: Gene Hackman, Al Pacino, Ann Wedgeworth
Academy Awards: None

PREVIEW: Two drifters have various experiences as they travel across the country together.

NOW SHOWING: "Crows Are Laughing"

Some viewers call *Scarecrow* (1973) an overlooked classic, but maybe there's a reason it's overlooked: it's not classic. Too bad, because the movie offers two amazing actors, Gene Hackman (Best Actor for 1971's *The French Connection*) and Al Pacino (nominated for 1972's *The Godfather*), in their primes. These two well-matched forces of nature partner up, travel together, and share experiences. As appealing as that sounds, the result is slightly disappointing.

Scarecrow is a road movie, similar to *Easy Rider* (1969) but without the motorcycles, drugs, and cool music. Max (Hackman) and Lionel (Pacino) play downtrodden drifters who are hitchhiking separately but decide to bum rides together as they head from the rural west to eastern cities. Throughout their intermittently interesting travels, they handle episodes differently. Volatile Max continually gets into stupid brawls, and his idea of a witticism that'll impress women is a loud burp. Vulnerable Lionel is sweeter and wards off trouble with humor. ("You think crows are scared of a scarecrow? … Crows are laughing," he declares, thus explaining his clownish behavior and the movie's title.) Lionel dances around, tells goofy jokes, and chants, "Keep 'em happy"; Max even calls him "Mr. Scarecrow."

It's not unreasonable to expect more laughs, especially with Lionel trying so hard to be funny, but there are only two comic highlights—a ludicrous sprint through a store, and an impromptu striptease to defuse a fight. The characters bond closely as friends after one of them is shockingly beaten up, but eventually their slow, meandering adventures just seem sad and desperate. The melodramatic ending with one man catatonic in a hospital feels like it's from a different movie. Impressive cinematography and the determined efforts of two superstars don't compensate for an aimless, downbeat character study with unrealized artistic ambitions. Many critics at the time were fairly underwhelmed by *Scarecrow*, but both stars quickly rebounded—Pacino with *Serpico* (1973) and Hackman with *The Conversation* (1974).

Scarecrow's director, Jerry Schatzberg, had previously collaborated with Pacino in *The Panic in Needle Park* (1971), a brutally realistic drama set in the seamy underworld of lowlife heroin addicts. Pacino, in his first starring role, convincingly plays a manic hustler who steals and deals. Equally good is Kitty Winn as a desperate junkie who turns to prostitution. Presented with gritty documentary-style images, raw language, and no music, *Needle Park* is a stark, unrelenting, and important '70s movie.

ADDED ATTRACTION: Criminal Pairs

Other 1970s movies besides *Scarecrow* pair two outlaws or two drifters together. Here are sixteen, listed chronologically.

- *The Honeymoon Killers* (1970): Tony Lo Bianco, Shirley Stoler
- *Wild Rovers* (1971): William Holden, Ryan O'Neal
- *Boxcar Bertha* (1972): David Carradine, Barbara Hershey
- *The Getaway* (1972): Steve McQueen, Ali MacGraw
- *Emperor of the North* (1973): Lee Marvin, Keith Carradine
- *Badlands* (1973): Martin Sheen, Sissy Spacek
- *Paper Moon* (1973): Ryan O'Neal, Tatum O'Neal
- *The Sting* (1973): Paul Newman, Robert Redford
- *Thieves Like Us* (1974): Keith Carradine, Shelley Duvall
- *The Sugarland Express* (1974): Goldie Hawn, William Atherton
- *Dirty Mary Crazy Larry* (1974): Peter Fonda, Susan George
- *Thunderbolt and Lightfoot* (1974): Clint Eastwood, Jeff Bridges
- *Aloha, Bobby and Rose* (1975): Paul Le Mat, Dianne Hull
- *Dog Day Afternoon* (1975): Al Pacino, John Cazale
- *Harry and Walter Go to New York* (1976): James Caan, Elliott Gould
- *Up in Smoke* (1978): Cheech Marin, Tommy Chong

The Day of the Jackal

Released: May 1973
Director: Fred Zinnemann
Stars: Edward Fox, Michael Lonsdale, Derek Jacobi
Academy Awards: One nomination (Best Editing)

PREVIEW: An assassin plans to kill Charles de Gaulle, but a cunning detective is on his trail.

NOW SHOWING: *C'est Magnifique*

Newcomers, be aware that *The Day of the Jackal* (1973) isn't *The French Connection* (1971), a more concise thriller with an intense investigation that's highlighted by an unforgettable chase; *The Day of the Jackal* is for patient viewers ready to indulge in a sprawling 143-minute thriller that builds slowly and carefully until it achieves fast, final moments of nail-biting excitement.

The movie tells two complementary sides of the same absorbing story. Propelling the action is the Jackal (Edward Fox), the code name for an aristocratic contract killer who is hired to kill France's President Charles de Gaulle. We watch the Jackal's meticulous preparations, admiring his detached, business-like precision even when the reasons for his actions aren't immediately apparent (his early purchase of old clothes and medals, for instance). Especially intriguing are scenes involving his unique gun, an intricate design of separate components that he can ingeniously hide until they're needed.

The Jackal's counterpart is Lebel (Michael Lonsdale), a methodical French inspector who is introduced a third of the way into the movie after the elusive Jackal already has a huge head start. Lebel is equally precise as he sifts through clues and tries to anticipate the Jackal's moves; he's unemotional and logical, only becoming a gun-toting hero in the last moments. Throughout, both men are simply doing their jobs—expertly, relentlessly, and, when necessary, ruthlessly. It's a fascinating cat-and-mouse duel.

What's amazing is that the movie succeeds so well, even though everyone knows the outcome in advance. Charles de Gaulle wasn't assassinated, yet the movie is so convincing that we truly believe he could be shot. Director Fred Zinnemann, an Oscar winner for *From Here to Eternity* (1953) and *A Man for All Seasons* (1966), makes some perfect choices to intensify the unfolding drama. He gives the movie a realistic documentary feel by filming on actual streets throughout Europe, and he lets street sounds replace a traditional soundtrack. His boldest choices are his two relatively unknown leads: having a straightforward inspector (not a dashing James Bond-style charmer) pursue an anonymous assassin (not some glory-seeking killer) keeps the focus on the step-by-step details, not on big movie stars and outrageous personalities.

There might be small flaws in the tale (a few post-1963 vehicles, a woman effortlessly strangled in total silence, some lucky hunches). Nevertheless, the movie's magnetic power draws you in and keeps you riveted until that climactic flurry of shots.

ADDED ATTRACTION: Movies Based on Bestsellers, Part Two

The Day of the Jackal was based on Frederick Forsyth's 1971 bestselling novel. The following 1973–1974 movies were also based on bestsellers. See a similar list about 1970–1972 movies in the entry for *Catch-22* (1970).

Movie (Year)	Book's Author (Publication Year)
Bang the Drum Slowly (1973)	Mark Harris (1956)
Charlotte's Web (1973)	E.B. White (1952)
Conrack (1974)	Pat Conroy (1972)
The Day of the Dolphin (1973)	Robert Merle (1967)
The Exorcist (1973)	William Peter Blatty (1971)
Thieves Like Us (1974)	Edward Anderson (1937)
The Great Gatsby (1974)	F. Scott Fitzgerald (1925)
Jonathan Livingston Seagull (1973)	Richard Bach (1970)
The Long Goodbye (1973)	Raymond Chandler (1953)
Lost Horizon (1973)	James Hilton (1933)
The Man with the Golden Gun (1974)	Ian Fleming (1965)
Murder on the Orient Express (1974)	Agatha Christie (1934)
Papillon (1973)	Henri Charrière (1969
Serpico (1973)	Peter Maas (1973)
The Taking of Pelham One Two Three (1974)	John Godey (1973)
The Terminal Man (1974)	Michael Crichton (1972)
Tom Sawyer (1973)	Mark Twain (1876)
Where the Red Fern Grows (1974)	Wilson Rawls (1961)

Don't Look in the Basement

Released: May 1973
Director: S.F. Brownrigg
Stars: Rosie Holotik, Anne MacAdams, Bill McGhee
Academy Awards: None

PREVIEW: A young nurse at a creepy mental asylum learns that she is in a horrifying situation.

NOW SHOWING: Don't Think Too Much

No wonder *Don't Look in the Basement* (1973) was a drive-in hit. Being in a car half-drunk and/or half-dressed might help viewers half-enjoy this low-budget thriller that puts the "ick" in "horror flick." It opens with the staff at an isolated sanitarium getting killed and a young pretty nurse (Rosie Holotik) arriving for her first day. She's immediately told that one of the patients "viciously attacked" and murdered the head doctor, but she doesn't ask which one or register any dismay about the no-locks-on-doors policy. For the slow first hour various disturbing patients torment each other and suggest the oncoming violence by occasionally wielding a knife or axe. Director S.F. Brownrigg uses shadows, the claustrophobic building, and extreme close-ups to generate mild scares, but the horror finally focuses into a two-minute section when an eyeball is stabbed, a throat is slit, and the nurse's perilous situation is blurted out. The last twenty minutes feature frightening, even bizarre encounters, especially a nymphomaniac's necrophilia with a bloody corpse (even the nurse retches at that one). After the patients mount a final gory attack, the credits showcase the cast individually, nine of them as slashed-up victims. Radical!

Brownrigg followed up with *Don't Open the Door* (1974). A child finds her mother's murdered body in their house. Thirteen years later, that child is now a blonde twentyish girl (Susan Bracken) who returns to claim the house. Some of the locals, however, want to drive her away for their own interests. She resists. That's the premise of this weak misfire that tries for atmospheric terror but achieves tedium. A sadistic obscene caller is quickly identified, so any potential suspense dissipates; additionally, this weirdo's frequent calls are so slow and tiresome viewers might wish the movie's title was *Don't Pick Up the Phone*. A two-minute hallucinatory sequence near the end suggests some transformation inside the girl and leads to the surreal ending when she's apparently in a demon-possessed state a la *The Exorcist* (1973). After she bludgeons to death the one person who's trying to help her (a baffling out-of-left-field finale), the audience is left to wonder: Is she insane? Is the house haunted? Is she going to stay? Passionate horror fans who can watch any scary movie may want to try to figure out where this peculiar movie is going, but casual viewers will be happier if they just don't.

ADDED ATTRACTION: There's a Basement? And a Door?

In both *Don't* movies, the titles don't really have any bearing on the action. The word "basement" is never spoken in *Don't Look in the Basement*, and the audience doesn't know a basement even exists until the eightieth minute when the nurse accidentally wanders into it. Similarly, the audience isn't aware of any special door in *Don't Open the Door*. During the movie the girl opens thirteen doors, including one on a car, and there are no advance warnings about any of them. Later in the decade, an unrelated *Don't* movie appeared that was made by a different director, Joseph Ellison. *Don't Go in the House* (1979) is about a disturbed man who was psychologically abused by his now-dead mother—shades of Hitchcock's *Psycho* (1960). Ellison's psycho lures women to his basement and then immolates them with a flamethrower. Why can't victims ever heed the stern warnings in these movie titles?

Pat Garrett & Billy the Kid

Released: May 1973
Director: Sam Peckinpah
Stars: James Coburn, Kris Kristofferson, Bob Dylan
Academy Awards: None

PREVIEW: In 1881, Sheriff Pat Garrett goes in pursuit of his friend, the outlaw Billy the Kid.

NOW SHOWING: James Coburn & Kris the Kid

In the early 1970s, western legends Pat Garrett and William Bonney (aka Billy the Kid) were portrayed in several movies. Both characters are in *Chisum* (1970), a John Wayne western, and *The Last Movie* (1971), Dennis Hopper's incoherent experiment. Next, thirty-three-year-old Michael J. Pollard took the title role in *Dirty Little Billy* (1972), offering a gritty, unromanticized version of the outlaw's early life (with no Garrett character, Billy, rendered as a shaky, homicidal dim-wit, survives).

The most high-profile telling is Sam Peckinpah's *Pat Garrett & Billy the Kid* (1973), but high-profile doesn't mean great. This dreary movie meanders through the rudiments of the factual story without delivering any real excitement. Some critics and fans have come to admire *Pat Garrett* in recent decades, but it still feels like a step backward from Peckinpah's riveting *Straw Dogs* (1971) and *The Getaway* (1972).

Part of the problem is the casting. The actual Garrett was thirty-one when he killed the twenty-one-year-old Kid. James Coburn, forty-five, plays Garrett, and musician Kris Kristofferson, thirty-seven, plays Billy. While Kristofferson brings bright-smile charisma and maverick spirit to the part, he's no kid, and he ends up ambling through the movie without really committing to it. The supporting cast includes able western veterans (Slim Pickens, Jack Elam, etc.) and two conspicuous newcomers: singer Rita Coolidge in a tiny, virtually silent role, and Bob Dylan as a sullen, mysterious sidekick who hangs around with little to do. Dylan also provides the soundtrack's songs, but his best moments are the melancholy instrumentals.

After a pre-title sequence setting up Garrett's death in 1909, the movie flashes back to 1881. Because they're long-time friends, Garrett warns Billy that "times have changed" and he needs to disappear. Billy defiantly stays, Garrett becomes sheriff, and most of the movie is Garrett's long pursuit so he can bring Billy in. Mexican locations, western slang, and lots of drinkin', whorin', and gunplay make it a rugged, masculine movie. Naturally, Peckinpah kills off dozens of men, occasionally with slow-motion blood spurts reminiscent of *The Wild Bunch* (1969). He also shows his typical disgusting cruelty against animals, here with cowboys giddily shooting the heads off live chickens. There are ten minutes of mild suspense near the end as the principals gather in Fort Sumner and the final showdown looms, but it's over quickly and, surprisingly for Peckinpah, bloodlessly. Appropriately enough, it's an underwhelming climax for this disappointing movie.

Kris Kristofferson and Bob Dylan.

ADDED ATTRACTION: Newman's Own Western

Another early-'70s movie about a real person is *The Life and Times of Judge Roy Bean* (1972), based on the self-appointed judge who was "the law west of the Pecos" in the 1800s. Presenting Bean's life as a playful tall tale, director John Huston puts bearded star Paul Newman under a sombrero and has characters, even dead ones, talk directly to the camera. As Bean, Newman declares that in his tiny town "there's gonna be order, progress, civilization, and peace ... and I don't care who I have to kill to get it." The hangin's start comin' reg'lar. It's an uneven, mildly diverting movie comprised of colorful episodes, a fiery final shoot-out, and a touch of sentimentality. Anthony Perkins, Tab Hunter, Roddy McDowall, Ava Gardner, and Huston himself have small roles, while Victoria Principal makes her movie debut co-starring as a sweet-faced *señorita*.

Emperor of the North

Released: May 1973

Director: Robert Aldrich

Stars: Lee Marvin, Ernest Borgnine, Keith Carradine

Academy Awards: None

PREVIEW: A legendary train-hopping hobo tries to ride the train run by a sadistic conductor.

NOW SHOWING: Clash of the Titans

Brutal, powerful, but also a little philosophical, *Emperor of the North* (1973) is an underappreciated drama that captures a distant time and subculture. Robert Aldrich, veteran director of potent movies like *The Dirty Dozen* (1967), here goes back to the Depression for another battle story, this one about trains and the nomadic hobos who sneak free rides.

The combatants (both played by Oscar winners) are Shack (Ernest Borgnine), who rules the #19 train with maniacal determination, and A-No. 1 (Lee Marvin), a dignified hobo who relies on guile and experience to go where he wants. Since it's 1933, Shack might represent the era's unsympathetic establishment, with A-No. 1 as the down-trodden common man who only wants to get somewhere during those impoverished times. Tagging along with A-No. 1 is Cigaret (Keith Carradine), an obnoxious young braggart probably named for his slender frame, not his habits (he doesn't smoke). A-No. 1 becomes Cigaret's reluctant mentor: "You've got a chance to be a good bum," says A-No. 1. "You can be a meat eater, kid," as he teaches him tricks of the trade.

The tone is set before the opening credits when Shack (Ernest Borgnine) literally hammers an unwary hobo, causing him to fall under the train and get sliced in two. Shack smiles sadistically; this psychopath loves his work. A-No. 1 proves he's equally tough when he defends himself from thieves by brandishing a live chicken.

When A-No. 1 announces he'll hop Shack's #19 train across Oregon, everyone places bets (Shack is so mean to everyone, even his co-workers want to see him get his comeuppance). The two foes then try to outwit and torment each other as A-No. 1 and Cigaret ride for over half the movie. There are some talky sections and a tense sequence involving an oncoming train, but mainly the movie builds to the titanic *mano-y*-sicko fight on the moving train. For five minutes A-No. 1 and Shack whale away with lumber, a hammer, heavy chains, and a fireman's axe. Blood flows, sweat pours, and Shack's eyes bulge demonically.

Remove the startling violence and this would still be a significant movie. Director Aldrich has staged the action masterfully and photographed the vintage trains meticulously (this is a must-see movie for rail fans). He gets the period details right, too, especially the colorful, almost poetic hobo lingo. *Emperor of the North* is a gritty, hard-hitting, and impressive ride.

Ernest Borgnine and Lee Marvin.

ADDED ATTRACTION: Violent Movies of the '70s

Violent movies of the late 1960s, especially *Bonnie and Clyde* (1967), *Night of the Living Dead* (1968), and *The Wild Bunch* (1969), paved the way for the violent movies of the 1970s. Here are twenty-two of the many movies released during the decade that, like *Emperor of the North*, had bloody reputations.

- *A Clockwork Orange* (1971)
- *Apocalypse Now* (1979)
- *Boxcar Bertha* (1972)
- *Coffy* (1973)
- *Dawn of the Dead* (1979)
- *Death Wish* (1974)
- *Dillinger* (1973)
- *Dirty Harry* (1971)
- *The Godfather* (1972)
- *The Hills Have Eyes* (1977)
- *I Spit on Your Grave* (1978)
- *Jaws* (1975)
- *Joe* (1970)
- *The Last House on the Left* (1972)
- *A Man Called Horse* (1970)
- *Prime Cut* (1972)
- *Rollerball* (1975)
- *Slaughter* (1972)
- *Straw Dogs* (1971)
- *Taxi Driver* (1976)
- *The Texas Chain Saw Massacre* (1974)
- *The Warriors* (1979)

Coffy

Released: June 1973

Director: Jack Hill

Stars: Pam Grier, Booker Bradshaw, Robert DoQui

Academy Awards: None

PREVIEW: Coffy, nurse by day and vigilante by night, hunts the pushers who hooked her sister.

NOW SHOWING: Strong *Coffy*

A highlight of the blaxploitation genre, *Coffy* (1973) is a slam-bang revenge movie with a terrific heroine, crazy-good fight scenes, and a wild villain. It's one of the first kick-ass action movies with a female star, and that star is convincing as an ordinary hard-working woman, a sexy seductress, and an athletic superhero. Seriously, who does that?

Pam Grier, that's who. She plays Nurse Coffen, who's got a real job and a nice white Mustang, but she becomes a tough vigilante to kill the dealers who hooked her sister on drugs. In the first eight minutes Coffy brutally slays a pusher and a junkie, but there are many more bad guys to come, especially a big bad pimp flamboyantly decked out in a gold jump-suit, gold accessories, and a hat with a feather in it.

Doing whatever's necessary, Coffy poses as a Jamaican prostitute, hides a blade in her Afro, and substitutes sugar for heroin so she can be harmlessly injected and pretend to be high. The take-no-prisoners violence is startling: a drug pusher's head explodes, Coffy beats up a group of hookers, and the pimp is sadistically dragged behind a car. Coffy finally shoots her lying boyfriend by blasting him with a shotgun ... in the groin. It's so satisfying to see this exotically beautiful wonder woman get pushed down but emerge as the last person standing. Wham/bam/thank you, Pam.

With a hit on its hands, American International Pictures rushed *Foxy Brown* (1974) into theaters just ten months later. It's not exactly a sequel, though writer/director Jack Hill returns, the plot is similar, and, have no fear, Grier is here as Foxy, dispensing violent vigilante justice (which, she says, is "as American as apple pie"). "She's a whole lotta woman," we're reminded, as if we couldn't tell from Foxy's dazzling array of cleavage-revealing outfits. Like Coffy, Foxy is self-reliant and uses her sex appeal to her advantage, this time infiltrating a call-girl ring to avenge her boyfriend's murder. She gets in a brawl in a lesbian bar, she's tied up/drugged/and raped, she slices an enemy in half with an airplane propeller, and she castrates another villain. *Foxy Brown* isn't quite as good or believable as *Coffy*, and it's a little raunchier, but as usual there's some humor and Grier plays her role seriously. No wonder Quentin Tarantino built *Jackie Brown* (1997) around this formidable star. Grier's great.

ADDED ATTRACTION: Wonder Women

Here are eighteen alphabetically listed 1970s movies that, like *Coffy* and *Foxy Brown*, show women in powerful leading roles. Not all of these women are violent in their movies, but at some point they're all tough and resilient. Lead actresses are identified.

- *Alien* (1979): Sigourney Weaver
- *Bloody Mama* (1970): Shelley Winters
- *Carrie* (1976): Sissy Spacek
- *Cleopatra Jones* (1973): Tamara Dobson
- *'Gator Bait* (1974): Claudia Jennings
- *Grease* (1978): Stockard Channing
- *Halloween* (1978): Jamie Lee Curtis
- *Hannie Caulder* (1971): Raquel Welch
- *Harold and Maude* (1971): Ruth Gordon
- *I Spit on Your Grave* (1978): Camille Keaton
- *Man of La Mancha* (1972): Sophia Loren
- *McCabe & Mrs. Miller* (1971): Julie Christie
- *Network* (1976): Faye Dunaway
- *Norma Rae* (1979): Sally Field
- *One Flew Over the Cuckoo's Nest* (1975): Louise Fletcher

- *The Spy Who Loved Me* (1977): Barbara Bach
- *Star Wars* (1977): Carrie Fisher
- *Stingray* (1978): Sherry Jackson

Dillinger

Released: June 1973
Director: John Milius
Stars: Warren Oates, Ben Johnson, Michelle Phillips
Academy Awards: None

PREVIEW: The FBI's Melvin Purvis pursues dangerous criminals, especially John Dillinger.

NOW SHOWING: Public Enemy No. 1

Makers of youth-oriented horror, biker, and beach movies from the 1950s to the 1980s, the prolific independent studio American International Pictures helped launch the careers of several soon-to-be-famous directors: Woody Allen, Peter Bogdanovich, Francis Ford Coppola, Brian De Palma, and Martin Scorsese all made some of their first movies for AIP. Joining this group in 1973 was John Milius. He'd already written successful screenplays (1972's *Jeremiah Johnson*), but *Dillinger* (1973) established him as an up-and-coming director.

Unlike most low-budget AIP productions, *Dillinger* has relatively high-brow aspirations. It boasts stars who had won Oscars (Ben Johnson, Cloris Leachman), impressive Depression Era details (vintage cars, settings, and costumes), and black-and-white montages that add authenticity. The fast-paced story presents the illegal activities of "Public Enemy No. 1," John Dillinger (Warren Oates), and the simultaneous pursuit by FBI man Melvin Purvis (Johnson). We see Dillinger on his crime spree, his capture and vow that "no jail can hold me," and his brash escape using a gun carved from soap. Purvis, meanwhile, first hunts down other notorious criminals before finally confronting Dillinger. Their one face-to-face meeting comes in the last five minutes when "the lady in red" (Leachman) accompanies Dillinger to his doom outside a Chicago movie theater. Purvis narrates events with low-key understatement: "I knew I'd never take him alive; I didn't try too hard neither."

This action-packed movie is violent—bullets fly, blood pours, cars explode, pedestrians are run over, etc.—but the carnage is well-staged, especially the long shoot-out that wipes out Dillinger's gang. Like the leads in *Bonnie and Clyde* (1967), Dillinger is occasionally charming and is sometimes sympathetic to his victims. Other villains, however, especially hot-headed Baby Face Nelson (Richard Dreyfuss), kill wantonly with no remorse. Yet as vicious as the criminals are, some of their deaths are surprisingly poignant, like when Pretty Boy Floyd (Steve Kanaly) flees a friendly sanctuary and dies alone in a field. The cast includes some charismatic personalities, including singer Michelle Phillips as Dillinger's girlfriend and Harry Dean Stanton as a hard-luck minion.

While everything is based on actual events, history gets slightly rearranged (the real Dillinger died before Nelson, not after). Still, even if the movie isn't always accurate, it's almost always entertaining.

ADDED ATTRACTION: *The Friends* of Robert Mitchum

A week after *Dillinger* blasted into theaters, a more subdued crime movie, *The Friends of Eddie Coyle* (1973), premiered to critical acclaim. Audiences, though, didn't rush to this slow, downbeat movie that emphasizes fascinating talk and authentic atmosphere over thrilling action and bloody violence. True, guns are shown or discussed in most scenes, but only two people get shot, and there are no other fights. Director Peter Yates, whose *Bullitt* (1968) includes an iconic car chase, here stages a mild twenty-second pursuit that never leaves the parking lot. *Eddie Coyle*'s strength is its ensemble acting. Robert Mitchum, tahkin' wit' a realistic Boston accent in one of his most understated and impressive performances, is Eddie, a world-weary small-time criminal whose sad life has come down to either a long prison sentence or a deal with the feds that'll make him rat on his "friends," the unlikeable losers around him who are pulling off crimes. They're in the movie as much as Eddie is, and at the end they triumph when he meets the fate inevitably coming to someone who's backed into a desperate corner and has "to turn permanent fink."

live and let Die

Released: June 1973
Director: Guy Hamilton
Stars: Roger Moore, Yaphet Kotto, Jane Seymour
Academy Awards: One nomination (Best Song)

PREVIEW: James Bond goes to New Orleans and a Caribbean island in pursuit of a heroin kingpin.

NOW SHOWING: Moore, Roger Moore

Live and Let Die (1973) was the third consecutive movie with a different actor playing James Bond (George Lazenby in 1969 and Sean Connery in 1971 were the previous 007's). Newcomer Roger Moore was the oldest of the three (forty-five years old, plus-eleven over Lazenby, and plus-five over Connery, who turned down a huge offer to return). But nervous fans could relax: Moore immediately made the role his own, and his success here would lead him to six more Bond movies.

Live and Let Die tweaks the familiar Bond formula, which is instantly apparent as soon as Paul McCartney and Wings crank up their Oscar-nominated theme song, the series' first rock anthem. More importantly, this movie is more interracial than earlier Bond films, perhaps acknowledging the decade's popular blaxploitation genre (*Live and Let Die* debuted in the same month as *Coffy* and *Shaft in Africa*). Thus, black musicians and dancers perform at different times, Harlem is one of the early settings, the villain and his minions are black, and, new for the Bond movies, 007 sleeps with a black girl (Gloria Hendry). Further distancing himself from Sean Connery's portrayal in six previous movies, Moore's 007 goes hatless, prefers bourbon and long cigars to Connery's martinis and cigarettes, and doesn't wear a tuxedo. They're both suave, of course, but Moore has a more tongue-in-cheek delivery. He's even called "Jim."

The plot involves "a simple matter of heroin smuggling," with free distribution ready to create a nation of addicts dependent on the villain's high-priced product. Bond travels to New York, a Caribbean island, and New Orleans on the trail of the formidable

Jane Seymour and Roger Moore.

Kananga (Yaphet Kotto, who will play Parker in 1979's *Alien*). A fifteen-minute sequence that launches from a lethal crocodile farm and segues to a chase on the bayou includes, thrillingly, some exciting speedboat stunts and, regrettably, an excitable Southern sheriff (Clifton James) who distracts with unnecessary humor. The grab-bag return to the island includes voodoo rituals, snakes, sharks, and an underground monorail from some other movie. Kananga gets his, Bond gets his girl (Jane Seymour).

The audience gets plenty of action, appearances by familiar characters—M, Moneypenny, CIA man Felix Leiter (not Q, though)—and a rare look inside Bond's flat. Most of all it gets satisfaction—*Live and Let Die* was a huge hit, meaning there'd soon be more Moore in *The Man with the Golden Gun* (1974).

ADDED ATTRACTION: Interracial Couples

Mixed-race couples appeared in other 1970s movies besides *Live and Let Die*. In the following movies, a black actor or actress (listed first) and a white actor or actress are paired romantically (or, as in *Mandingo* and *Shaft*, paired physically without any romance).

- *Blazing Saddles* (1974): Cleavon Little, Madeline Kahn
- *The Eiger Sanction* (1975): Vonetta McGee, Clint Eastwood
- *The Grasshopper* (1970): Jim Brown, Jacqueline Bisset
- *The Great White Hope* (1970): James Earl Jones, Jane Alexander
- *Honky* (1971): Brenda Sykes, John Nielson
- *The Landlord* (1970): Diana Sands, Beau Bridges
- *The Liberation of L.B. Jones* (1970): Lola Falana, Anthony Zerbe

- *Mahogany* (1975): Diana Ross, Anthony Perkins
- *Mandingo* (1975): Ken Norton, Susan George
- *The Omega Man* (1971): Rosalind Cash, Charlton Heston
- *Shaft* (1971): Richard Roundtree, Margaret Warncke
- *Super Fly* (1972): Ron O'Neal, Polly Niles
- *Together for Days* (1972): Clifton Davis, Lois Chiles

American Graffiti

(One of 1973's five **FAR-OUT** movies)

Released: August 1973

Director: George Lucas

Stars: Richard Dreyfuss, Ron Howard, Charles Martin Smith

Academy Awards: Five nominations (Best Picture; Best Supporting Actress—Candy Clark; Best Director; Best Writing; Best Editing)

PREVIEW: In 1962, teens cruise the streets in classic cars and wrestle with major decisions.

FINE LINE: "The night is young and I'm not hittin' the rack till I get a little action." (Carol, the youngest of the cruisers, talking tough to the oldest cruiser as he tries to get her off his hands by driving her home.)

CLOSE-UP: Eighty minutes into the movie, the Pharaohs pull their destructive prank on the lurking cop car. Down the street is Petaluma's State Theater, its marquee reading *Dementia 13*. This inside joke points to Francis Ford Coppola's 1963 movie (Coppola was one of *American Graffiti*'s producers). But 1963, obviously, is a year *after* the time setting for *American Graffiti*. Other *Graffiti* anachronisms we've spotted: the last song is the Beach Boys' 1964 hit, "All Summer Long," the license plate on John Milner's yellow hot rod—THX 138—references George Lucas's *THX 1138* (1971), a 1967 Chevy Caprice is parked on a street, and Curt's car appears to be a 1967 Citroën.

NOW SHOWING: American Classic

Routinely included among the hundred best American movies *ever* (and among the top dozen of the 1970s), *American Graffiti* (1973) is truly a marvel, especially when you consider what preceded it. Writer/director George Lucas's previous movie was an ambitious science-fiction drama, *THX 1138* (1971). Visually and sonically impressive, it presents a bleak future where dehumanized laborers with shaved heads and numbers for names live in sterile underground cities. Compulsory pills repress feelings; extreme surveillance and robot police enforce strict laws; and love is forbidden.

American Graffiti veers about as far from that stark, high-tech experience as you can get. Set in 1962, this small, sweet movie, glowing with warm humanity and sparkling dialogue, perfectly captures an innocent moment tied to the recent past but right on the cusp of a new era (the Kennedy assassination, the Beatles, and Vietnam are just around the corner). And whereas everyone in *THX 1138* basically looks and acts the same, *American Graffiti* assembles a colorful ensemble cast of distinctive personalities. Except for Ron Howard, most of the actors and actresses were unknown at the time, with Harrison Ford, Paul Le Mat, Mackenzie Phillips, Kathleen Quinlan, and Suzanne Somers all getting their first significant screen roles.

Mood, not story, dominates *THX 1138*; in contrast, *American Graffiti* overlaps four plot lines that intricately weave back and forth. Throughout the movie, main characters continually splinter off and then reconnect, updating each other and affecting the events that all happen in one night. For instance, nerdy Toad (Charles Martin Smith) ditches his Vespa scooter and borrows a majestic '58 Chevy Impala from another lead, Steve (Howard). Toad drives off, has romantic adventures, and later intersects with Steve when the car is stolen. Toad gets in a fist-fight but is rescued by another lead, John (Paul Le Mat). After witnessing the show-stopping act of youthful defiance perpetrated by yet another lead, Curt (Richard Dreyfuss), Toad sets the climactic car race in motion. This is just one example of what Lucas and co-screenwriters Gloria Katz and Willard Huyck do so brilliantly, this constant interlacing of subplots and characters that is complex to summarize but a joy to watch.

The movie's spine is its exuberant soundtrack. The very first sounds we hear—someone moving a radio dial—precede the opening titles. From then on, music leans in and out from background to foreground but is always present, with Wolfman Jack, a real DJ, providing a steady stream of commentary, advice, and nostalgic songs from rock's Golden Age. After *American Graffiti*, many movies (including dozens by Woody Allen) would back scenes with relevant popular songs instead of a newly composed score.

But it's not just the presence of old songs on the soundtrack that's important. It's the way those songs are used that is so creative. Listen carefully as Curt runs down the street and stands in an intersection forty-four minutes into the movie. He isn't carrying a radio, but music swirls around him, intensifying and fading as car radios pass by; it's like he's breathing the floating music. Fifty minutes later, the radio inspires him to make a desperate visit to the station outside of town. He arrives with hope, gets

Wolfman Jack.

some encouragement, and leaves with both a lesson and a little disillusionment from the music man. At once funny, illuminating, and poignant, this powerful scene is one of the movie's dramatic highlights.

All the major characters are touched by unexpected events. Ambitious Steve is determined to break up with his long-time girlfriend and leave "this turkey town" (supposedly Modesto, Lucas' actual hometown, but actually Marin County's San Rafael and Petaluma). Ironically, Steve ends up reuniting with his girlfriend and settling down as an insurance salesman. Curt is tormented by indecision and seems ready to stay, but he's the one who climbs aboard the getaway plane. Tough-guy John resists but then befriends the young girl played by Mackenzie Phillips, and they share a memorable scene walking through the car graveyard before he gently delivers her home in his '32 deuce coupe. Nice girl/head cheerleader Laurie (Cindy Williams) defiantly climbs into a wicked '55 Chevy and almost gets killed in a dramatic drag race; in a movie full of car-related stunts and surprises, this last race is the most dangerous.

One final flourish comes just before the end credits, when text summarizes the future lives of the four main guys (a missed opportunity—the girls should've been included, too). After the thrilling, funny, emotional night we've all shared, it's genuinely touching to read the sad destinies that await two main characters when adult concerns catch up to them in a hurry. Other movies, including *The French Connection* (1971), had done something similar, but at the time these short biographical projections still felt fresh, and they would soon be parodied in *Animal House* (1978).

Inventive, charismatic, and sincere—like we said, *American Graffiti* is truly a marvel. Amazingly, studio executives were so unhappy with Lucas' finished product, which he made in under a month on a shoestring budget, that they almost didn't release it (they got their come-uppance when *American Graffiti* earned a Best Picture Oscar nomination and became a box-office blockbuster). Not only is it beloved, *American Graffiti* has been influential: viewers who like *Grease* (1978), *Fast Times at Ridgemont High* (1982), *Dazed and Confused* (1993), TV's *Happy Days*, and many other high school-themed productions have got this witty, wonderful classic to thank.

ADDED ATTRACTION: Lee's Last

Opening in the same month as *American Graffiti* was *Enter the Dragon* (1973), another influential movie with many imitators. Bruce Lee was already well-known to American audiences as a lightning-fast martial arts pioneer, thanks to TV's *The Green Hornet* and several Chinese-language kung fu movies. *Enter the Dragon* gives him his only starring role for a major American studio, and this thrilling, stylish spectacle about international espionage is his masterpiece. Showcased as a lean, muscular whirling wonder, the thirty-two-year-old Lee died tragically just weeks before the movie opened to critical and popular acclaim.

Westworld

Released: August 1973
Director: Michael Crichton
Stars: Richard Benjamin, James Brolin, Yul Brynner
Academy Awards: None

PREVIEW: Two friends visit a futuristic theme park where everything eventually goes wrong.

NOW SHOWING: Go *Westworld*, Young Man

In *Westworld* (1973), two pals (Richard Benjamin and James Brolin) visit "the ulti-mate resort" for "an unforgettable vacation." Of the three fantasy areas guests can explore—Roman World, Medieval World, and Westworld—the guys choose to experi-ence "lawless violence on the American frontier of the 1880s." In the Westworld area, realistic western sets serve as the backdrops for rough-and-tumble cowboy action, and life-like robots simulate everyone from sexy saloon girls to pistol-packing villains. And with the "reliable computer technology" (that's what a recorded announcement calls it), "nothing can go wrong." For a while that seems to be true as the friends relish the detailed environment, triumph in a shoot-out, and even take a trip to a brothel. Eventually, of course, *everything* goes wrong, and the last third of the movie is one long, suspenseful chase as a technologically enhanced gunslinger (Yul Brynner), relentless and unemotional like the humanoid machine that will arrive from the future in *The Terminator* (1984), pursues Benjamin's character as he flees through the entire resort past dead guests.

Writer/director Michael Crichton, who will later invent another location plagued by dysfunctional technology, Jurassic Park, presents an exciting tale in a taut eighty-eight minutes. Everything, from the control room to the dismantled robot faces to the com-puterized view from a robot's perspective, feels real and believable. There are a few plot holes—the park is run from a control room that the employees somehow can't get out of, a violent free-wheeling bar-room brawl should easily injure the paying customers, and unfathomably the robots are shooting real bullets—plus there's some silliness with dopey guests, but nothing diminishes the high-tech fun and the last-act tension, especially when it becomes apparent that the killer robot is like the Energizer bunny and will just keep going and going. Already ahead of its time in 1973, the *Westworld* saga has endured with a sequel called *Futureworld* (1976) and two later TV series. Like a thoroughly entertaining Disneyland ride, *Westworld* is an E-ticket experience.

ADDED ATTRACTION: Bad Signs

Between the start of the movie and the death of the first guest about an hour later, we see small signs that things may not be perfect in Westworld.

- 5 minutes into the movie:
  The introductory video on the flight incorrectly calls the park Western World.
- 10 minutes:
  The control room reports minor problem with the "balance controls"; a techni-cian realizes that the stagecoach may arrive late, and if it does, "I don't know what to do."

- 19 minutes:
Medieval World's malfunctioning Black Knight is being repaired.

- 25 minutes:
In the brothel, the girl's robotic eyes suddenly flash alert.

- 30 minutes:
In the repair lab, a robot occasionally falls over, and a different robot is having a serious "central malfunction"; also, the robots have been designed by other computers, so technicians admit that they "don't know exactly how they work."

- 32 minutes:
Lab technicians aren't "getting sound pickup from the tenth quadrant."

- 42 minutes:
Problems with the laundry delivery and the air-conditioning.

- 46 minutes:
A mechanical rattlesnake bites a guest; in the control room, a supervisor tries to use a malfunctioning telephone and disgustedly asks, "Doesn't anything work around here?"

- 53 minutes:
A "sex model" in Medieval World has a "program breakdown" and slaps a guest.

- 59 minutes:
Supposedly repaired, Medieval World's Black Knight stabs and kills a guest.

Mean Streets

(One of 1973's five **FAR-OUT** movies)

Released: October 1973

Director: Martin Scorsese

Stars: Robert De Niro, Harvey Keitel, David Proval

Academy Awards: None

PREVIEW: A low-level New York mobster deals with guilt as he tries to help his foolish friend.

FINE LINE: "You don't make up for your sins in church. You do it in the streets. You do it at home." (Opening narration spoken by Martin Scorsese.)

CLOSE-UP: Forty-one minutes into the movie, an assassin arrives to shoot a drunk. The shooter is played by nineteen-year-old Robert Carradine, the drunk by his half-brother, twenty-seven-year-old David Carradine.

NOW SHOWING: Life on the *Mean Streets*

Imagine attending 1973's New York Film Festival. It opened with François Truffaut's *Day for Night* (1973), closed with Terrence Malick's *Badlands* (1973), and in between gave viewers their first look at Martin Scorsese's *Mean Streets* (1973). Instantly acclaimed by festivalgoers, *Mean Streets* is now regarded as a seminal '70s movie and one of the most important in Scorsese's illustrious career.

One year earlier, Scorsese had made *Boxcar Bertha* (1972), an interesting but lesser crime drama set in the Depression and reminiscent of *Bonnie and Clyde* (1967); *Mean*

Streets is set in modern times and is reminiscent of … nothing else. At the time *Mean Streets* felt like a new kind of movie. *Taxi Driver* (1976), Scorsese's breakthrough masterpiece, isn't as shocking if you've already seen *Mean Streets*.

In *Mean Streets*, the gritty New York streets are indeed mean when that word is defined as malicious and hostile, but they are also mean in the sense of small and of low stature. The criminal element here isn't the powerful, wealthy family of *The Godfather* (1972); *Mean Streets'* criminals are unimportant hustlers and bookies trying to make a few bucks. It's like Scorsese remade *The Godfather* about the lowlife hoodlum Paulie, not Don Corleone.

The most common complaint about *Mean Streets* is its central storyline. There isn't one. Instead, the movie presents realistic characters and culture to study. Things happen, arguments start, fights erupt, but not until the last ten minutes do we realize that a main character may not survive. The first scene introduces Charlie (Harvey Keitel), the diplomat among uneducated neighborhood friends in New York's Little Italy. These are guys who insult and shove each other, but ultimately they're loyal to the group. Charlie's got a crucifix around his neck and another on his wall, he goes to church, he whispers directly to God, and he wants "to help people." It's not easy for him, though, given his many crime associates and their usual hangout, a sleazy topless bar perpetually lit in hellish red. All movie long he's tormented by guilt; "those things," he says about Catholic confessions and prayers, "they don't mean anything to me, they're just words." The movie presents his attempts to reconcile his inner feelings with his outer life.

Charlie's biggest burden is his friend Johnny Boy (Robert De Niro). Johnny Boy enters as a senseless prankster who recklessly blows up a corner mail box (later he'll toss a cherry bomb off a roof and shoot into a window, all for some juvenile thrills). De Niro is electrifying as a lean, rash jerk who borrows money from everyone, doesn't go to work, and is described as "half-crazy," "crazy," "an insane person," a "crazy bastard," "a punk bastard," a "punk kid," a "bum," and "stupid." Charlie tries to help him with counsel and cash, but it eventually becomes clear that Johnny Boy is doomed.

It's a hard movie to enjoy, but an easy one to appreciate as something original and startling. For one thing, *Mean Streets* boldly takes movie profanity to an authentic new level with vocabulary that is raw and racist. Johnny Boy has his own streetwise way of talking, flinging the F-word like confetti and pronouncing "beautiful" as "beeyooteeful" and "joint" as "jurnt." Characters have names like Joey Clams and Frankie Bones, and sentences sometimes sound like this: "Bla bla bing bing, comin' home I run into Jimmy Sparks. … bing bing bing, I lose $400." One of the most memorable scenes involves a big brawl in a pool hall when one of the guys gets called a "mook," a word they don't recognize.

For modern audiences, it's fascinating to see how *Mean Streets* heralds Scorsese's later successes. His first movie, the black-and-white *Who's That Knocking at My Door* (1967), incorporated some of his recognizable characteristics—it stars Harvey Keitel, uses similar settings, and, as in many later movies, has Scorsese's own mother in a small role; while it's inventive, it's also an unpolished work. Building on that impressive debut, Scorsese really becomes Scorsese with *Mean Streets*. Importantly, it's his first of nine movies with Robert De Niro, leading to one of Hollywood's most thrilling collaborations. As he will later, Scorsese uses a handheld camera, slow-motion, and long unbroken shots effectively (he even mounts a camera on a taxi cab, like in *Taxi Driver*). *Mean Streets'* soundtrack includes the Rolling Stones, whose songs will play in both *Goodfellas* (1990) and *Casino* (1995). A question asked eleven times in *Mean*

Streets—"What's the matter with you?"—will reappear in many of Scorsese's later movies (three times in 1980's *Raging Bull*). At the end of *Mean Streets* and *Taxi Driver*, De Niro's character takes a bullet in the throat. In both movies, Scorsese himself brandishes handguns in the back seats of cars.

In many ways, *Mean Streets* is the key hinge in Scorsese's career. While not his best work, it's a major tour de force that firmly establishes his signature style and thus influences future gangster movies, not just his own (the title will be echoed in non-Scorsese movies like 1997's *Mean Guns*, 2004's *Mean Girls*, and 2016's *Mean Dreams*). From seeds planted in his first two movies, *Mean Streets* is where Scorsese's art blooms into a dark, dark flower.

ADDED ATTRACTION: Movie Marquees, Part Two

Characters in *Mean Streets* see *The Searchers* (1956) and *The Tomb of Ligeia* (1964) in theaters. Here are other 1973–1974 movies where marquees, or actual clips, announce other movies. For more movie marquees, see the entry for *Bless the Beasts & Children* (1971).

- *Airport 1975* (1974): *American Graffiti* (1973) is the in-flight movie.
- *American Graffiti* (1973): During the police-car prank, *Dementia 13* (1963) is on a background marquee.
- *Black Caesar* (1973): Seventy-nine minutes into the movie, a theater is showing *The Godfather* (1972).
- *Blazing Saddles* (1974): In the Grauman's Chinese Theater climax, *Blazing Saddles* itself is playing.
- *Breezy* (1973): The main characters see *High Plains Drifter* (1973), directed, like *Breezy*, by Clint Eastwood.
- *Crazy Joe* (1974): The movie opens in a theater where *Kiss of Death* (1947) is playing.
- *Dillinger* (1973): *Manhattan Melodrama* (1934) is on the Biograph's marquee when Dillinger is killed.
- *Earthquake* (1974): When the earthquake strikes, Rosa is in a theater watching *High Plains Drifter* (1973).
- *Paper Moon* (1973): Nine minutes in, a theater across from the diner is showing *Steamboat Round the Bend* (1935).
- *The Sugarland Express* (1974): When the leads hide at the drive-in, *Sssssss* (1973) is playing.
- *The Way We Were* (1973): The first minute shows a marquee with *Counter-Attack* (1945) and *Go West* (1940).

Badlands

(One of 1973's five **FAR-OUT** movies)
Released: October 1973
Director: Terrence Malick
Stars: Martin Sheen, Sissy Spacek, Warren Oates
Academy Awards: None

PREVIEW: In the 1950s, two young lovers kill people as they drive across the Dakota badlands.

FINE LINE: "The world was like a faraway planet to which I could never return." (Holly, acknowledging how different her life is halfway through the movie.)

CLOSE-UP: Thirteen minutes into the movie, Kit and Holly have sex outdoors. For Holly it's her first time, and she is totally naïve about the experience: "Did it go the way it's supposed to," she asks while getting dressed. "Is that all there is to it? … Gosh, what was everybody talkin' about?" Kit, distant and untalkative for once, saunters down to the river. "You don't care about anything I say," says Holly. They'll kiss later, but for these two young lovers this is the only sexual contact we see in the movie.

NOW SHOWING: "Suppose I Shot You? How'd That Be?"

Some great directors, including Hal Ashby, Michael Cimino, Jonathan Demme, George Lucas, Steven Spielberg, and Oliver Stone, made their first major movies between 1970 and 1974. Typically their debuts were lesser-known works that pale in comparison to their later masterpieces; *Caged Heat* (1974) by Demme (he'd direct 1991's *The Silence of the Lambs*) and *Seizure* (1974) by Stone (1986's *Platoon*) are two good examples. Twenty-nine-year-old Terrence Malick also directed his first feature film during this period, but his debut, *Badlands* (1973), was different. Strong, assured, and startling, it was one of the decade's high points and is still one of his best movies ever. What's more, Malick not only directed *Badlands*, he wrote and produced it, and he even briefly appears in it. If other debuts were interesting signposts on the Hollywood highway, *Badlands* was a blazing billboard announcing the sudden arrival of an important new artist.

Though the closing credits claim that the movie "is fictional and is not intended to depict real events or persons," Malick based *Badlands* on actual history. In 1958 nineteen-year-old Charles Starkweather and his fourteen-year-old girlfriend, Caril Ann Fugate, drove around Nebraska and Wyoming on a prolific murder spree. After eleven deaths, both teenagers were caught; Starkweather was executed seventeen months later, while Fugate served seventeen years in prison. *Badlands* changes the story a bit. Kit Carruthers (Martin Sheen) is twenty-five, and Holly Sargis (Sissy Spacek) is fifteen. Set in South Dakota, the movie shows eight murders. Kit is executed six months after the crimes, while Holly gets "probation and a lot of nasty looks."

There's also a connection to *Bonnie and Clyde* (1967), and indeed at the end of *Badlands* Malick thanks the director of that influential classic, Arthur Penn. Both movies are set in the past, both show a young murderous couple on the lam, and nobody escapes happily. But there are big differences, too. Unlike the romanticized Bonnie Parker and Clyde Barrow, who are portrayed as Robin Hood-style bank robbers with sympathies for the poor, Malick doesn't sentimentalize his criminals. Kit and Holly have no goals and no sympathy for anyone (one of their victims is Kit's own friend). Clyde is gentle while visiting with Bonnie's mother; Kit shoots Holly's father in cold blood. Bonnie and Clyde stay with each other and share one last loving look before they die; Holly leaves Kit to fend for himself.

So confident is Malick in his ability to tell his story in a compelling and poetic way, he doesn't attempt to explain Kit's motivations. It's a daring strategy, frustrating to some viewers but chillingly enigmatic to many others. Holly is easier to understand because she adds her observations in voice-over narration throughout the entire movie. Occasionally she infuses some homespun imagery into her commentary—something feels "just kind of blah, like when you're sittin' there and all the water has run out of the bathtub"—but generally her tone is flat and impassive.

Sissy Spacek and Martin Sheen.

She starts the movie as a freckle-faced barefoot girl who's twirling her baton when Kit, a chatty garbage man in flashy cowboy boots, swaggers over and introduces himself. "He was handsomer than anybody I'd ever met," she narrates, "he looked just like James Dean." Holly also mentions that Kit "came from the wrong side of the tracks, so-called," but she's too immature to try to comprehend or judge his actions, even after he kills her father. "I sensed that my destiny now lay with Kit, for better or for worse," she concedes as they take off in Kit's dusty 1951 Mercury.

Hiding in a forest, they build a treehouse, make a simple life, fall in love, and have some nice moments, like their impromptu dance to the 1956 hit "Love Is Strange." But when Kit shoots three bounty hunters, they're back on the road across vast landscapes. After he kills three more people, Holly calls Kit "the most trigger-happy person" she's ever met and "kind of odd," but still she doesn't offer any real protests. He remains a detached, unemotional mystery, impulsively shooting without getting angry or making declarations. "I shoot people every now and then" is all the explanation he can muster. As they both drift along, seven times in the movie one of them says, "I don't know."

Stealing a big '59 Caddy they head "across endless miles of open range" toward Montana. Holly seems to evolve and decides "to never again tag around with the hell-bent type, no matter how in love" she is. There's another sweet moment when they slow-dance to Nat King Cole's "A Blossom Fell," but eventually Holly abandons Kit. Just before he surrenders to the pursuing police, Kit adjusts the car's mirror so he can fix his hair. Now acting like a celebrity big shot, he charms everyone in a remarkable scene at an airport. As usual, when he has a final conversation with Holly, he speaks seventy-one words, and she mumbles one: "Yeah."

In this first impressive effort, Malick is already displaying characteristics that will be common to his later movies: dreamy, plain-spoken narration; restrained, thoughtful performances; beautiful shots of pastoral nature and colorful skies; arresting images there just for visual interest; and distinctive instrumental music (here the child-like "Musica Poetica" with hints of sadness that echo Holly's lost innocence). Malick's later movies may be more philosophical and heartbreaking, but they aren't more powerful and mesmerizing than *Badlands*.

ADDED ATTRACTION: The NFPB's NFR

Since 1989, the National Film Preservation Board has been adding movies to its National Film Registry. Up to twenty-five "culturally, historically, or aesthetically significant films" join the list each year. *Badlands* was added in 1993; here are other 1970–1974 feature films included in the NFPB's NFR, grouped according to the years when the movies came out.

- **1970**: *Five Easy Pieces, Little Big Man, M*A*S*H, Patton, Wanda*

- **1971**: *Dirty Harry, The French Connection, Harold and Maude, The Hospital, The Last Picture Show, McCabe & Mrs. Miller, Shaft, Two-Lane Blacktop, Willy Wonka & the Chocolate Factory*

- **1972**: *Cabaret, Deliverance, The Godfather, Lives of Performers*

- **1973**: *American Graffiti, Enter the Dragon, The Exorcist, Mean Streets, The Spook Who Sat by the Door, The Sting*

- **1974**: *Blazing Saddles, Chinatown, The Conversation, The Godfather: Part II, A Woman Under the Influence, Young Frankenstein*

The Paper Chase

Released: October 1973

Director: James Bridges

Stars: Timothy Bottoms, Lindsay Wagner, John Houseman

Academy Awards: One win (Best Supporting Actor—John Houseman), plus two more nominations (Best Writing; Best Sound)

PREVIEW: A student balances his love life and academics while in his first year at law school.

NOW SHOWING: "Bring on the Test"

After the phenomenal success of *Love Story* (1970), more college-life movies were inevitable. One of the first to follow was also one of the best, *The Paper Chase* (1973). An intelligent, authentic, and insightful look at students trying to survive Harvard Law School, this excellent movie probably inspired, and drove away in equal numbers, people interested in law careers.

A late suicide attempt notwithstanding, little actually happens. Serious academics, not dramatic action or comedic pranks, dominate the movie, with about twenty-five percent taking place in a classroom. Friends sneak into the library to access scholarly notes that they then read aloud; a student declines a sexy weekend getaway so he can do research; a professor quietly grades exams. For college life, it's about as far as you can get from *Animal House* (1978).

Surprisingly, all this is engrossing. We follow James Hart (Timothy Bottoms), a likeable student with unruly hair (many of the actors wear long 1970s hairstyles).

Hart's biggest problem is the class taught by Professor Kingsfield (John Houseman). Houseman is riveting as Kingsfield, an unsmiling tyrant who forcefully commands without ever shouting. Kingsfield uses the Socratic Method and prompts analysis with streams of questions. These classroom exchanges are fascinating. Hart starts out timid and unprepared, and he even throws up after his first class, but he's determined to succeed. Around him, struggling students leave the study group and even drop out.

Complicating Hart's studies is Susan (Lindsay Wagner), who happens to be Kingsfield's daughter. Hart tries to stay focused: "You cannot balance girls and law school at the same time," he concedes. He seems to be right. School is so demanding that near the end Hart completely forgets about an important birthday party.

The ambiguous conclusion has long been a subject of debate. We know Kingsfield gives Hart an A (we see the grade), but Hart doesn't. When his grades finally arrive, Hart tosses them, unopened, into the sea as a paper airplane. After his year-long slog, he's not a little interested? Is he safely assuming he got an A? Was the experience, not the grade, what he really wanted? Or has Susan convinced him that life and love, not "your little diploma," are what's important? This topic would make an interesting series of questions in Kingsfield's class.

ADDED ATTRACTION: Oscars Old and Young

The same year that seventy-one-year-old John Houseman won the Oscar as Best Supporting Actor and became the oldest winner ever in his category, ten-year-old Tatum O'Neal won Best Supporting Actress for *Paper Moon* (1973) and became the youngest winner ever in *her* category. Houseman wasn't the only seventy-something, and O'Neal wasn't the only ten-or-under child, to get an Oscar or an Oscar nomination for acting in a 1970s movie. Here are nine more with their ages in the years their movies came out.

- **Won**
  George Burns, 79: *The Sunshine Boys* (1975)
  Melvyn Douglas, 78: *Being There* (1979)
  Helen Hayes, 70: *Airport* (1970)

- **Nominated**
  Fred Astaire, 75: *The Towering Inferno* (1974)
  Lee Strasberg, 73: *The Godfather: Part II* (1974)
  Chief Dan George, 71: *Little Big Man* (1970)
  Laurence Olivier, 71: *The Boys from Brazil* (1978)
  Quinn Cummings, 10: *The Goodbye Girl* (1977)
  Justin Henry, 8: *Kramer vs. Kramer* (1979)

The Way We Were

Released: October 1973

Director: Sydney Pollack

Stars: Barbra Streisand, Robert Redford, Lois Chiles

Academy Awards: Two wins (Best Song; Best Music), plus four more nominations (Best Actress—Barbra Streisand; Best Cinematography; Best Art Direction; Best Costume Design)

PREVIEW: Two college students with opposite styles meet in 1937 and fall in love in the 1940s.

NOW SHOWING: "Misty Watercolor Memories"

Imagine studio executives monitoring the success of *Love Story* (1970). If a modern tear-jerker with two relative unknowns could become the year's top box-office hit, think what old-fashioned schmaltz with two superstars could do! Thus, Barbra Streisand, Robert Redford, *The Way We Were* (1973), multiple Oscars, a hit song, and one of 1973's biggest money-makers.

Streisand gets top billing and dominates the movie. She's Katie, an outspoken political activist who can argue world peace anytime with anyone. The movie opens in 1944 when she gasps upon seeing Hubbell (Redford) in his Navy uniform. Cue the theme song about memories, and for twenty-five minutes the movie flashes back to 1937 when she's president of her college's Young Communist League and he's a track star (Redford displays convincing athleticism, though at thirty-seven he's a little old for an undergrad). They don't fall in love, however, until the movie returns to 1944. Hubbell becomes a successful screenwriter, and they move to Malibu for a life of sailing and parties. He enjoys their affluence and thinks her continued activism is "stupid and dangerous"; she wants to live in France and believes "people are their principles!" Unable to compromise, they sadly split up; the finale finds them later in Manhattan, both with other people and doing what they do (he's writing for TV, she's protesting the bomb).

Viewers swooned then, and many still do (*The Way We Were* regularly makes "most romantic movies" lists). Polished and pretty, the movie is impeccably nostalgic. And the commercial formula works: Redford is charismatic and handsome, Streisand is sassy, vulnerable, and unconventionally appealing (twice we're reminded that she's "beautiful"). For all their tender moments, their best scenes together are when they're having emotional arguments.

To the movie's credit, it's perhaps the first to incorporate 1947's "Hollywood Ten" (*The Front* would tackle blacklisting head-on in 1976). Alas, the ending seems implausible, even unflattering—Hubbell glimpses his newborn baby, leaves for good while Katie's in the hospital, and she's okay with that. Really? We later learn he has zero relationship with his daughter. Again, really? What's more, Katie, moments after childbirth, is as radiant as Jenny was when she died in *Love Story*.

If some fantasy aspects are the way we weren't, there's still something effective about this well-made movie. It's like the title of Hubbell's novel, *A Country Made of Ice Cream*— irresistibly alluring, and gooey in a nice way.

Barbra Streisand and Robert Redford.

ADDED ATTRACTION: Eastern Intrigue

In the 1970s, director Sydney Pollack and actor Robert Redford made four movies together: *Jeremiah Johnson* (1972), *The Way We Were* (1973), *Three Days of the Condor* (1975), and *The Electric Horseman* (1979). Between numbers two and three Pollack directed another American movie star, Robert Mitchum, in *The Yakuza* (1974). Two heavyweights wrote the noirish screenplay: first Paul Schrader (who later wrote 1976's *Taxi Driver*), then a rewrite by Robert Towne (1974's *Chinatown*). Mitchum, typically tough, world-weary, and excellent, goes to Japan to find a friend's kidnapped daughter and gets entangled with family secrets, criminal gangs (the Yakuza), betrayals, an old flame, and fascinating rituals that include self-mutilation. Dark and intricate, *The Yakuza* has violent action sequences, especially a titanic few-against-many sword fight that seemingly inspired scenes in *Kill Bill: Vol. 1* (2003).

Charley Varrick

Released: October 1973
Director: Don Siegel
Stars: Walter Matthau, Joe Don Baker, Andy Robinson
Academy Awards: None

PREVIEW: A bank robber accidentally steals Mafia money, bringing on both cops and mobsters.

NOW SHOWING: Good-Time Charley

A smart little thriller, *Charley Varrick* (1973) is another worthy effort from director Don Siegel, who's better known for *Dirty Harry* (1971). As usual in Siegel's films, we end up rooting for an anti-hero who isn't always admirable, sometimes not even likeable. That's Charley (Walter Matthau), leading a team of robbers in a New Mexico bank heist where everything goes horribly wrong: Charley's wife and another robber are killed (Charley grieves for about ten seconds), cops are shot, and the getaway car is half-demolished. Charley and his sole remaining partner, an intense hothead played by Andy Robinson (*Dirty Harry*'s cackling villain), have stolen $765,118 in laundered mob money, which means not only are the cops after them, but so is Molly (Joe Don Baker), a menacing Mafia hit man.

   As beautifully underplayed by Matthau, Charley politely goes around setting up some mysterious scheme that isn't revealed until the end. To set up the clever switch-eroo finale, he double-crosses his partner by secretly switching their dental records. Then he sequesters the stolen money and manages to pit the hit man against his own boss. An exciting four-minute car-vs.-biplane chase finally brings Charley's plan to an explosive conclusion.

   Fans may lament that Hollywood doesn't make tightly focused crime movies like this anymore. In a way that's good, because two disturbing scenes with women weaken the movie. In the first, Molly the tough hit man slaps Sheree North's character, who responds by ... smiling and taking him to bed. Later, Charley somehow seduces a younger secretary he's just met and rolls around with her on silk sheets. That this bizarre pick-up might be an inside joke—the secretary is played by Felicia Farr, wife of Matthau's pal Jack Lemmon—doesn't change how preposterous the scene is. Still, there's plenty to recommend, including some snappy dialogue: Clint Eastwood, star of five Siegel-directed movies, gets mentioned, and one line about working a suspect over "with a pair of pliers and a blowtorch" was appropriated by Quentin Tarantino for *Pulp Fiction* (1994).

ADDED ATTRACTION: Go Direct Yourself, Part Two

Charley Varrick has one additional distinction: the director, Don Siegel, has a tiny role as a ping-pong player forty minutes into the movie. Here are other 1973–1974 movies in which the directors gave themselves cameo roles. We're not including leading roles, like when Clint Eastwood starred in his own movies. For director cameos in 1970–1972 movies, see the entry for *Frenzy* (1972).

- *Badlands* (1973): Fifty-eight minutes into the movie, a well-dressed Terrence Malick leaves a message at the elegant house.
- *Breezy* (1973): As the two leads walk through Marina del Rey's Fisherman's Village, Clint Eastwood is nearby standing at the rail.
- *Chinatown* (1974): Roman Polanski is the well-dressed gangster who slices Jake Gittes' nose (Polanski is later glimpsed outside the rest home).
- *Harry and Tonto* (1974): Ninety-nine minutes in, Paul Mazursky is the male hooker glimpsed near the bus.
- *The Last Detail* (1973): Fifty-four minutes in, Hal Ashby sits in a bar and watches other customers play darts.
- *Mean Streets* (1973): Martin Scorsese appears as a low-level gangster; he's also the shooter in the car at the end.
- *Pat Garrett & Billy the Kid* (1973): Late in the movie, Sam Peckinpah plays a coffin-maker.
- *Phantom of the Paradise* (1974): Sixty-three minutes in, Brian De Palma sits on the stage behind Phoenix for five seconds.

Robin Hood

Released: November 1973
Director: Wolfgang Reitherman
Stars: Brian Bedford, Phil Harris, Roger Miller
Academy Awards: One nomination (Best Song)

PREVIEW: Cunning Robin Hood battles greedy Prince John and tries to earn Maid Marian's love.

NOW SHOWING: The Legend of *Robin Hood*

Robin Hood (1973) is an easy film for children to love. It has funny sight gags, cute animals, and a simple story played out against colorful backgrounds. Objective adults, however, might rank *Robin Hood* in the lower tier of Disney's animated achievements.

The studio's twenty-first animated feature, *Robin Hood* opens with a traditional story book and turning pages. These initial illustrations of men are the last humans in the movie. Every subsequent character is an anthropomorphized animal who sometimes shares physical characteristics with the person providing the voice; for instance, Sir Hiss,

Little John and Robin Hood.

the snake, has a gap in his front teeth just like actor Terry-Thomas. And as in previous Disney animated movies, natural enemies, such as a fox and chicken, here become allies.

Hiss and some others are new to the story, but most of the main characters—Robin, Maid Marian, Little John, etc.—derive from the original English legend. The episodic plot starts with Robin and Little John (both in drag) pitted against the thumb-sucking Prince John; then comes a raucous archery tournament; at the end, Robin and Little John steal the prince's ill-gotten gold, and Robin marries Marian.

Distractingly, the movie introduces anachronisms drawn from recent centuries. Songs ("Rock a Bye Baby," eighteenth century), games (badminton, nineteenth century), items (hubcaps, twentieth century), and slang ("that's a gas," twentieth century) pull the story from its twelfth-century origins. In addition, this traditional English tale has a narrator (twangy Texan Roger Miller) and some main characters with strong American accents. A few of the characters are very similar to those in *The Jungle Book* (1967): Little John and Baloo are twins with the same voice (Phil Harris), and the snakes in both movies, Hiss and Kaa, have the same hypnotizing eyes. What's more, *Robin Hood* doesn't have a single memorable song. In a musical, that's a problem. The Oscar-nominated "Love" is pretty, but few viewers will remember the melody.

The movie does have an easy comedic style with touches of adult humor (a couple of cleavage gags) and one moment of real suspense, the forty seconds near the end when Robin appears to have drowned in the moat. While it's not as great as Disney's earlier animated classics, *Robin Hood* nevertheless endures as a pleasant, good-hearted addition to the Disney canon.

ADDED ATTRACTION: Charlotte's Shermans

Unlike *The Aristocats* (1970) and *Bedknobs and Broomsticks* (1971), *Robin Hood* is a Disney musical that *doesn't* have songs written by the prolific Sherman brothers, Richard and Robert. Instead, the movie's songs are by Roger Miller and other composers. The Shermans, however, did write songs for another animated movie in 1973, but it was made by Hanna-Barbera, famous for the Flintstones and other TV cartoon characters. Their *Charlotte's Web* (1973) is a warm, respectful version of E.B. White's classic 1952 children's story about a "runty pig" that is twice saved from slaughter by a deep-thinking, web-writing spider. The sad death near the end might depress kids, but the animations are colorful and pretty (if a little flat and lacking Disney's detail), and the vocal performances, especially by Debbie Reynolds as Charlotte, are charming (Rex Allen, Disney's frequent narrator, is also the folksy narrator here). The Shermans' unremarkable songs, though, which are frequently simple-minded and reliant on nonsense rhymes ("thingamajig of a pig"), won't make anyone forget their masterpieces for *Mary Poppins* (1964).

Breezy

Released: November 1973

Director: Clint Eastwood

Stars: William Holden, Kay Lenz, Roger C. Carmel

Academy Awards: None

PREVIEW: A reserved older man has a romantic relationship with an enthusiastic hippie girl.

NOW SHOWING: Oh Kay

The first movie Clint Eastwood directed that he didn't also star in, *Breezy* (1973) is a soft, warm *divertissement* that quickly blew in and out of theaters. *Breezy*'s most daring feature is the thirty-five-year gap between the romantic leads, William Holden, fifty-five and closer to his craggy golden-years future than his sleek golden-boy past, and Kay Lenz, a ripe, perky twenty. The ages work, however, because the twist is that *she* avidly seduces *him*.

Frank (Holden) is an upper-class Hollywood realtor whose rigid, dignified life is defined by deals, tennis, and a vindictive ex-wife. In her first major role, Lenz plays Edith Breezerman, a personable, well-endowed hippie from Intercourse, Pennsylvania. In the first scene she wakes up naked next to some guy who doesn't even know her name, so obviously she's a free-loving girl. Plus, she constantly mentions things she loves: fireplaces, California, "the smell of new clothes," the dog, and "being horizontal." Her life's-a-picnic optimism propels the movie.

After she randomly appears on Frank's doorstep, Breezy, who wasn't born yesterday, steadily insinuates herself into his well-appointed home above Sunset Boulevard. Initially Frank resists her chatty attempts to get personal: (She: "Do you think God is dead?" He: "I didn't even know he was sick.") Once Frank relaxes, the relationship accelerates. She whispers "I love you" nine times, but he holds the words back, even after she undresses and tenderly invites him to build a bridge over the river Kwai. Balancing their courtship scenes are awkward moments in public that highlight their age difference, but Breezy remains unconcerned, blithely orders Shirley Temples in restaurants, and implores him to loosen up. Frank regains "that old zing," but he never becomes a towering inferno of passion and so leaves. Realizing what he's lost, he orchestrates a reunion and finally uses the L-word in the last scene.

Holden is appealing, as always. But it's Lenz's movie. Without her convincing sweetness and sincere emotions, the title might've been *Sleazy*. To win over viewers who think the whole premise could also be called *Wheezy* or *Queasy*, Eastwood handles everything sensitively and films his scenes beautifully. Actually, a good alternative title would indicate how well the movie incorporates a network of '70s artifacts—a wild bunch including Frank's battleship-size Lincoln Continental, hippie crash pads, authentic L.A. locations, Breezy's casual fashions, and poetic folk songs—to capture the era's zeitgeist. Love is a many-splendored thing.

ADDED ATTRACTION: High Plains Eastwood

Eighty minutes into *Breezy*, the couple goes to see *High Plains Drifter* (1973), the movie Clint Eastwood directed before *Breezy* (what a year 1973 was for him—he directed a movie, directed and starred in another, and starred in *Magnum Force*). *High Plains Drifter* is Eastwood's first attempt at directing a western, and it's a success. He's at his squintiest playing "the Stranger," a solemn, fast-drawing roughneck who rides into a remote town, promptly kills three men, and rapes a woman. Intimidated by his brutality, the desperate locals, who share a sinister secret, hire him to defeat three incoming villains. He organizes everyone, renames the town Hell, symbolically paints it red, and by the light of hellish flames wreaks violent retribution. Then he literally vanishes. Supernatural elements—eerie music, dark flashbacks, a bathtub ambush where he's seemingly unkillable, a final grave marker—suggest this drifter isn't an actual man, he's—ready?—an avenging apparition. In a Clint Eastwood western? Freaky!

Serpico

Released: December 1973

Director: Sidney Lumet

Stars: Al Pacino, Tony Roberts, Jack Kehoe

Academy Awards: Two nominations (Best Actor—Al Pacino; Best Writing)

PREVIEW: A young honest New York cop is threatened for not taking bribes like his colleagues.

NOW SHOWING: Dirty Laundry

With a diverse résumé that includes *Murder on the Orient Express* (1974), *Dog Day Afternoon* (1975), *Network* (1976), and *The Wiz* (1978), Sidney Lumet was one of the decade's most versatile directors. His fourth movie of the 1970s, *Serpico* (1973), is the gritty true story of an honest cop's lonely and courageous fight against a corrupt system.

The movie opens with a wailing police siren and a close-up of Frank Serpico (Al Pacino), who's literally been shot in the face; meanwhile, various officers wonder if "a cop did it," since "six cops said they'd like to." (In about two hours, we'll see how he got this hideous wound.) A flashback takes us to young Serpico's graduation from the academy and his first day as a clean-cut rookie in New York City. Immediately he questions the free lunch that cops get at the local diner. Called a "weirdo cop" and "pretty weird" by the others, he never fits in and transfers several times, eventually going

Al Pacino.

totally undercover with a beard and long hair (like the young Cat Stevens), plus hippie shirts, an earring, and sandals. His undercover get-up is so believable that other cops mistakenly shoot at him.

Forty-three minutes in, the movie changes dramatically when Serpico is handed a $300 bribe by a dirty cop. Serpico returns the money and transfers yet again to a supposedly "clean" unit, but corruption is everywhere. With low-key restraint, Serpico continually refuses bribes and repeatedly takes his case to his unhelpful superiors. As he becomes more isolated and threatened, he eventually goes to the newspapers. In a powerful outdoor scene, Serpico tells the captain he's going to "outside agencies" while he's dwarfed by a huge bridge looming behind him, showing his insignificance relative to the massive institution he is challenging.

Pacino is riveting in one of his best performances, which comes between his two *Godfather* movies. He's tough, obstinate, usually intense with controlled rage, sometimes fiery and explosive, but he's also surprisingly sweet (he plays with kids on the street and dances happily at a party). The profane language and grimy city help make this long movie feel authentic, like we're actually witnessing real events. Those events conclude with an epilogue about Serpico's medal, retirement, and move to Switzerland; while we wish Lumet had included summaries of the fates of the corrupt cops and officials, this is still an extremely satisfying movie.

ADDED ATTRACTION: *MAD* Magazine's Parodies of 1973 Movies

Serpico got its own movie parody, "Serpicool," in *MAD* magazine (the parody ran in September 1974). Below are nine other 1973 movies that were similarly honored, followed by the titles of the parodies. *MAD*'s parodies of 1974 movies are with the entry for *Airport 1975* (1974).

- *American Graffiti*: "American Confetti"
- *Class of '44*: "The Clods of '44"

- *The Exorcist*: "The Ecchorcist"
- *Live and Let Die*: "Live and Let Suffer"
- *Lost Horizon*: "Least Horizon"
- *Paper Moon*: "Caper Goon"
- *Papillon*: "Popicorn"
- *The Sting*: "The Zing"
- *The Way We Were*: "The Way We Bore"

The Three Musketeers

Released: December 1973
Director: Richard Lester
Stars: Michael York, Oliver Reed, Raquel Welch
Academy Awards: None

PREVIEW: Four dashing swordsmen try to defeat a devious plot to ruin the queen's reputation.

NOW SHOWING: Fun for All

The comic inventiveness that director Richard Lester brought to the Beatles' first two movies and *A Funny Thing Happened on the Way to the Forum* (1966) bubbles joyously throughout *The Three Musketeers* (1973). Released in Europe in late 1973 and stateside in early 1974, this opulent, sprawling epic was a hit then and remains an entertaining experience today.

The serious plot—young swordsman D'Artagnan (Michael York) joins France's "all for one and one for all" musketeers and helps defuse a dastardly conspiracy against the queen—occasionally slows down the swashbuckling action. The real energy is in the creative fight sequences, the nutty slapstick and sight gags, and the delightful performances from major stars having a lark. Purists devoted to Alexandre Dumas's historical novel might question the light tone, but everyone else will have a grand old time.

The four heroes have distinct personalities and skills (the musketeer played by burly Oliver Reed is ferocious, for instance, while Richard Chamberlain's debonair musketeer is more refined). The musketeers aren't perfect, however, and it's amusing to see them sometimes fall and fail (the movie darkens seventy minutes in when three of the four *really* fail and apparently die). Charlton Heston has a sly turn as a wicked cardinal, Christopher Lee is a menacing villain, and Faye Dunaway is a deliciously duplicitous seductress, but the biggest surprise is voluptuous Raquel Welch, who steals all her scenes as a clumsy seamstress.

Overlook the decidedly non-French accents. Instead, indulge in the spectacular palaces and the extravagant costumes (how did this movie *not* get an Oscar nomination for Best Costume Design?). And notice the fascinating details, such as the seventeenth-century dentistry, flashlights, and undergarments that certainly look convincing (though we could've done without the gruesome falconry exhibition). Happily, the leads all survive, so the final announcement of an imminent sequel is welcome.

At least, welcome for the *audience*. The cast was initially mortified by news of *The Four Musketeers* (1974) because they weren't paid for it (it uses footage not included in the first movie), resulting in successful litigation and new contractual

Raquel Welch.

language that specifies how many movies the actors are actually making. Fortunately, the sequel is almost as satisfying as the first movie. Director Lester and the principals return for a more somber story that alarmingly kills off D'Artagnan's lady love and ends with bloody revenge. This time the lavish costumes get their well-deserved Oscar nomination.

ADDED ATTRACTION: Lester Goes to Sea

After *Four Musketeers*, director Richard Lester had another successful movie come out in 1974. Unlike his entertaining musketeer adventures, *Juggernaut* (1974) is a taut thriller that anticipates *The Taking of Pelham One Two Three*, which followed a week later with its own unique hostage crisis. In *Juggernaut*, an extortionist named with the movie's title plants booby-trapped explosives on an ocean liner and demands ransom money. Richard Harris commands a bomb squad that parachutes to the ship and struggles to disarm the devices, and Anthony Hopkins leads the search for the clever criminal. Lester avoids disaster-movie clichés (there's no song, like there was in another ocean-goer, 1972's *The Poseidon Adventure*) and minimizes the humor so he can concentrate on building up genuine suspense. Smartly, he delays revealing Juggernaut's identity as long as possible (by contrast, 1970's *Airport* shows its bomber relatively early), and the climactic scene of Harris making his critical which-wire-to-cut decision is heart-stopping.

The Last Detail

Released: December 1973

Director: Hal Ashby

Stars: Jack Nicholson, Randy Quaid, Otis Young

Academy Awards: Three nominations (Best Actor—Jack Nicholson; Best Supporting Actor—Randy Quaid; Best Writing)

PREVIEW: Two career sailors give a young criminal new experiences as they take him to prison.

NOW SHOWING: In the Navy

Usually we say someone swears like a sailor, but in *The Last Detail* (1973) the sailors swear like Jenny in *Love Story* (1970).

Okay, they're a *little* worse. By 1973 Hollywood had overcome various restrictions on violence and sex, but few movies had tested the profanity barrier. *M*A*S*H* (1970) is considered the first major American movie to use the F-word (once, and quickly). *Mean*

Streets (1973) took it up several notches, but two months later *The Last Detail* was the dynamite that blasted open the doors to raw language. Different characters in this compelling movie say the F-word about sixty times, a puny amount compared to later movies like *Scarface* (1983). At the time, though, *The Last Detail*'s abundant expletives were so noteworthy that they were spelled out with symbols—#@!*—four times on the movie's poster to alert audiences.

The character in *The Last Detail* who swears the most (forty-two times) is a crude career Navy man, "Bad Ass" Buddusky (Jack Nicholson, with a moustache). Buddusky's assignment—his detail—is to join with another sailor, Mulhall (Otis Young), and escort Meadows (Randy Quaid), an eighteen-year-old convicted criminal, from Virginia to prison in New Hampshire. Soft-spoken and naïve, Meadows doesn't swear, but he shoplifts. Pathetically, he can't help himself, and often he doesn't even want the small things he takes.

The journey starts with this awkward trio taking a bus and a train up the coast. Meadows makes one feeble escape attempt, but mostly he's docile and obedient. Stopping in Washington, D.C. and New York, the guys bond as they share hotel rooms and experiences. Buddusky gets paternal and proudly introduces Meadows to "the finest Italian-sausage sandwiches in the world" and "the finest beer in the world." The big leap comes when Buddusky and Mulhall pay for Meadows' visit to a Boston whorehouse; his first encounter lasts all of twenty seconds, but he seems changed.

On the last day, Meadows tries to run, the swabbies manage to deliver him to prison, and he's abruptly taken away. Buddusky and Mulhall exit bragging about how well they did their jobs (a departure from the original book, where Buddusky is killed in a skirmish, thus he really was on his "last detail"). The audience, meanwhile, leaves with haunting impressions—of the poor kid's grim future, of Nicholson's perfect performance, and of the startling profanity that has intensified the realism of this underappreciated tragi-comedy.

ADDED ATTRACTION: Diner Scene, Take Two

Twenty-four minutes into *The Last Detail*, the three sailors stop in a Washington, D.C. diner. There, Buddusky starts to make an issue out of something that's been served to them. Seeing this in 1973, perceptive viewers might have been holding their breaths, since a famous diner scene in *Five Easy Pieces* (1970) had ended with Nicholson's character telling the defiant waitress what to do with the chicken from his chicken-salad sandwich—"I want you to hold it between your knees"—and then dramatically clearing the table with his arm. In *The Last Detail* he politely asks the waiter to melt the cheese on the cheeseburger. He then tells the young sailor at the table, "See Meadows? It's just as easy to have it the way you want it." It can't be a mere coincidence that the word "easy" is in that sentence.

Papillon

Released: December 1973
Director: Franklin J. Schaffner
Stars: Steve McQueen, Dustin Hoffman, Robert Deman
Academy Awards: One nomination (Best Music)

PREVIEW: A prisoner is sent to a harsh penal colony, where he makes repeated escape attempts.

NOW SHOWING: "I'm Still Here!"

Several appealing factors successfully unite in *Papillon* (1973). First, it's based on a bestselling nonfiction book by Henri Charrière, the real-life Papillon (French for "butterfly," and his conspicuous tattoo). Next, director Franklin J. Schaffner had already won an Oscar for *Patton* (1970), and his two stars, Steve McQueen and Dustin Hoffman, were among Hollywood's most popular actors. Add in exciting action, exotic locations, and Jerry Goldsmith's Oscar-nominated score, and the result is a robust epic that became a box-office hit.

The sprawling story covers fourteen grim years in the life of Papillon (McQueen), a "safecracker" who is sent to French Guiana's infamous penal colony in 1933. Not only is escape supposedly impossible, but mere survival is unlikely thanks to trigger-happy guards, knife-wielding prisoners, vampire bats, sharks, starvation, and malaria. Schaffner shows these perils with gruesome close-ups (a guillotined head splatters into the camera) and wide panoramic shots that emphasize how remote and vast this jungle prison is. Only a few moments of comic relief, as when prisoners are ordered to retrieve an angry crocodile, ease the tension.

Papillon's freedom-loving spirit is indefatigable, though he's betrayed at every step (by the judicial system that framed him, by greedy villains he pays to help him, even by a nun he trusts). The movie shows three escape attempts, beginning with an impulsive swim that quickly fails. Later, a carefully planned breakout gets him into a sailboat to Honduras, where he finds a temporary home on a serene beach. His last scheme, involving a sack of coconuts drifting across the sea, seems ludicrous but is successful.

Throughout, McQueen makes a convincing protagonist, suitably heroic for the physical exploits but also surprisingly effective when years of solitary confinement reduce

Steve McQueen and Dustin Hoffman.

him to a haggard, bug-eating old man. Hoffman, playing his loyal, less-adventurous friend, provides an excellent contrast. Their harrowing ordeal is, at 151 minutes, too exhausting for some critics who could also quibble about the absence of French accents. But most viewers will come to admire Papillon and the full range of exertion, inspiration, madness, disappointment, and endurance his prison experiences represent.

The last minutes are triumphant and emotional: having exposed the barbaric, degrading system that never even pretended to rehabilitate prisoners, the movie announces that Papillon outlived the penal colony. After everything we have witnessed, it's moving to see footage of the real buildings, now ruined and overwhelmed by the jungle. Hope wins.

ADDED ATTRACTION: *Papillon's* Players

For all its A-list star power, *Papillon* has some interesting players in minor parts.

- Don Gordon: He gets his throat slit forty-two minutes into the movie; later he's one of the main firemen alongside McQueen in *The Towering Inferno* (1974).
- Anne Byrne Hoffman: Three minutes into the movie, Dustin Hoffman's then-wife plays the wealthy woman who sees her husband off.
- Victor Jory: The Honduran chief who gets a butterfly tattoo; Jory had starred in a similar prison movie, *Escape from Devil's Island* (1935).
- Billy Mumy: The eighteen-year-old prisoner shot at the twenty-two-minute mark; he's a long way from TV's *Lost in Space*.
- Gregory Sierra: For several late scenes, he's the fellow prisoner on the run with Papillon; he's the bartender in another McQueen movie, *The Towering Inferno*.
- Dalton Trumbo: The movie's co-writer, this multiple Oscar winner appears a minute into the movie and briefly addresses the prisoners.

Sleeper

Released: December 1973
Director: Woody Allen
Stars: Woody Allen, Diane Keaton, John Beck
Academy Awards: None

PREVIEW: A man from 1973 comes out of a coma in 2173 to find himself in an oppressive society.

NOW SHOWING: Light *Sleeper*

For the uninitiated, *Sleeper* (1973) is the perfect gateway movie into Woody Allen's canon. The most accessible of his early movies, it's got a terrific set-up, hilarious one-liners, and wonderfully silly slapstick. Fans, non-fans, kids, adults—everyone smiles with *Sleeper*.

It's a distinctive movie for Allen. First, it's his only feature-length attempt at science-fiction (the title and basic story come from H.G. Wells's 1898 sci-fi novel *When the Sleeper Awakes*). It's also the first of five consecutive Allen-directed movies with the brilliant Diane Keaton. She plays Luna, an airhead poet living in the year 2173. Timid Miles Monroe (Allen) meets her when he goes into the hospital in 1973 and somehow wakes up two-hundred years later. Not only is the future strange to him, he's dragged into a political rebellion. With Luna's reluctant help Miles destroys the despotic leader, and he even wins Luna's affections.

Allen originally intended *Sleeper* to last three hours and be split between 1973 and 2173, with *no* second-half dialogue. Besides cutting everything from the present, he also deleted a dream sequence (with himself as a chess pawn) and an ending where Luna chose between Miles and the brawny Erno (John Beck), instead of simply escaping with Miles. Also notable is the location: since Allen hadn't yet established New York as his primary movie setting, he shot *Sleeper* in California and Colorado. And, atypically for his movies, he wears some unusual costumes, dressing as a tuxedoed robot, an acolyte in an all-white suit, and a doctor for the terrific nose-cloning sequence.

Sleeper is filled with wonderful inventions. The blissful Orb, the ecstasy-inducing Orgasmatron, the portable flying pack, the futuristic kitchen with the giant pudding blob—you'll wake up to these in comedy heaven. There are also creative references to past classics: Allen's inflatable "hydrovac suit" echoes one in Buster Keaton's *The Navigator* (1924), his talking computer evokes *2001: A Space Odyssey* (1968), his "gyro-mirror" antics mimic *Duck Soup* (1933), and Allen plays Blanche DuBois in a parody of *A Streetcar Named Desire* (1951).

Sleeper also takes some big strides toward what will become Allen's familiar cinematic style. It's his first movie to have credits of white text on a black background, for instance (Allen and his jazz band play the bouncy ragtime on the soundtrack). More consistent and polished than his previous movies, *Sleeper* satisfies, and it accelerates his progress toward his masterpiece, *Annie Hall*.

ADDED ATTRACTION: *Sleeper* Goes *Bananas*

Sleeper borrows two things from Allen's own *Bananas* (1971). One is Howard Cosell, who's the basis for some comedy. In *Bananas*, Cosell is in on the joke as he delivers blow-by-blow descriptions, just like the sportscaster he actually is, of an assassination in the opening scene and then of the couple's wedding night at the end of the movie (Cosell can barely keep from laughing out loud in that last scene); in *Sleeper*, Cosell becomes the *butt* of a joke when it's said that prisoners were once punished with forced viewings of his TV appearances. The second borrowing is musical. In *Bananas* the rebel leader motivates his troops with "the song of the rebels": "Rebels are we, born to be free, just like the fish in the sea!" Late in *Sleeper*, Luna, the fragile poet who is converted into a militant jungle guerrilla, strums a guitar and confidently sings the exact same "rebels" song.

The Day of the Dolphin

Released: December 1973

Director: Mike Nichols

Stars: George C. Scott, Trish Van Devere, Paul Sorvino

Academy Awards: Two nominations (Best Music; Best Sound)

PREVIEW: Scientists discover that two trained dolphins are to be used for an assassination.

NOW SHOWING: "Fa Love Pa"

After directing *The Graduate* (1967), *Catch-22* (1970), and *Carnal Knowledge* (1971), three movies that invigorated drama with smart humor, Mike Nichols went full thriller with a humorless movie about talking cetaceans. While the premise seems implausible, it's based on actual scientific research, so the notion of talking dolphins isn't totally far-fetched. Besides, *The Day of the Dolphin* (1973) tells its story with such conviction that most audiences are willing to suspend disbelief, even if the movie doesn't totally succeed.

For *Dolphin*, Nichols recruited some of the collaborators on his previous movies, notably Buck Henry, the co-screenwriter on *The Graduate* and sole screenwriter on *Catch-22*; Nichols also brings in Jon Korkes, who played Snowden (*Catch-22*'s wounded airman) and now becomes *Dolphin*'s villain. The plot starts with a marine biologist (the formidable George C. Scott) and his isolated team (including his then-wife Trish Van Devere) who are raising dolphins from birth and teaching them basic English at a special seaside research facility.

After an hour-long buildup that showcases the amazing dolphins and their revolutionary training, the movie quickly and dramatically darkens. The supposedly benevolent foundation paying for the facilities turns out to be evil: they murder someone in the lab, get an infiltrator to kidnap the two star dolphins, and then attempt to use the dolphins as political assassins by strapping to their heads small bombs that will detonate underneath the presidential yacht (we told you it seemed implausible, but somehow this whale of a tale works). Happily the brilliant dolphins figure out on their own how to outwit the bad guys, but sadly the heartrending finale has Scott releasing his beloved students out to sea forever.

In the original book the dolphins spoke almost fluent English, but in the movie their language skills have been simplified to rudimentary syllables ("Fa love Pa," for instance) to make the story a little more convincing (supposedly Buck Henry helped supply the dolphins' sounds). As good as Scott always is, the sleek dolphins are the real stars. They're the most emotive dolphins since the title character in *Flipper* (1963).

This moderately entertaining movie is at its best when it's presenting fascinating information about them and showing their remarkable swimming and leaping abilities, stylish scenes enhanced by Georges Delerue's beautiful Oscar-nominated score. In the water, *The Day of the Dolphin* is no fluke; only when it's on land pursuing espionage thrills does it start to flounder.

ADDED ATTRACTION: Trish in Your Pocket

The Day of the Dolphin was Trish Van Devere's second movie of 1973. Earlier she co-starred in *Harry in Your Pocket*, a small, pleasant crime movie about a quartet of elegantly dressed pickpockets. James Coburn and Walter Pidgeon are veteran thieves mentoring newbies Van Devere and Michael Sarrazin. Together the four slip away with wallet after wallet using well-choreographed moves that are both fascinating and amusing to watch. The movie slows down in the second half as alliances rearrange, a team member gets busted, and a final big score ends disappointingly. Still, *Harry* is polished and generally entertaining, with some good lines—"If it's the milk of human kindness you're looking for, my boy, Harry ain't the cow"—and attractive Pacific Northwest locations. Van Devere is smart and lovely, Coburn is cool and professional, and the venerable Pidgeon is sympathetic and, surprisingly, a seventy-six-year-old cocaine sniffer!

The Sting

(One of 1973's five **FAR-OUT** movies)

Released: December 1973

Director: George Roy Hill

Stars: Paul Newman, Robert Redford, Robert Shaw

Academy Awards: Seven wins (Best Picture; Best Director; Best Writing; Best Editing; Best Art Direction; Best Costume Design; Best Music), plus three more nominations (Best Actor—Robert Redford; Best Cinematography; Best Sound)

PREVIEW: In the 1930s, two con artists team up to pull an elaborate scam on a vicious gangster.

FINE LINE: "Revenge is for suckers. I've been grifting thirty years and I never got any." (Henry Gondorff, trying to explain his motivation for going after the dangerous Doyle Lonnegan.)

CLOSE-UP: *The Sting* has the most creative nicknames since *Guys and Dolls* (1955). Forty-five minutes into the movie, Kid Twist and Dukey rattle off the names of possible candidates for their operation, among them Horse Face Lee, Suitcase Murphy, the Big Alabama, Crying Jonesy, Dippy Burke, and Limehouse Chappie. In addition, dozens of horses are named in the movie, including Dr. Twink, Ima Dreamer, and Chi Chi.

NOW SHOWING: "Everything's Jake Now!"

The late 1960s and early 1970s produced several good movies—including *The Flim-Flam Man* (1967), *The Producers* (1967), *Skin Game* (1971), and *Paper Moon* (1973)—about charismatic con artists. The granddaddy of them all, of course, the one that reset the bar for charming crime thrillers, is *The Sting* (1973). The Best Picture winner at the Oscars, and the year's second highest-grossing movie (close behind *The Exorcist*), *The Sting* quickly found an exalted place in moviegoers' hearts and in Hollywood history.

The Sting famously reunites the three heavyweights from *Butch Cassidy and the Sundance Kid* (1969), one of the most beloved and successful movies of the 1960s. That movie's director, George Roy Hill, had made an underappreciated space oddity, *Slaughterhouse-Five* (1972), just before returning to commercial glory with *The Sting*. Meanwhile, his two handsome stars were riding high: Paul Newman was already a screen icon, and Robert Redford had been in numerous recent hits (Redford would get the movie's Best Actor nomination, the only one of his career). Other notables include veteran music man Marvin Hamlisch, writer David Ward, and legendary costume designer Edith Head, who would all win Oscars for their *Sting* work.

At 129 minutes it's a necessarily long movie because the extremely complicated plot covers all aspects of an elaborate crime operation. Briefly, an army of con men led by Henry Gondorff (Newman) and Johnny Hooker (Redford) want revenge on Doyle Lonnegan (Robert Shaw), a vicious gangster who has killed one of their own. There's a righteousness to the effort—their target isn't a bank, store, or rich old lady, it's a savage villain who leaves one of his victims "in a quarry with a knife in his eye."

Their revenge takes the form of an intricate scam, a "big con" that leads to a "sting," the moment when Lonnegan unwittingly hands over a half-million dollars. The scammers take two movie hours to plan, organize, construct, test, and finalize the scheme that brings Lonnegan into a fake betting parlor where the trap will be sprung. For all their careful preparations, the con men have to do some major improvising to overcome unexpected problems: they quickly create a Western Union office when Lonnegan announces he wants to meet a nonexistent partner; they generate fake FBI men to tamp down a nosy detective; and when they can't afford a big pay-out on one of Lonnegan's bets, they orchestrate a "shut-out" so he can see what's happening without actually winning anything. There's a jovial tone to the proceedings, with the dozens of con men acting like a big, friendly family that uses a casual gesture to recognize its members. At the end, startling twists result in sudden gunfire and some shocking deaths.

All movie long Gondorff is the conductor of the crime orchestra, and Hooker is the brash soloist (Gondorff repeatedly calls him "kid," though Newman was only nine years older than the thirty-seven-year-old Redford). During the movie their mentor/student relationship gets contentious, and in the last act they don't even appear to be on the same side. This makes the climactic death scene convincing, since it seems logical that Gondorff would want to shoot Hooker after all he's done for this betraying upstart.

This great movie hasn't been unassailable, however. Critics note that *The Sting* isn't very funny, offering no jokes and only the occasional amusing situation. Also, this otherwise inoffensive movie unfortunately uses the N-word three times. More significantly, the movie isn't really *about* anything. There's no underlying message or theme. Revenge? Despite the happy ending, revenge is said to be unsatisfying and unattainable during the movie. The theme might have involved the Great Depression, but that crisis is totally downplayed. Set in 1936, *The Sting* does open with a scene of a sad line outside a Salvation Army and men sleeping on dirty streets; later a train roars past a garbage fire; and there are two sentences that mention the Depression. But other than these fleeting acknowledgements, it's as if this historic economic catastrophe doesn't exist. The old-fashioned sepia-toned Universal logo that turns at the beginning of the movie is apparently signaling, not merely a return to the 1930s, but to 1930s *movies*, when glamour and good cheer pushed the Depression into the

Paul Newman and Robert Redford.

background. By contrast, *Paper Moon*, with its more desperate references to the times and its frequent commentary about FDR's responses to the nation's ongoing troubles, seems weightier. *The Sting* is closer to *The Hot Rock* (1972), a lightweight crime comedy that also stars Robert Redford.

None of these quibbles detract from the sublime entertainment found here. The style and craftsmanship are obvious and impressive, with wonderful clothes, old cars, and realistic-looking locations (mostly L.A. sets, surprisingly) creating an entire world. While Scott Joplin's ragtime piano music comes from a quarter-century earlier, it perfectly expresses the movie's jaunty spirit, and it eloquently fills the minutes—Hooker getting spiffed up, Hooker getting chased, Hooker alone on the streets—when there's no dialogue. In a nice touch, the chapter headings—"The Set-Up," "The Hook," The Wire," etc.—evoke vintage magazine illustrations. Chapters had divided up earlier movies, especially *Meet Me in St. Louis* (1944) and *The Fortune Cookie* (1966), but this still seemed like an interesting novelty in 1973.

Challenging, rewarding, and impeccably polished, *The Sting* remains a thoroughly entertaining experience. Look up "timeless" in the dictionary, and you might find this movie's poster in the definition.

ADDED ATTRACTION: *Sting* Lingo

Throughout *The Sting*, various street-wise characters use atmospheric slang terms that aren't defined but are still understandable just from their context. Here are ten examples listed in the order they appear in the movie.

- "Everything's jake now!"
- "If you ain't a sharper in them linens!"
- "I lammed around a bunch of bohunk towns, one kick ahead of the G-men."
- "You tied into a loaded mark."
- "A huge duke is too simple. With no fix, we're gonna need a con with a sure-fire blow-off."
- "These boys have gotta be the quill."
- "Got in a fight with a raggle down on Thirteenth."
- "Don't crack wise with me, flatfoot."
- "You can forget the boodle, Eddie."
- "Stack me a cooler, Floyd."

The Exorcist

(One of 1973's five **FAR-OUT** movies)

Released: December 1973

Director: William Friedkin

Stars: Ellen Burstyn, Linda Blair, Max von Sydow

Academy Awards: Two wins (Best Writing; Best Sound), plus eight more nominations (Best Picture; Best Actress—Ellen Burstyn; Best Supporting Actor—Jason Miller; Best Supporting Actress—Linda Blair; Best Director; Best Editing; Best Cinematography; Best Art Direction)

PREVIEW: Two priests perform an exorcism to drive out a demon that has possessed a young girl.

FINE LINE: "I think the point is to make us despair. To see ourselves as animal and ugly. To reject the possibility that God could love us." (Father Merrin, answering Father Karras's question, "Why this girl?" in the Extended Director's Cut from 2000.)

CLOSE-UP: Thirty-one minutes into *The Exorcist*, when Regan's at the doctor's office, her eyes widen as she briefly sees a devilish face. This subliminal glimpse of the dreadful demon is one of the movie's most unnerving terror tricks. Here are more quick shots of the demon, as timed in the Extended Director's Cut (2000).

- 46 minutes into the movie:
  A flash of the demon's face as Karras runs to his mother at the subway.

- 58 minutes:
  As kitchen lights flicker, the demon's face appears on the hood over the stove.

- 107 minutes:
  During the exorcism, the lights go out and for a split second Regan morphs into the demon's ghastly face.

- 109 minutes:
  After the 360-degree head spin, Regan's face overlaps with the demon's.

NOW SHOWING: "What an Excellent Day for an Exorcism"

The scariest movie of all time debuted over 1973's Christmas holidays. Immediately there were news stories about long lines of people waiting to see *The Exorcist* (1973); significantly, there were also reports about viewers fainting, getting sick, or running out during the movie. People who did finish it recounted their experiences—scrunching down in seats, blocking their eyes, enduring subsequent sleepless nights—like they'd survived an actual demonic encounter. All the notoriety helped Warner Bros., of course, and *The Exorcist* soon became the studio's biggest hit ever. It also launched an entire subgenre of demonic-possession movies, and it was the first true horror movie ever to be nominated for the Best Picture Oscar. *The Exorcist* wasn't merely a movie; it was a phenomenon.

The key to the movie's horror is its in-your-face immediacy. The movie isn't taking place in the distant past or in strange haunted houses few people would want to visit. Nor does it incorporate hulking monsters—like *Frankenstein* (1931) did—or uniquely perverse killers—as in *Psycho* (1960). Instead, *The Exorcist* takes place in modern times in a normal town and in an ordinary house where a sweet, healthy, innocent twelve-year-old girl has unwittingly been overtaken by a powerful force. And, as nearly everybody knew at the time (early viewers received handouts to remind them), the movie was based on a true story. *The Exorcist* terrified viewers deeply and personally: if this realistic story could happen now, there, to her, then it could happen tomorrow, here, to anyone.

A ten-minute prologue establishes the good-vs.-evil confrontation to come. Set among ancient structures in Iraq, these eerie scenes introduce Father Merrin (Max von Sydow), an old priest and archaeologist who unearths an evil relic. Based on past encounters, Merrin instantly recognizes his familiar adversary and visits a horrible statue of the demon, where snarling dogs imply unchecked chaos (the movie doesn't identify the demon, but the bestselling novel calls it Pazuzu). The prologue also reveals Merrin's vulnerability when he shakily takes heart medication, an important plot point later (Merrin looks to be in his seventies, though von Sydow himself is only forty-four).

From here the movie shifts to the Georgetown neighborhood of Washington, D.C., where the battle for Regan (Linda Blair) commences. We see Regan's mother, Chris (Ellen Burstyn), Chris' work, and everybody's daily routines, which just happen to be punctuated by unsettling moments (noises in the attic, a candle that suddenly flares, a misbehaving Ouija board). However, nothing about Regan, a happy kid with typical interests, suggests that she's about to transition into a hideous creature.

Soon, though, manifestations of demonic possession appear. Regan's bed moves violently, she punches someone, she lets loose with vicious profanities, and she starts to look ... different. "What's wrong with me," she asks, and to find out Chris takes her to clinics for various tests. One of these, an arteriogram, is shown step-by-step documentary-style, a disturbing sight that has doctors torturing her almost as much as the demon does. Ultimately, all medical science, including psychiatry, fails Regan. When Regan brutally kills a houseguest, Chris has only one hope, a last resort suggested by a frustrated doctor: the ancient ritual of exorcism, "to drive out the so-called invading spirit."

Balancing Regan's chilling story is a religious one about the inner struggle of a young local priest, Father Karras (Jason Miller). With his elderly mother dying, and with suffering all around him, Karras is experiencing a spiritual crisis: "I can't cut it anymore," he tells a friend, "I've lost my faith." The profound guilt he feels when his mother dies will be a vital weapon the demon later uses against him.

Two-thirds of the way through the movie, the beast completely possesses Regan. The horror that so far has been hinted at now becomes intensely and repulsively real as director William Friedkin, already an Oscar winner for *The French Connection* (1971),

unleashes state-of-the-art (and over-the-top) special effects. Her face gruesomely mutilated, her genderless voice a low, fearsome croak, Regan spins her head twice, spews green vomit, and levitates. Merrin finally reappears and, alongside Karras, chants "the power of Christ compels you!" fourteen times during the famous exorcism, an astonishing sequence that surprisingly takes up only about ten minutes of the movie.

By now the answer to a question the audience has probably posed—why did the demon claim this insignificant little girl?—becomes clear. The demon doesn't want her; it wants the priests. To destroy Karras' faith forever, the demon attacks him psychologically, using his own guilt against him—"You killed your mother" it shouts, at one point even turning into his mother. Then, having used Regan as bait to lure Merrin close, the demon giggles in delight when the aged priest dies.

Ultimately Karras finds his faith and re-ascends to Regan's room for the concluding duel. When the healing Regan resurfaces in the riveting last scene, the exhausted audience studies her fading scars and calm demeanor with renewed admiration. The final hand-off of a meaningful religious medal shows that, despite the priests' deaths, good has triumphed and their spirit endures. It's a symbolic gesture but shows the intelligence at work here. Many later movies exploited *The Exorcist*'s shocking tricks and themes without achieving its lasting power. That's because *The Exorcist*, as nightmarish as it is, is artistic, intellectual, and ultimately reassuring. Religion matters, the movie argues convincingly, it saves when nothing else can.

ADDED ATTRACTION: *The Exorcist*'s Celebrities

Playing a movie producer in an early scene is William Peter Blatty, the actual author of the bestselling novel (he's one of at least four recognizable authors who are in the '70s movies of their books—we caught Michael Crichton as a doctor in 1971's *The Andromeda Strain*, James Dickey as the sheriff in 1972's *Deliverance*, Peter Benchley as a reporter in 1975's *Jaws*, and Ann Beattie as a waitress in 1979's *Head Over Heels*). Besides showing Blatty, *The Exorcist* mentions some real people, including these famous names (the names are compiled from the different versions of the movie, the 1973 original and the slightly altered 2000 "Version You've Never Seen," which was re-released as the Extended Director's Cut).

- Lucille Ball
- Humphrey Bogart
- Napoleon Bonaparte
- Walt Disney
- John Garfield
- Jackie Gleason
- Joseph Goebbels
- Groucho Marx
- Sal Mineo
- Ho Chi Minh
- Paul Newman
- Claude Rains
- Debbie Reynolds

1974

In Film

- Oscar for Best Picture: *The Godfather: Part II.*
- Most Oscar wins (six): *The Godfather: Part II.*
- Most Oscar nominations (eleven): *Chinatown, The Godfather: Part II.*
- Top-grossing movie: *The Towering Inferno.*
- Top-grossing comedy: *Blazing Saddles.*
- Top-grossing horror or sci-fi: *The Texas Chain Saw Massacre.*
- *Earthquake* introduces the new Sensurround audio system.
- MGM celebrates its fiftieth anniversary with a musical retrospective, *That's Entertainment!*
- Five memorable actors: Jeff Bridges, Art Carney, Robert De Niro, Dustin Hoffman, Burt Reynolds.
- Five memorable actresses: Ellen Burstyn, Diahann Carroll, Faye Dunaway, Valerie Perrine, Gena Rowlands.
- Movie debuts: Jeff Goldblum, directors Michael Cimino, Jonathan Demme, Steven Spielberg, Oliver Stone.
- Deaths include Bud Abbott, Jack Benny, producer Samuel Goldwyn.

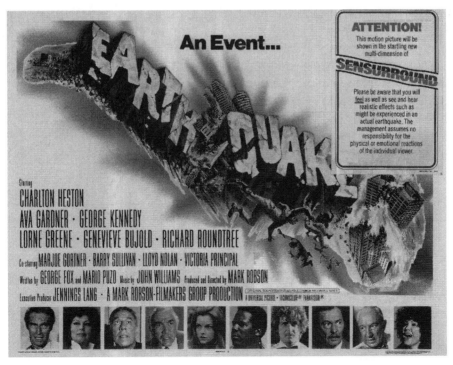

In America

- President Nixon resigns; Vice President Gerald Ford becomes president.
- An oil crisis and a stock market crash; inflation jumps to 12% (triple the 1972 rate).
- National highway speed limit lowered to 55 mph.
- Average price for a gallon of gasoline: fifty-nine cents.
- Heiress Patricia Hearst is kidnapped.
- Expo '74, a world's fair that lasts six months, is held in Spokane, Washington.

- The first UPC (Universal Product Code) is scanned on a pack of gum at an Ohio grocery store.
- Evel Knievel attempts to jump the Snake River Canyon in a rocket cycle.
- New transportation: B-1 bomber, F-16 fighter jet, Ford Elite, Jeep Cherokee.
- Hank Aaron breaks Babe Ruth's home run record; at "Ten Cent Beer Night" in Cleveland, violence erupts and the home team, baseball's Cleveland Indians, is forced to forfeit the game.
- Muhammad Ali defeats George Foreman to reclaim boxing's heavyweight crown.
- Sports champions: Miami Dolphins in Super Bowl VIII, Philadelphia Flyers in hockey, Milwaukee Bucks in basketball, Oakland Athletics in baseball.
- A nude streaker runs across the stage at the televised Oscar ceremony.
- Philippe Petit makes a famous high-wire walk between New York's Twin Towers.
- *People* magazine debuts; Stephen King publishes his first novel, *Carrie*.
- Music: Joni Mitchell's *Court and Spark*, the Beach Boys' *Endless Summer*, and debut albums from Kiss and Rush are released; John Lennon makes his final public performance when he plays alongside Elton John at Madison Square Garden.
- TV debuts: *Happy Days*, *Little House on the Prairie*, *Police Woman*.
- Deaths include Dizzy Dean, Duke Ellington, Cass Elliot, Charles Lindbergh, Karen Silkwood, Ed Sullivan, Jacqueline Susann, Earl Warren.

Ladies and Gentlemen:
The Rolling Stones

Released: January 1974
Director: Rollin Binzer
Stars: Mick Jagger, Keith Richards, Mick Taylor
Academy Awards: None

PREVIEW: One of the world's great rock groups, playing in its prime, is shown live in concert.

NOW SHOWING: Concert at the Movies

Ladies and Gentlemen: The Rolling Stones (1974) is a daring concert movie because of what it's not. Significantly, it's not *Woodstock* (1970), the three-hour Oscar-winning documentary that includes split-screens, interviews with townspeople, and lots of footage of spectators arriving or surviving. It's also not *Gimme Shelter* (1970), the fascinating documentary about 1969's disastrous Altamont concert.

Instead, *Ladies and Gentlemen* is a tight, disaster-free blast of epic performances by the Rolling Stones culled from several 1972 shows in Texas. Nothing distracts from the band and its familiar anthems—the audience isn't really seen until the last two songs, there are no stage props or dazzling special effects (just a black background), and nothing outside is shown.

At this moment in music history the Stones, coming off a string of landmark hits, were probably the world's most popular rock group. They were also promoting their recent masterpiece, *Exile on Main Street*. The band's lineup features the usual suspects—Mick Jagger (vocals), Keith Richards (guitar), Bill Wyman (bass), and Charlie Watts (drums)—and a relative newcomer, baby-faced Mick Taylor, the guitarist who had replaced Brian Jones, plus an onstage horn section and a barely glimpsed Nicky Hopkins on piano.

Director Rollin Binzer moves the camera around the stage, blending wide shots with extreme close-ups but always keeping the focus on the musicians. Everyone plays with energy and confidence, tearing into the rousing opening number, "Brown Sugar," and roaring through fourteen other recent classics.

Jagger, wearing sequins on his face and a yam in his pants, commands the stage with his cocky strut and thrusting pelvis. Highlights include Taylor stealing the spotlight with his "Gimme Shelter" and "Love in Vain" solos, pre-dental-work Richards singing lead on "Happy," powerful extended versions of "Tumbling Dice" and "Midnight Rambler," and a triumphant "Street Fighting Man" finale. Among the lowlights: the few times Jagger talks to the audience, his brief comments add little. And the ending arrives abruptly: after Jagger's "thank you very much, good night" farewell, the audience can't believe that no encore is forthcoming (twice the announcer reminds everyone that the show is indeed over).

Anyone who knows the Rolling Stones only as craggy old men will be interested to see these seminal rockers when everyone was young and energized. And anyone who is a Stones fan needs to see this terrific concert movie that shows the group at the peak of its awesome powers.

ADDED ATTRACTION: *Ladies and Gentlemen,* the Concert

In the early '70s there were other concert films besides *Woodstock, Gimme Shelter,* and *Ladies and Gentlemen: The Rolling Stones.* Among the rest: *Soul to Soul* (1971), a concert in Ghana featuring Wilson Pickett and Roberta Flack; *Fillmore* (1972), with legendary Bay Area bands like Santana and the Grateful Dead; and two movies starring the King, *Elvis: That's the Way It Is* (1970) and *Elvis on Tour* (1972). None of these movies, however, got the kind of special release that *Ladies and Gentlemen* did. When the movie opened in America, initially it was shown in only a handful of cities, and the few theaters where it played were outfitted with special speakers for a more realistic concert experience.

Blazing Saddle*r*

(One of 1974's five **FAR-OUT** movies)

Released: February 1974

Director: Mel Brooks

Stars: Cleavon Little, Gene Wilder, Madeline Kahn

Academy Awards: Three nominations (Best Supporting Actress—Madeline Kahn; Best Editing; Best Song)

PREVIEW: A black sheriff tries to stop corrupt politicians from destroying a frontier town.

FINE LINE: "I'm through being Mr. Goodbar. The time has come to act and act quickly." (Hedley Lamarr in 1874, anachronistically mentioning a 1925 candy bar as he assembles his villainous army.)

CLOSE-UP: Ninety-seven minutes into the movie, Hedley Lamarr buys a $3 movie ticket to go see *Blazing Saddles.* A glass case in the background displays *"Black Bart,"* which originally was going to be the movie's title. *"Black Bart"* was later used for a 1975 TV series based on the movie, but only the pilot episode was aired.

NOW SHOWING: "Excuse Me While I Whip This Out"

Mel Brooks had already won an Oscar by parodying Broadway musicals in *The Producers* (1967), and he was about to stylishly spoof old horror movies with *Young Frankenstein* (1974). In between he co-wrote, directed, and co-starred in the all-time classic send-up of traditional westerns, *Blazing Saddles* (1974). This gleefully anarchic comedy isn't for every taste, but it was so popular that it became one of the few '70s movies to gross over $100 million. By now *Blazing Saddles* is routinely included near the top of any list of the funniest movies ever made.

This giddy movie does have something resembling a plot, though it's more like an excuse to assemble an inspired grab bag of hilarious one-liners, goofy puns, outrageous sight gags, and wonderfully silly situations (some groaners, too, but another joke is always just seconds away). The lunacy revolves around an 1874 land grab orchestrated by two corrupt politicians (Harvey Korman and Brooks). To take over a vital town, the pair installs a sheriff "who so offends the citizens of Rock Ridge that his very appearance would drive them out." Thus is Bart (Cleavon Little), a black railroad worker (Black Bart, get it?), promptly appointed. Smart and hip, he finds an ally in the gun-slingin' Waco Kid (Gene Wilder), wins over the town's residents, and rallies them when the frustrated politicians launch a final assault with an army of cutthroats. A bawdy musical number fifty-three minutes into the movie by Madeline Kahn as the linguisti-cally challenged Lili Von Shtupp is a show-stopping highlight.

Throughout the movie, Brooks and company satire every cliché in the history of westerns. A wagon train stretches for a mile; an old desert rat shouts unintelligible "authentic frontier gibberish"; tired lines like "head 'em off at the pass" are quickly scorned; eating beans for every meal produces the expected results in a famous camp-fire scene; and the heroes ride off into the sunset—in a limousine. Long-time western star Randolph Scott even gets mentioned. The more westerns you've seen, the more jokes you'll recognize.

What's most interesting about *Blazing Saddles* is how subversive it is. It isn't just making fun of things to be funny; it's mocking things to destroy them. Its most controversial, politically incorrect attack is on racism. Blatant in-your-face racism fills the movie: the N-word is spoken over a dozen times, there are two slurs against the Chinese, and stereotypes pop up in casual conversation (Indians are "the little red devils"; Lili asks Bart, "Is it true … you people are *gifted*"; and Bart gets attention by yelling, "Hey, where are the white women at?"). But Brooks and his writers (including Richard Pryor) aren't laughing *with* the racists, they're laughing *at* them by using racist attitudes to expose how ridiculous the racists really are. After all, the movie's black characters are bright, noble, and hard-working, while most of the white characters are ignorant, dishonest idiots or crooks (Brooks himself plays one of the biggest buffoons). Observe: hero getting applauded at the end—the black sheriff, Bart. Villain getting shot—the white evil mastermind, Hedley Lamarr.

Brooks doesn't stop there. Add in jokes about Jews, gays, preachers, breasts, plus lots of vulgarities, and this becomes an equal-opportunity movie with insults enough for everybody. But when everybody becomes the butt of rapid-fire over-the-top jokes, nobody can be more offended than anyone else, so theoretically everything balances out, everyone laughs at everyone, and nobody takes the abuse personally. Theoretically. Not everyone agrees, of course, and there are plenty of offended viewers who are disgusted by the language and attitudes on display. To appease them, Brooks will soon rein himself in with less-aggressive parodies like *Silent Movie* (1976) and *High Anxiety* (1977).

The radical ending also divides viewers. Throughout the movie, Brooks incorporates many allusions to modern times, thus preparing the audience for what he's going to unleash in the last ten minutes. The first anachronism comes in the first three minutes when black railroad workers sing Cole Porter's "I Get a Kick Out of You" (1934), followed quickly by the question, "What in the wide wide world of sports is a-goin' on here," referencing a modern TV show. Later, characters share a doobie and use the word "groovy" (see more anachronisms in "Added Attraction"). What's more, characters know they're in a movie and occasionally break the "fourth wall" (an old lady asks the audience, "Have you ever seen such cruelty?"; Bart looks at the camera and says, "Always like to keep my audience *riveted*"; and Hedley Lamarr poses a rhetorical question, looks at the camera, and wonders, "Why am I asking you?"). Thus is the audience braced for the chaotic last sequence. Brooks segues from a Rock Ridge brawl to a 1970s Warner Bros. sound stage, where a Busby Berkeley-style musical is underway. The *Blazing Saddles* cowboys burst in and mention Mel Brooks by name, the chase moves to Hollywood's modern streets, and the main characters assemble at Grauman's Chinese Theater. Conveniently, *Blazing Saddles* is showing, so the characters watch themselves play out the final duel and goodbyes.

Some critics felt that Brooks had no real ending to his western and so threw in this one out of desperation, but the theater audience surrounding us in 1974 gasped in delight as it watched surprise follow surprise follow surprise. And like us they left the theater deliriously babbling about coming back to see *Blazing Saddles* again.

Cleavon Little and Gene Wilder.

ADDED ATTRACTION: Blazing Anachronisms

We've already mentioned several anachronisms in *Blazing Saddles*. Here are fifteen more, in the order in which they're heard or seen.

- Hedy Lamarr (actress, born 1914)
- Howard Johnson's Ice Cream Parlor (Howard Johnson's, opened 1925)
- Richard Dix (actor, born 1893)
- Paddle ball (invented 1920s)
- Van Johnson (actor, born 1916)
- Bart's Gucci-made uniform (Gucci, founded 1921)
- Count Basie (born 1904) plays "April in Paris" (1932)
- Cecil B. DeMille (director, born 1881)
- Western Union Candygram (introduced 1959)
- Vitamin E (discovered 1922)
- Twentieth-century Nazis and motorcyclists
- "We don't need no stinkin' badges," from *The Treasure of the Sierra Madre* (1948)
- Jesse Owens (athlete, born 1913)
- "An almost-certain Academy Award nomination for Best Supporting Actor" (first Academy Awards, 1929)
- "Now go do that voodoo that you do so well" (echoing Cole Porter's "You Do Something to Me," 1929)

Thieves Like Us

Released: February 1974
Director: Robert Altman
Stars: Keith Carradine, Shelley Duvall, John Schuck
Academy Awards: None

PREVIEW: In the Depression, three bank robbers are on the run when one meets a young farm girl.

NOW SHOWING: On the Road

By 1974, director Robert Altman had already redefined war movies (1970's *M*A*S*H*), westerns (1971's *McCabe & Mrs. Miller*), and detective stories (1973's *The Long Goodbye*). Next genre up: 1930s gangster movies. Generally unloved at the time, *Thieves Like Us* (1974) is now often regarded as "good Altman." It's not his masterpiece, but *Thieves Like Us* is accessible and interesting, two things you can't say about every movie in Altman's long, idiosyncratic career.

Dipping into *Bonnie and Clyde* (1967) territory, Altman tells a relaxed, frequently charming, sometimes violent story of Depression-era bank robbers on the run. Altman's poignant movie is longer and slower than *Bonnie and Clyde*, and he defies the expectations created by that iconic classic: he doesn't present a stream of big, dramatic robberies, there's no exciting "getaway" music during escapes, and the movie doesn't conclude with graphic, bloody violence (the final slaying is behind closed doors). This atmospheric, beautifully photographed movie exists to observe characters, not to thrill with crowd-pleasing action. And Altman wants to study the period in all its detail, from the constant chatter on old radio shows to the vintage cars, costumes, and lingo. It all feels so accurate that we really believe we're down south with these poor, simple people.

The actors perfectly inhabit their roles and generate convincing chemistry. As in Terrence Malick's *Badlands* (1973), *Thieves Like Us* spotlights a youthful criminal, Bowie (Keith Carradine), and an adoring small-town girl, Keechie (Shelley Duvall). Both are thin, almost adolescent characters who constantly swig Coca-Cola (see "Added Attraction"). Early in their courtship they're like a couple of immature kids (virginal Keechie brags about playing a game at school, while Bowie boyishly asks, "Do you like me a whole lot ... a hundred million billion trillion bushels full?"). As if to remind us that this couple is both young and doomed, Altman has a radio drama of *Romeo and Juliet* playing the first time they're in bed together.

Altman stays pretty true to Edward Anderson's 1937 novel, with one major exception: in the novel, Bowie and Keechie both get ambushed and killed, but Altman spares the pregnant girl so she can leave this life of crime and move on to motherhood. It's a sympathetic touch appropriate for this elegiac movie.

ADDED ATTRACTION: Thieves Like Coke

Coca-Cola is ubiquitous in *Thieves Like Us*. Robert Altman's DVD commentary notes that the Coke placements were realistic. "Everything was Coca-Cola. ... You couldn't move down there without kicking a Coke bottle or seeing a sign," he says. But is he also showing how limited the options were back then? Consider that as you examine this sample of Coke sightings in the movie (an average of one every eight minutes).

- Coke signs: on the service station, the prison, and the prison's mess hall.
- Coke bottles: stacked near a Coca-Cola ice box; characters hold Coke bottles in different scenes; prominent empties are on a windowsill, on tables, and beside Keechie's bed.
- Coke mentions: Bowie requests "a cold Coke" and says Keechie's constantly "drinking Cokes."
- Coke truck: with a six-foot bottle and a salesgirl offering Cokes.
- Last scenes: Keechie returns five empties to the motel office, gets a fresh one, and holds two bottles as the final ambush begins. In the train station she sips a Coke, and three kids holding Cokes walk up the stairs.

The Great Gatsby

Released: March 1974
Director: Jack Clayton
Stars: Robert Redford, Mia Farrow, Sam Waterston
Academy Awards: Two wins (Best Costume Design; Best Music)

PREVIEW: The rich and mysterious Jay Gatsby romances his long-lost love, who is now married.

NOW SHOWING: "Rich Girls Don't Marry Poor Boys"

Derided by many critics, *The Great Gatsby* (1974) was still a financial success. With Watergate and Vietnam on TV and *The Exorcist* (1973) in theaters, audiences chose to escape to the sumptuous world of Scott Fitzgerald's exquisite novel. There they indulged in elegant cars, shimmering costumes, and "glittering white palaces" so opulent they upstage the actors. Additionally, Robert Redford's fans came to see their handsome hero in a passionate love story. Looks, however, aren't everything.

The movie is generally true to the familiar story. Everything takes place over a single 1920s summer when the mysteriously wealthy Gatsby romances his past love, Daisy, who's now a wife and mother. As in the book, the sad story contrasts with wild champagne-filled parties; there's a doomed roadside couple living under a billboard's watchful gaze; and a flurry of three deaths desolates the last act. Working between his two *Godfather* movies, screenwriter Francis Ford Coppola keeps most of Fitzgerald's action and some of his memorable lines ("Can't repeat the past? Why of course you can!"). But Coppola also removes characters (Gatsby's mentor, Dan Cody), adds new scenes (a gift of a green ring, a candlelit dance), invents dialogue ("rich girls don't marry poor boys," spoken twice), and ends this 143-minute movie before the book's magnificent "boats against the current" terminus. While Coppola captures Fitzgerald's tone, he can't deliver the one thing that makes the book a masterpiece: the full majesty of Fitzgerald's gorgeous prose. Admittedly, no movie could, unless an omniscient narrator simply recited eloquent text like, "So he waited, listening for a moment longer to the tuning fork that had been struck upon a star."

Also missing is the real Gatsby. On the page, he's "an elegant young rough-neck, a year or two over thirty," who possibly "killed a man." On the screen, golden-hunk Redford, thirty-eight in 1974, isn't convincing as a tragic, broken-hearted "rough-neck" with a dark past. Even worse is Mia Farrow's Daisy. A vapid "beautiful little fool" forcing an aristocratic accent, Daisy comes across as a spoiled flibbertigibbet unworthy of the adoration she somehow commands. Director Jack Clayton, known for a Victorian thriller, *The Innocents* (1961), gets background settings right but foreground characters wrong. The only history the actors made involves publishing: Farrow, in costume, landed *People* magazine's first cover (March 4, 1974). The movie's a noble effort, but the melodramatic, overlong result is more like *The Pretty Good Gatsby*.

ADDED ATTRACTION: A Different Daisy

Besides *The Great Gatsby*, two other literary classics became 1974 movies. *Huckleberry Finn* is a lackluster family musical that incorporates songs by the Sherman brothers (of Disney fame) and takes many liberties with Mark Twain's masterpiece. In contrast, *Daisy Miller* (1974) is a faithful adaptation of Henry James' 1878 novella about Americans mingling with European society, yet it's more commonly remembered as the disappointing movie that snapped director Peter Bogdanovich's streak of early-'70s hits. Bogdanovich reunites three actresses from *The Last Picture Show* (1971)—Eileen Brennan, Cloris Leachman, and Cybill Shepherd—and puts everyone in elegant costumes and in spectacular Swiss and Italian settings. Unfortunately, this sophisticated, slow-moving movie is tedious, even at just ninety-one minutes. Shepherd is pretty, and she tries hard as the headstrong "terrible, frightful flirt" who chatters at high-speed through long scenes, but critics were generally unimpressed and audiences were decidedly uninterested.

Mia Farrow and Robert Redford.

The Sugarland Express

Released: March 1974
Director: Steven Spielberg
Stars: Goldie Hawn, William Atherton, Michael Sacks
Academy Awards: None

PREVIEW: After they steal a police car, an impetuous married couple is pursued across Texas.

NOW SHOWING: Sweet Ride

The Sugarland Express (1974) is notable for being Steven Spielberg's first theatrical feature. Only twenty-eight at the time, he impressed everyone—studio executives, critics, and small, appreciative audiences—with this entertaining debut and was quickly on to his early masterpiece, *Jaws* (1975).

Based on a real event, the movie starts like an offbeat comedy. The beguiling Goldie Hawn plays the headstrong, manipulative Lou Jean, who quickly busts her submissive husband, Clovis (William Atherton), out of a Texas prison so they can go rescue their baby from foster parents. After wrecking their stolen Buick, they kidnap a police officer and commandeer his car. Scores of police vehicles are in pursuit, yet the amiable vibe in the movie's first half suggests the possibility of a happy ending.

Once the sharpshooters arrive fifty minutes in, the light mood darkens. Though TV crews turn the chase into a media frenzy and giddy locals cheer the getaway car as it passes, there's this increasingly foreboding feeling that two solemn rangers, who can "at three-hundred yards hit a dime" with their powerful rifles, are eventually going to "drop that ol' boy." Tragedy finally arrives via a loudly echoing shot that rips

Goldie Hawn.

through Clovis. Unlike *Bonnie and Clyde* (1967), which violently killed both outlaws, *The Sugarland Express* is like *Thieves Like Us* (1974), which opened a month earlier and spared its country girl. The last scene takes a lingering look at the freed cop, who's as dejected as viewers are at this point. The closest we get to a happy ending is closing text that summarizes Lou Jean's fate—prison, parole, and a quiet life with her baby.

The Sugarland Express may be a modest achievement, but it does present remarkable images that demonstrate Spielberg's dynamic visual skills, even at this early stage in his career. Watch how the camera maneuvers inside the claustrophobic car, or the long line of police cars snaking along the highways, or the amber silhouettes in the final melancholy shot. This movie also represents Spielberg's first teaming with composer John Williams, whose score here is memorable, not for grand orchestrated marches, but for poignant harmonica solos. Their collaboration will ultimately span decades and produce some of the greatest cinematic experiences in Hollywood history. *The Sugarland Express* isn't one of them, but it's a confident beginning.

ADDED ATTRACTION: The Rookies

Like Steven Spielberg, the following prominent directors made their first movies in the 1970s. Except for Elaine May, each of the names below earned an Oscar nomination as Best Director at some point in their careers; their first movies, and their later movies that *won* the Oscar for Best Director, are noted.

- Hal Ashby: *The Landlord* (1970)
- Warren Beatty: *Heaven Can Wait* (1978); *Reds* (1981)
- Robert Benton: *Bad Company* (1972); *Kramer vs. Kramer* (1979)
- Michael Cimino: *Thunderbolt and Lightfoot* (1974); *The Deer Hunter* (1978)
- Jonathan Demme: *Caged Heat* (1974); *The Silence of the Lambs* (1991)
- Clint Eastwood: *Play Misty for Me* (1971); *Unforgiven* (1992); *Million Dollar Baby* (2004)
- Ron Howard: *Grand Theft Auto* (1977); *A Beautiful Mind* (2001)
- George Lucas: *THX 1138* (1971)
- David Lynch: *Eraserhead* (1977)
- Terrence Malick: *Badlands* (1973)
- Elaine May: *A New Leaf* (1971)
- Alan Parker: *Bugsy Malone* (1976)
- Ridley Scott: *The Duellists* (1977)
- Oliver Stone: *Seizure* (1974); *Platoon* (1986); *Born on the Fourth of July* (1989)

The Golden Voyage of Sinbad

Released: April 1974
Director: Gordon Hessler
Stars: John Phillip Law, Caroline Munro, Tom Baker
Academy Awards: None

PREVIEW: Sinbad and his crew sail to a mysterious island and fight extraordinary opponents.

NOW SHOWING: "A Very Strange Trip"

The three great Indiana Jones adventures of the 1980s seem to echo *The Golden Voyage of Sinbad* (1974). Consider: all are ripping yarns set in the past in exotic locations; all of them star a dashing headgear-wearing hero. Like *Golden Voyage*, the early Indy trilogy includes a spell-casting villain, a sea voyage to a mysterious island, sequences inside temples and caverns, symbolic gold objects, a marketplace fight, a frantic horseback ride, and a pretty girl who gets captured. With all these similarities, you almost expect Sinbad to declare, "That belongs in a museum!"

What Sinbad has that Indy doesn't is Ray Harryhausen. The legendary stop-motion animator provides the story and visual effects that make *Golden Voyage* golden. Harryhausen had already made *The 7th Voyage of Sinbad* (1958) with a different Sinbad (Kerwyn Mathews), a cyclops, and a dragon. Sixteen years later he's got John Phillip Law doing an indeterminate accent and battling a range of fantasy opponents highlighted by a bat-like "homunculus," a six-armed sword-wielding statue, and a centaur and griffon that have their own clash of the titans. Orchestrating these foes is Prince Koura (Tom Baker), a sorcerer with "black and ugly ambitions" who can "summon the demons of darkness." Both men are trying to unravel "a great and mighty secret" that involves a journey to "a place of untold dangers" and a Fountain of Destiny.

As a crewmember says, "a very strange trip, this one," starting with Sinbad himself: he gets no introduction or back story, as if we're continuing some ongoing TV series. Next, the pace is a little slow, and almost forty minutes elapse before we get the first big animation showcase, the fight with the ship's angry wooden figurehead. Along for the expedition is a "worthless slave girl," the stunningly sexy Margiana (played by the tanned, glistening, architecturally amazing Caroline Munro). Sinbad says, "She finds favor in my eyes," his version of "hubba-hubba," but unfortunately she's given little to do or say. Also, for some reason much of this movie takes place in darkness or in caves, and even when Sinbad sails away at the end it's at night.

Saturday-afternoon kids and nostalgic adults will be enjoying the imaginative pre-digital spectacle too much to worry about these minor issues. For now there's popcorn to munch, and soon there'd be another fun Harryhausen epic sailing over the horizon, *Sinbad and the Eye of the Tiger* (1977).

ADDED ATTRACTION: Sintax

Sinbad and the Eye of the Tiger introduces Patrick Wayne, the Duke's son, as the next Sinbad. The movie has new monsters (including a saber-toothed tiger and a "walrus *giganticus*") and a bigger budget, but it makes a smaller impression, especially coming out three months after the game-changing *Star Wars* (1977). Both *Golden Voyage* and *Eye of the Tiger* offer stilted dialogue that mixes old-sounding proverbs and strange observations, like the following half-dozen examples. The second entry is spoken three times in *Golden Voyage*, and the fourth one is delivered by that movie's villain, so heed at your peril.

- "He who walks on fire will burn his feet."
- "Trust in Allah, but tie up your camel."
- "Every voyage has its own flavor."
- "He who is patient, obtains."
- "For one who enjoys the hashish, you should be more at peace."
- "I have been dreaming of his roasted sheep's eyes."

The Conversation

Released: April 1974

Director: Francis Ford Coppola

Stars: Gene Hackman, John Cazale, Harrison Ford

Academy Awards: Three nominations (Best Picture; Best Writing; Best Sound)

PREVIEW: A professional wire tapper makes a recording he fears could lead to deadly results.

NOW SHOWING: "This Is No Ordinary Conversation"

One of the impressive early-'70s movies remembered as quintessential artistic achievements—an esteemed group that includes *Five Easy Pieces* (1970) and *The Last Picture Show* (1971)—is *The Conversation* (1974), the low-key tour de force that Francis Ford Coppola made between his high-profile *Godfather* movies. With no Italian mobsters, period setting, or guns, *The Conversation* is so unlike those operatic Best Picture winners that one might think it's from another director altogether.

The qualities that make this movie special are exactly what impatient viewers disparage. *The Conversation* is a moody, quiet character study that slowly builds into a tense thriller. It starts with random sounds in San Francisco's Union Square while the camera follows someone who's silent, a mime. A surveillance team, we realize, is surreptitiously recording a strolling couple. Their conversation is replayed throughout the movie as the team leader, Harry Caul (Gene Hackman), gradually recognizes that the couple is plotting ... something.

A hired professional, Caul simply wants a "nice, fat recording" without responsibilities, but once he peruses the tapes he acknowledges that "this is no ordinary conversation" (shades of 1966's *Blow-Up*, where enlarged photographs reveal a hidden gunman). Caul considers delivering the incriminating tapes to his clients (Robert Duvall and Harrison Ford), but he's tormented because when he did something similar in the past, murders resulted. Warned that "these tapes are dangerous," Caul gets paranoid, realizes he's being followed, and considers destroying the reels. When they're stolen, he conducts his own investigation. The last act includes unexpected images that might be imaginary—a toilet overflows with blood, glimpses of violence, a corpse. Caul ultimately destroys his apartment in a search for microphones—the wiretapper, ironically, has become the wiretapped.

Hackman is brilliant as a nerdy, obsessed loner who's the opposite of the volatile powerhouse he played in *The French Connection* (1971). Caul is so secretive, not even his long-time mistress (Teri Garr) knows his age or occupation, yet Hackman manages to express this introvert's innermost anxieties and suppressed anger. Coppola, meanwhile, displays true mastery of the medium. He isolates Caul in empty spaces, uses swirling piano music to evoke the turning tape reels, and keeps Caul and the audience guessing with complex sound collages. In the final shot, a ceiling camera discreetly conducts a surveillance sweep of Caul's room. How perfect. A technical marvel and an intelligent mystery, *The Conversation* is a triumph of nuance over spectacle.

Gene Hackman.

ADDED ATTRACTION: Consecutive Oscars

Between 1972 and 1979, Francis Ford Coppola directed four movies in a row—*The Godfather, The Conversation, The Godfather: Part II, Apocalypse Now*—that got Oscar nominations for Best Picture (both *Godfathers* won). Here are other directors with consecutive Oscar nominations for Best Picture during the decade. Note number seven—like Coppola in 1974, Herbert Ross directed two Best Picture nominees in the same year.

- Hal Ashby: *Bound for Glory* (1976); *Coming Home* (1978)
- Bob Fosse: *Cabaret* (1972); *Lenny* (1974); *All That Jazz* (1979)
- William Friedkin: *The French Connection* (1971, winner); *The Exorcist* (1973)
- Stanley Kubrick: *A Clockwork Orange* (1971); *Barry Lyndon* (1975)
- George Lucas: *American Graffiti* (1973); *Star Wars* (1977)
- Sidney Lumet: *Dog Day Afternoon* (1975); *Network* (1976)
- Herbert Ross: *The Turning Point* (1977); *The Goodbye Girl* (1977)
- Franklin J. Schaffner: *Patton* (1970, winner); *Nicholas and Alexandra* (1971)

The Groove Tube

Released: April 1974
Director: Ken Shapiro
Stars: Ken Shapiro, Richard Belzer, Chevy Chase
Academy Awards: None

PREVIEW: An irreverent hit-and-miss anthology of skits spoofing TV shows and commercials.

NOW SHOWING: Groovin' on the Tube

Raunchy, irreverent, generally funny and occasionally hilarious, *The Groove Tube* (1974) is a good way to gauge your friends' sense of humor. Not everyone will like it, and even those who do might not agree on which segments are the highlights. But if you're a fan, and many people were in 1974, you'll find plenty to laugh at in this wildly diverse anthology movie.

The Groove Tube jams two-dozen skits into seventy-five R-rated minutes. Most of them are parodies of TV shows and commercials, though the five-minute opener clones the early scenes of *2001: A Space Odyssey* (1968), but now the man-apes discover a TV instead of a monolith. It's a long sequence with no dialogue, and that's something impressive about *The Groove Tube*—it often lets the visuals carry the laughs. Other examples of this are the prolonged three-minutes of awkward silence that conclude the newscast, the laugh-out-loud make-out scene in a movie theater, and the exuberant wordless frolic down a Manhattan street. The movie also includes a surreal animation sequence, nudity, some bad lighting, tasteless images, and juvenile humor (three separate ads for the Uranus Corporation, all right already).

Some of it will seem pretty dated to modern audiences, since a few skits mock specific commercials from the 1970s, like the silly "let your fingers do it" bit that plays off the Yellow Pages' old "let your fingers do the walking" slogan. But when it really hits its groove, this movie delivers. Favorites include "The Koko Show" in which a clown stops the antics on his children's TV show to read adult literature aloud; the gut-busting "Kramp TV Kitchen" that spoofs cooking shows; and the mock-serious "Wild World of Sports" live broadcast from the International Sex Games in Tijuana, Mexico.

Chevy Chase and comedian Richard Belzer both make their movie debuts with appearances in various sketches, but producer/director/co-writer/and co-star Ken Shapiro was the main man behind the *Tube*. The movie proved to be quite influential: the newscast that includes "good night, and have a pleasant tomorrow" in its sign-off seems to have been lifted directly into *Saturday Night Live*, and the longest bit, the eighteen-minute "The Dealers in *Wasted*," predates the Cheech and Chong movies. More importantly, this low-budget movie was a surprising commercial hit, thus paving the way for later zany anthologies. So if you like *The Kentucky Fried Movie* (1977), thank *The Groove Tube*.

ADDED ATTRACTION: Anthology Movies

Besides *The Groove Tube*, these American movies compiled three or more separate sections during the 1970s.

- *The Bugs Bunny/Road Runner Movie* (1979): Classic Warner Bros. cartoons.
- *California Suite* (1978): Guests stay at the Beverly Hills Hotel.
- *Everything You Always Wanted to Know About Sex* But Were Afraid to Ask* (1972): Woody Allen answers seven sex-related questions.
- *Fantastic Animation Festival* (1977): Fourteen award-winning short films.
- *The Kentucky Fried Movie* (1977): A collection of movie parodies.
- *The Many Adventures of Winnie the Pooh* (1977): Three animated stories about Christopher Robin and friends.
- *Plaza Suite* (1971): Guests stay at New York's Plaza Hotel.
- *Screams of a Winter Night* (1979): Students share scary stories.

- *Ten from Your Show of Shows* (1973): Classic skits from the 1950-1954 TV show.
- *The Three Stooges Follies* (1974): Stooges' shorts from the 1930s and '40s.
- *Visions of Eight* (1973): Eight directors show different events at the 1972 Summer Olympics.

Claudine

Released: April 1974
Director: John Berry
Stars: Diahann Carroll, James Earl Jones, Lawrence-Hilton Jacobs
Academy Awards: One nomination (Best Actress—Diahann Carroll)

PREVIEW: A struggling garbage man romances a woman on welfare who is trying to raise six kids.

NOW SHOWING: It's the Story of a Lovely Lady

A single mother, a single father, six kids, some humor, some drama—what is this, *The Brady Bunch*? Kind of. *Claudine* (1974) is a small-but-pleasing movie that boasts excellent performances and gritty Harlem locations where mice run through apartments. Most importantly, *Claudine* respectfully presents believable black characters dealing with realistic problems, unlike the violent blaxploitation movies of the early 1970s—*Super Fly* (1972), *Coffy* (1973), etc.—that were dominated by outrageous villains and implausible situations. Poverty and unruly kids, not pimps and drug dealers, are *Claudine*'s concerns.

The title's lovely lady is Diahann Carroll, fresh off an award-winning TV series, *Julia*, where she played a widowed nurse with one son. Here she's a divorcée struggling to raise six kids, including a militant teenage son who gets a vasectomy and a defiant teenage daughter who gets pregnant. Carroll swears, smokes, drinks beer, lies, and offers tough love by beating her daughter with a hair brush, but she is convincing and captivating in the role.

Even more compelling is James Earl Jones as Rupe, a smooth charmer who downplays himself as an "ugly ol' smelly ol' garbage man" and admits he's an irresponsible deadbeat dad with kids he never sees or supports. He's smart, though, and says memorable things like, "You gotta make the best of each day because when you're dead life isn't worth living." He also quickly identifies a key topic when they first meet: Claudine is fraudulently collecting welfare while simultaneously earning unreported income. Rupe and Claudine sleep together on their memorable first date, and from there the movie shows their growing romance as they deal with that troubling welfare issue (if he sticks around, her aid could be cut).

Considering that Jones will soon be immortalized as the powerful voice of Darth Vader in *Star Wars* (1977), it's interesting to see him here as a vulnerable, flawed hero who weeps, wears tightie-whities, gets beaten up by a teenager, and petulantly threatens to move away. Happily, he's redeemed in a crazy wedding ceremony that somehow ends with the entire wedding party being hauled off in a paddy wagon. In the joyful final scene, the smiling family walks down a city street together with "we can make it" as the hopeful last line from the great Gladys Knight & the Pips soundtrack. That they'll face their unsolved problems with unity and dignity makes this warm, compassionate movie a continued inspiration.

ADDED ATTRACTION: One '70s Movie, One Oscar Nomination

With *Claudine*, Diahann Carroll earned an Oscar nomination for Best Actress. Somehow this is Carroll's only movie of the 1970s; she did TV movies and TV shows during the decade, but no other theatrically released movies until the 1990s. Shown below are four more stars who got acting nominations for the one and only movie he or she made during the '70s (other '70s stars got nominations for their *first* movies—Diana Ross in 1972's *Lady Sings the Blues* and Tatum O'Neal in 1973's *Paper Moon*—but they went on to star in other '70s movies). The stars below all earned Best Supporting Actor/Best Supporting Actress nominations, but none of them won the Oscar.

- Mikhail Baryshnikov: *The Turning Point* (1977)
- Leslie Browne: *The Turning Point* (1977)
- Justin Henry: *Kramer vs. Kramer* (1979)
- Quinn Cummings: *The Goodbye Girl* (1977)

That's Entertainment!

Released: May 1974
Director: Jack Haley Jr.
Stars: Frank Sinatra, Gene Kelly, Liza Minnelli
Academy Awards: None

PREVIEW: Clips from classic movies spotlight the greatest musical scenes in MGM's history.

NOW SHOWING: That's Surprising!

"Boy, do we need it now." That was the poster for *That's Entertainment!* (1974), addressing a nation weary from Watergate, war, and brutal movies like *The Exorcist* (1973). America responded, making this nostalgic documentary one of 1974's most surprising block-busters. *That's Entertainment!* was so successful, sequels followed in 1976 and 1994.

"Thank God for film! It can capture a performance and hold it right there forever," declares one of the narrators, Liza Minnelli; her ardent words could also summarize the movie's mission. Honoring Metro-Goldwyn-Mayer's fiftieth anniversary in 1974, and helmed by Jack Haley Jr. (son of the actor who played the Tin Woodsman in 1939's *The Wizard of Oz*), *That's Entertainment!* celebrates MGM's famous musicals with 134 minutes of glorious, sometimes rare, and always entertaining clips that spotlight eighty songs and almost a hundred stars through the 1950s.

That's narration! Eleven Hollywood legends present a dozen sections, with these highlights: Frank Sinatra describing MGM's earliest hits; James Stewart and the transition to talkies; Gene Kelly talking about Fred Astaire, and Astaire talking about Kelly; Donald O'Connor spotlighting Esther Williams and the "swimming musical"; Debbie Reynolds on MGM's twenty-fifth anniversary lunch in 1949 and 1951's *Show Boat*; and Liza Minnelli discussing her mother, Judy Garland, and *Oz*. While more behind-the-scenes info would have been welcome, there are plenty of smile-induc-ing moments to enjoy, including the stiff dance moves of hard-working Clark Gable and the awkward crooning by young Jimmy Stewart; the exuberant performances by Mickey Rooney and Judy Garland in Busby Berkeley's "backyard musicals"; the medley of Astaire's ingenious dance numbers; and the generous footage given to some great stars (Eleanor Powell) and razzle-dazzle musicals (1955's *Hit the Deck*) that are sometimes overlooked.

It's especially poignant to watch *That's Entertainment!* today and see the now-deceased stars in their prime as they perform in memorable movies from long ago. They sure don't make 'em like that anymore. Adding to the sentiment is the sad realization that the scenes of the narrators on the old MGM backlot were the last scenes ever shot there, because the dilapidated structures were soon demolished and the land was sold to developers so they could build townhouses.

ADDED ATTRACTION: And the Oscar Goes to...

That's Entertainment! is old-fashioned feel-good fun; its polar opposite is *Hearts and Minds* (1974), that year's Oscar winner as Best Documentary. This powerful, provocative movie, which has no narrator and limited music, uses direct words (from politicians, advisors, ex-soldiers, ex-POWs, disabled vets, Vietnamese refugees, and ordinary Americans) and vivid images (from black-and-white newsreels, current combat footage, new interviews, and old Hollywood movies) to explore America's involvement in the Vietnam War. All the era's key figures—American presidents, generals, Daniel Ellsberg, even Bob Hope—make appearances, and hawks and doves express their attitudes. Director Peter Davis pairs scenes for maximum impact: American pilots describe "the sense of excitement" as they drop their bombs, and then Vietnamese peasants lament "the heap of rubble" that used to be their simple house; a football coach and LBJ rouse their audiences to victory; the heart-wrenching wails of mourning Vietnamese civilians contrast Commanding General William Westmoreland's assertion that "life is cheap in the Orient." While some scenes are harrowing to watch—an actual execution, for instance—the most unbearable are those with sobbing, suffering children. *Hearts and Minds* is essential viewing for anyone interested in this controversial period in American history.

Herbie Rides Again

Released: June 1974
Director: Robert Stevenson
Stars: Helen Hayes, Ken Berry, Stefanie Powers
Academy Awards: None

PREVIEW: A greedy developer covets an old lady's house, but Herbie the VW comes to her rescue.

NOW SHOWING: Ride On!

The Love Bug (1968) was a likeable car comedy that became one of that year's surprise blockbusters. Six years later, *Herbie Rides Again* (1974) similarly cruised to box-office success. This agreeable sequel reunites two of Disney's movie-making veterans, director Robert Stevenson and screenwriter Bill Walsh; however, the first movie's stars, Dean Jones, Michele Lee, and Buddy Hackett, are all missing (it's explained that Jones and Hackett's characters are in Europe and Tibet, respectively, but Lee's isn't mentioned). Fortunately, the first movie's biggest star, the adorable white VW bug with a mind of his own, shows he's still got plenty of mileage left in him.

The sequel takes a sharp detour from *The Love Bug*'s racing action. Greedy, growly developer Alonzo Hawk (Keenan Wynn) wants his "nauseatingly innocent" nephew, Willoughby (Ken Berry), to eliminate the one obstacle standing between Hawk and his plans to erect "the world's highest building." That obstacle is the widow Steinmetz (Helen Hayes), the aunt of Buddy Hackett's *Love Bug* character, who lives right where Hawk Plaza will rise. Willoughby is called "incredibly dumb," but he soon sympathizes with Mrs. Steinmetz, falls for her spirited granddaughter (Stefanie Powers), and turns against his villainous uncle. The movie's second half presents zany chases and confrontations as Hawk tries to take the house.

Berry, Powers, and Hayes are pleasant enough, but it's sentient, independent Herbie who delivers the high-octane fun. When Hawk steals Herbie, he insults Herbie as "a one-cylinder old hair dryer" and quickly elicits Herbie's violent retaliation. However, when the friendly Mrs. Steinmetz drives Herbie, she doesn't even have to steer because Herbie is safely in control. Herbie's spectacular stunts include rooftop leaps, a drive up a Golden Gate Bridge cable, and an ocean swim. For the demolition crew's last charge, Herbie recruits another dozen VW's to chase them off for good.

Unlike *The Love Bug*, which raced across all of California, this movie stays in the Bay Area and really shows off San Francisco. It also tries to stay hip with lines like, "You win the bread, man," and girls wearing miniskirts and shag haircuts. The best scene might be Hawk's bizarre minute-long dream sequence when he imagines a pack of voracious Herbies chomping toward him and then a squadron of Herbies flying around him. While it's slightly disconcerting to watch an Oscar-winning legend, Helen Hayes, converse with a car, kids won't care and should enjoy Herbie's madcap antics.

Ken Berry, Helen Hayes, and Stefanie Powers.

ADDED ATTRACTION: Disney's Fantasy Island

Herbie Rides Again was Disney's summertime hit; six months later the studio released its big holiday hopeful, *The Island at the Top of the World* (1974). Like *Herbie*, *Island* was directed by Robert Stevenson, the Englishman who helmed *Mary Poppins* (1964) and other Disney hits. Potentially, *Island* might've been an exciting masterpiece a la *20,000 Leagues Under the Sea* (1954), but without that classic's charismatic stars, memorable monster, or philosophical themes, *Island* simply doesn't have the same majesty. Set in 1907, the movie sends a search party in a whale-shaped airship to the Arctic, where they find a strange, verdant island and a lost Viking colony. As with other Disney live-action movies, there's a cute pet, a pretty girl, vivid nature footage, and looming disasters before the requisite happy ending. While it's decent popcorn entertainment for a Saturday afternoon, *Island*'s lackluster box-office performance put Disney out of the epic-adventure business until *The Black Hole* (1979).

Uptown Saturday Night

Released: June 1974

Director: Sidney Poitier

Stars: Sidney Poitier, Bill Cosby, Harry Belafonte

Academy Awards: None

PREVIEW: When a winning lottery ticket is stolen, two friends battle mobsters to get it back.

NOW SHOWING: Get Down

Uptown Saturday Night (1974) pairs two likeable stars, Sidney Poitier and Bill Cosby, and lets their great chemistry bring off a simple story. They play hard-working ordinary guys in Chicago (Poitier's a steel worker, Cosby a bearded cab driver) who treat themselves one Saturday night to an after-midnight trip away from their wives and into a ritzy pleasure palace. While they're happily gambling and checking out the seductive scenery, robbers break in and steal everyone's valuables, including Poitier's lottery ticket worth $50,000. For the rest of the movie, the two buddies visit various locations to recover the stolen ticket. Along the way they encounter an all-star team of terrific actors and entertainers, including Harry Belafonte, Richard Pryor, Flip Wilson, Rosalind Cash, Paula Kelly, Roscoe Lee Browne, and legendary dance-man Harold Nicholas. After a lengthy run-in with some dangerous gangsters, a car chase, and a couple of death-defying leaps off a bridge, the stars and the ticket emerge relatively unscathed.

Wisely, director Poitier makes himself the dignified, polite straight man and leaves the comedy to the pros, especially Cosby, who always seems to be improvising and insti-gating. Cosby talks their way into the nightclub and enjoys a hilarious run at the dice table; later he comically erupts at Poitier and then provokes him to insult the gangsters. By the end "young blood" and "homeboy" (as they call each other) will both have played the action hero and survived encounters with some pretty wild '70s fashions. Of the supporting cast, Pryor has only one five-minute scene as an anxious con man, but he nails it. As the head gangster, Belafonte stuffs his cheeks and growls out an impression of Don Corleone from *The Godfather* (1972) that was probably a lot funnier then than it is now. Roscoe Lee Browne plays a two-faced congressman who wears a conservative suit and displays a Nixon portrait when he's meeting with two "gentlemen" from "the Mayor's office," but he flips the picture to Malcolm X and puts on an exotic African robe as soon as he finds out that the two "rather ordinary" men outside are his "constituents."

Modern audiences may choke at the occasional racial epithet, the jokes about fried chicken and picking cotton, and the bar that serves chitlins and pig's feet. Nevertheless, 1970s audiences so embraced this generally harmless comedy that it was soon followed by two sequels (see "Added Attraction").

ADDED ATTRACTION: Multiple Movies

Sidney Poitier and Bill Cosby co-starred in *Uptown Saturday Night*'s sequels, *Let's Do It Again* (1975) and *A Piece of the Action* (1977). Both were successful and received generally positive reviews. Besides Poitier and Cosby, other actors and actresses shared multiple movies during the decade, including these.

- **Woody Allen/Diane Keaton**
  Play It Again, Sam (1972); *Sleeper* (1973); *Love and Death* (1975); *Annie Hall* (1977); *Manhattan* (1979)

- **Warren Beatty/Julie Christie**
  McCabe & Mrs. Miller (1971); *Shampoo* (1975); *Heaven Can Wait* (1978)

- **Clint Eastwood/Sondra Locke**
  The Outlaw Josey Wales (1976); *The Gauntlet* (1977); *Every Which Way But Loose* (1978)

- **Elliott Gould/Donald Sutherland**
  M*A*S*H (1970); *Little Murders* (1971); *S*P*Y*S* (1974)

- **Al Pacino/John Cazale**
  The Godfather (1972); *The Godfather: Part II* (1974); *Dog Day Afternoon* (1975)

- **Burt Reynolds/Sally Field**
  Smokey and the Bandit (1977); *The End* (1978); *Hooper* (1978)

- **Gene Wilder/Madeline Kahn**
  Blazing Saddles (1974); *Young Frankenstein* (1974); *The Adventure of Sherlock Holmes' Smarter Brother* (1975)

The Parallax View

Released: June 1974
Director: Alan J. Pakula
Stars: Warren Beatty, Hume Cronyn, William Daniels
Academy Awards: None

PREVIEW: Investigating an assassination, a journalist uncovers a sinister organization.

NOW SHOWING: Different Perspective

Not everyone will see *The Parallax View* (1974) the same way, which is appropriate: parallax, after all, is defined as the change in perspective from different viewing positions. Some might see this somber movie as a frustrating story with no easy answers; others will celebrate its ambiguities and atmosphere. Either way, *The Parallax View* ranks high among the paranoid political thrillers of the 1970s (see "Added Attraction").

Warren Beatty, with groovy hair and hip clothes similar to what he'll wear in *Shampoo* (1975), plays Joe, a renegade journalist. After a senator is shot in a scene resembling the Robert Kennedy assassination, Joe gradually realizes that some of that event's witnesses have coincidentally died in "accidents" (why there's a need to eliminate witnesses is never clear, since the actual assassin dies at the scene, so the case could have been immediately closed). Joe starts poking around and finds that he himself has become a target: he survives a drowning attempt, an explosion on a boat, and a time bomb on an airliner. Uncovering the mysterious Parallax Corporation, he infiltrates the organization as a new applicant and learns that "whoever's behind this is in the business of recruiting assassins." Sent out on his first assignment, Joe is at the scene of another assassination as an observer. Recognizing that he's been set up as a patsy, he tries to escape, only to be gunned down. A follow-up investigation smears Joe by declaring him a deranged, solitary killer.

The movie's strengths are its eerie mood and imagery. In over his head, Joe is frequently depicted among huge buildings, vast spaces, and deep shadows, all signifying that the conspiracy he's investigating is simply too big to be truly understood and conquered. A memorable five-minute montage at the Parallax headquarters midway through the movie presents a fascinating mix of recurring images, from the patriotic and comforting to the erotic and disturbing, that are being used either to brainwash Joe or to test his reactions. Eventually the movie heads to a suspenseful climax that echoes *The Manchurian Candidate* (1962) as we watch the details of an assassination unfold. In that earlier classic, the enemies were foreign, working from the outside; here the enemies are a powerful corporation, working from within. It's a significant shift but appropriate for a Watergate-era movie made after a decade of assassinations. *The Parallax View* was an unsettling movie for an unsettling time.

ADDED ATTRACTION: Conspiracy Theories

Fifteen additional 1970s movies that feature conspiracies, listed chronologically with their stars.

- *THX 1138* (1971): Robert Duvall
- *Soylent Green* (1973): Charlton Heston
- *Executive Action* (1973): Burt Lancaster
- *The Conversation* (1974): Gene Hackman
- *Chinatown* (1974): Jack Nicholson
- *Three Days of the Condor* (1975): Robert Redford
- *All the President's Men* (1976): Robert Redford
- *Logan's Run* (1976): Michael York
- *Twilight's Last Gleaming* (1977): Burt Lancaster
- *The Domino Principle* (1977): Gene Hackman
- *Telefon* (1977): Charles Bronson
- *Capricorn One* (1977): James Brolin
- *Coma* (1978): Geneviève Bujold
- *Good Guys Wear Black* (1978): Chuck Norris
- *Winter Kills* (1979): Jeff Bridges

Chinatown

(One of 1974's five **FAR-OUT** movies)

Released: June 1974

Director: Roman Polanski

Stars: Jack Nicholson, Faye Dunaway, John Huston

Academy Awards: One win (Best Writing), plus ten more nominations (Best Picture; Best Actor—Jack Nicholson; Best Actress—Faye Dunaway; Best Director; Best Editing; Best Cinematography; Best Art Direction; Best Costume Design; Best Music; Best Sound)

PREVIEW: A private detective investigates a mysterious real estate swindle in Los Angeles.

FINE LINE: "Most people never have to face the fact, at the right time and the right place, they're capable of anything." (Noah Cross, rationalizing his evil actions.)

CLOSE-UP: Eighty-five minutes into the movie, Jake reveals something significant about his past and foreshadows the ending. In bed with Evelyn, he tells her that Chinatown was "bad luck": "I was trying to keep someone from being hurt. I ended up making sure that she *was* hurt." When she asks if there was "a woman involved," he says, "Of course."

NOW SHOWING: "A Nosy Fellow"

Chinatown (1974) represents the perfect union of *what* a movie is doing (presenting a labyrinthine mystery) with *how* a movie is doing it (blending an ideal cast, haunting music, and rich visuals). Powered by the decade's most intricate screenplay, *Chinatown* unspools a serpentine, almost unfathomable plot that requires repeat viewings for full comprehension. But the journey through the mystery from its innocuous start to its grim conclusion is so entertaining, so watchable, so impressive, that repeat viewings are welcome. Of the many questions viewers could ask after watching *Chinatown*, one of them might be to wonder why it didn't win more than one Oscar.

The story is far too complicated for a full summary here. Essentially, a private investigator is hired by a wife to produce evidence that her husband is having an affair, but when that husband suspiciously drowns it becomes apparent that there is some kind of conspiracy at work. Eventually a massive real estate swindle and a truly terrible family secret are exposed. A newspaper dateline, classic clothes, and vintage cars set the year at 1937.

Private eye Jake Gittes (Jack Nicholson) is in every scene, and the movie is often shot from his perspective. This unites the audience with him, so that we see only as much as he sees (there's no scene of criminals plotting or pulling off a job with nobody else around). Director Roman Polanski puts the camera behind Gittes' shoulder so we see the subjects as he's taking photos; we look through his binoculars at distant action; as he drives through an orange grove, we watch through the windshield from his perspective; when Gittes gets clobbered and blacks-out, the camera blacks-out, too; we peer through windows, right along with Jake; and we share his viewpoint as he walks through a murder scene. Throughout, viewers have no more clues than Jake has.

Intriguingly, he's consistently in the dark. Unlike Agatha Christie's brilliant detectives, Jake has no uncanny gift for solving crimes and often gets things wrong. Here are just a few of his many mistakes: he's instantly duped by an imposter posing as Evelyn Mulwray (Faye Dunaway); he incorrectly assumes the El Macondo apartment belongs to Hollis, Evelyn's husband; he arrives at the dam to interview Hollis, who's already dead; he wrongly guesses that Hollis died in a fight with Evelyn at their backyard pond; and he's too late when he tries to rush through a final explanation and shouts, "He's rich … thinks he can get away with anything!" At the very end, when the tragedy has abruptly and horribly played out despite his best intentions, Jake stares into space, possibly overwhelmed by sadness, but perhaps wondering what just happened.

While Jake isn't as sharp as his obvious movie ancestors, Sam Spade and Philip Marlowe, he's also not as smooth. "This business requires a certain amount of finesse," he counsels an associate, but he himself is constantly blundering. Early on he accidentally kicks a tile off the roof and almost falls as he's surreptitiously taking photos. He loudly tells a vulgar joke, unaware that elegant Evelyn is directly behind him. He gets swept through a water channel and loses an expensive shoe. At a rest home he attempts an impersonation and is quickly exposed. Worst of all he suffers a hideous nose wound (appropriate for "a nosy fellow") and has to wear an undignified bandage across his face for thirty-nine minutes of the movie.

Verbally, though, Jake is thoroughly accomplished. He rattles off one-liners (his sliced nose hurts "only when I breathe") and glib dialogue ("I'm not in business to be loved, but I *am* in business"). And he amusingly toys with underlings and minor characters: he noisily smokes, hums, and whistles around the busy secretary at the Department of Water and Power to hurry her along; he torments the Hall of Records "weasel"; he taunts a low-level cop with a mean joke about his wife. Nicholson brings just the right amount of arrogance to make these encounters delightful for everybody except his victims.

Equally good are Dunaway as the doomed femme fatale and John Huston as Noah Cross, her vile father whose enormous crime against the city is paralleled by his depraved crime against his then-fifteen-year-old daughter. Watch her as she slightly tips off her secret with nervous words and tics in the movie's first two-thirds; watch him to see the embodiment of charming, menacing, overpowering evil (he's so unstoppable, he's shot point-blank with little effect). That Cross gets away with both

Jack Nicholson and Faye Dunaway.

his profitable plan and his granddaughter is a glaring departure from the typical noir thriller that would have brought him to justice. Robert Towne's original screenplay had Evelyn shooting and killing Cross at the end, but as Polanski explains on the DVD's special features, Polanski was "absolutely adamant that she has to die at the end if the film is to have any kind of meaning."

This demanding movie challenges audiences to keep up. Impatient viewers complain that it's too long and doesn't have enough action, but *Chinatown* rewards close scrutiny. Observe how it opens with black-and-white images, drawing us into Dashiell Hammett's and Raymond Chandler's world; note the word pairs—apple-core/albacore, grass/glass, Gittes/Gitts, sister/daughter; connect the cracked eyeglasses, Jake's broken sunglasses, the broken taillight, the "flaw" in Evelyn's iris, and the bullet through that eye. As with all masterpieces, the more you study *Chinatown*, the more there is to see.

ADDED ATTRACTION: Famous Film Quotes

The movie's last line—"Forget it, Jake, it's Chinatown"—is ranked seventy-fourth on the American Film Institute's list called "AFI'S 100 Greatest Movie Quotes of All Time." Here are five other famous quotes from 1970–1974 movies that made the AFI list. Number one, by the way, is "Frankly, my dear, I don't give a damn" from *Gone with the Wind* (1939).

- AFI #2, *The Godfather* (1972): "I'm gonna make him an offer he can't refuse."
- AFI #13, *Love Story* (1970): "Love means never having to say you're sorry."
- AFI #51, *Dirty Harry* (1971): "You've gotta ask yourself one question: 'Do I feel lucky?' Well, do ya, punk?"
- AFI #58, *The Godfather: Part II* (1974): "Keep your friends close, but your enemies closer."
- AFI #77, *Soylent Green* (1973): "Soylent Green is people!"

Death Wish

Released: July 1974

Director: Michael Winner

Stars: Charles Bronson, Vincent Gardenia, Hope Lange

Academy Awards: None

PREVIEW: When his wife is killed and his daughter is raped, a quiet man gets frontier justice.

NOW SHOWING: Pistol-Packin' Paul

Following in the footsteps of *Walking Tall* (1973), a smash hit about a southern sheriff who uses violent methods to clean up his crime-filled town, *Death Wish* (1974) brings old-fashioned frontier justice to a modern city. Audiences enraged by out-of-control urban crime rates made it a box-office success. While those audiences may have come to cheer on a lone vigilante, what they got was actually a little more thought-provoking.

Charles Bronson is effective as Paul, a soft-spoken architect who was a conscientious objector during the Korean War. Twelve minutes into the movie, Paul's wife is killed and his daughter is raped by three vicious thugs in their Manhattan apartment.

Charles Bronson.

Frustrated by the unproductive police investigation, he takes matters into his own hands. First he stops a mugger by clubbing him with a sock filled with quarters, an experience that leaves Paul shaking but resolute. Then, armed with a pistol he's received as a gift, he starts courting trouble by loitering at night in parks and on subways. Soon he shoots and kills a mugger; Paul gets physically sick afterwards, but from then on he's aggressive in his new role as an impassive, remorseless crime crusader. Eventually, he kills nine more muggers in an alley, a subway station, and a park, some of them even as they're lying wounded or running away.

The story elevates beyond *Walking Tall*-style vengeance once the police close in via ballistics tests and solid detective work. The question is, should they arrest this law-breaking killer? Maybe not: with the mysterious vigilante now a front-page story, a billboard sign, and a regular TV-news topic, the crime rate is dropping precipitously. It's an interesting dilemma made even more complicated when other citizens (even little old ladies) are inspired to physically fight back against criminals, setting up potentially dangerous situations.

The mayor suggests scaring the vigilante off but letting the public think he's still active. Consequently, when Paul is injured and captured, the inspector on the case tells him he needs to move away (when he's told he should get out of town, Paul answers with a frontier cliché: "By sundown?"). The last we see of Paul, he's smiling as he pretends to shoot vandals in Chicago's busy airport terminal. If that sounds like sequels are coming, you're right: four more *Death Wish* movies with Bronson followed in the 1980s and '90s. In Hollywood, violence really does beget violence.

ADDED ATTRACTION: Vigilante Movies

A dozen more '70s movies that show one person cleaning up a town or getting revenge against villains. Stars are noted.

- *Billy Jack* (1971): Tom Laughlin
- *Bucktown* (1975): Fred Williamson
- *Carrie* (1976): Sissy Spacek
- *Coffy* (1973): Pam Grier
- *Dirty Harry* (1971): Clint Eastwood
- *High Plains Drifter* (1973): Clint Eastwood
- *I Spit on Your Grave* (1978): Camille Keaton
- *Rage* (1972): George C. Scott
- *Rolling Thunder* (1977): William Devane
- *Taxi Driver* (1976): Robert De Niro
- *Walking Tall* (1973): Joe Don Baker
- *White Line Fever* (1975): Jan-Michael Vincent

Bank Shot

Released: July 1974
Director: Gower Champion
Stars: George C. Scott, Joanna Cassidy, Clifton James
Academy Awards: None

PREVIEW: A wacky gang steals an entire bank and then struggles try to hide it and blow the safe.

NOW SHOWING: Trying to Make a *Bank Shot*

A brisk little farce that zips by in only eighty-three minutes, *Bank Shot* (1974) presents an ingenious twist on bank heists: don't just steal the money, steal the entire bank. At a construction site, the current bank has relocated into a temporary trailer. Master criminal Walter Ballantine (George C. Scott) gets one look and instantly devises an elaborate plan. Soon he and his goofy gang (including a young Bob Balaban) manage to tow away the trailer, paint it, and stash it in a mobile-home park. Unfortunately, while trying to blow the seemingly indestructible safe they end up demolishing the entire trailer. In an abrupt ending, the last we see of Walter he's ditching his pursuers by swimming into the Pacific Ocean ... to Samoa, according to the final narration.

A few of the scenes really are comical, as when Walter drives a huge lumbering earth-moving vehicle out of prison, demolishing everything in his path while the warden (Clifton James) chases him in a tiny three-wheeled golf cart. Walter is also quick to change costumes (he briefly masquerades as a bearded biker) and steal vehicles (a police motorcycle, a Pantera, an antique car, and an ice cream truck, among others). As he proved in *Dr. Strangelove* (1964), Scott excels in comedic roles, but here he seems slightly miscast, blending his cantankerous growl from *Patton* (1970) with a strange speech impediment and the most conspicuous eyebrows since Groucho Marx. Fortunately, there's enough mindless amusement to keep this *Bank Shot* from being a total miss.

Four months later, George C. Scott made a radical shift from lightweight comedy to sluggish drama. Scott had already directed himself in a dark movie, the vigilante-themed *Rage* (1972); he goes from dark to disturbing in *The Savage Is Loose* (1974).

Again both starring and directing, Scott and his real-life wife, Trish Van Devere, play parents to a young son in the early 1900s. After a shipwreck strands them on a deserted island, they manage to survive like the Swiss Family Robinson. Midway through the movie, though, the boy grows to become a studly young man who lusts for the only girl around—mom. The intensifying tensions culminate when the son plots against his dad so he can claim his mom. Though Scott tries to treat the unsavory topic of incest carefully, critics and audiences were uneasy, and this awkward, ponderous disaster marked the end of Scott's directing career.

ADDED ATTRACTION: The Donald

Bank Shot is based on a 1972 novel by Donald E. Westlake, the author of many clever crime stories. Earlier movies based on his works include *Point Blank* (1967); later he'd get an Oscar nomination for his screenplay for *The Grifters* (1990). During the 1970s the following movies were based on his works. All of these movies have a comedic touch, except for number three, which is a violent thriller. Westlake himself wrote the screenplay for the second movie and he co-wrote the screenplay for the fifth. Stars are noted.

- *The Hot Rock* (1972): Robert Redford
- *Cops and Robbers* (1973): Cliff Gorman
- *The Outfit* (1973): Robert Duvall
- *Bank Shot* (1974): George C. Scott
- *Hot Stuff* (1979): Dom DeLuise

Macon County Line

Released: August 1974
Director: Richard Compton
Stars: Alan Vint, Jesse Vint, Cheryl Waters
Academy Awards: None

PREVIEW: In 1954, two rowdy brothers are chased when they are wrongly identified as killers.

NOW SHOWING: Crossing the *Macon County Line*

Even compared with other low-budget drive-in movies, *Macon County Line* (1974) isn't great, but somehow it had enough appeal to become a box-office hit. Credit goes to Max Baer Jr., familiar as Jethro on TV's *The Beverly Hillbillies*. Not only did Baer produce this movie, he also invented the story and plays an important character.

Set in 1954 Louisiana, the movie begins as a whoop-it-up comedy, thanks to cheerful opening music and two spirited brothers (played by brothers Alan and Jesse Vint) who are introduced during a sexual encounter with a howling hooker. Soon they leap out the window, dine-and-dash at a café, destroy a police car in a prank similar to the one in *American Graffiti* (1973), and pick up a pretty girl as they drive along shirtless in a vintage convertible. With military service pending, they proclaim they're "out cattin' around and havin' us a ball." Raucous road-trip fun ahead, right?

Nope. Their car continually breaks down, the guys are flat broke, and they're hassled by a local sheriff (Baer). The tone darkens midway through the movie when two mean-looking drifters rob a random house, which turns out to be the sheriff's. They kill his wife and later shoot a deputy. Unfortunately for the brothers, the enraged sheriff mistakenly thinks they've committed these crimes, and the last twenty minutes are dominated by a nighttime foot chase that culminates with a surprise shooter and bloodshed. Text at the beginning and end announces this as a true story, though that's a dubious claim.

The movie engages its target audience with lovely southern sunsets, tons of guns, and a Bobbie Gentry theme song. Additionally, there are mentions of moonshine, cockfights, and character names like Hamp, Gooch, and Gurney. Oh yeah, there's a tender sex scene in a barn, too. The brothers are mildly charming and get off a few lines ("If the Lord was gonna give the world an enema," one says at a run-down gas station, "right here is where he'd stick the hose."). Interestingly, the law-enforcement officers come off pretty bad: the racist sheriff steers his son away from black playmates, and a colleague forces confessions with his pistol.

Producer Baer scored big with *Macon County Line*, one of the early-1970s movies made for southern viewers (see "Added Attraction"). *Return to Macon County* (1975), with Nick Nolte and Don Johnson as two new rowdies, was a rushed, forgettable follow-up.

ADDED ATTRACTION: Southern-Centric Cinema, 1970–1974

Like *Macon County Line*, the following twelve movies use southern settings (we're including Texas) to tell southern stories. Some entries in this chronological list show good ol' boys havin' fun and gettin' in trouble, while others present serious, even violent conflicts involving racism, criminals, guns, vehicles, smuggling, and more. But all could be considered examples of southern-centric cinema in the early 1970s. Stars are noted.

- *...tick...tick...tick...* (1970): Jim Brown
- *The Last Picture Show* (1971): Timothy Bottoms
- *Deliverance* (1972): Burt Reynolds
- *Sounder* (1972): Cicely Tyson
- *Walking Tall* (1973): Joe Don Baker
- *The Last American Hero* (1973): Jeff Bridges
- *White Lightning* (1973): Jan-Michael Vincent
- *The Sugarland Express* (1974): Goldie Hawn
- *'Gator Bait* (1974): Claudia Jennings
- *The Longest Yard* (1974): Burt Reynolds
- *The Texas Chain Saw Massacre* (1974): Marilyn Burns
- *The Klansman* (1974): Lee Marvin

Harry and Tonto

Released: August 1974

Director: Paul Mazursky

Stars: Art Carney, Larry Hagman, Josh Mostel

Academy Awards: One win (Best Actor—Art Carney), plus one more nomination (Best Writing)

PREVIEW: Evicted from his New York apartment, an old man travels cross-country with his cat.

NOW SHOWING: Lone Ranger

With *Bob & Carol & Ted & Alice* (1969) and *Blume in Love* (1973), writer/director Paul Mazursky had already made well-received, insightful satires about new social attitudes. In *Harry and Tonto* (1974), he presents an unconventional exploration of the Me Decade by using a resilient old man with a hearing aid as a prism through which we see changing times and a dignified way to cope with them.

Sort of a toned-down version of Maude in *Harold and Maude* (1971), Harry (Art Carney) is a likeable, smart, seventy-two-year-old New Yorker who makes friends easily, recites poetry, plays piano, and sings to his old cat, Tonto. He's also amazingly accepting of life's difficulties ("mugged four times this year," he mentions nonchalantly). Evicted from his apartment, he first relocates into his son's suburban home and then heads west to visit his other kids. Wherever he goes, Harry improvises his transportation without fear or urgency: he abandons an airport for a bus, leaves the bus to buy a '55 Chevy, spontaneously gives away the car in Arizona, and confidently catches rides until he reaches L.A. There he finds contentment, a part-time tutoring job, companionship, and, after Tonto dies, a new cat. Throughout his episodic road trip (which even includes a brief stay in jail), Harry converses amiably with relatives and fellow travelers.

The movie is packed with small true-to-life vignettes that span every emotion, from the comical (the vow-of-silence grandson talks in his sleep) to the poignant (Harry's ex-love is now confused by dementia). That Harry meets so many different people is slightly frustrating because attention-grabbing characters, like the enthusiastic hooker played by Barbara Rhoades, are introduced and quickly left behind (it would be interesting to know what happens when she picks up Harry in her car and eagerly pulls off the road, but Mazursky immediately moves on). Throughout, Harry reserves judgement as he discusses current topics (communes, drugs, Zen Buddhism) and observes different lifestyles. Open to adjustment, he swaps his old chapeau for a Lone Ranger-style white cowboy hat—perfect for someone traveling with Tonto—and even wears beads.

When his road adventures finally end, Harry isn't dying or depressed, he's flourishing. Art Carney, a TV favorite from *The Honeymooners*, fully inhabits this sensitive character and won that year's Best Actor Oscar. "The times change, and we change with it," Harry declares, an ungrammatical but appropriate summation of this warm, wise movie.

ADDED ATTRACTION: Harry and Lenny

One of the intense young actors nominated alongside Art Carney for 1974's Best Actor Oscar was Dustin Hoffman, who gave an incendiary performance that year as the controversial, groundbreaking comedian Lenny Bruce in *Lenny* (1974). Based on Julian Barry's award-winning Broadway play, directed by Bob Fosse, and filmed in black and white, *Lenny* is a powerful depiction of a tragic life (as shown in the movie, Bruce died in 1966 at age forty of a drug overdose). *Lenny* was up for Best Picture and other top Oscars including Best Actress for Valerie Perrine's performance as Bruce's wife, who's a stripper. Lenny Bruce's mother, Sally Marr, is played in the movie by actress Jan Miner; coincidentally, the actual Sally Marr appears in *Harry and Tonto* for two minutes at the end as Celia, the convivial cat lady at Venice Beach who invites Harry to move in.

The Longest Yard

Released: August 1974

Director: Robert Aldrich

Stars: Burt Reynolds, Eddie Albert, Ed Lauter

Academy Awards: One nomination (Best Editing)

PREVIEW: A former football star leads a team of prisoners in a game against the prison guards.

NOW SHOWING: Burt Scores

The Longest Yard (1974) opens with a disgraced ex-jock who is seemingly beyond redemption, but after he applies two hours of swaggering charm, sex appeal, and athletic prowess, Burt Reynolds transforms this unappealing lowlife character into a hero and this rough-and-tumble movie into a blockbuster.

In the first eight minutes Paul Crewe (Reynolds) shoves around a scantily-dressed woman, leads cops on a dangerous car chase through a busy city, and drunkenly resists arrest. He lands in a Florida prison, where his macho moustache is shaved off and he's beaten by guards. Borrowing lingo and atmosphere from *Cool Hand Luke* (1967), the movie shows the hardships of his degrading prison life, making Crewe slightly more sympathetic as he tries to endure.

Formerly "pro football's most valuable player," Crewe is invited to assemble a prison football squad to challenge the guards' championship-caliber semi-pro team. In the middle third of the movie, Crewe recruits the toughest prisoners and organizes them into an enthusiastic "mean machine." These murderers and rapists are called "scum," but they're also colorful and united, so the audience roots for them, especially after the despicable warden (Eddie Albert) instructs his vicious captain to "inflict as much painful damage on the prisoners as is humanly possible."

Director Robert Aldrich, known for manly movies like *The Dirty Dozen* (1967) and *Emperor of the North* (1973), gets the football scenes right with split-screen footage and believable easy-to-follow gridiron action. The actual game fills thirty-nine minutes, exactly triple the length of the rowdy contest that concludes *M*A*S*H* (1970). As in *M*A*S*H*, Crewe's game starts with the opponents returning the opening kick for a touchdown and following up with a quick safety. To fulfill a secret arrangement, Crewe, playing quarterback, attempts to throw the game, but eventually his feelings change and he engineers a crowd-pleasing comeback. With seven seconds left and the ball on the one-yard line, the final slow-motion play lasts ninety seconds and ends in "his-to-ry." A short coda adds the potential for a literal "sudden death" finish.

Simplistic but undeniably winning, *The Longest Yard* inspired both a mini-run of football-themed movies—*Semi-Tough* (1977), *Heaven Can Wait* (1978), *North Dallas Forty* (1979)—and a 2005 remake (Reynolds plays the older coach). For Reynolds, *The Longest Yard* pulls him from the serious drama of *Deliverance* (1972) and instead cements the wise-cracking good-ol'-boy persona that will dominate upcoming hits like *Smokey and the Bandit* (1977).

ADDED ATTRACTION: From NFL Stars to Movie Stars

One reason the football action in *The Longest Yard* seems so realistic is that actual players are on the field. (Burt Reynolds played in college, so even he enhances the believability.) Here are ten NFL stars who appeared in various 1970–1974 movies.

- Jim Brown: Thirteen '70s movies, including *Slaughter* (1972).
- Ben Davidson: The defender ejected from the big game in *M*A*S*H* (1970).
- Roosevelt Grier: Co-star of *The Thing With Two Heads* (1972).
- Joe Kapp: *The Longest Yard*'s "walking boss."
- Alex Karras: Many movie roles, especially Mongo in *Blazing Saddles* (1974).
- Joe Namath: Star of *C.C. & Company* (1970).
- Ray Nitschke: The most menacing opponent in *The Longest Yard*.
- Merlin Olsen: A supporting role in *Something Big* (1971).
- O.J. Simpson: Prominent security guard in *The Towering Inferno* (1974).
- Fred Williamson: Star of numerous blaxploitation hits like *Hammer* (1972).

The Taking of Pelham One Two Three

Released: October 1974
Director: Joseph Sargent
Stars: Walter Matthau, Robert Shaw, Martin Balsam
Academy Awards: None

PREVIEW: Four dangerous men hijack a New York City subway car and hold passengers for ransom.

NOW SHOWING: Pain Train

The Taking of Pelham One Two Three (1974) is an excellent blend of substance and style. The substance is the clever crime: "four very dangerous men armed with machine guns" hijack a New York subway train and hold eighteen hostages for ransom. Their scheme seems ludicrous—"There is no way you can get away with this," Lt. Garber (Walter Matthau) says over the radio, "you are underground in a tunnel!" So how do these "friggin' pirates" hope to escape with the money, despite being surrounded by an army of policemen? Eighty-two minutes elapse before their ingenious getaway becomes clear.

Meanwhile, the movie's straightforward style delivers the story directly and effectively. There are no laborious pre-crime planning sessions, no lame side stories or romances to slow events down. In the opening scenes the well-organized gang calmly starts the hijacking; significantly, the first sound anyone makes is one of the criminals sneezing. Once the Command Center understands what's going on, the movie (which is named after a subway station and departure time) becomes a war of wits as Garber tries to anticipate the gang's moves while conducting sarcastic radio conversations with the smart, disciplined leader (Robert Shaw, coolly doing crossword puzzles during the crime).

Nobody is what he seems to be: the hijackers dress like ordinary businessmen, wear fake moustaches, and use colors for names (Mr. Green, Mr. Blue, etc., an idea Quentin Tarantino borrows for 1992's *Reservoir Dogs*); the supposedly non-English-speaking Japanese visitors are actually fluent (a funny, unexpected reveal); the buffoonish mayor is no leader; a long-haired hippie is actually an undercover cop (Garber later mistakes him for a girl); Garber makes an embarrassing assumption about the chief inspector; near the end Garber incorrectly declares "that's our man right there"; when he does confront the one remaining hijacker, Garber walks away until a memorable final sneeze brings him back.

Critics deride the plan's implausibility (seriously, how realistic are subway trains with zero graffiti on them?) and all the racist and profane language. But the movie does so many things well—from the urban atmosphere captured by Owen Roizman (cinematographer for 1971's *The French Connection*) to the jazzy, jagged, unsettling score, to the strong performances and authentic New York accents (they "woik" in the "noive centah")—that it overcomes any obstacles. Influential and suspenseful, surprising and entertaining, *The Taking of Pelham One Two Three* hurtles along like a speeding express train.

Walter Matthau.

ADDED ATTRACTION: Take This Vehicle to Cuba

Seventy-two minutes into *The Taking of Pelham One Two Three*, an official claims that the hijackers are "gonna fly the train to Cuba." Someone else adds, "What do you mean you haven't got any buses? Go out and hijack some!" Hijacking was a hot topic in 1974. There had already been dozens of real-life hijackings, including D.B. Cooper's famous escape from a hijacked 727 over the Pacific Northwest in November 1971 and a failed attempt to crash a hijacked DC-9 into the White House in February 1974. Here are some other 1970s movies that include various hijacked or ransomed vehicles.

- Airliner: *Airport '77* (1977), *Lost Horizon* (1973), *Magnum Force* (1973), *The Out-of-Towners* (1970), *Skyjacked* (1972)
- Blimp: *Black Sunday* (1977)
- Elevated train: *The French Connection* (1971)
- Ocean liner: *Juggernaut* (1974)
- Roller coasters: *Rollercoaster* (1977)
- School bus: *Dirty Harry* (1971)
- Space shuttle: *Moonraker* (1979)

Airport 1975

Released: October 1974
Director: Jack Smight
Stars: Charlton Heston, Karen Black, George Kennedy
Academy Awards: None

PREVIEW: After a 747 is damaged in a collision, a stewardess flies the jet until help arrives.

NOW SHOWING: Crash Landing

Airport (1970), one of the decade's earliest and biggest blockbusters, got its first sequel, *Airport 1975* (1974), and most critics shot it down right after takeoff. The *Airport* series didn't crash and burn, however. Audiences so enjoyed the movie's suspenseful situations and campy fun that *Airport 1975* became a high-flying hit, guaranteeing more sequels.

Except for the upgraded jet (from 707 to 747), nearly everything that made *Airport* a multiple-Oscar-nominated epic is diminished in *Airport 1975*. Take the midair disasters. *Airport*'s bomb explosion produced realistic effects that were explained to us and seem plausible; *Airport 1975*'s head-on collision rips opens a huge hole that instantly sucks out the jet's co-pilot, but later, when a stewardess reaches out through the hole, all the 192 mile-per-hour wind does is muss her hair. Additionally, *Airport* juggled five troubled relationships, whereas *Airport 1975* has a disgruntled stewardess who's "tired of one-night stands." *Airport*'s memorable soundtrack evokes thrilling spectacle; *Airport 1975*'s unremarkable music suggests TV movies. *Airport*'s passengers deplane with dignity; *Airport 1975*'s passengers slide ungracefully down emergency chutes.

Airport 1975 makes no reference to *Airport*'s events, and only one major character is in both movies, George Kennedy (formerly a mechanic, now a V.P.). The new heroes are Charlton Heston, wearing a yellow turtleneck, and Karen Black, the emoting stewardess who flies the ruptured jet until Heston's character literally drops in. The entertaining cast is filled with recognizable names, including Hollywood legend Myrna Loy, TV's Sid Caesar, singer Helen Reddy, and, a year after *The Exorcist*, a cheerful Linda Blair. The most ridiculous passenger is seventy-five-year-old Gloria Swanson, playing herself and getting so many gratuitous compliments (she's "lovely," has "eternal youth," "looks terrific") that she must've required them in her contract.

Airport 1975's greatest contribution to film history comes when many of the movie's elements—a lady singing to a sick girl, famous athletes getting recognized, a panicked stewardess at the controls, the autopilot— are brilliantly parodied in *Airplane!* (1980). But there's so much old-fashioned slang ("I can dig it," "neat"), so many dated attitudes (a stupid racial joke, pilots ogling stewardesses and calling them "baby," "mama," and "honey"), and so many laugh-out-loud lines ("The people are so interesting!" says Blair) that for modern audiences *Airport 1975* is already its own parody. Viewers, please enjoy the flight, but stow your serious expectations under the seat in front of you.

ADDED ATTRACTION: *MAD* Magazine's Parodies of 1974 Movies

Airport 1975 got its own movie parody, "Airplot '75," in *MAD* magazine (July 1975). Here are ten other 1974 movies that were similarly honored, followed by the titles of the parodies. *MAD*'s parodies of 1970 movies are with the entry for *Airport* (1970); *MAD*'s

1971 parodies are with *Willard* (1971); *MAD*'s 1972 parodies are with *The Godfather* (1972); and *MAD*'s parodies of 1973 movies are with the entry for *Serpico* (1973).

- *Chinatown*: "Chinaclown"
- *Death Wish*: "Death Wishers"
- *Earthquake*: "Mirthquake"
- *The Godfather: Part II*: "The Oddfather Part, Too!"
- *The Great Gatsby*: "The Great Gasbag"
- *The Longest Yard*: "The Longest Yardbird"
- *Murder on the Orient Express*: "Muddle on the Orient Express"
- *The Tamarind Seed*: "The Tommy-Red Seed"
- *That's Entertainment!*: "What's Entertainment?"
- *The Towering Inferno*: "The Towering Sterno"

Phantom of the Paradise

Released: November 1974
Director: Brian De Palma
Stars: William Finley, Paul Williams, Jessica Harper
Academy Awards: One nomination (Best Music)

PREVIEW: A disfigured songwriter seeks revenge on the wicked music mogul who took his songs.

NOW SHOWING: Music of the Night

We were *Phantom* phans from the first time we saw *Phantom of the Paradise* (1974) in theaters. Okay, at times it's campy, silly, and outrageous, but it's also romantic, imaginative, and surprising. And it's directed by Brian De Palma, a visual stylist who had already snagged us with *Sisters* (1972) and would soon terrify us with *Carrie* (1976). In *Phantom* De Palma's got his tongue firmly in his cheek and is going for outlandish entertainment instead of scares. He springs lots of tricks on the audience—split-screen, for instance, which he had used effectively in *Sisters*. He also showcases various music parodies (1950s' doo-wop groups, surf music, heavy metal) and presents cool homages to many archetypal stories (see "Added Attraction"). Fans of old-school rock music and iconic movies will have a field day.

The lively story is a blend of *Faust* and *The Phantom of the Opera*, updated into the rock milieu with evocative pop songs by Paul Williams. Winslow, a brilliant but naïve songwriter (William Finley), is swindled by a record producer (Williams) and accidentally disfigured. Transforming himself into the masked Phantom, Winslow falls for a beautiful singer (Jessica Harper), signs a contract with the Devil, and seeks revenge at an over-the-top final concert. That's the big picture, all brought off with wit, creative costumes, and actors who seem to relish being in on the joke (Williams is especially good and goes through the movie with a twinkle in his evil eye). Plus there are many small details to watch for, like the receptionist's index that includes Dick Clark, Alice Cooper, Peter Fonda, Kris Kristofferson, George McGovern, Bette Midler, and Randy Newman (what a client roster!), and Sissy Spacek in the credits as Set Dresser (her husband was the production designer). Comedy and horror; spirit and style; major fun and a minor classic.

ADDED ATTRACTION: *Phantom's* References

Music, horror, comedy—homage? Consider these conspicuous allusions to classic tales in *Phantom of the Paradise*.

William Finley.

- Edgar Allan Poe's "The Cask of Amontillado": Poe's story is echoed when Swan builds a brick wall across a door to trap Winslow.

- Bram Stoker's *Dracula*: Swan's assistant announces that Swan, wearing a Dracula-style cape, has flown in from Transylvania.

- The *Faust* legend: Winslow writes "a whole series of songs that tell the story of Faust"; Swan calls it "the first rock version of *Faust*."

- Mary Shelley's *Frankenstein*: *Phantom*'s elaborate stage show includes creepy nurses sewing together body parts and electrifying them into a living rock star.

- Gaston Leroux's *The Phantom of the Opera*: As in the original story, De Palma shows a mutilated, costumed composer trying to reclaim his stolen music for his preferred female singer; Winslow is called the Phantom fifty-four minutes into the movie.

- Oscar Wilde's *The Picture of Dorian Gray*: A high school photo shows that Swan, like Dorian Gray, hasn't aged in twenty years, but he finally reverts to his old, scarred self.

- *Psycho* (1960): Mimicking Hitchcock's shower scene, Winslow wields a plunger, not a knife.

- *Touch of Evil* (1958): De Palma's two-minute tracking shot of a bomb being put into a car trunk is similar to Orson Welles' famous three-minute opener to *Touch of Evil*.

- *The Twilight Zone*: Rod Serling, who introduced the episodes on the famous TV show, narrates *Phantom*'s prologue.

Earthquake

(One of 1974's five **FAR-OUT** movies)

Released: November 1974

Director: Mark Robson

Stars: Charlton Heston, George Kennedy, Geneviève Bujold

Academy Awards: Two wins (Best Sound; Special Achievement Award for Visual Effects), plus three more nominations (Best Editing; Best Cinematography; Best Art Direction)

PREVIEW: When a massive earthquake destroys L.A., the survivors face various emergencies.

FINE LINE: "Earthquakes bring out the worst in some guys." (Sgt. Slade, after killing a psychotic survivor.)

CLOSE-UP: Oscar voters who gave *Earthquake* its Special Effects award must not have remembered the elevator scene fifty-seven minutes into the movie. When a falling elevator finally hits bottom and causes violent deaths, the screen suddenly fills with big blobs of cartoon blood. Eager to skirt the R rating that might've resulted from a more realistic portrayal of the carnage, Universal instead opted for a cheesy animation that unfortunately inspires only surprised snickers.

NOW SHOWING: The Big One

By 1974, Hollywood had shown spectacular disasters in the air—*Airport* (1970)—and at sea—*The Poseidon Adventure* (1972)—so everyone was ready for a disaster on land. Two high-profile movies ran with this concept in different directions: *The Towering Inferno* (1974) burned down a skyscraper, while *Earthquake* (1974) destroyed a city. *Earthquake* wasn't as good as its fiery Best Picture-nominated rival, but it may have been more ambitious.

Whereas some previous disaster movies had presented implausible situations—we're looking at you, *Airport 1975* (1974)—*Earthquake* was grounded in historical precedent, the devastating 1971 earthquake that wreaked death and destruction in California's San Fernando Valley. Thus, with earthquakes a realistic threat, audiences were primed for *Earthquake*, a realistic movie. And it's the realism that makes *Earthquake* so memorable. Earthquakes had been shown before, of course, as in the Best Picture-nominee *San Francisco* (1936), but in 1974 the effects in *Earthquake* seemed like a completely new experience.

The first tremor, magnitude 3.1, hits just five minutes into the movie and delivers some jiggling-camera effects. Then the Big One arrives forty-five minutes later and rumbles steadily for eight dramatic minutes (that's not impossible—a 1960 Chilean earthquake lasted almost ten minutes). In *Earthquake*, buildings sway and topple, streets lift and split, and a dam cracks and bursts, destruction that's even more resonant because many of the buildings—the Capitol Records tower, for instance—are familiar landmarks. After Los Angeles is ruined and millions of people die, the survivors are confronted with dangerous gas leaks, fires, downed power lines, and flash floods. Director Mark Robson shows these conditions with impressive wide-angle shots, not with cheating close-ups of shattering windows and spurting fire hydrants.

Where the movie producers really got ambitious was with their patented Sensurround audio system. Developed for the movie and installed in major theaters, Sensurround's low-frequency speakers produced gut-churning bass effects. Legends quickly circulated that ceiling plaster in some theaters had fallen during the most intense moments, publicity that only strengthened the allure. Armed with Sensurround, *Earthquake* became an "event" movie and thundered its way to blockbuster status. The visual and sonic presentation of "the greatest natural disaster in the history of the United States" (as it's described in the movie) won *Earthquake* multiple technical-achievement Oscars.

Viewers who disparage *Earthquake* usually bring the movie's characters into their argument. Blending earnest scientists, romantic lovers, and clownish lowlifes, *Earthquake* has an all-star cast but simply doesn't know what kind of movie it wants to be. The subplots range from the barely relatable to the overtly ridiculous, as if the producers wanted weirdness and comedy alongside catastrophe and heartbreak. *Earthquake* is an hour-long story padded to 123 minutes with campy subplots, dated attitudes (the phrase "sexy broads" comes up), and a couple of bizarre casting choices.

Following the disaster template established by *Airport*, *Earthquake* has more than one hero, and, as per the template, one of them is played by George Kennedy. As he was in *Airport*, here Kennedy is the everyman lug with a regular job (he's a cop) who acts first and thinks later, but viewers know his heart is in the right place. It's Kennedy's cop who is chasing stolen cars, punching guys who have smart mouths, shooting dangerous kidnappers, and literally rescuing a puppy.

Balancing Kennedy is another stalwart of epic movies, Charlton Heston. He's the Shakespearean hero, high-ranking and strong, but haunted and pitiable. As a cutting-edge architect he knows that most of L.A.'s buildings won't survive a major earthquake, but his attempts early in the movie to rally support for better designs are defeated by economic realities. Trapped in a failing marriage with a spoiled, rich wife, the architect's affections wander to a lithe widow who is nineteen years his junior (Geneviève Bujold). At the end of the movie, the architect has to choose between them. His self-destructive choice confirms that thou shalt not commit adultery.

Ava Gardner, as the architect's wife, is one of *Earthquake*'s mistakes. Her father is played by Lorne Greene, who at fifty-nine years old is only seven years older than his "daughter." It's not the decade's strangest age disparity; that would probably be *Barry Lyndon* (1975), where twenty-eight-year-old Marisa Berenson is only a year older than the son played by Leon Vitali, but the Ava/Lorne pairing is still jarring.

Victoria Principal is another supporting character, and she stays stunningly beautiful under an indestructible sky-high Afro. Unfortunately, her role calls for her to stand still and be ogled in a bar by men who brazenly stare at her cleavage, ostensibly for comic effect but actually an insult in a decade blooming with feminist causes. Richard Roundtree, the iconic, cool detective in *Shaft* (1971), plays a goofy role that seems beneath him; Marjoe Gortner, in the most disconnected, off-putting subplot of them all, is a disturbed National Guardsman in an embarrassing wig who shoots other survivors; and for no discernable reason Walter Matthau (billed under the name Walter Matuschanskayasky) has an unfunny, pointless role as a mumbling, wildly dressed drunk.

Despite its obvious faults, *Earthquake* was a smashing success at the box office. In addition, its primary technical contribution, Sensurround, made it into two other Universal movies, *Midway* (1976) and *Rollercoaster* (1977), before high costs and the proliferation of small multiplex theaters ended this brief audio experiment. Nobody would claim it's the Great One, but in many ways *Earthquake* was the Big One.

ADDED ATTRACTION: All-Star Casts

Long before *Earthquake*, producers had been presenting classic all-star casts. Two good examples are two Best Picture winners, *Grand Hotel* (1932) and *Around the World in Eighty Days* (1956), which were both populated with famous faces. Representing the early 1970s are the next five movies and some of their venerable stars.

- *Airport* (1970): Helen Hayes, Van Heflin, George Kennedy, Burt Lancaster, Dean Martin, Jean Seberg, Maureen Stapleton
- *Airport 1975* (1974): Dana Andrews, Sid Caesar, Charlton Heston, George Kennedy, Myrna Loy, Helen Reddy, Gloria Swanson
- *Murder on the Orient Express* (1974): Lauren Bacall, Ingrid Bergman, Sean Connery, Albert Finney, John Gielgud, Wendy Hiller, Anthony Perkins, Vanessa Redgrave, Richard Widmark
- *That's Entertainment!* (1974): Fred Astaire, Bing Crosby, Gene Kelly, Liza Minnelli, Donald O'Connor, Debbie Reynolds, Mickey Rooney, Frank Sinatra, James Stewart, Elizabeth Taylor
- *The Towering Inferno* (1974): Fred Astaire, Faye Dunaway, William Holden, Jennifer Jones, Steve McQueen, Paul Newman

Murder on the Orient Express

Released: November 1974

Director: Sidney Lumet

Stars: Albert Finney, Lauren Bacall, Ingrid Bergman

Academy Awards: One win (Best Supporting Actress—Ingrid Bergman), plus five more nominations (Best Actor—Albert Finney; Best Writing; Best Cinematography; Best Costume Design; Best Music)

PREVIEW: A brilliant detective tries to figure out who the murderer is on the *Orient Express*.

NOW SHOWING: "The Murderer Is with Us Now"

Keep a scorecard when you watch *Murder on the Orient Express* (1974) for the first time. As with another complicated 1974 movie, *Chinatown*, new viewers can understand the ending but may need lots of notes to fully comprehend how everyone got there.

Before *Murder on the Orient Express*, there had been many adaptations of Agatha Christie's books, notably the Best Picture-nominee *Witness for the Prosecution* (1957), but no great ones for the next decade. Would 1970s audiences embrace her cerebral 1934 whodunit? The answer to that risky question was a resounding yes, because this classy movie is so smart, stylish, and enjoyable that it launched a mystery mini-trend (1978's *Death on the Nile* was the next Christie hit).

Surprisingly, *Murder on the Orient Express* doesn't offer thrilling suspense. The first six minutes present a shadowy depiction of a 1930 crime (the kidnapping and killing of a young girl, a la the 1932 Lindbergh-baby murder), and then the movie jumps to 1935 aboard the glamorous *Orient Express*. A third of the way into the movie, a single passenger is killed. There's no threat of more deaths: this isn't *Ten Little Indians* (1965), with characters being picked off one by one. Instead, for the rest of the movie a shrewd detective, Christie's fussy Belgian, Hercule Poirot (Albert Finney), investigates, interrogates, and deduces (other characters also make guesses, one of which is literally "the butler did it"). Viewers see and hear the same things Poirot does, but what we miss, he catches.

Albert Finney.

Soon Poirot acknowledges the possibility of multiple killers and uncovers the victim's true identity. Eventually he gathers everyone together and masterfully proposes *two* solutions in a twenty-eight minute explanation that includes quick, helpful flashbacks. His "simple answer" involves a "mysterious stranger" who has left the train; his "more complex" solution assumes that the murderer is someone in the room, so he confronts each person individually. Christie's ingenious conclusion is one of the most famous in the genre.

The fascination is watching Poirot. The fun is watching the stellar cast ("Look, it's James Bond! With a big moustache!"). Unfortunately, most stars only get a few minutes in the spotlight, and the array of accents and alibis at times make this the disorienting express. However, with its elegant costumes, lavishly appointed train (this movie is a must-see for rail fans), and lush music, *Murder on the Orient Express* is a thoroughly delightful ride.

ADDED ATTRACTION: Train Set

Hollywood has a long history of movies that have been set on or around trains. The pre-1970s list includes *Shanghai Express* (1932), *Terror by Night* (1946), *Strangers on a Train* (1951), and *The Train* (1964). *Murder on the Orient Express* is the most elegant of the train-focused movies from the '70s; here are nine more of the decade's train tales, in chronological order (we're not including movies that have only a few train scenes, like 1973's *The Sting*).

- *Boxcar Bertha* (1972)
- *Emperor of the North Pole* (1973)
- *The Taking of Pelham One Two Three* (1974)
- *Breakheart Pass* (1975)
- *Silver Streak* (1976)
- *The Cassandra Crossing* (1976)
- *The Billion Dollar Hobo* (1977)
- *The Great Train Robbery* (1978)
- *Avalanche Express* (1979)

Alice Doesn't Live Here Anymore

Released: December 1974

Director: Martin Scorsese

Stars: Ellen Burstyn, Diane Ladd, Alfred Lutter

Academy Awards: One win (Best Actress—Ellen Burstyn), plus two more nominations (Best Supporting Actress—Diane Ladd; Best Writing)

PREVIEW: A woman and her son gain insight and hope as they drive from New Mexico to California.

NOW SHOWING: Alice in Struggleland

In *Alice Doesn't Live Her Anymore* (1974), thirty-five-year-old Alice (Ellen Burstyn) spends most of the movie struggling to cope after her domineering husband dies in an accident. But with only five minutes left to go, Alice announces, "I'm not gonna let anybody stop me this time," a declaration of hard-won independence that shows she's transitioned from a traditional housewife into an assertive modern woman. Finally she feels like she can achieve anything, including the singing career she barely started long ago.

Alice is a triumphant movie, and a surprise. Consider: it is set in the American Southwest and includes scenes with cows and horses. It is told from a woman's perspective. It's got children in major roles. And it opens with a three-minute homage to the Kansas scenes in *The Wizard of Oz* (1939). Yet it was directed by Martin Scorsese in between two of his gritty urban classics, *Mean Streets* (1973) and *Taxi Driver* (1976). While the feminist theme and restrained style of *Alice* may be different from those two, there are some elements consistent with the Scorsese canon. For instance, there's an unforgettable lead, Ellen Burstyn, in a powerful Oscar-winning role. Jodie Foster and Harvey Keitel are here before they co-star in *Taxi Driver*; Foster plays a rebellious kid who drinks wine and shoplifts, and Keitel, with a cowboy's hat and twang, goes from zero to ferocious in a heartbeat (also watch for seven-year-old Laura Dern in her uncredited movie debut near the end). Like other Scorsese movies, there's great rock music on the soundtrack, and his camera is in motion, swooping in through windows, traveling along bars and countertops, or switching to handheld views, perhaps to mimic Alice's restless, improvised life.

Alice is something of a road movie because it sends a mother and her bright eleven-year-old son on a sometimes-depressing quest for a safe haven. It could also be labeled a "buddy movie," since the two of them trade wisecracks but remains allies (she even calls him "buddy" at one point). In the movie's satisfying last scene, they decide to stay in Tucson, Alice ready to get serious about her singing career and beau, and Tommy (Alfred Lutter) eager to start school. As they walk together, a restaurant sign ahead of them beckons with the name of the destination Alice has been aiming for throughout the movie: Monterey. Happily, even that hard-won dream comes true.

ADDED ATTRACTION: On the Road Again

A dozen more road movies from the early 1970s with two or more travelers sharing long trips (their reasons vary, from family reunions to crime-scene getaways). Stars are noted.

- *Badlands* (1973): Martin Sheen, Sissy Spacek
- *Dirty Mary Crazy Larry* (1974): Peter Fonda, Susan George

- *Five Easy Pieces* (1970): Jack Nicholson, Karen Black
- *The Getaway* (1972): Steve McQueen, Ali MacGraw
- *Harry and Tonto* (1974): Art Carney, "Tonto"
- *The Last Detail* (1973): Jack Nicholson, Otis Young, Randy Quaid
- *Paper Moon* (1973): Ryan O'Neal, Tatum O'Neal
- *Scarecrow* (1973): Gene Hackman, Al Pacino
- *The Sugarland Express* (1974): Goldie Hawn, William Atherton
- *Thieves Like Us* (1974): Keith Carradine, Shelley Duvall
- *Two-Lane Blacktop* (1971): James Taylor, Dennis Wilson
- *Two Mules for Sister Sara* (1970): Clint Eastwood, Shirley MacLaine

The Godfather: Part II

(One of 1974's five **FAR-OUT** movies)

Released: December 1974

Director: Francis Ford Coppola

Stars: Al Pacino, Robert De Niro, John Cazale

Academy Awards: Six wins (Best Picture; Best Supporting Actor—Robert De Niro; Best Director; Best Writing; Best Art Direction; Best Music), plus five more nominations (Best Actor—Al Pacino; two for Best Supporting Actor—Michael V. Gazzo, Lee Strasberg; Best Supporting Actress—Talia Shire; Best Costume Design)

PREVIEW: Michael, son of the deceased Don Corleone, now controls the powerful crime family.

FINE LINE: "Keep your friends close, but your enemies closer." (Michael, explaining to Frankie Pentangeli something he learned from his father.)

CLOSE-UP: Poor Kay. In both *Godfather* movies, the last time we see Michael's wife (played by Diane Keaton) she is watching a door being closed on her, sealing her off from her husband's life. Her final scene 186 minutes into *Part II* is particularly crushing as she stands outside on the doorstep, looking into the room where her children are. She's grieving as Michael (Al Pacino) approaches the door, but he's now totally estranged from her, refuses to even speak to her, and coldly shuts the door in her face.

NOW SHOWING: The Son Also Rises

The saga continues, as brilliant, and as lauded, as ever. Often called the greatest movie sequel in Hollywood history, *The Godfather: Part II* (1974) was the first sequel ever to win the Best Picture Oscar. What makes *Part II* so good is that it doesn't just extend the story of the first movie, which many sequels do; it develops and enriches *The Godfather* (1972) with new scenes that could easily have been blended into that first movie. Except for a top *capo*, Richard Castellano, all of the major players who survived the first movie make it into *Part II*, and all of the major crew members— director Francis Ford Coppola, co-writer Mario Puzo, cinematographer Gordon Willis, composer Nino Rota, production designer Dean Tavoularis, and others—are back. How often does *that* happen in a sequel? See *Jaws 2* (1978) for a classic example of how quickly the magic can disappear.

Almost a half-hour longer than *The Godfather*, *The Godfather: Part II* takes the sprawling Corleone story both forward and backward through the decades, making *Part II* as much a prequel as it is a sequel to the original movie. *The Godfather* covered the years from 1945 to 1955; *Part II* opens in 1958, when a somber, humorless Michael (Al Pacino), his father now dead for three years, fully commands the powerful Corleone crime family. They've abandoned New York for Nevada, but Michael hopes to forge a major partnership that will lead to lucrative investments in Cuba. However, an assassination attempt in Michael's own home makes him realize that there is a traitor inside his family (it's interesting how often assassination attempts fail: Don Corleone and Michael each survive one in *The Godfather*, and in *Part II* Michael, Pentangeli, and Roth all live through assassination attempts; it's hard to get good help, evidently). Throughout *Part II* Michael tries to uncover the traitor by playing other important characters off of each other, telling each of them different stories about the suspects and seemingly switching his allegiance. Ultimately, Michael learns that nobody can be trusted, and his transition from idealistic war hero to ruthless villain becomes complete once Michael aims his gunman at his own blood relative, something his father could never have done. The assassination is heartbreaking.

Weaving in and out of Michael's story is a long flashback to the early life of his father, Vito Corleone. Some viewers may quibble with the constant interruptions; after all, they might ask, these flashbacks show the early life of a character who is already dead when this movie starts, and Marlon Brando, who famously played him in the first movie, doesn't appear at all in the second. Nevertheless, the scenes of the young Don are fascinating. We meet Vito at nine years old, a "dumb-witted" and "weak" orphan in Sicily who witnesses his mother's murder (and is almost murdered himself) before he manages to escape to Ellis Island in 1901. Later episodes show him in 1917, a struggling

John Cazale and Al Pacino.

young father played by Robert De Niro, making the friends who will become his life-long allies and beginning his rise through the underworld. De Niro captures the old man's quiet authority, getting the raspy voice and the measured, confident delivery right. During this period we meet young Clemenza and Tessio, and we get to hear Vito say, "I'll make an offer he don't refuse," an early version of what becomes an iconic quote. Photographed with warm, nostalgic light, these evocative scenes beautifully capture the formative years of the titan we watched in *The Godfather*.

An interesting side note involves a trait the sequel shares with the first movie: intriguing casting choices for smaller roles. *The Godfather* had a role, Connie, for Coppola's actual sister, Talia Shire, plus tiny parts for Coppola's father Carmine and baby daughter Sofia; also, the role of Clemenza's wife was played by Ardell Sheridan, who became the actual wife of the actor playing Clemenza, Richard Castellano. Similarly, *Part II* makes senators out of Roger Corman and Phil Feldman, two real-life producers of Coppola's early movies; what's more, Connie's fiancé, Merle Johnson, is played by Troy Donahue, whose real name, curiously enough, actually *is* Merle Johnson.

In the first movie, it was the Don's hope that one day Michael "would be the one to hold the strings." In *Part II*, he really does, easily outmaneuvering an insulting senator who can be helpful to him and then steering his way through a tough investigation. Of all the three sons, Michael is the one who emulates the Don's temperament: Sonny was an undisciplined hothead, Fredo is a pitiable, dim-witted clown, but Michael, like his father, intimidates with controlled force behind a calm exterior. Nearly always wearing business suits and refusing to smile, he embodies smart, dignified strength. But Michael's power comes at a terrible cost. In *The Godfather* his father, older brother, and young bride all died; in *Part II* he loses his mother, his unborn son, and, most tragically, his other brother; his marriage seems to be over; by the end, the *capi* Michael has known all his life—Clemenza, Tessio, Frankie Pentangeli—are all dead; he is even reminded that "one by one, our old friends are gone." Thus, the image of Michael sitting alone at the end, dwelling on a family memory from 1941, is both sad and appropriate. Great gain, this magnificent movie shows us, is balanced by great loss.

ADDED ATTRACTION: Sons of *The Godfather*

The two *Godfathers* weren't the only early-'70s movies about the mob. The over-whelming success of *The Godfather* (1972) inspired many imitators, including the ten 1972–1974 movies listed below. All of these chronologically listed American movies are about the Mafia or similar crime organizations, and all were released between *The Godfather* and *The Godfather: Part II*.

- *The Valachi Papers* (1972)
- *Across 110th Street* (1972)
- *The Stone Killer* (1973)
- *Mean Streets* (1973)
- *Charley Varrick* (1973)
- *The Outfit* (1973)
- *The Don Is Dead* (1973)
- *Crazy Joe* (1974)
- *The Black Godfather* (1974)
- *Massacre Mafia Style* (1974)

Young Frankenstein

Released: December 1974

Director: Mel Brooks

Stars: Gene Wilder, Marty Feldman, Peter Boyle

Academy Awards: Two nominations (Best Writing; Best Sound)

PREVIEW: Dr. Frankenstein and his assistants make a monster and then struggle to control it.

NOW SHOWING: "Come Over Here, You Hot Monster"

First the bad news, what little there is. *Young Frankenstein* (1974) starts slowly. It has some comical early moments—Elizabeth (Madeline Kahn) at the train station, the "Chattanooga Choo Choo" arrival in Transylvania—but the movie really accelerates fifteen minutes in, when Igor (Marty Feldman) appears (by comparison, 1931's original *Frankenstein* opened *in media res* with the digging-up-the-grave scene).

Next, a few unnecessary jokes interrupt the otherwise consistent tone, especially when Igor makes comments directly into the camera or incorporates cheap show-biz shtick. Similarly, the "walk this way" vaudeville bit was already old when the Three Stooges used it in 1951 (Brooks recycles it in several movies). Some jokes—"what knockers!" and "could be worse … could be raining"—are simply too juvenile or obvious (admittedly, they're amusing). We're probably over-thinking this, but the last medical procedure is nonsensical, considering the results—it's a skull-to-skull brain transference, not a below-the-waist organ transplant. Finally, Frederick Frankenstein (Gene Wilder) sure shouts a lot; perhaps he's imitating Colin Clive's hyper-theatrical acting style in the original *Frankenstein*, but in *Young Frankenstein* Frederick commands like a strident general. He even shouts in his sleep and on the movie's poster.

Enough nitpicking; now for the abundant good news. *Young Frankenstein* is a masterpiece and director Mel Brooks' most stylish, well-rounded triumph (his previous hit, *Blazing Saddles*, has more laughs, but it's not nearly as polished). Brooks and co-screenwriter Wilder lift entire sequences—the monster's encounter with a little girl, the blind hermit's cabin, etc.—from the horror classics *Frankenstein* and *Bride of Frankenstein* (1933) and brilliantly twist them. They've added their own wonderful inventions, too, like the revolving bookcase, the darts game, the show-stopping "Putting on the Ritz" musical number, and the "hot monster" cave seduction. Any movie with Madeline Kahn, Cloris Leachman, Teri Garr, and Kenneth Mars can't help but be hilarious.

But there's more than just parody here; there's real affection for these classic old movies. Brooks shows off some of their actual lab machinery in a perfectly replicated high-ceilinged lab, and throughout he gets the vintage black-and-white look right. Also, he reins in his anarchic impulses, something he didn't do in *Blazing Saddles*. Several long sequences have no laughs (as when Frederick brings the monster to life), and, thanks to Peter Boyle's innate sweetness as the misunderstood "zipperneck," *Young Frankenstein* is touching.

Monsters, mirth, emotions—an abby normal combination, and Brooks' best movie.

ADDED ATTRACTION:
Background Brooks

Young Frankenstein is one of Mel Brooks's most controlled, consistent movies, partly because Brooks himself doesn't have a main supporting role in it; recall that he played *two* characters in the rowdier *Blazing Saddles*, and he's later the star of *Silent Movie* (1976) and *High Anxiety* (1977). Even if he's not a conspicuous character in *Young Frankenstein*, Brooks's image and voice might still be in the movie, as noted here.

Gene Wilder and Teri Garr.

- 18 minutes into the movie:
  Most likely that's Brooks providing the wolf's howl for the "there wolf" joke.

- 30 minutes:
  Gargoyles on the lab's wall and in the library slightly resemble Brooks.

- 48 minutes:
  In the town meeting, is Brooks the bearded, white-haired villager toward the back on the center aisle? Fifty-one minutes later, this figure is glimpsed again as Inspector Kemp speaks.

- 60 minutes:
  During the darts game, Brooks definitely provides the screeching-cat sound.

The Towering Inferno

(One of 1974's five **FAR-OUT** movies)

Released: December 1974

Director: John Guillermin

Stars: Steve McQueen, Paul Newman, Faye Dunaway

Academy Awards: Three wins (Best Editing; Best Cinematography; Best Song), plus five more nominations (Best Picture; Best Supporting Actor—Fred Astaire; Best Art Direction; Best Music; Best Sound)

PREVIEW: Fire crews battle an uncontrollable inferno raging through a soaring skyscraper.

FINE LINE: "You know, we were lucky tonight. The body count is less than two hundred. One of these days, they're gonna kill ten thousand in one of these firetraps." (Chief O'Hallorhan, standing outside of the smoking ruin in the last scene.)

CLOSE-UP: Orange seems to be the movie's color scheme. In the first six minutes we see orange on a helicopter, on Paul Newman's shirt, and on office furniture. Later a kid's shirt, fixtures in the utility and control rooms, and Faye Dunaway's négligée are all orange. Orange may have been a groovy 1974 design choice, but some of the rooms and clothes look like they're already on fire long before any flames arrive.

NOW SHOWING: Blaze of Glory

Producer Irwin Allen succeeded with *The Poseidon Adventure* (1972) and then triumphed with *The Towering Inferno* (1974). With the first movie he helped establish the disaster genre; with the second, he perfected it.

The Towering Inferno does indeed tower as one of the decade's most entertaining movies. It's a real *movie* movie, a showy extravaganza filled with spectacle, excitement, and glamour. The year's top-grosser at the box office, it won multiple Oscars and was nominated for Best Picture. It was also the first major production jointly produced by two competing studios. Warner Bros. and 20th Century-Fox each owned rights to different novels about flame-engulfed skyscrapers, so rather than compete they decided to unite. The movie also was one of the first to use "diagonal billing" for its two main actors; the movie's poster and opening credits place Paul Newman's name nearer to the top and Steve McQueen's name farther to the left, so each star could believe his name was being read first.

In style and in scale, *The Towering Inferno* improves and expands the disaster template created by *Airport* (1970), *The Poseidon Adventure*, and *Earthquake* (1974). With a runtime of 165 minutes it's by far the longest of the four (the others are closer to two hours than three). It also boasts the biggest all-star cast, blending 1970s superstars McQueen and Newman with Hollywood legends like Fred Astaire, William Holden, and Jennifer Jones, plus some interesting novelties like O.J. Simpson (making his movie debut), Paul Newman's son Scott as a fireman, and Mrs. Irwin Allen as the mayor's wife. Imagine this movie being made today with not one, not two, but a half-dozen current superstars and legends. The payroll would bust the budget.

The main story is simple: after fire breaks out inside the world's tallest skyscraper, beleaguered fire crews (led by McQueen) battle for control while the people inside (led by Newman) struggle for survival. Unlike other disaster epics where a single event (a bomb, a wave, an earthquake) leads to catastrophe, there's no solitary cause for all the havoc in *The Towering Inferno*. Among the many mistakes and mishaps that lead up to *Inferno*'s inferno: cheap sub-standard wiring; sprinklers, electrical systems, and other safety features that either don't work or haven't yet been installed; and, as a survivor mentions, the complete absence of any fire drills.

Compounding these pre-fire mistakes are the bad decisions made *after* flames have ignited: all the lights in the building are turned on, dangerously overloading the power system; warned about using the hazardous express elevator, passengers still rush into it to their doom; a disorganized panic at the breeches buoy kills several more guests. The biggest mistake, of course, might have been building such a tall structure—especially in earthquake-prone San Francisco—in the first place. Fires had been killing people in tall buildings long before the movie was made, and in fact a skyscraper fire earlier that year had killed 179 people in Brazil. As in every *Titanic* movie, man's hubris has to be punished.

Multiple subplots add interesting drama, and even romantic melodrama, to the main disaster. Unlike *Earthquake*, which had silly, unrelated side stories that seemed more like filler than integral additions, the subplots in *The Towering Inferno* intensify the disaster. The best example is the small story of two lovers who enjoy a romantic after-hours tryst in an upstairs office, only to later find the rooms outside totally ablaze. Left alone in a burning room, Susan Flannery's character desperately leaps through a sixty-fifth-floor window. Of all the many deaths in the movie, hers may be the most poignant.

Admittedly, there are some pretty unrealistic situations that defy logic. For instance, at the end, colossal water tanks two floors above the upper Promenade Room are detonated to drown the fire with literally a million gallons of water, but the enormous sheets of water pouring from the exterior of the ruined building never seem to reach the streets, which should be flooded. Nevertheless, nothing can stop this movie once it gets going. Unlike *The Poseidon Adventure*, which delivered its biggest capsizing effect early, *The Towering Inferno* slowly gathers momentum for two-and-a-half hours until that raging fire is literally right outside the door where the last survivors are huddled.

All the fire and explosion scenes, directed by Allen himself, are spectacular, an impressive achievement considering that he was working in the pre-digital era with models of the building and full-size sets being consumed by real fires and real water. The tensest moments, as when McQueen rescues the scenic elevator and women ride the high-wire cable one at a time to a nearby building, are excruciating to watch. When Newman and McQueen set their explosive charges on the water tanks in the last minutes and then wait for the clock to tick down, the suspense becomes almost unbearable. And the last sad shot of the dead firemen lined up on the sidewalk is genuinely affecting. So much has happened since this movie came out—including real-life scenes of people jumping to their deaths from the smoking towers on 9/11, and bigger disaster movies like *Titanic* (1997)—yet nothing has diminished the power of Irwin Allen's masterpiece.

Steve McQueen, Faye Dunaway, and Paul Newman.

ADDED ATTRACTION: Oscar-Winning Hit Songs

Among its many accomplishments, *The Towering Inferno* claimed the Oscar for the year's Best Song. Listed in chronological order are all of the decade's Oscar-winning songs, their movies, and the performers of those songs in the movies.

- "For All We Know": *Lovers and Other Strangers* (1970), Larry Meredith
- "Theme From *Shaft*": *Shaft* (1971), Isaac Hayes
- "The Song from *The Poseidon Adventure*, aka The Morning After": *The Poseidon Adventure* (1972), Renée Armand
- "The Way We Were": *The Way We Were* (1973), Barbra Streisand
- "We May Never Love Like This Again": *The Towering Inferno* (1974), Maureen McGovern
- "I'm Easy": *Nashville* (1975), Keith Carradine
- "Evergreen (Love Theme from *A Star Is Born*)": *A Star Is Born* (1976), Barbra Streisand
- "You Light Up My Life": *You Light Up My Life* (1977), Kacey Cisyk
- "Last Dance": *Thank God It's Friday* (1978), Donna Summer
- "It Goes Like It Goes": *Norma Rae* (1979), Jennifer Warnes

The Man with the Golden Gun

Released: December 1974
Director: Guy Hamilton
Stars: Roger Moore, Christopher Lee, Britt Ekland
Academy Awards: None

PREVIEW: Agent 007 tracks an expert assassin to his remote island and confronts him in a duel.

NOW SHOWING: Duel in the Sun

With *The Man with the Golden Gun* (1974), the movie series with the golden touch at the box office almost got scuttled. The decade's third James Bond movie and the second with Roger Moore as 007, it was only a modest financial success and was heavily criticized as being uninspired and silly (fans often rank it near the bottom of all the Bond movies). Ironically, director Guy Hamilton had helmed one of the series' finest entries, the great *Goldfinger* (1964), plus *Diamonds Are Forever* (1971) and *Live and Let Die* (1973), but after this movie he quit Bond for good.

Many flaws make *Golden Gun* misfire. For instance, some of Bond's own actions seem beneath him, especially when he shoves a bothersome child from a moving boat. He also slaps an unarmed woman hard and threatens to keep doing it; Sean Connery had slapped Jill St. John across the face in *Diamonds Are Forever* (1971), but it's still alarming to see it here. In addition, in *Golden Gun* Bond has taken to smoking giant stogies, which looks odd. And his greatest stunt in the movie, a truly spectacular leap over a river in a small car, is diminished by a ludicrous slide-whistle accompaniment. Stunning Britt Eklund plays a daffy agent whose biggest contribution is some bikini exposure at the end; elegant Maud Adams, later the star of *Octopussy* (1983), is regrettably killed off mid-movie; and inexplicably the goofball sheriff from *Live and Let Die*

Christopher Lee and Roger Moore.

(Clifton James) returns. Finally, the electrified theme song that Lulu belts out is one of the weakest in the Bond *oeuvre*.

That's the bad news. In contrast, the urbane white-suited villain, Scaramanga (Christopher Lee), is a worthy foe. A "spectacular trick-shot artist" and ex-KGB assassin with a gold pistol, he now charges a million dollars per hit. Scaramanga lures Bond to his remote island for a "duel between titans." Then, as usual in these movies, he can't resist explaining his entire operation and business plan to Bond before their lackluster final confrontation in a weird funhouse (the obvious outcome is signaled well in advance). Enhancing the movie are breathtaking women (including Chew Mee, a naked swimmer), exotic locations, and familiar Bond characters—M, Q, Moneypenny—who make appearances. *The Man with the Golden Gun* may be imperfect, but the franchise still had plenty of ammo and would reload with *The Spy Who Loved Me* (1977).

ADDED ATTRACTION: Bond Makes the Scene, Man

The Man with the Golden Gun is based on Ian Fleming's 1965 novel, but the movie attempts to stay current with 1970s events. "The energy crisis is still with us," Bond observes, and indeed it was in 1974; thus, part of the movie's plot involves solar-cell data and a much-needed Solex Agitator, which can supposedly "convert radiation from the sun into electricity." In addition, martial arts movies were becoming extremely popular in the mid-'70s, and 1974 even welcomed Carl Douglas's hit song "Kung Fu Fighting." Consequently, there are six minutes of martial arts fights in *Golden Gun* (some martial arts action had appeared in earlier Bond movies, including 1967's *You Only Live Twice*). Finally, when Bond pitches a few hours of romance to Mary Goodnight, she tells him his suggestion "isn't quite my scene." As if that lingo isn't hip enough, there's an Oriental character actually named Hip!

Black Christmas

Released: December 1974

Director: Bob Clark

Stars: Olivia Hussey, Keir Dullea, Margot Kidder

Academy Awards: None

PREVIEW: During the holiday season a psycho starts murdering girls in their sorority house.

NOW SHOWING: Silent Night

Before Bob Clark directed a beloved holiday classic, *A Christmas Story* (1983), he made a slightly more sinister seasonal movie. *Black Christmas* (1974) is an influential, well-made creepshow.

Black Christmas opened in America in December 1974 with the title *Silent Night, Evil Night*. Later it was successfully re-released as *Black Christmas*, and that's how it's been known as it has risen in stature to become a cult favorite. The plot seems simple enough—an unseen psycho kills sorority sisters until one is left for a final scary chase. But *Black Christmas* offers more than just visceral scares, and it firmly established several themes that will appear in later horror movies. For instance, it's one of the first movies to have eerie, taunting phone calls being dialed from *inside* the victims' own house; *When a Stranger Calls* (1979) famously magnifies this same terrifying premise. Also, *Black Christmas* is considered an early slasher movie, a horror sub-genre probably started by *Psycho* (1960) and revved up by movies like *The Last House on the Left* (1972). *Black Christmas* is also one of the first calendar-themed horror movies, a long list that includes *Halloween* (1978), *Friday the 13th* (1980), and *April Fool's Day* (1986).

The movie achieves its biggest surprise through misdirection. Conspicuous clues make the audience assume the killer is a troubled boyfriend. This character is even involved in the movie's truly thrilling climax when the only girl left alive is chased into a hellish basement. But in a daring departure from typical horror movies, *Black Christmas* ends ambiguously, with maniacal giggles in the attic and a ringing phone downstairs indicating that the real killer remains unknown.

Don't bother wondering why the police comb the town house-to-house but never peek into the attic. Focus instead on the good gifts *Black Christmas* delivers, including a drinking house mother and a bad Santa as comic relief, extremely effective camera movement, and very unnerving sounds (the "moaner" is genuinely disturbing, if unnecessarily profane). Keir Dullea (with shaggy hair) and pretty Olivia Hussey both starred in classic 1968 movies, *2001: A Space Odyssey* and *Romeo and Juliet*, respectively; Margot Kidder (in a cool black choker) is the feistiest girl and bloodiest victim, stabbed brutally as a beautiful carol is sung. Andrea Martin dies, too, but she'll later live on as a comedy legend.

ADDED ATTRACTION: The Black Pack

Interestingly, American studios didn't produce a single nostalgic Christmas movie during the '70s like they did in other decades with *A Christmas Carol* (1938), *It's a Wonderful Life* (1946), etc. In fact, *Black Christmas* is the only '70s movie with "Christmas" in its title, and here it's used ominously to play off the joyous holiday musical *White Christmas* (1954). Other American movies made in the 1970s also had titles that led with "Black." Here's a baker's dozen from the decade, in alphabetical order, with their stars noted.

- *Black Belt Jones* (1974): Jim Kelly
- *The Black Bird* (1975): George Segal
- *Black Caesar* (1973): Fred Williamson
- *The Black Gestapo* (1975): Rod Perry
- *Black Girl* (1972): Peggy Pettit
- *Black Gunn* (1972): Jim Brown
- *The Black Hole* (1979): Maximilian Schell
- *Black Mama White Mama* (1973): Pam Grier
- *Black Rodeo* (1972): Documentary
- *Black Shampoo* (1976): John Daniels
- *The Black Six* (1973): Robert Howard
- *The Black Stallion* (1979): Kelly Reno
- *Black Sunday* (1977): Robert Shaw

Tom Skerritt has starred in a long list of acclaimed movies that include some of Hollywood's biggest hits. Fans of '70s movies will quickly recall him as Duke, one of the main doctors in *M*A*S*H* (1970), and as the heroic Captain Dallas in *Alien* (1979), shown in the photo at top-left. His later movies include key roles in *Top Gun* (1986), *Steel Magnolias* (1989), and *Contact* (1997), among many others in an impressive big-screen career that is still going strong. Skerritt continues to be a frequent presence on major television shows, and in 1993 he won the Emmy Award as the year's Outstanding Lead Actor in a Drama Series for *Picket Fences*. He is also the founder and chairman of Heyou Media, Inc. (heyoumedia.com), a Seattle-centered company that provides cutting-edge mobile, online, and multiplatform digital entertainment. He graciously answered seven questions for us about '70s movies.

What's the first title that comes to mind when you hear the phrase "1970s movie"?

"*M*A*S*H.*"

Do you have favorite films or directors from the 1970s?

"Stanley Kramer, Hal Ashby, Bob Altman, Ridley Scott, Italian, and French."

Is there a particular director whose work in the 1970s you admire?

"But for Altman, I don't know that I'd be an actor. He was my mentor for a few years prior to *M*A*S*H.*"

What was your favorite movie-going experience of the 1970s?

"Weeks before we finished production on *M*A*S*H*, Altman told me he was making a two-, maybe a three-ticket movie. That is, he was planting so much to take in, you'd have to return a couple of times to get it all. I watched him develop the final cut of *M*A*S*H*, a film the studio hated and had written off, and in fact the screenwriter wanted his name removed from credits. When it was finished, I wanted to see *M*A*S*H* for the first time with an objective ticket-buying audience, so I went to the Bruin Theatre in Westwood Village near UCLA. When I got there, the line already went down the block and around the corner. I couldn't get a ticket. Irony was present, because suddenly I had an acting career in front me."

Many fans and movie critics have called the 1970s a "golden age" for movies. Did you have a sense at the time that you were part of a "golden age"?

"As it was happening, I knew I was surrounded and influenced by great storytellers."

Can you identify any 1970s movie trends that continued in later decades?

"The importance of storytelling began to favor special effects, as seen in the decade's new science-fiction movies."

What forces were at work to make '70s movies so distinctive?

"Good storytelling engages audiences and always inspires the best from those involved."

—Tom Skerritt

Movies by Genre: 1970–1974

The book's main entries, divided into genres and then listed alphabetically.

Animation

The Aristocats
Robin Hood

Blaxploitation

Black Caesar
Coffy
Shaft
Super Fly
Sweet Sweetback's Baadasssss Song

Comedy

American Graffiti
Bananas
The Barefoot Executive
Brewster McCloud
Carnal Knowledge
Everything You Always Wanted to Know About Sex * But Were Afraid to Ask
The Groove Tube
Harry and Tonto
Herbie Rides Again
The Million Dollar Duck
Now You See Him, Now You Don't
Paper Moon
Play It Again, Sam
Plaza Suite
Sleeper
Start the Revolution Without Me
Up the Sandbox
Uptown Saturday Night
What's Up, Doc?
Where's Poppa?

Crime

Badlands
Bank Shot
Bloody Mama
Boxcar Bertha
Charley Varrick
Chinatown
A Clockwork Orange
The Conversation
The Day of the Dolphin
The Day of the Jackal
Death Wish
Diamonds Are Forever
Dillinger
Dirty Harry
The French Connection
Frenzy
The Getaway
The Godfather
The Godfather: Part II
Klute
Live and Let Die
The Long Goodbye
Macon County Line
The Man with the Golden Gun
Mean Streets
Murder on the Orient Express
Papillon
The Parallax View
Play Misty for Me
The Private Life of Sherlock Holmes
Serpico
Sleuth
The Sting
Straw Dogs
The Sugarland Express
The Taking of Pelham One Two Three
Thieves Like Us

Disaster

Airport
Airport 1975

Earthquake
The Poseidon Adventure
Skyjacked
The Towering Inferno

Documentary

Gimme Shelter
The Hellstrom Chronicle
Ladies and Gentlemen: The Rolling Stones
On Any Sunday
That's Entertainment!
Woodstock

Drama

Alice Doesn't Live Here Anymore
Bless the Beasts & Children
C.C. & Company
Deliverance
Diary of a Mad Housewife
Emperor of the North
Fat City
Five Easy Pieces
The Golden Voyage of Sinbad
Husbands
Joe
The Last Detail
The Last Picture Show
Le Mans
Little Fauss and Big Halsy
The Longest Yard
The Molly Maguires
Napoleon and Samantha
The Paper Chase
Save the Tiger
Scarecrow
Sounder
The Three Musketeers
The Unholy Rollers
Vanishing Point
Zabriskie Point

Horror/Horror Comedy

Black Christmas
Don't Look in the Basement
The Exorcist
The Last House on the Left
Sisters
Willard
Young Frankenstein

Musical

Bedknobs and Broomsticks
Cabaret
Lady Sings the Blues
Lost Horizon
Man of La Mancha
On a Clear Day You Can See Forever
Phantom of the Paradise
Willy Wonka & the Chocolate Factory

Romance

Breezy
Butterflies Are Free
Claudine
The Great Gatsby
Harold and Maude
The Heartbreak Kid
Love Story
Summer of '42
The Way We Were

Science-Fiction

The Andromeda Strain
Beneath the Planet of the Apes
Conquest of the Planet of the Apes
Escape from the Planet of the Apes
The Omega Man
Silent Running
Slaughterhouse-Five
Westworld

War/War Comedy

Catch-22
Kelly's Heroes
M*A*S*H
Patton
Tora! Tora! Tora!

Western/Western Comedy

The Ballad of Cable Hogue
Blazing Saddles
The Cowboys
Dirty Dingus Magee
Jeremiah Johnson
Little Big Man
A Man Called Horse
McCabe & Mrs. Miller
Pat Garrett & Billy the Kid
Support Your Local Gunfighter
Two Mules for Sister Sara

Most Popular Movies: 1970–1974

According to the rankings at boxofficemadness.wordpress.com, these thirty-five titles are the biggest box-office hits of the early 1970s, separated into the years of release and then listed in order (highest earnings first).

1970
Love Story
Airport
M*A*S*H
Patton
The Aristocats
Little Big Man
Woodstock

1971
Fiddler on the Roof
Billy Jack
The French Connection
Summer of '42
Dirty Harry
A Clockwork Orange
Diamonds Are Forever

1972
The Godfather
The Poseidon Adventure
What's Up, Doc?

Deliverance
Cabaret
Jeremiah Johnson
The Getaway

1973
The Exorcist
The Sting
American Graffiti
Papillon
The Way We Were
Magnum Force
Robin Hood

1974
The Towering Inferno
Blazing Saddles
Young Frankenstein
Earthquake
The Trial of Billy Jack
The Godfather: Part II
Airport 1975

Daring Movies: 1970–1974

There are others, of course, but these thirty-five movies from 1970–1974 all pushed the boundaries of violence, sex, or profanity, or they introduced special-effects technology, radical themes, or a unique cinematic artistry (sometimes combining several of these simultaneously). These aren't the thirty-five *best* movies of the early '70s, but they are some of the most distinctive. Listed chronologically.

1970
M*A*S*H
Zabriskie Point
Woodstock
Diary of a Mad Housewife
Five Easy Pieces
Husbands

1971
THX 1138
Sweet Sweetback's Baadasssss Song
Shaft
Carnal Knowledge

Two-Lane Blacktop
The Last Picture Show
The French Connection
A Clockwork Orange
Dirty Harry
Straw Dogs

1972
Cabaret
Slaughterhouse-Five
Deliverance
The Last House on the Left
Up the Sandbox

1973

Coffy
American Graffiti
Everything You Always Wanted to Know About Sex * But Were Afraid to Ask
Westworld
Mean Streets
Badlands
The Last Detail

Serpico
The Exorcist

1974

Blazing Saddles
Claudine
The Conversation
Earthquake
Phantom of the Paradise

Top Oscar Winners: 1970–1974

Major categories, year by year.

1970

Most Oscar Wins: *Patton* (seven)

Best Picture (in bold): *Airport, Five Easy Pieces, Love Story, M*A*S*H,* **Patton**

Best Actor, Actress: George C. Scott (*Patton*), Glenda Jackson (*Women in Love*)

Best Director: Franklin J. Schaffner (*Patton*)

1971

Most Oscar Wins: *The French Connection* (five)

Best Picture: *A Clockwork Orange, Fiddler on the Roof,* **The French Connection**, *The Last Picture Show, Nicholas and Alexandra*

Best Actor, Actress: Gene Hackman (*The French Connection*), Jane Fonda (*Klute*)

Best Director: William Friedkin (*The French Connection*)

1972

Most Oscar Wins: *Cabaret* (eight)

Best Picture: *Cabaret, Deliverance, The Emigrants,* **The Godfather**, *Sounder*

Best Actor, Actress: Marlon Brando (*The Godfather*), Liza Minnelli (*Cabaret*)

Best Director: Bob Fosse (*Cabaret*)

1973

Most Oscar Wins: *The Sting* (seven)

Best Picture: *American Graffiti, Cries and Whispers, The Exorcist,* **The Sting**, *A Touch of Class*

Best Actor, Actress: Jack Lemmon (*Save the Tiger*), Glenda Jackson (*A Touch of Class*)

Best Director: George Roy Hill (*The Sting*)

1974

Most Oscar Wins: *The Godfather: Part II* (six)

Best Picture: *Chinatown, The Conversation,* **The Godfather: Part II**, *Lenny, The Towering Inferno*

Best Actor, Actress: Art Carney (*Harry and Tonto*), Ellen Burstyn (*Alice Doesn't Live Here Anymore*)

Best Director: Francis Ford Coppola (*The Godfather: Part II*)

Top Oscar Nominees: 1970–1974

Movies released in the first half of the decade that earned three or more Oscar nominations.

Eleven nominations

Chinatown (1974)
The Godfather: Part II (1974)

Ten

Airport (1970)
Cabaret (1972)
The Exorcist (1973)
The Godfather (1972)
Patton (1970)
The Sting (1973)

Eight

Fiddler on the Roof (1971)
The French Connection (1971)
The Last Picture Show (1971)
The Poseidon Adventure (1972)
The Towering Inferno (1974)

Seven

Love Story (1970)

Six

Lenny (1974)
Murder on the Orient Express (1974)
Nicholas and Alexandra (1971)
The Way We Were (1973)

Five

American Graffiti (1973)
Bedknobs and Broomsticks (1971)
Cries and Whispers (1973)
The Emigrants (1972)
Lady Sings the Blues (1972)
Mary, Queen of Scots (1971)
M*A*S*H (1970)
Tora! Tora! Tora! (1970)
A Touch of Class (1973)

Four

A Clockwork Orange (1971)
Earthquake (1974)
Five Easy Pieces (1970)
Kotch (1971)
Paper Moon (1973)
Ryan's Daughter (1970)
Scrooge (1970)
Sounder (1972)
Sleuth (1972)
Summer of '42 (1971)
Sunday Bloody Sunday (1971)
Travels with My Aunt (1972)
Women in Love (1970)

Three

Alice Doesn't Live Here Anymore (1974)
Blazing Saddles (1974)
Butterflies Are Free (1972)
Cinderella Liberty (1973)
The Conversation (1974)
Darling Lili (1970)
Day for Night (1974)
Deliverance (1972)
I Never Sang for My Father (1970)
The Last Detail (1973)
Lovers and Other Strangers (1970)
The Paper Chase (1973)
Save the Tiger (1973)
Tom Sawyer (1973)
Woodstock (1970)
Young Winston (1972)

The 1970-1974 Movies on the American Film Institute's "Greatest-Hits" List

The American Film Institute, established in 1967 with Gregory Peck as its first chair-person, is an esteemed body of critics and filmmakers that works to preserve America's film heritage, to celebrate achievements in film, and also to educate with advanced film-studies programs. In 1998 and 2007 the AFI created "greatest-hits" lists called "100 Years … 100 Movies." As mentioned in our Introduction, both lists included more movies from the 1970s than from any other decade. Here are the 1970–1974 movies that the AFI recognized (numbers indicate the movies' positions on the lists). The number-one movie on both lists, by the way, was *Citizen Kane* (1941).

1998

3. *The Godfather* (1972)
19. *Chinatown* (1974)
32. *The Godfather: Part II* (1974)
46. *A Clockwork Orange* (1971)
56. *M*A*S*H* (1970)
70. *The French Connection* (1971)
77. *American Graffiti* (1973)
89. *Patton* (1970)

2007

2. *The Godfather* (1972)
21. *Chinatown* (1974)
32. *The Godfather: Part II* (1974)
54. *M*A*S*H* (1970)
62. *American Graffiti* (1973)
63. *Cabaret* (1972)
70. *A Clockwork Orange* (1971)
93. *The French Connection* (1971)
95. *The Last Picture Show* (1971)

The Best of the '70s: 1970–1974

Our top thirty-five titles, in alphabetical order.

Airport (1970)
American Graffiti (1973)
Badlands (1973)
Blazing Saddles (1974)
Cabaret (1972)
Carnal Knowledge (1971)
Chinatown (1974)
A Clockwork Orange (1971)
The Conversation (1974)
Deliverance (1972)
Dirty Harry (1971)
The Exorcist (1973)
Five Easy Pieces (1970)
The French Connection (1971)
The Godfather (1972)
The Godfather: Part II (1974)
Harold and Maude (1971)
The Last Picture Show (1971)

Little Big Man (1970)
M*A*S*H (1970)
Mean Streets (1973)
Paper Moon (1973)
Papillon (1973)
Patton (1970)
Serpico (1973)
Shaft (1971)
Silent Running (1972)
Sleeper (1973)
Sleuth (1972)
Sounder (1972)
The Sting (1973)
The Taking of Pelham One Two Three (1974)
The Towering Inferno (1974)
Woodstock (1970)
Young Frankenstein (1974)

Best Movie: *The Godfather* (1972)

Coming Attractions: 1975–1979

Movies covered in *The Daring Decade: Volume Two, 1975-1979*:

Adventures of the Wilderness Family

Agatha

Airport '77

Alice, Sweet Alice

Alien

All That Jazz

All the President's Men

Aloha, Bobby and Rose

American Hot Wax

The Amityville Horror

...and justice for all.

Animal House

Annie Hall

An Unmarried Woman

Apocalypse Now

The Apple Dumpling Gang

The Apple Dumpling Gang Rides Again

At Long Last Love

Attack of the Killer Tomatoes!

At the Earth's Core

Avalanche

The Bad News Bears

The Bad News Bears Go to Japan

Barracuda

Barry Lyndon

Being There

The Bermuda Triangle

The Betsy

Big Bad Mama

The Big Bus

The Big Fix

The Big Sleep

Big Wednesday

Bite the Bullet

The Black Bird

The Black Hole

The Black Stallion

Black Sunday

Blue Collar

Boulevard Nights

Bound for Glory

A Boy and His Dog

The Boys from Brazil

Breakheart Pass

Breaking Away

A Bridge Too Far

The Brink's Job

The Buddy Holly Story

Buffalo Bill and the Indians

Burnt Offerings

California Dreaming

California Suite

Candleshoe

Capricorn One

Car Wash

Carrie

The Cat from Outer Space

The Cheap Detective

The Children of Theatre Street

The China Syndrome

City on Fire

Close Encounters of the Third Kind

Coma

Coming Home

Convoy

Cooley High

Corvette Summer

Damien: Omen II

Dawn of the Dead

Days of Heaven

Death on the Nile

Death Race 2000

The Deep

The Deer Hunter

Dog Day Afternoon

Dracula

Drive-In Massacre

The Driver

The Duchess and the Dirtwater Fox

Eat My Dust!

Eaten Alive

The Eiger Sanction

The Electric Horseman

Embryo

Empire of the Ants

The End

The Enforcer

Eraserhead

Escape from Alcatraz

Escape to Witch Mountain

Every Which Way But Loose

Exorcist II: The Heretic

Eyes of Laura Mars

Family Plot

Farewell, My Lovely

FM

The Fortune

Foul Play

Freaky Friday

French Connection II

Friday Foster

From Noon Till Three

The Front

Fun with Dick and Jane

The Fury

Gable and Lombard

The Gauntlet

The Giant Spider Invasion

Girlfriends

Goin' South

The Goodbye Girl

Goodbye, Norma Jean

Go Tell the Spartans

Grand Theft Auto

Gray Lady Down

Grease

The Great Santini

The Great Train Robbery

The Great Waldo Pepper

Halloween

Hanover Street

Harlan County U.S.A.

Harper Valley P.T.A.

Heaven Can Wait

Herbie Goes to Monte Carlo

Hester Street

High Anxiety

The Hills Have Eyes

The Hindenburg

Hooper

Hot Lead and Cold Feet

Hustle

Interiors

Invasion of the Body Snatchers

I Spit on Your Grave

Jaws

Jaws 2

The Jerk

Julia

The Kentucky Fried Movie

King Kong

Kramer vs. Kramer

The Land That Time Forgot

The Last Remake of Beau Geste

The Last Tycoon

The Last Waltz

A Little Romance

Logan's Run

Looking for Mr. Goodbar

Love and Death

Lucky Lady

MacArthur

Mahogany

The Main Event

Mandingo

Manhattan

The Man Who Would Be King

The Many Adventures of Winnie the Pooh

Marathon Man

Mean Dog Blues

Meteor

Midnight Express

Midway

Mikey and Nicky

The Missouri Breaks

Moment by Moment

Moonraker

More American Graffiti

The Muppet Movie

Murder by Death

Nashville

Network

New York, New York

Night Moves

1941

Norma Rae

The North Avenue Irregulars

North Dallas Forty

Oh, God!

Old Boyfriends

Oliver's Story

The Omen

The One and Only

One Flew Over the Cuckoo's Nest

One of Our Dinosaurs Is Missing

Orca

The Other Side of Midnight
The Other Side of the Mountain
The Outlaw Josey Wales
The People That Time Forgot
Pete's Dragon
Piranha
Pretty Baby
Pumping Iron
Quadrophenia
Quintet
Rabbit Test
The Rescuers
Robin and Marian
Rock 'n' Roll High School
Rocky
The Rocky Horror Picture Show
Rocky II
Rollerball
Rollercoaster
The Rose
Saint Jack
Same Time, Next Year
Saturday Night Fever
Sextette
Sgt. Pepper's Lonely Hearts Club Band
The Shaggy D.A.
Shampoo
Sheba, Baby
The Shootist
Silent Movie
Silver Streak
Slap Shot
Smile
Smokey and the Bandit
The Song Remains the Same
Sorcerer

The Spy Who Loved Me
A Star Is Born
Star Wars
Starting Over
The Stepford Wives
Stingray
The Strongest Man in the World
The Sunshine Boys
Superman
The Swarm
Taxi Driver
10
Tentacles
Thank God It's Friday
That's Entertainment, Part 2
Three Days of the Condor
3 Women
Time After Time
Tommy
Treasure of Matecumbe
The Turning Point
Two-Minute Warning
Unidentified Flying Oddball
Walk Proud
The Wanderers
The War at Home
The Warriors
W.C. Fields and Me
A Wedding
The White Buffalo
The Wind and the Lion
Wise Blood
The Wiz
Wizards
The World's Greatest Lover
You Light Up My Life

Books

Biskind, Peter. *Easy Riders, Raging Bulls: How the Sex-Drugs-and-Rock 'n' Roll Generation Saved Hollywood*. New York: Simon & Schuster, 1998.

Bordwell, David. *The Way Hollywood Tells It: Story and Style in Modern Movies*. Berkeley, CA: University of California Press, 2006.

Ebert, Roger. *Awake in the Dark: The Best of Roger Ebert*. Chicago, IL: The University of Chicago Press, 2006.

———. *Scorsese by Ebert*. Chicago, IL: The University of Chicago Press, 2008.

Friedman, Lester D., and Brent Notbohm, eds. *Steven Spielberg: Interviews*. Jackson, MS: The University Press of Mississippi, 2000.

Geissman, Grant, ed. *MAD About the Seventies: The Best of the Decade*. Boston, MA: Little, Brown and Company, 1996.

Hanson, Steve. *Lights, Camera, Action! A History of the Movies in the Twentieth Century*. Los Angeles, CA: *The Los Angeles Times*, a Times Mirror Company, 1990.

Hogan, Ron. *The Stewardess Is Flying the Plane! American Films of the 1970s*. New York: Bulfinch Press, 2005.

Kael, Pauline. *For Keeps*. New York: Dutton, 1994.

Kirshon, John W., ed. *Chronicle of America*. New York: DK Publishing, Inc., 1997.

Kline, Sally, ed. *George Lucas: Interviews*. Jackson, MS: The University Press of Mississippi, 1999.

Maltin, Leonard. *The Disney Films*. New York: Popular Library, 1978.

———. *Leonard Maltin's 2015 Movie Guide: The Modern Era*. New York: Plume, 2014.

O'Neill, Tom. *Movie Awards: The Ultimate, Unofficial Guide to the Oscars, Golden Globes, Critics, Guild & Indie Honors*. New York: Perigee, 2001.

Osborne, Robert. *85 Years of the Oscar: The Official History of the Academy Awards*. New York: Abbeville Press Publishers, 2013.

Peary, Danny. *Guide for the Film Fanatic*. New York: Simon & Schuster, 1986.

Pfeiffer, Lee and Dave Worrall. *The Essential Bond: The Authorized Guide to the World of 007*. New York: HarperCollins Publishers, 2000.

Phillips, Gene D., ed. *Stanley Kubrick: Interviews*. Jackson, MS: The University Press of Mississippi, 2001.

Roberts, Jerry. *The Complete History of American Film Criticism*. Santa Monica, CA: Santa Monica Press, 2010.

Schickel, Richard. *Keepers: The Greatest Films—and Personal Favorites—of a Moviegoing Lifetime*. New York: Alfred A. Knopf, 2015.

Stern, Jane and Michael Stern. *Jane & Michael Stern's Encyclopedia of Pop Culture*. New York: HarperPerennial, 1992.

Thomson, David. *The New Biographical Dictionary of Film*, 6th edition. New York: Alfred A. Knopf, 2014.

DVDs

Years indicate when the DVDs were released, not the years of the original movies.

American Grindhouse. Kino Lorber, Inc., 2010.

The Aristocats (DVD special features). Walt Disney Home Entertainment, 2008.

BaadAssss Cinema: A Bold Look at 70's Blaxploitation Films. IFC Entertainment, 2002.

Black Caesar (DVD special features). MGM Home Entertainment, 2001.

Boffo! Tinseltown's Bombs and Blockbusters. Home Box Office, Inc., 2006.

Chinatown/L.A. Confidential: Double Feature (DVD special features). Warner Home Video, 2014.

Corman's World: Exploits of a Hollywood Rebel. Anchor Bay Entertainment, 2012.

A Decade Under the Influence. IFC Entertainment, 2003.

Freaky Friday (DVD special features). Buena Vista Home Entertainment, Inc., 2004.

Going to Pieces: The Rise and Fall of the Slasher Film. Thinkfilm, 2007.

Midnight Movies: From the Margin to the Mainstream. Starz Home Entertainment, 2007.

One Flew Over the Cuckoo's Nest (DVD special features). Warner Home Video, 2002.

Silent Running (DVD special features). Universal Studios, 2002.

Thieves Like Us (DVD special features). MGM Home Entertainment , 2007.

Up the Sandbox (DVD special features). Warner Home Video, 2003.

INDEX

List of Photographs

ABOUT THE AUTHOR

Since 2000 Chris Strodder has had ten books published. Half of them are nonfiction books that celebrate popular culture, including *Swingin' Chicks of the '60s*, *The Encyclopedia of Sixties Cool*, and *The Disneyland Encyclopedia* (named one of the year's "Best Reference Books" by the national *Library Journal*). Strodder's writing has also appeared in many print magazines, including *Los Angeles*, *The Hollywood Reporter*, *Parade*, and *Movieline*. Following the 2019 publication of *The Daring Decade: Volume One, 1970–1974*, the second volume covering 1975–1979 movies will be released in 2020. And after that, well, as Timmy Lupus says at the end of *The Bad News Bears* (1976), "Just wait till next year."

The author's classic Mustang in front of one of his hometown movie houses, the old Rio Theatre on Soquel Avenue in Santa Cruz, California.

Made in the USA
Columbia, SC
27 December 2019

85865632R00172